THE VAGRANT MOOD

TEN NOVELS
AND THEIR AUTHORS

W. SOMERSET MAUGHAM

THE VAGRANT MOOD

MOOD

—

TEN NOVELS AND THEIR AUTHORS

Distributed by
HERON BOOKS

Published by arrangement with
William Heinemann Ltd.

The illustrations in this book were
reproduced by courtesy of
John R. Freeman & Co. :
facing pp. 16, 46, 136, 176 and between pp. 107 and 108
The Mansell Collection : facing p. 78
The Radio Times Hulton Picture Library : facing p. 218

Edito-Service S.A., Geneva, Publishers

CONTENTS

CONTENTS

THE VAGRANT MOOD

CONTENTS

Three of the essays in this volume appeared in *The Cornhill*. One was delivered as a lecture at the Philosophical Colloquium of the University of Columbia, but I have rewritten it in the hope of making it more easily readable. Part of the final essay appeared many years ago in *Life and Letters*.

W. S. M.

AUGUSTUS

I

I THINK I must be one of the few persons still alive who knew Augustus Hare. I had published a first novel which had had some success and he asked a common friend, a minor canon of St. Paul's, to invite me to dinner so that we might meet. I was young, twenty-four, and shy; but he took a fancy to me, because, tongue-tied though I was, I was content to listen while he discoursed, and shortly afterwards he wrote to me from Holmhurst, his house in the country, and asked me to come down for the week-end. I became a frequent guest.

Since the kind of life he lived there is lived no longer, I think it may be not without interest to describe the daily round. Sharp at eight in the morning a maid in a rustling print dress and a cap with streamers came into your room with a cup of tea and two slices of thin bread and butter, which she placed on the night table; if it was winter a tweeny followed her, in a print dress too, but not so shiny nor so rustling, who raked out the ashes of the fire which had been lit the night before, and laid and lit another. At half-past eight the maid came in again with a small can of hot water. She emptied the basin in which you had made a pretence of washing before going to bed, put the can in the basin and covered it with a towel. While she was thus occupied the tweeny brought in a sitz-bath, laid a white mat so that water should not splash the carpet, and on it, in front of the blazing fire, placed the sitz-bath. On each side of this she set a large can of hot water and a large can of cold, the soap-dish from the washing-stand and a bath-towel. The maids retired. The sitz-bath must be unknown to the present generation. It was a round tub perhaps three feet in diameter, about eighteen inches deep, with a back that rose to your shoulder-blades when you were sitting in it. Outside it was japanned a bilious yellow and inside painted white. As there was no room for your legs, they dangled outside, and you had to be something of a contortionist to wash your feet. You could do nothing about your back but trickle water down it from your sponge. The advantage of the contraption was that as your legs and back were out of the water you had no occasion to dawdle as you do in a bath in which you can lie full length, so that though you lost the happy thoughts and fruitful reflections which you might otherwise have had, you were ready to go downstairs at nine o'clock when the breakfast bell rang.

Augustus was already in his chair at the head of the table, laid for the hearty meal he was soon to partake of. In front of him was the great family Bible and a large Prayer Book bound in black leather. Seated, he looked solemn and even imposing. Standing, however, because he had a long body and short legs, he lost something of his impressiveness and indeed looked a trifle ridiculous. The guests took their seats and the servants trooped in. A row of chairs had been placed

6

for them in front of the sideboard, on which, besides a
noble ham and a brace of cold pheasants, various good
things to eat were kept hot in silver entrée dishes by
the thin blue flames of methylated spirit. Augustus read
a prayer. He had a strident, somewhat metallic voice
and he read in a tone that seemed to suggest that he was
not one to stand any nonsense from the deity. Sometimes it happened that a guest was a minute or two
late; he opened the door very cautiously and slunk in
on tiptoe, with the air of one who seeks to make himself
invisible. Augustus did not look up; he paused in the
middle of a sentence and remained silent till the late-
comer had seated himself, and then proceeded from
where he had left off. The air was heavy with reproof.
But that was all: Augustus made no reference afterwards to the sluggard's tardiness. When he had read
a certain number of prayers Augustus closed the book
and opened the Bible. He read the passages marked
for the day, and having finished, uttered the words:
'Let us pray.' This was the signal for us all to kneel,
the guests on hassocks and the servants on the Turkey
carpet, and we recited in chorus the Lord's Prayer.
Then we scrambled to our feet, the cook and the maids
scuttled out of the room; in a moment the parlour-
maid brought in tea and coffee, removed Bible and
Prayer Book, and put the tea-kettle and coffee-pot in
their place.

I was accustomed to family prayers and I noticed that
some of the prayers Augustus read sounded strangely
in my ears. Then I discovered that he had neatly inked
out many lines in the Prayer Book he read from. I
asked him why.

'I've crossed out all the passages in glorification of God,' he said. 'God is certainly a gentleman, and no gentleman cares to be praised to his face. It is tactless, impertinent and vulgar. I think all that fulsome adulation must be highly offensive to him.'

At the time this notion seemed odd to me and even comic, but since then I have come to think that there was some sense in it.

After breakfast Augustus retired to his study to write the autobiography on which he was then engaged. He neither smoked himself, nor allowed smoking in the house, so that such of his guests as hankered for the first pipe of the day had to go out of doors, which was pleasant enough in summer when you could sit down with a book in the garden, but not so pleasant in winter when you had to seek shelter in the stables.

Luncheon, a substantial meal of eggs or macaroni, joint, if there were no left-overs from the night before, with vegetables and a sweet, was at one; and after a decent interval Augustus, in a dark town suit, black boots, a stiff collar and a bowler hat, took his guests for a walk in the grounds. The property was small, rather less than forty acres, but by planning and planting he had given it something of the air of a park in a great country house. As you walked along he pointed out the improvements he had made, the resemblance he had achieved here to the garden of a Tuscan villa, the spacious view he had contrived there, and the wooded walks he had designed. I could not but observe that notwithstanding his objection to treating God with fulsome adulation, he accepted the compliments of his guests with a good deal of complacency. The promenade ended with a visit to the Hospice. This was a cottage he had arranged for the entertainment of gentle-women in reduced circumstances. He invited them for a month at a time, supplied them with their travelling expenses, farm and garden produce and groceries. He enquired if they were comfortable and had everything they wanted. No duchess, bringing calves-foot jelly and half a pound of tea to a cottager on the estate, could have combined condescension with beneficence with a more delicate sense of the difference that exists between the conferring of favours and the accepting of them.

After that it was time to go back to tea. This was a copious repast of scones, muffins or crumpets, bread and butter, jam, plain cake and currant cake. The better part of an hour was spent over this, and Augustus talked of his early life, his travels and his many friends. At six he went to his study to write letters and we met again when the second bell called us down to dinner. We were waited on by maids in black uniforms, white caps and aprons, and were given soup, fish, poultry or game, sweet and savoury; sherry with the soup and fish, claret with the game, and port with the nuts and fruit. After dinner we returned to the drawing-room. Some-times Augustus read aloud to us, sometimes we played an intolerably tedious game called Halma, or, if he thought the company worthy, he told us his famous stories. The clock struck ten and Augustus rose from his chair by the fire. We marched out into the hall, where candles in silver candle-sticks were waiting for us, lit them and walked upstairs to our respective bed-rooms. There was a can of hot water in the basin and a fire blazed in the hearth. It was difficult to read by the light of a single candle, but it was enchanting to lie in a four-poster and watch the glow of the fire till the sleep of youth descended upon you.

Such was a day in one of the smaller country houses at the end of the nineteenth century, and such, more or less, throughout the land was the day in hundreds upon hundreds of houses belonging to persons who, without being rich, were well enough off to live in the great comfort which they looked upon as the way in which gentlefolk should live. Augustus was house-proud, and nothing pleased him more than to show guests the relics of a 'wealthy past', with which Holmhurst was filled. It was a rambling house of no architectural merit, with wide corridors and low ceilings, but by adding another room or two, building archways in the garden, decorating it here and there with urns and statues, among which was one of Queen Anne and her four satellites which had once stood in front of St. Paul's, Augustus had managed to give the place an air. It might have been the dower-house on the estate of a great nobleman, which, if there was no dowager to inhabit it, might be appropriately lent to an aunt who was the relict of a former ambassador to the Ottoman court.

II

Augustus was profoundly conscious of the fact that he was the representative of an ancient county family, the Hares of Hurstmonceux, connected, though distantly, with members of the aristocracy; and though its fortunes were fallen, his sense of the consequence this gave him remained unabated. He was like an exiled king, surrounded with such objects of departed grandeur as he has saved from the wreck, who is hail-fellow-well-met with the rag-tag and bobtail his altered circumstances force him to frequent, but who is alert to watch for the bobs and bows that his graciousness might induce ill-conditioned persons to omit.

Though Augustus was apt to mention with a deprecating smile that he was descended from a younger son of King Edward I, the family fortunes were founded by Francis Hare, a clever parson who had the good luck to be Sir Robert Walpole's tutor at King's College, Cambridge. Walpole's advancement, as we know, was furthered by Sarah, Duchess of Marlborough, and it may be surmised that it was by her influence that Francis Hare was appointed Chaplain-General to the forces in the Low Countries. He rode by the side of the great general at the battles of Blenheim and Ramillies. With such powerful friends it is not surprising that his merits did not go unrewarded. He was made Dean of Worcester and then of St. Paul's; and the second of these lucrative offices he continued to hold when he was created first Bishop of St. Asaph's and then Bishop of Chichester. He made two very profitable marriages. By his first wife, Bethaia Naylor, he had a son, Francis, who inherited the vast and romantic castle of Hurstmonceux and a handsome estate, and then added the name of Naylor to that of Hare. By his second wife, a great heiress, he had a son Robert, whose godfather, Sir Robert Walpole, as a christening present bestowed on him the sinecure office of sweeper-ship of Gravesend, worth £400 a year. This he held to the day of his death. Sir Robert took sufficient interest in his old tutor's son to advise that he should adopt the Church as his profession, since he could thus best provide for his future. Robert took orders and was given first a living and then a canonry at Winchester. The bishop was a prudent man and while Robert was still very young arranged a marriage for him with the heiress of a property close to that of his own wife. By her he had two sons, Francis and Robert, and soon after her death he married another heiress. His elder brother died childless and the Canon of Winchester inherited Hurstmonceux Castle. The bishop must have been well satisfied with his son's station in life.

The bishop's descendants, however, seem to have inherited little of his worldly wisdom, for from that time the fortunes of the family began to decline. The first step was taken by the canon's second wife. She dismantled the castle and from it took the floors, doors and chimney-pieces for a large new house called Hurst-monceux Place which she built in another part of the park. The canon's eldest son, Francis Hare-Naylor, the grandfather of our Augustus, was a good-looking ne'er-do-well, bold, witty and extravagant; he seems to have got himself periodically arrested for debt and in order to extricate himself from his difficulties was obliged to raise money on his prospects from the Hurst-monceux estates. He had taken the fancy of Georgiana, Duchess of Devonshire, who introduced him to her cousin Georgiana, daughter of Jonathan Shipley, Bishop of St. Asaph. The pair eloped, whereupon their respective families 'renounced them with fury' and neither the Bishop of St. Asaph nor the Canon of Winchester ever saw them again. They went abroad and lived on the two hundred pounds a year which the Duchess allowed them. They had four sons, Francis, Augustus, Julius and Marcus. When Francis Hare-Naylor, the husband of Georgiana Shipley, eventually succeeded his father he sold the remnants of his ancestral estates for sixty thousand pounds. On his death, in 1815, his eldest son Francis Hare, for since he no longer owned Hurstmonceux he abandoned the additional name of Naylor, came into possession of what remained of the family fortunes, and proceeded to live a life of pleasure till his circumstances obliged him, like many another spendthrift at that time, to take up his residence on the Continent. But he was apparently still well enough off to give large dinner parties twice a week. He kept good company and counted Count D'Orsay and Lady Blessington, Lord Desart, Lord Bristol, Lord Dudley among his more intimate friends. In 1828 he married Anne, a daughter of Sir John Paul, the banker, and by her had a daughter and three sons. The youngest of these, born in 1834, was the Augustus who is the subject of this essay.

Though the Hurstmonceux estates had been sold the family had retained the advowson of the rich living. The incumbent was the Reverend Robert Hare, the younger son of Francis Hare-Naylor, and it was understood that he should be succeeded by the Reverend Augustus Hare, one of Francis Hare's three brothers. Of Marcus, the youngest of the three, I have been able to discover nothing except that he married a daughter

13

of Lord Stanley of Alderley, had a 'place' at Torquay, complained when he was staying at Hurstmonceux Rectory that the water with which the tea was made was never on the boil, and died in 1845. Julius was a Fellow of Trinity and a very learned man. With his brother Augustus he was the author of a book called *Guesses at Truth*, which in its day was popular with the devout. When the Reverend Robert Hare died his nephew the Reverend Augustus Hare did not wish to leave the parish of Alton Barnes, to which he had been appointed, and persuaded his brother Julius to accept the living of Hurstmonceux in his place. It was a wrench to Julius to leave Cambridge, but he had too great a sense of duty to allow a valuable piece of property to go out of the family and so consented to the sacrifice. He eventually became Archdeacon of Lewes.

The Reverend Augustus Hare married Maria, daughter of the Reverend Oswald Leicester, Rector of Stoke-upon-Terne. He died in Rome, whither he had gone for his health, in 1834, the year in which our Augustus was born. It was after him that my hero was named and the widow, Mrs. Augustus Hare, was his godmother. Francis and Anne Hare, the child's parents, found it none too easy to live in the style suitable to their position and at the same time support a family, and they were very much annoyed when their last son was born. Maria Hare was childless, and on her return to England after burying her husband it occurred to her that they might be willing to let her adopt her godson. She wrote to her sister-in-law and shortly afterwards received from her the following letter:

'My dear Maria, how very kind of you. Yes, certainly the baby shall be sent as soon as it is weaned; if anyone else would like one, would you kindly remember that we have others.'

The child in due course was 'sent over to England with a little green carpet-bag containing two little white night-shirts and a red coral necklace.'

Maria Hare's father, the Reverend Oswald Leicester, belonged to a family of great antiquity, which claimed direct descent from Gunnora, Duchess of Normandy, grandmother of William the Conqueror. He belonged thus to the same class as the Bertrams of Mansfield Park and Mr. Darcy of Pemberley. The Reverend Oswald Leicester was a sincere Christian, but he had a very proper notion of what befitted an English gentleman. He would have agreed with Lady Catherine de Bourgh that Elizabeth Bennet was not the sort of person Mr. Darcy should marry. Reginald Heber, the hymn-writer, afterwards Bishop of Calcutta, was Rector of Hodnet, which was only two miles from Maria Leicester's home, and she spent long periods with him and his wife. Reginald Heber had a curate called Martin Stow and since we are told nothing about his antecedents we must conclude that he was not 'a gentleman born'. Maria Leicester and Martin Stow fell in love with one another, but her father would not hear of his daughter's union with 'a mere country curate', and she was too dutiful a daughter to marry without his consent. When Reginald Heber was appointed to the bishopric of Calcutta he offered his Indian chaplaincy to Martin Stow, who accepted it in the hope that this preferment would induce the

Reverend Oswald Leicester to look upon his suit with favour. His hope was frustrated, Maria and Martin met and parted, and a few months later the sad news was brought her that Mr. Stow had died of fever. Now, the Reverend Augustus Hare was a cousin of Mrs. Heber's and a friend of Martin Stow. He was the confidant of the lovers. His was a willing ear when they needed to pour out their troubles. On hearing of Martin Stow's death Maria Leicester wrote to Augustus Hare as follows:

'I must write a few lines, although I feel it almost needless to do so, for Augustus Hare knows all my feelings too well to doubt what they must be now . . . it is to you I turn as the sharer, the fellow sufferer in my grief . . . I know that if you can you will come here. When we have once met it will be a comfort to mourn together.'

They met, they corresponded, and, as Maria wrote in her Journal, 'unconsciously and imperceptibly the feelings of esteem and friendship,' with which she had regarded Augustus, 'assumed a new character, and something of the tenderness and beauty attending a warmer interest' took their place. Two years after the death of Martin Stow Augustus asked her to marry him and she agreed. 'Secure in the affection of Augustus,' she wrote again in her Journal, 'I feel no longer a blank in life, and everything takes a new and bright colouring.' But it was not till a year later that she received her father's consent to the engagement. It may be surmised that he gave it because he thought it would be for the happiness of his daughter, thirty-one years old by this time, an age then at which a

A portrait of Maria Hare, Augustus Hare's godmother

maiden, as Mr. Wordsworth somewhat ungallantly put it, was withering on the stalk; but also because he thought an alliance between the Hares of Hurstmonceux, descended from a younger son of King Edward I, and the Leicesters of Toft, descended from Gunnora, Duchess of Normandy, could not but be regarded as suitable. Moreover, with the rich living of Hurstmonceux to fall to Augustus on the death of his Uncle Robert, Maria would be able to live in the style appropriate to a gentleman's daughter. Though both families were sincerely imbued with the conviction that this life was merely a post-inn, as it were, in which they sojourned for a brief space on their way to their heavenly home, they saw no reason why they should not make their temporary abode as comfortable as possible.

After the death of her husband Maria Hare spent some months with Julius, her brother-in-law, at Hurstmonceux and then took a house near-by, called Lime, which remained her home for twenty-five years. When she adopted the little Augustus, her godson, it was with the idea that he should be brought up to take Holy Orders and in due course succeed his Uncle Julius as Rector of Hurstmonceux. She started to train him in virtue from the beginning. When he was only eighteen months old she wrote in her Journal: 'Augustus has grown much more obedient, and is ready to give his food and playthings to others.' His religious education was her constant care and when he was three, by which time he could read and was learning German, she took pains to explain to him the mystery of the Trinity. When he was four his playthings were taken away from him and banished to the loft, so that he should learn that there were more serious things in life than toys. He had no companions of his own age. There was a poor woman who lived close to the gate of Lime whom Maria Hare often visited to relieve her necessities and by her pious exhortations persuade her to accept her lot as a special blessing of Providence. This woman had a little boy, whom Augustus longed to play with, and once did in a hayfield, but he was so severely punished for it that he never did again. To Mrs. Hare (Miss Leicester of Toft as was) it was not only a duty, it was a labour of love to visit the poor, but it was out of the question to allow a gentleman's son to play with a working-man's.

On March 13, 1839, she wrote in her Journal: 'My little Augustus is now five years old. Strong personal identity, reference of everything to himself, greediness of pleasure and possession, are I fear prominent features in his disposition. May I be taught how best to correct his sinful propensities with judgment, and to draw him out of self to live for others.'

Notwithstanding everything, however, Augustus was sometimes naughty. Then he was sent upstairs 'to prepare', which, I take it, means to take down his knicker-bockers and bare his little bottom, and Uncle Julius was bidden to come from his rectory to beat him. This he did with a riding-whip. Mrs. Hare was afraid of over-indulging the child and he only had to express a wish to have it refused. On one occasion she took him to visit the curate's wife and someone gave him a lollypop, which he ate, but when they got home the smell of peppermint betrayed him and he was given a large dose of rhubarb and soda with a forcing spoon to teach him in future to avoid carnal indulgence.

Meanwhile Maria Hare had made the acquaintance of the Misses Maurice, Priscilla and Esther, sisters of Frederick Maurice, the evangelist. They kept a school at Reading, but every year came to stay at Lime for a period. They were intensely, even aggressively, religious and they acquired a great influence over Mrs. Hare. One of its results was that she adopted more stringent measures so to form the character of Augustus that he might become a worthy minister of Christ. Till then he had had roast mutton and rice pudding every day for dinner. An occasion came when he was told that a delicious pudding was to be served. It was talked of till his mouth watered. It was placed on the table and he was just about to eat the helping he had been given when it was snatched away from him and he was told to get up and take it to some poor person in the village. Mrs. Hare wrote in her Journal: 'Augustus would, I believe, always do a thing if *reasoned* with about it, but the necessity of obedience without reasoning is especially necessary in such a disposition as his. The will is the thing that needs being brought in subjection.' And again: 'Now it seems to be an excellent discipline whereby daily some self-denial and command may be acquired in overcoming the repugnance to doing from duty that which has in itself no attraction.'

Mrs. Hare in this sentence did not express herself with her usual clarity. I think she must have meant that if Augustus, aged then five, was forced to do every day something he didn't want to do, he would eventually want to do it.

Once a year Maria took Augustus to stay with her parents at Stoke. They went in their own chariot, spending the night at post-inns, and even after the railway was built they continued to go in their chariot placed on a truck. When at last they came to use ordinary railway carriages they still had post-horses to meet them at a station near London, because Mrs. Hare would not have it known that she did anything so excessively improper as to enter London in a railway carriage.

Mrs. Leicester, Maria's step-mother, was severe but kind to Augustus. If he made a noise at home he was at once punished, but at Stoke Mrs. Leicester would say: 'Never mind the child, Maria, it is only innocent play.' She knew her duty as a clergyman's wife. She taught in the village school and when she thought it necessary to chastise her pupils, would take a book from the table and on using it say to the offender: 'You don't suppose I'm going to hurt my fingers in boxing your ears,' and then: 'Now we mustn't let the other ear be jealous,' upon which she soundly smacked it. The curates came to luncheon at the Rectory on Sundays, but they were not expected to talk, and if they ventured on a remark were snubbed. After they had eaten their cold veal they were called upon to give Mrs. Leicester an account of what they had been doing during the week, and if they had not done what she wished they were harshly chidden. They were obliged to come in by the back door, except Mr. Egerton, who was allowed to come in by the front door because he was a gentleman born. When Augustus told me this story, I, being young, was shocked.

'Don't be so silly,' he said when I expressed my indignation, 'it was perfectly natural. Mr. Egerton was a nephew of Lord Bridgewater. The others were nobodies. It would have been very impertinent of them to ring the front-door bell.'

'D'you mean to say that if they happened to come to the Rectory together, one would have gone to the front door and the other to the back?'

'Of course.'

'I don't think it speaks very well for Mr. Egerton.'

'I dare say you don't,' Augustus answered tartly. 'A gentleman knows his place and he takes it without giving it a second thought.'

Mrs. Leicester ruled the maids as strictly as she ruled the curates. When annoyed with them she had no hesitation in boxing their ears, which, such were the manners of the time, they never thought of resenting. The washing was done every three weeks and it was a rule of the house that it must begin at one in the morning. The ladies'-maids, who were expected to do the fine muslins, had to be at the wash-tubs at three. If one was late the housekeeper reported it to Mrs. Leicester, who gave her a good scolding. But Mrs. Leicester had a lighter side. Maria Hare thought it sinful to read fiction and in the evenings read Miss Strickland's *Queens of England* to her parents. *Pickwick* was coming out then in monthly numbers and Mrs. Leicester took them in. She read them in her dressing-room, behind closed doors, with her maid on the watch against intruders, and when she had finished a number she tore it up into little pieces which she threw in the waste-paper basket.

21

When Augustus was nine Mrs. Hare, on the insistence of the Misses Maurice, sent him to a preparatory school, and in the summer holidays, after the usual visit to Stoke, she took him for a tour of the English lakes. Uncle Julius accompanied them, and Maria, wishing to give Esther Maurice a rest after her arduous work at Reading, invited her to join the party. It was a dangerous kindness. Julius Hare proposed to Esther Maurice and was accepted. Maria Hare shed bitter tears when they told her of their engagement. Esther shed bitter tears and Julius 'sobbed and cried for days'. Ever since her husband's death Julius had been Maria's constant companion. He came to dinner at Lime every evening at six, leaving at eight, and Maria constantly drove up to the Rectory in the afternoon. Julius 'consulted her on every subject, and he thought every day a blank when they had no meeting.' Doubtless, since the Prayer Book and the laws of England forbade her to feel any warmer emotion for him, her affection remained strictly that of a sister-in-law for her brother-in-law, but she would have been more than human if she had welcomed the notion of another woman, a protégée of her own, becoming the mistress of Hurstmonceux Rectory. But however distasteful such a prospect was, she had a more serious objection to the marriage. Mr. Maurice was a scholar and a clergyman, but he was not a gentleman born, and the manners of the Misses Maurice, high-minded and worthy as they were, were not the sort of manners she was accustomed to. They were not ladies. Martin Stow perhaps was not a gentleman born, but her dear dead Augustus had been the first to admit his excellence and nobility of character. She loved him, but she had accepted her father's decision that he was not the sort of person it was proper for her to marry.

The marriage took place. Mrs. Julius Hare, now Aunt Esther to Augustus, was a deeply religious woman, but of a harsh and domineering character. 'She looked upon pleasure as a sin and if she felt that the affection for somebody drew her from the thorny path of self-sacrifice she tore that affection from her heart.' To such of the poor as accepted her absolute authority she was kind, generous and considerate; and to 'her husband, to whom her severe creed taught her to show the same inflexible obedience she exacted from others, she was utterly devoted.' For his soul's good she set herself to subdue the little Augustus. Since she was determined that her marriage should make no difference in the habits of the two families, and Julius had dined every night at Lime, she insisted that Maria Hare and Augustus should dine every night at the Rectory. In winter it was often impossible for them to go home after dinner and they passed the night at the Rectory. Augustus was a delicate boy and suffered badly from chilblains so that there were often large open sores on his hands and feet. Aunt Esther put him to bed in an unfurnished damp room with a deal trestle to sleep on, a straw palliasse and a single blanket. The servants were not allowed to bring him hot water and in the morning he had to break the ice in the pitcher with a brass candlestick or, if that had been taken away, with his wounded hands. Still for the good of his soul, because the smell of sauerkraut made him sick he was made to eat it. Sunday was a day of respite. Owing to her religious duties Maria Hare did not go to the Rectory, but Aunt Esther, fearing that Maria would indulge him, persuaded her to let Augustus be locked up in the vestry between services with a sandwich for his dinner. He had a cat to which he was devoted, and when Aunt Esther discovered this she insisted that it should be given up to her. Augustus wept, but Maria Hare said he must be taught to give up his own way and pleasures to others. With tears he took it to the Rectory and Aunt Esther had it hanged.

It is almost inconceivable that a pious, God-fearing woman could have treated a child of twelve with such inhumanity. I have wondered whether her behaviour to him, besides her determination to train him in the way of virtue and self-sacrifice, was not occasioned also by a desire, of which she may well have been unconscious, to give the adopted mother who adored him a needful lesson. Maria Hare had been very good to Esther Maurice, but had there not been something in her manner which never let the humble friend forget that Mrs. Hare was her benefactress and that there was a great gulf fixed between a young woman, of the highest principles certainly, but of humble origins, and Maria Leicester of Toft, the widow of a Hare of Hurstmonceux? Is it not possible that Esther Maurice, like Charlotte Brontë in her situation as a governess, saw slights when only kindness was intended, and in a dozen little ways felt that the subservience of her position was never entirely absent from Maria's mind? When she became Mrs. Julius Hare did it never cross her mind that it could only do dear Maria good to suffer? And she did suffer. But she accepted her distress at the miseries inflicted on the boy as a fiery trial that must be patiently endured.

I shall pass over the next few years of Augustus's life. On leaving his preparatory school, he went to Harrow, but owing to illness only stayed there for a year and until he was old enough to go to Oxford lived with tutors. He took his degree in 1857 and then started on the main business of his life. This was to paint in water-colours, see sights and mix in high society. He made his first sketch from nature when he was seven. Maria Hare drew well, and as she could not but look upon this accomplishment as harmless, she fostered Augustus's inclinations and gave him useful lessons. She would look at a drawing carefully and then say: 'And what does this line mean?' 'Oh, I thought it looked well.' 'Then, if you don't know exactly what it means, take it out at once.' This was sound advice. As Maria Hare deprecated colour, he was allowed to use only pencil and sepia, and it was not till he was grown up that she permitted him to paint in water-colour. He made endless sketches. The walls of Holmhurst were papered with the best of them in handsome frames and he had albums full of them. At this distance of time I cannot judge of their quality. Years later Maria Hare showed some of them to Ruskin, who examined them very carefully and at last pointed out one as the least bad of a very poor collection. Augustus had an eye for the picturesque and as I look back I have a suspicion that the critic was unduly severe. They were painted in the style of the mid-nineteenth century, and if they are still in existence might be found now to have a certain period charm.

III

When Augustus was only fourteen, at a tutor's at Lyncombe, he was already an indefatigable sight-seer. To visit an ancient house or a fine church he would often walk twenty-five miles a day. So that he should not be led astray Mrs. Hare sent him back to his tutor's with only five shillings in his pocket and he went on these excursions without a penny to buy himself a piece of bread. Many a time he sank down by the wayside, faint with hunger, and was glad to accept food from the 'common working people' he met on the road. But neither his delight in painting the picturesque nor his passion for sights was as important to him as to get into society. In this endeavour he started with certain advantages. Through his parents he was connected with a number of noble and county families, and through his adopted mother with several more. However distant the relationship he counted all their members as his cousins.

Maria Hare had been in poor health for some years and the doctors advised her to try living in a climate milder than that of Hurstmonceux. She had before this taken Augustus for short trips on the Continent, but soon after he left Oxford it was decided that they should make a prolonged sojourn abroad. So that they should be properly waited on they took Mrs. Hare's maid and manservant with them. Julius Hare, to the sorrow of his relations and the relief of his parishioners, had died two years before and Maria, while she was away, lent Lime to his widow. They travelled slowly, of course by carriage, through Switzerland and Italy, visiting places of interest and making abundant sketches; they had a goodly supply of books in their roomy chariot and during the journey read the 'whole of Arnold, Gibbon, Ranke and Milman'. It looks like a formidable undertaking. On reaching Rome they took an apartment in the Piazza del Popolo. Augustus's father had died some years before and his widow, whom Augustus called Italima, a contraction of Italian mamma, was living in Rome with her daughter Esmeralda. Of her two other sons, Francis and Robert, Augustus's elder brothers, one was in the Guards and the other in the Blues. Since he knew them but slightly and did not care for them I need only say that they lived as extravagantly as their father had done, with even smaller resources, and died destitute. Francis had further outraged his family by marrying 'a person with whom he had long been acquainted', which, I presume, was Augustus's delicate way of saying that she was his mistress. In his autobiography he dismissed her in a footnote: 'The person whom Francis Hare had married during the last months of his life vanished, immediately after his death, into the chaos from which she had come.'

Augustus had seen little of his real mother and she had never taken any interest in him. But now he became better acquainted with her. She moved with her daughter in the best Roman society, and when Maria Hare could spare him she took Augustus with her. The list of princes and princesses, dukes and duchesses, he thus frequented is impressive. Italima

27

liked to see Augustus more often than his adopted mother quite approved of, and sometimes when he had a particular engagement with her, Maria Hare would demand his presence. It looks as though the saintly woman was not entirely devoid of the unpleasant failing of jealousy.

Maria Hare and Augustus remained abroad for eighteen months and would have remained longer but that Mrs. Hare began to suspect that her adopted son had leanings to Roman Catholicism, and though he was ill and the doctors told her he could not survive the rigour of an English winter she insisted on taking him back to a staunchly Protestant country. She felt that the hazard to his soul was of more consequence than the hazard to his body. She was well aware how much pleasure he took in the religious processions that so often passed through the streets of Rome, the sight of cardinals in their red robes driving in their coaches, the splendid ceremonies of the Church and the pomp of the Eternal City when the Pope was still a temporal sovereign. She knew Augustus well and she dreaded his levity. One day she told him that she had never known anyone who enjoyed things as much as he did; she said it not by way of blaming him, but perhaps with the feeling at the back of her mind that there was danger in such an attitude towards life.

During this period there was a wave of conversions to Catholicism. There had been the notorious instances of Newman and Manning; their example had been followed by others of lesser note, though by some of greater social importance, and it had caused dissension in many families. Italima and Esmeralda had become

Catholics, though to Italima's credit it had to be admitted that she had sought to dissuade her daughter from taking the step, because she had expectations from her grandmother, Lady Anne Simpson, and the old lady would certainly disinherit her if she changed her religion. Sir John Paul, Augustus's grandfather, had turned his daughter out of the house and refused ever to see her again when she was received into the Church of Rome, and when Mary Stanley, Maria's niece and the daughter of the Bishop of Norwich, forsook the faith of her Protestant fathers, Maria could not but fear for her dear Augustus.

The reader will remember that from his earliest years he had been destined for the Church. It was on this account that Maria Hare had brought him up so strictly. It was on this account that he had been taught to sacrifice himself for others. It was on this account that his toys were taken away from him. It was on this account that Aunt Esther, when she came on the scene, had insisted that he should be inured to hardship and privation, and that he should learn that pleasure, a snare of the devil, was something he must eschew. Though the Hares had lost their land and most of their money, there still remained the rich living of Hurst-monceux, and as the youngest son of Francis Hare it was his right in due course to have it. Unfortunately Augustus's eldest brother had been driven by his financial necessities to sell the advowson, so that Maria Hare could never hope to see her adopted son occupy the Rectory with which she had so many pleasant and edifying associations, but that did not make it less desirable that Augustus should adopt the profession for which he had been so well prepared. His ancestry and his family connections marked him out to pursue the useful and profitable life of a clergyman who was a gentleman born. The founder of the family fortunes had held two bishoprics besides the Deanery of St. Paul's, one of Augustus's grandfathers had been Bishop of St. Asaph, another Canon of Winchester, his two uncles had taken Holy Orders; Maria's brother-in-law, Edward Stanley, had been Bishop of Norwich, and his son Arthur Stanley was already a Canon of Canterbury and would in due course no doubt occupy a position of even greater dignity. He did in fact become Dean of Westminster, marry Lady Augusta Bruce and grow to be a close friend of Queen Victoria. Then there were the Strathmores, the Ravensworths, the Stanleys of Alderley. With such connections Augustus could surely look forward to preferment. The good old days of pluralism were past, but there was no reason why with his ability and so many influential relations he should not achieve distinction in the Church.

It was a shock to Maria Hare when Augustus, while they were still in Italy, informed her, we can imagine how nervously, that he did not wish to be ordained. From every point of view, from the earthly as well as from the heavenly, this seemed as foolish as it was ungrateful. She shed bitter tears. But she was a sincerely Christian woman and what could she do when he told her that he felt himself unfitted to take Holy Orders? She loved him devotedly, and though it almost broke her heart, at last acquiesced in his determination. But when they got back to England and the family were informed, there was hell to pay. They asked him his reasons for refusing to be ordained. He could give none that was adequate. He merely said that it was uncongenial. Aunt Esther thought that made it all the more desirable that Maria should insist on it. Had he religious doubts? No. He had come back from Italy as true a Protestant as when he left. It was obvious then that if he persisted in his obstinacy it could only be that he wanted to lead an idle, useless life of self-indulgence.

The truth was simply that Augustus was bored with religion. He had been bored by the two services he had been forced to attend every Sunday and bored by the long, incomprehensible sermons of his Uncle Julius, bored by the elevating conversations on the power of faith which Maria Hare held with her friends and relations, exasperated by the evangelical fanaticism of the Maurice women and made miserable by the severities to which for his spiritual welfare he had been so long subjected. When I knew him Augustus had ceased going to church on Sundays, and if he continued to have family prayers it was as a social gesture becoming to a gentleman of ancient lineage.

Then came the question as to what he should do. He tried to get a clerkship at the Library of the British Museum, but did not succeed, and finally through the good offices of Arthur Stanley he was commissioned by John Murray to write the *Handbook of Berks, Bucks and Oxfordshire*. It was a job that just suited him, for it enabled him to do a great deal of sight-seeing and at the same time must bring him in contact with the sort of people he liked to know. He did in fact make a

number of desirable acquaintances, discovered a
number of new cousins and stayed at a number of
grand houses. At about this time Lime was sold over
Maria's head and she moved to Holmhurst, which
then became Augustus's home for the rest of his life.
The handbook was so well received that Murray asked
him to choose any counties he liked for another work
of the same kind. He chose Northumberland and
Durham. So began the long series of guide-books
which made the name of Augustus Hare well-known
to at least two generations of travellers in Europe. They
were written on a plan that had novelty, for inter-
spersed with useful information were long quotations
from the New Testament, Fathers of the Church,
historians, art critics and poets. The earnest sight-
seer must have been flattered to find in his guide-book
quotations from Virgil, Horace, Ovid, Martial,
Suetonius, and even from a work which few can have
read, Prudentius *contra Symmachum*. Augustus paid his
readers the compliment of leaving these passages
untranslated and the compliment was doubtless appreciated.

But his habit of extensively quoting from other
authors sometimes got him into trouble. In his *Cities
of Northern and Central Italy* he quoted largely from some
articles by Freeman, the historian, without receiving
permission, whereupon Freeman charged him with
bare-faced and wholesale robbery. Augustus was very
much hurt. He felt that the real interest of Freeman's
articles had been overlooked owing to the 'dogmatic
and verbose style in which they were written', and he
had introduced extracts from them in order to attract

notice to them and so do the historian a good turn. 'I need hardly say,' he adds in a footnote to his account of the incident, 'that as soon as possible thereafter I eliminated all reference to Mr. Freeman, and all quotations from his works from my books.' He was satisfied that he had thus swept the historian back into the obscurity from which he had delivered him. What Augustus describes as a most virulent and abusive article appeared upon this work in the *Athenæum*, in which he was accused of having copied from Murray's *Handbooks* without acknowledgement and as proof quoting passages in which the same curious mistake occurred. And in fact that is exactly what he had done. But the books were very popular. By the end of the nineteenth century there had been fifteen editions of *Walks in Rome*, five of *Florence and Venice*, and six of *Walks in London* and *Wanderings in Spain*. Spain, Holland and Scandinavia, all of which he wrote books about, he knew very superficially, but he knew Italy and France as few people did then or are likely to do now.

During the next ten years Maria and Augustus Hare spent a great deal of time in France and Italy. She was often ill and, when she was, Augustus nursed her devotedly. In the intervals he moved in high circles, took parties of well-born ladies to paint in water-colour with him, and in Rome conducted them on sight-seeing tours during which, the centre of a little crowd of admiring females, he discoursed on the artistic merit and the historical associations of the objects he showed them.

Italima had been greatly reduced in circumstances

33

by the failure of her father's bank and lost what she had left by the defalcation of the attorney who attended to her affairs. She died in 1864. Her daughter Esmeralda died four years later and Maria Hare in 1870. For a while after this event Augustus was in acute financial anxiety, for the relation between his adopted mother and himself had been so close that she could not bring herself to believe that he would long survive her. She failed in consequence to make what he calls the usual arrangements for his future provision, and it looked as though he would be left with nothing but Holmhurst and sixty pounds a year. He does not explain how things were arranged, but the upshot seems to have been that he succeeded to her fortune. He complained bitterly that, since he was no legal relation, he had to pay ten per cent duty on everything he inherited. He was always reticent about his income and I have no notion what it was; it was sufficient to enable him to keep up Holmhurst in some style, entertain constantly, and travel whenever he had a mind to. He had at least enough to lose a few hundred pounds now and then on a wild-cat speculation. He did not look upon himself as a professional author, but as a gentleman who from purely altruistic motives wrote books which would help travellers profitably to enjoy the beauties of nature and art. He published them at his own expense and they must have brought him in considerable sums.

From the time of Maria Hare's death Augustus's life followed a course of some regularity. He went abroad a good deal, generally for his work on the guide-books; and when in England he spent some time at Holmhurst, receiving a succession of guests, and made a round of country house visits. When in London he had a bedroom in Jermyn Street and went to the Athenaeum for breakfast, where he always occupied the same table; he spent the morning at work in the library and went out to lunch; in the afternoon there were calls to pay, a tea-party or a reception at which he had to make *acte de présence*, and at night he dined out. There is a note in his Journal which strikes a sinister note: 'May 15. Drawing-party in dirty, picturesque St. Bartholomew's. For the first time this year no one asked me to dinner, and I was most profoundly bored.' Augustus never married. There is a cryptic remark in his autobiography which suggests that on one occasion he had an inclination to do so. 'This year (1864) I greatly wished something that was not compatible with the entire devotion of my time and life to my mother. Therefore I smothered the wish, and the hope that had grown up with it.' If this means what I think it does I should say it was safe to surmise that the object of his affections was a well-connected young woman of some fortune; but of course he was financially dependent on Maria Hare, and though there is no reason to believe that his reasons for smothering the wish were not such as he said, he cannot but have been aware that if he married without her consent she was capable of cutting him off without a shilling. It was a tradition in the family. I do not think he was of a passionate nature. He told me once that he had never had sexual intercourse till he was thirty-five. He marked the occasions on which this happened, about once every three months, with a black cross in his

Journal. But this is a matter on which most men are apt to boast, and I dare say that to impress me he exaggerated the frequency of his incontinence.

During the last months of Mrs. Hare's life Augustus had discussed with her his desire to write a book about her which should be called *Memorials of a Quiet Life*. She laughed at the notion when first he put it before her, but after reflecting for a day or two said that she could not oppose his wish if he thought that the simple experiences of her life, and God's guidance in her case, might be made useful to others; she gave him many journals and letters which he might use, and directed the arrangement of others. He set to work at once and was able to read to her the earlier chapters before she died. He spent the winter after her death in seclusion until he had finished the book. His cousins, especially the Stanleys, were very angry when they found out what he was up to, and even threatened to bring an action against him if he published any of the letters of Mrs. Stanley, Maria's sister. Arthur Stanley, by this time Dean of Westminster, went so far as to persuade John Murray to go to Augustus's publishers to try to stop the publication. The book was issued and three days after its appearance a second edition was called for. It was in fact a great success both in England and in the United States, and pilgrims came from America to visit the various places Augustus had written about. Carlyle, whom he met at luncheon, told him: 'I do not often cry and am not much given to weeping, but your book is most profoundly touching, and when the dear Augustus (Maria's husband) was making the hay I felt a lesson deep down in my heart.'

The world that read these two stout volumes with emotion has long ceased to exist. To me they have seemed tedious. There is, of course, a great deal about the Hares and the Leicesters; the members of the two families wrote immensely long letters to one another, and one can only marvel at the patience they must have had to read them. The pious consolations, the pious exhortations which these people wrote to one another on the death of a relation or a friend were so unctuous that one can hardly believe in their sincerity. But one must not judge of the sentiments of one generation by those of another. God was constantly in their thoughts and their conversation turned frequently on the life to come, but Augustus somewhat maliciously noticed that though in youth they talked of longing, pining for 'the coming of the Kingdom', as they grew older they seemed less eager for it. 'By and by would do.'

The success of *Memorials of a Quiet Life* brought Augustus other work of the same kind, and in course of time he published *Life and Letters of Frances, Baroness Bunsen*, *The Story of Two Noble Lives*, *The Gurneys of Earlham*, and others. The subjects of *The Story of Two Noble Lives* were Louisa, Lady Waterford and Charlotte, Lady Canning. It is still readable; indeed the chapters that deal with the period during which their father, Lord Stuart de Rothesay, was ambassador in Paris, from 1815 to 1830, are very interesting. Augustus had made the acquaintance of Lady Waterford when he was getting together his material for Murray's *Handbook on Durham and Northumberland*; and after this he paid her a yearly visit first at Ford and then at Highcliffe. This was not an isolated case. He was apparently a welcome guest at a vast number of great houses, and there seem to have been few to which he could not count on an invitation year after year. He went from castle to castle, from park to park and from hall to hall. He was not what people call a man's man. He could play no games. He had never touched a card in his life. He neither shot, fished nor hunted. Though he had a few male friends of his own age, men he had known at Oxford, and a few others whose religious proclivities he could sympathise with, the men with whom he got on best were older. They liked the enthusiastic interest he took in their noble mansions and their contents. Sometimes, however, his enthusiasm was put to a more severe test than he appreciated. When he went to stay at Port Eliot his host met him at the station and almost walked him off his feet while he showed him every picture in the house, every plant in the garden and every walk in the woods. 'There is a limit to what ought to be shown,' Augustus wrote acidly in his diary, 'and Lord Eliot has never found it out.'

It was with the ladies that Augustus found himself most at ease. They liked to go sketching with him, they were flattered by his eagerness to see the local sights and took him daily for drives to visit a neighbouring great house, a fine church or a romantic ruin. In those days, days long before the gramophone and the radio, when the gentlemen came home from their day's sport, after tea the ladies retired to rest till it was time to dress for dinner and Augustus went to his room to write his Journal. The interval between dinner and bedtime was devoted to conversation and music. Augustus showed the party his sketches and those who sketched showed him theirs. Anyone who played the piano was invited to play and anyone who had a voice was pressed to sing. It was then that Augustus came into his own. He was a famous teller of stories. He had discovered his gift when he was a boy at Harrow and early in life had begun assiduously to collect them. He wrote them all down in his Journal. A great many were ghost stories, for there were few of the houses he visited that did not harbour a ghost who appeared either to frighten a guest who had been put in the haunted room or to announce the death of a member of the family. There appears to be a lack of initiative in the conduct of ghosts and there is a certain tediousness in their behaviour; Augustus, however, told his stories very well and when people asked him whether he believed in them he answered that he had no doubt at all of their existence. A little shudder of apprehension would pass through his listeners. But ghost stories by no means exhausted his repertoire. He could tell stories of telepathy, of clairvoyance and of precognition. He could tell blood-curdling tales about the Italian and Spanish aristocracy. It was a 'turn' that he did, and he took pains to perfect himself. In fact it was the greatest of his social assets. He relates that when he was staying at Raby, if ever he escaped to his room after tea a servant would tap on the door and say: 'Their Graces want you to come down again.' 'Always,' he adds, 'from their insatiable love of stories.' His renown grew to such a height that on one occasion a party was arranged at Holland House so that he might tell Princess Louise some of his stories, 'which she had graciously wished to hear'.

The houses he visited were mostly those of high-minded people and the conversation often turned on religious subjects. On these Augustus, who had heard them discussed at home from his earliest youth, was quite at home. Sometimes, however, his hosts went to lengths that he thought unnecessary. When, for instance, he was staying with the George Liddells he found Sunday 'a severe day'. It was spent in going to church, reading prayers and listening to long sermons at home. Even on week-days, after morning prayers, the Psalms and Lessons for the day, verse by verse, were read before anyone was allowed to go out.

Augustus did not consort much with men of letters and I think his interest in them was only in so far as they gave occasion for an anecdote which he could tell at the luncheon or the dinner table. On one of her journeys Maria Hare took him to see Wordsworth, who read to him, 'admirably', some of his verses. Augustus said that the poet talked a good deal about himself and his own poems, 'and I have a sense of his being not vain, but conceited.' The distinction is delicate and I think Augustus must have meant that Wordsworth had an overweening opinion of himself without caring much what other people thought of him. We are all more tolerant of vanity than of conceit, for the vain man is sensitive to our opinion of him and thereby flatters our self-esteem; the conceited man is not and thereby wounds it.

Mrs. Greville took Augustus to see Tennyson: 'Tennyson is older looking than I expected so that his

40

unkempt appearance signifies less. He has an abrupt, bearish manner, and seems thoroughly hard and *un*-poetical: one would think of him as a man in whom the direct prose of life was absolutely ingrained.' Tennyson insisted that Augustus should tell him some stories, but he 'was atrociously bad audience and constantly interrupted with questions.' 'On the whole,' Augustus adds, 'the wayward poet leaves a favourable impression. He could scarcely be less egotistic with all the flattery he has. . . .' 'Mr. Browning', whom he met at Lady Castletoun's, failed to make an impression on him, though he quotes, I suspect with approval, Lockhart's remark: 'I like Robert so much because he is not a damned literary person.' Carlyle had been to stay at Hurstmonceux Rectory, where 'they had not liked him very much', when Augustus was a child, and during the period with which I am now concerned he met him from time to time in London. Once Lady Ashburton took him to see the sage of Chelsea in Cheyne Row. 'He complained much of his health, fretting and fidgeting about himself, and said that he could form no worse wish for the devil than that he might be able to give him his stomach to digest with through all eternity.' On another occasion, at Lady Ashburton's, Carlyle 'talked in volumes, with fathomless depths of adjectives, into which it was quite impossible to follow him, and in which he himself often got out of his depth.' Augustus met Oscar Wilde at Madame du Quaine's. 'He talked in a way intended to be very startling, but she startled him by saying quietly, "You poor dear foolish boy, how can you talk such nonsense?" Another friend had met him at a

41

country house and one day he came down looking very pale. "I am afraid you are ill, Mr. Wilde," said one of the party. "No, not ill, only tired," he answered. "The fact is, I picked a primrose in the wood yesterday, and it was so ill, I have been sitting up with it all night." '

So much for Augustus's association with men of letters. When he was still quite a young man he had been impressed by the Speaker of the House of Commons, Denison, with whom he was a fellow-guest at Winton Castle, because he had 'a wonderful fund of agreeable small talk.' Augustus realised how useful an accomplishment this was. I don't know whether he deliberately sought to acquire it, but from my own recollection I can vouch for his having done so. If he could dine out every night he was in London it was because he gave his hosts good value for their money. He could listen as well as talk. I think one can get some idea of the sort of conversation which was then in favour by an incident Augustus relates. Rogers, the banker-poet, was a great talker and there was a brash young man by the name of Monckton Milnes, whom people called The Cool of the Evening, and who was a great talker too. 'If Milnes began to talk, Rogers would look at him sourly, and say, "Oh, you want to hold forth, do you?" and then, turning to the rest of the party, "I am looking for my hat, Mr. Milnes is going to entertain the company." ' But by the time Augustus came to know the brash young man he had become Lord Houghton, and 'in spite of his excessive vanity' he grew sincerely attached to him. He could not but deplore that Lord Houghton sometimes entertained 'a quaint collection of anybodies and nobodies'; on one occasion indeed he asked Augustus to a party where he met 'scarcely anyone but authors, and a very odd collection—Black, Yates, and James the novelists; Sir Francis Doyle and Swinburne the poets; Mrs. Singleton, the exotic poetess (Violet Fane), brilliant with diamonds; Mallock, who had suddenly become a lion from having written a clever squib called "The New Republic", and Mrs. Julia Ward Howe with her daughter'. This was not the sort of company Augustus was used to keep.

Lord Houghton could tell as many stories as he could and had a fund of small talk as agreeable. Augustus was wise enough not to compete with him. But it was different when he came in contact with persons of no social consequence who sought to make themselves heard at the dinner tables of the great. Abraham Hayward, whom he often to his disapproval met in society, he dismisses in two footnotes: 'Constantly invited by a world which feared him, he was always determined to be listened to, and generally said something worth hearing'; but nothing that Augustus thought fit to record. In another footnote Augustus says that Hayward, 'who had been articled in early life to an obscure country attorney, always seemed to consider it the *summum bonum* of life to dwell among the aristocracy as a man of letters; and in this he succeeded admirably, and was always witty and well-informed, usually satirical, and often very coarse.'

IV

Augustus's social career was crowned by an event that came about through his writing of the memoirs of the Baroness Bunsen. When this work was approaching completion he went to Germany to see her two unmarried daughters and on the way paid a long visit to the Dowager Princess of Wied, who had been a close friend of hers. Here he met her sister, the Queen of Sweden, who told him that she must consider him a friend, since in a life of trouble his *Memorials of a Quiet Life* had been a great comfort to her and that she never went anywhere without them. She was sending the Prince Royal to Rome that winter 'to learn his world' and expressed a wish that Augustus should go there too. She invited him to visit her in Sweden and shortly afterwards he did so. He made a good impression on the King and it was agreed that Augustus should act as guide and mentor to the Prince during his sojourn in the Eternal City. The Queen begged him to sow some little seeds of good in her son's young heart and the King talked to him of the places and people he should see. Augustus accordingly went to Rome for the winter. He saw the Prince twice a day and showed him the necessary sights. He took care that he should make acquaintance with the right people. He read English with him and delivered lectures at places of interest not only attended by the Prince and Baron Holtermann, Marshal of the Palace, but by a choice selection of distinguished persons. At the end of the winter Augustus was able to write: 'On looking back, I have unmixed satisfaction that I came. He leaves Rome quite a different person from the Prince I found here—much strengthened, and I am sure much improved in character as well as speaking English and French (which he did not know before), and being able to take a lively animated part in a society in which he was previously a cypher.'

In May the Prince arrived with his suite at Claridge's. Augustus took him to see the Royal Academy, the National Gallery, the Tower of London and accompanied him to Oxford, where he was given an honorary degree. Throughout the season he went to a great many parties, where royalties, English and German, were present in numbers, dukes and duchesses past counting, and in fact everyone who was anyone. At a ball at Lady Salisbury's Augustus presented so many of his relations to the Prince that he said what astonished him more than anything in England was the multitude of Mr. Hare's cousins.

The years wore on. Augustus continued to travel, to go to house parties, and when in London to dine out. The period when visits to country houses often lasted weeks, and even months, was long since a thing of the past. It was become usual to have guests for the week-end. Augustus rarely accepted such invitations; he preferred to spend his Sundays in London. He went to church to hear the preacher who was the fashion of the day, and then, perhaps after a stroll in the Park, went out to lunch. Luncheon parties on Sunday, not yet quite killed by the week-end habit of going into the country, were popular. The most famous of these were given by Lady Dorothy Neville and to them Augustus often went. In the afternoon there was generally a tea-party to go to, and someone was sure to ask him to dinner or supper.

But even dukes and duchesses are mortal. The day comes when the chatelaines of great castles are displaced by their daughters-in-law and either retire to a dower house or establish themselves in Bath or Bournemouth. Augustus began to spend more time at Holmhurst, and was apt to come up to London only when a brilliant marriage or an important funeral made it necessary. The company he kept was not so choice as it had been. He had never much frequented that of Americans or Jews. In his early years he found the Americans he met on his travels vulgar, but he grew more tolerant with age, and when Mr. Astor bought Cliveden and asked him to stay he thought him genial and unassuming. Money was becoming a power. Aforetime, when a person of title married the daughter of a wealthy manufacturer, Augustus, on mentioning the fact, passed it over lightly and it was almost with surprise that he noted in his Journal that the new countess was unaffected and ladylike. Now not only younger sons but heirs to great titles were marrying into Jewish families.

The nineties came. Augustus did not like them. He was getting on for sixty and many of his old friends had died. The pace of life had increased. A different generation amused itself in a different way. There were no longer ladies of artistic inclinations to go on a drawing-party with him to 'dirty, picturesque St. Bartholomew's'; there were no longer ladies of high

Augustus Hare (1834-1903)

rank with whom he could have edifying conversation on religious subjects; no longer could he spend pleasant evenings with his portfolio showing his sketches to an appreciative circle, and no longer was he pressed to tell his famous stories. There was no more conversation. The size and lateness of dinners had killed society. The time had passed when a brilliant talker could 'hold forth' and the company was prepared to listen. Now everybody wanted to talk and nobody wanted to listen. Perhaps Augustus was beginning to seem a bit of a bore; and as the decade wore on there was more than one evening in the year when no one asked him to dinner. He had an affectionate disposition, and by the time I came to know him he still had a number of friends who were attached to him, but when they spoke of him it was with as it were a shrug of the shoulders, with a smile kindly enough, but with a suspicion of apology. He had become faintly ridiculous.

The reader can hardly have read so far without its having crossed his mind that Augustus was something of a snob. He was. But before I deal with this I should like to point out that the word has in the course of years somewhat changed its significance. When Augustus was young, gentlemen 'wore straps to their trousers, not only when riding, but always: it was considered the *ne plus ultra* of snobbism to appear without them' (so in the days of my own youth it was considered to wear brown boots in London). I take it that when Augustus wrote this, snobbish was equivalent to vulgar or common. I have a notion that the sense it now has was given it by Thackeray. Of course Augustus was a snob. But here, like Thomas Diafoirus in *Le Malade*

Imaginaire, I am inclined to say: '*Distinguo, Mademoiselle.*'
The Oxford Dictionary defines the snob as 'one who
meanly or vulgarly admires and seeks to imitate, or
associate with, those of superior rank or wealth; one
who wishes to be regarded as a person of social importance.' Well, Augustus didn't *wish* to be regarded as a
person of social importance; it had never occurred to
him that he was anything else. Not to have regarded
him as such would have seemed to him merely a proof
of your crass ignorance. He did not meanly or vulgarly
seek to associate with those of superior rank. His grandfather was Mr. Hare-Naylor of Hurstmonceux, and he
counted at least three Earls as his cousins, several times
removed certainly, but cousins none the less. He had
always moved in the highest circles of society, indeed
it was for them that he had written one of his most
successful books, *The Story of Two Noble Lives*, and he
regarded no one as his superior. He had not, like
Abraham Hayward, wormed his way into those circles
by intelligence, or wit, but taken his place in them by
right of birth. Yet most people looked upon Augustus
as an outrageous snob.

On one occasion, after I had known him for some
years, I happened to be at a party when the conversation turned upon this trait of his, not with malice, but
with an amused indulgence. At that time when you
had dined out it was polite to call within a week, and
though you hoped to find your hostess not at home it
was only decent to ask whether she was. Sometimes,
in my nervousness, when the butler opened the door
to me I could not for the life of me remember the name
of the lady on whom I was paying this visit of courtesy.

I spoke of this and added that when I told Augustus how great my embarrassment was when this occurred, he answered: 'Oh, but that often happens to me, but I just say, "Is her ladyship at home?" and it's always right.' Everyone laughed and said: 'How exactly like Augustus!' I was somewhat taken aback when twenty years later I read this little quip of mine in a book of memoirs, for there was not a word of truth in it; I had invented it on the spur of the moment merely to amuse the company. But it was sufficiently characteristic of Augustus to be remembered. I have written this essay partly to make reparation to his memory.

It was inexcusable of me thus to make fun of Augustus, because his kindness to me was great. He took an interest in my career as a novelist. 'The only people worth writing about,' he told me, 'are the lower classes and the upper. No one wants to read about the middle classes.' He could not have foreseen that a time would come when, so low has the stock of the upper classes fallen, no self-respecting novelist would introduce a person of rank into his fiction except as a figure of fun. Augustus felt that as a medical student at St. Thomas's Hospital I must have learnt as much as was needful about the lower orders, but he thought I should acquire more than a superficial knowledge of the manners and customs of the nobility and gentry. With this object in view he took me to call on various of his old friends, and finding I had not made too bad an impression, asked them to invite me to their parties. I was glad enough to have the opportunity to enter a world new to me. It was not the great world, for by then Augustus

had lost touch with it; it was a world of elderly gentlefolk who lived in discreet, rather dull splendour. I was
no credit to Augustus and if they continued to invite
me it was for his sake rather than for mine. Like most
young men, then and now, I thought my youth a
sufficient contribution to the entertainment of the
company. I had not learnt that when you go to a
party it is your business to do your best to add to its
success. I was silent and even if I had had anything
to say would have been too shy to say it. But I kept
my eyes and my ears open, and I learnt one or two
things that I have since found worth knowing. I was
once at a great dinner of twenty-four people in Portland Place. Of course all the men were in tails and
white ties and the women, in satins and velvets, with
long trains, were richly jewelled. We walked down the
stairs to the dining-room in a long procession, giving
our arm to the lady whom we had been instructed to
'take down'. The table blazed with old silver, cut
glass and flowers out of season. The dinner was long
and elaborate. At the end of it the ladies, on catching
the hostess's eye, rose and trooped up to the drawing-
room, leaving the men to drink coffee and liqueurs,
smoke and discuss the affairs of the nation. I found
myself sitting then next to an old gentleman whom I
knew to be the Duke of Abercorn. He asked me my
name and, when I gave it, said: 'I'm told you're a very
clever young man.' I made an appropriately modest
reply, and he took out of his tail pocket a large cigar-
case.

'Do you like cigars?' he asked me, as he opened it and
displayed to my view a number of handsome Havanas.

'Very much,' I said.

I didn't see fit to tell him that I couldn't afford to buy them and smoked one only when it was offered me.

'So do I,' he said, 'and when I come to dinner with a widow lady I always bring my own. I advise you to do the same.'

He looked carefully over those in his case, picked one out, put it up to his ear and slightly pressed it to see that it was in perfect condition, and then snapped the case shut and put it back in his pocket. It was good advice he gave me, and since I have been in a position to do so I have taken it.

Augustus, though indulgent, did not spare reproof when he thought it was good for me. One Tuesday morning, when I had been spending the week-end with him, the post brought me a letter which he must have written soon after my departure. 'My dear Willie,' it ran. 'Yesterday when we came in from our walk you said you were thirsty and asked for a *drink*. I have never heard you vulgar before. A gentleman does *not* ask for a *drink*, he asks for *something to drink*. Yours affectionately. Augustus.'

Dear Augustus! I'm afraid that if he were alive now he would find the whole English-speaking world as vulgar as he found me then.

On another occasion when I told him I had been somewhere by bus, he said stiffly: 'I prefer to call the conveyance to which you refer an omnibus'; and when I protested that if he wanted a cab he didn't ask for a cabriolet, 'Only because people are so uneducated today they wouldn't understand,' he retorted. Augustus was of opinion that manners had sadly deteriorated since his youth. Few young men knew how to behave in polite society, and how could you wonder when there was no longer anyone to teach them? In this connection he was fond of telling a story about Caroline, Duchess of Cleveland. She had rented Osterley and had a number of people staying with her. She was lame and walked with an ebony stick. One day when they were all sitting in the drawing-room the duchess got up, and a young man, thinking she wanted to ring the bell, sprang to his feet and rang it for her; whereupon she hit him angrily over the head with her stick and said: 'Sir, officiousness is not politeness.' 'And quite right too,' said Augustus, and then in an awe-struck tone: 'For all he knew she might have wanted to go to the water-closet.' Even duchesses are subject, his lowered voice indicated, to natural necessities. 'She was a very great lady,' he added. 'She's the last woman who ever smacked her footman's face in Bond Street.' He thought with nostalgia of his own grandmother, the wife of the Reverend Oswald Leicester, who habitually boxed the ears of her maids. Those were the brave days of old, when servants were prepared to suffer corporal punishment at the hands of their mistresses.

Augustus published the first three volumes of *The Story of My Life* in 1896 and the next three in 1900. Seldom can a work have been received with such a unanimity of hostile criticism, and it is true that one might cavil at an autobiography even of a very great man in six volumes of nearly five hundred pages each. The *Saturday Review* described it as a monument of self-sufficiency and found it wholly without delicacy. The

Pall Mall Gazette was filled with genuine pity for a man who could attach importance to a life so trivial. The *National Observer* had not for long met with an author so garrulous and so self-complacent. *Blackwood* asked: 'What is Mr. Augustus Hare?' Mr. Augustus Hare remained superbly indifferent. He had written the book for himself and his relations, as he had written *The Story of Two Noble Lives* for 'the upper circles of society', and not for the general public, and I suppose it never occurred to him that in that case it might have been better to print it privately. Even after the publication of the second three volumes, undeterred he went on with the story, writing every morning, to the very end of his life. There was no one, however, with sufficient piety to publish what was doubtless a bulky manuscript.

To refresh my memory I have recently re-read *The Story of My Life*. What the reviewers said was true enough, but it was not the whole truth. It was apparently the custom of the day when you went abroad to write long descriptions to your friends of the sights you saw, and these letters of his Augustus printed in full. They are tedious. Yet they describe a way of travel, by carriage or *vetturino*, which no longer obtains, and the look of old towns and historic cities the aspect and character of which the advance of civilisation has entirely changed. If a novelist wanted to write a story situated in Rome during the last years of the temporal power he would find in Augustus's pages not a little picturesque material that he could turn to good use. Of course the lists of important persons he met on his visits to great houses are intolerably dull. He had no gift for bringing people to life and they exist merely as names; though not himself a sayer of good things, he had a quick appreciation of those said by others, and a diligent reader is often rewarded by coming upon a nice repartee. I should have liked to be present when the lady on being reproached for burning the candle at both ends, said: 'Why, I thought that was the very way to make both ends meet.' Augustus inserted in the six volumes of this work all the stories, ghost stories and others, which he used to relate to a group of spell-bound ladies of high rank. Some of them are very good. It is unfortunate that they should be buried in a mass of twaddle. Augustus suffered from the persuasion that he was a gentleman, and an author, though a voluminous one, only by the way. If he had been a man of letters first and a gentleman next, he might, instead of writing the six volumes of his autobiography, with the material at his disposal have produced two or three books which would have been, not a lively, but at least an interesting, picture of the times.

V

Augustus had suffered from an affection of the heart for some years, and one morning, in 1903, when the maid went into his room to bring him his cup of tea and his two slices of thin bread and butter, she found him lying on the floor in his night-shirt, dead.

ZURBARAN

I

LONG ago, in the dim past of the thirteenth century, when Alfonso the Wise was King of Castile, some herdsmen were guarding their cattle near a place called Halia in Estremadura. One of them missed a cow that belonged to him and went to look for her, but after vainly ranging the plain for three days, he thought it well to pursue his search in the mountains, and there, not far from the River Guadalupe, he found her lying dead in a great grove of oak trees. He was surprised that the wolves had not mangled the carcase, and bewildered when he found no wound or injury to account for the creature's death. To make the best of a bad job, he took out his knife to skin it and, as the custom was, began by making two cuts on the chest in the form of a cross; upon which the cow rose to her feet, and the herdsman, terror-stricken, started away from her. As he did so Our Lady St. Mary the Virgin appeared to him and spoke as follows:

'Have no fear, for I am the Mother of God, through whom the race of mankind was redeemed. Take your cow and put her with the others, for from her you will get many more in memory of the apparition which you now see. And when you have put her with the others, go back to your dwelling-place and tell the priests and the people there to come to this place where I have appeared to you, and let them dig and they will find an image of me.'

The Blessed Virgin vanished from his sight, and the herdsman took his cow and put her with the others and told his companions what had happened to him. They jeered, but he answered and said:

'My friends, do not believe what I say, but believe the sign on the chest of the cow.'

Then they, seeing the sign in the form of a cross, believed him. He left them to return to his village, and as he went told whomsoever he met of the strange thing that had occurred to him. The cowherd was a native of Caceres, where he had a wife and children, and when he came to his house he found his wife weeping because her son was dead, whereupon he said:

'Do not be troubled nor weep, for I promise him to St. Mary of Guadalupe if she will restore him to me alive and well, and I will give him to be the servant of her house.'

And at that moment the boy rose, alive and well, and said to his father:

'Father, get ready, and let us go to St. Mary of Guadalupe.'

They that were there were amazed and believed all that the cowherd told them of the apparition of Our Lady. Then he went to the priests and said to them:

'Gentlemen, know that St. Mary the Virgin appeared to me in the mountains near the River Guadalupe; and she bade me tell you to go to that place and dig there, and you would find an image of her, and that you should take it from there and build her a house. And she told me further that those who were in charge of her house should give food once a day to all of the poor who came to it. And she told me further that she would make many people come to her house from many countries on account of the many miracles she would perform all over the world both on sea and on land. And she told me further that there, on that great mountain, she would cause a town to be built.'

No sooner had the priests, and others, heard these things than they betook themselves to the place where Our Lady had appeared. And when they got there they dug and found a cave like a sepulchre and they took the image of Our Lady which was there, and they built a little house of dry stones and of green wood for her, and they roofed it with cork because in that district there were many cork trees. Then the sick, suffering from various ills, came to that spot, and when they prayed to the image of Our Lady they were healed; and they returned to their own countries praising God and his blessed Mother for the great marvels and miracles she had performed. And the cowherd remained with his wife and children as guardian of the shrine, and his descendants as servitors of St. Mary the Virgin.

The attentive reader will have noticed that the cowherd, when he came to tell his story to the priests, somewhat enlarged upon the instructions which the Blessed Virgin had given him, and thus secured for himself a position of honour and perhaps of profit. The inhabitants of Estremadura have the reputation in Spain of being as canny as they are adventurous.

Notwithstanding that the sanctuary was in a wild and almost inaccessible place pilgrims came from afar off to do reverence to the image on account of the miracles and marvels which by means of it St. Mary performed. In course of time the little sanctuary fell into decay, and Alfonso XI, grandson of Alfonso the Wise, built in its place a great church so that all who came might find room to worship. At about this time he fought a desperate battle with the Moors, and in danger of defeat placed his cause in the hands of St. Mary of Guadalupe, who thereupon granted him a glorious victory. From then on, the Kings of Castile, and afterwards the Kings of Spain, showed great devotion to the sanctuary. They endowed it with lands, as also did private persons, and gradually it acquired great wealth. Houses were built for the priests, hospitals for the sick, dormitories for the pilgrims; and since their needs had to be provided for, Jews and Moors, in whose hands trade then was, lured by the prospect of gain, settled in the town which was built to accommodate them. Guadalupe underwent various vicissitudes, for its vast estates, its immense herds, the privileges which had been accorded it, excited the jealousy of neighbouring feudal lords, lay and ecclesiastic, and more than once it had to resist the assault of armed bands. Notwithstanding, by means of pious donations and the ability of its priors, its wealth increased. Towards the end of the fourteenth century the monks of the order of St. Jerome were charged with its custody and administration. Succeeding priors erected buildings of great splendour and spent enormous sums on their decoration. Kings continued to visit and befriend it. Christopher Columbus before his first journey went there to ask for the protection of the Blessed Virgin; later, Cortez, Pizarro and Balboa, all natives of Estremadura, went to thank Our Lady for the favours she had conferred upon them.

Now, early in the thirties of the seventeenth century, Philip IV being then King of Spain, Fray Diego de Montalvo, the prior, decided to build a sacristy more magnificent than any in Spain, and he engaged a painter called Francisco de Zurbaran to paint pictures to adorn its walls. He chose him doubtless because he had already won reputation for his paintings of monks, especially those who wore a white habit, as did those of St. Jerome, and perhaps also because he was a native of Estremadura. He was born in fact in a tiny village called Fuente de Cantos not very far from Guadalupe.

The date of Zurbaran's birth is unknown, but his certificate of baptism still exists, and this is dated November the seventh, 1598. His father was a peasant in easy circumstances and, like the peasant in Fuente de Cantos to this day, had, it may be supposed, a two-storey house in the village street, with unglazed windows, and he kept his cow and his pigs, his goats and his donkey on the ground floor, and lived in the upper one. While he attended to his land, the boy of a morning led the livestock to the pasture, and it is related that one day, when he was but twelve, some gentlemen who were hunting saw him drawing on the trunks of trees with a piece of charcoal, and struck by his cleverness took him to Seville. But stories more or less similar have been told of various painters, of

Giotto among others, and are merely an expression of the surprise laymen must feel when they discover talent in someone whose birth and antecedents give no reason for it. Talent is a mysterious gift of nature for which there is no accounting.

The story told of Zurbaran cannot be true, since there is a document extant which proves that he did not go to Seville till he was between fifteen and sixteen. This is an agreement, signed by his father towards the end of 1613, whereby he apprenticed his son for three years to a certain Pedro Diaz de Villanueva, who is described as an *imaginero*, a maker of images, and who by affixing his signature to the document early in January undertook to teach Francisco de Zurbaran his art such as he knew it without concealing anything from him, for which he was to receive sixteen ducats, half payable at once and the other half at the end of eighteen months. The ducat was worth about ten shillings, but ten shillings then was equivalent to five pounds or more today, so that the total sum paid would amount now to something between eighty and a hundred pounds. The agreement stipulated that for this the image-maker should provide his apprentice with board and lodging and pay for his treatment in sickness so long as this did not last longer than two weeks, in which case the expense was to be borne by the boy's father. His father was besides to provide him with clothes and foot-wear. A further condition was that if 'the said Francisco' during the three years of his apprenticeship chose to work on feast-days and holidays his earnings should belong to him.

Some surprise has been occasioned by the fact that

the lad should have been apprenticed not to one of the famous painters who were then living in Seville, but to an image-maker of so little repute that nothing is known of him but that he was Zurbaran's master. I should have thought the explanation was simple. It is true that the image-makers were often painters as well, Alonso Cano, for instance, was as highly esteemed for his polychrome statues as for his paintings, and though Pedro Diaz de Villanueva was chiefly occupied in carving the images, large and small, which were not only placed in churches but were also sought after by the laity for their private devotions, it is likely enough that he painted pictures; but if so, not one has survived. Francisco de Herrera, Juan del Castillo and Juan de las Roelas, who had studied with Titian, were at this time well-known teachers in Seville, and their paintings were highly thought of; it is not unreasonable to suppose that they would have refused to take a pupil for the modest sum Zurbaran's peasant father was prepared to pay. If he apprenticed the boy to an insignificant artisan it is surely because he was cheap.

The most interesting thing we know about the three years of Zurbaran's apprenticeship is that he became friends with Velasquez, who was studying with Herrera el Viejo. For long the influence of the Italian schools had been paramount in Spain, but about this time the paintings of Ribera began to be known, and because they appealed to marked idiosyncrasies of the Spanish character grew popular. Ribera was a Spaniard, but at an early age, after studying for some time with Ribalta at Valencia, he made his way to Rome. There he worked with Caravaggio, the head of the naturalistic school and a master of chiaroscuro. The violent contrasts of light and shade, the dramatic power, the sombre tones with which Ribera painted gruesome scenes of martyrdom were very much to the taste not only of the public, but also of the young painters who were impatient of the conventionality of masters who were still practising an art that had lost its savour. So great, indeed, was Ribera's influence on the young Velasquez and on the young Zurbaran that several of their early pictures have at various times been ascribed first to one and then to the other. For example, the *Adoration of the Shepherds* in the National Gallery, long considered to be by Velasquez, is now attributed to Zurbaran.

The Church frowned on the use in schools of the nude model, so the student, as exercises to prepare himself to paint the human figure, which was then the artist's only subject-matter, painted still-lifes and flower-pieces, but anything of the kind Zurbaran may have produced during this period has perished, and his first extant painting is an Immaculate Conception dated 1616. He was then eighteen. It is a hard, careful portrait of a young girl standing in space on the heads of eight cherubs, and it owes its composition very obviously to Italian influence. At about the same time he must have painted the *Virgin as a Child in Prayer*, for he has used the same homely, fat-faced wench as a model.

II

Zurbaran lived obscurely, and little can be told of him that is more than conjecture. That is not to be wondered at, for there is of necessity a great deal of monotonous regularity in a painter's life. His occupation is physically exhausting, and after his day's work is done he is unlikely to have much inclination to indulge in the kind of adventures that provide matter for a biographer. In Zurbaran's time a painter did not, as now, paint pictures because he had a mind to and trust to finding a patron to buy them; he had no money to buy colours and canvases, the appurtenances of his art, and painted on commission. His social position was humble, on a level with the goldsmith's and silversmith's, the cabinet-maker's and the book-binder's. He was a craftsman who led a modest and straitened life, and no one thought it worth his while to record its vicissitudes. If he had love-affairs they were no one's business but his own, and his comings and goings were of little interest to anyone but himself. But when an artist has won fame the world is curious to know what sort of man he was; it is hard to believe that someone who has produced work of a rare and original quality should have been to all seeming a very ordinary person whose life was no more exciting than a bank-clerk's. It happens then that legends arise and though there is no evidence for them they may so accord with the instinctive impression his work furnishes, or, if there are portraits of him, with the look of him, as to have a certain plausibility.

So it has happened with Zurbaran. The story goes that before he left Fuente de Cantos, never to return, he drew a vicious caricature of a gentleman of property who lived there. This gentleman, named Silverio de Luerca, on hearing of it, went to the boy's house and asked for him. His father told him that he had gone away, but refused to say where he was, upon which the incensed young man hit him so violent a blow on the head that within five days he died of it. Luerca fled to Madrid, where owing to influential friends he escaped the consequences of his crime, and in course of time came to occupy posts of some importance under Philip IV. Many years passed. Zurbaran went to Madrid, either because he had work to do there or because he was looking for work, and one night on his way home he came across two men who were taking leave of one another. One said: 'Good night, Luerca, see you tomorrow'; and walked away. Zurbaran went up to the man who had been thus addressed and asked him: 'Are you by chance Don Silverio de Luerca, a native of Fuente de Cantos?'

'I am.'

'Then draw your sword, for the blood of my father cries out for blood, and his life demands yours. I am Francisco de Zurbaran.'

They fought. The conflict was brief. Silverio de Luerca fell to the ground crying: 'I am a dead man,' and Zurbaran fled from the scene.

The story is certainly characteristic of the period, when the point of honour was an obsession with the Spaniards and everyone, not only gentlemen and soldiers, but haberdashers and lackeys, carried a sword and was quick to resent affront. There is in the gallery at Brunswick a portrait, said to be of Zurbaran, which gives a certain likelihood to the legend. It is that of a man of a swarthy complexion, with a head of untidy black hair, a black moustache and a black goatee, dark eyes and a stern, harsh look. You would not have said that this was a man to forget or to forgive an injury. There is in Madrid a drawing which is also presumed to be a portrait of Zurbaran, but when he was much older. The hair is thin and white, the expression mild. In neither case, however, are there better grounds for the ascription than that it has for a long time been made. He is said to have painted himself in one or other of his large compositions, in the great *Apotheosis of St. Thomas Aquinas*, for instance, and in the picture at Guadalupe of Henry III offering a bishopric to the prior. This again is mere guess-work.

But there is a small picture, recently acquired by the Prado, which one must be of a very sceptical temper not to accept as an authentic portrait of the artist in his old age. It is entitled *Jesus Christ with St. Luke in the guise of a painter*. Christ is on the Cross, and standing by his side, with a palette on his thumb and brushes in his fingers, is a painter. He is thin and worn, with a great Adam's apple protruding from his skinny neck, bald except at the back of his head, from which lank grey locks hang to his shoulders. He has the same high cheek-bones as in the Brunswick picture, but the cheeks are sunken; he has a bold, hooked nose, a long upper lip and a somewhat receding chin partly concealed by a sparse and straggling beard. He wears a loose brown smock such as Zurbaran or any painter today might wear to paint in. It is the portrait of a man broken by the years, by poverty, neglect and disappointment. His right hand is pressed to his heart and he looks up at his dying Lord with the humble, pathetic adoration of a dog unjustly beaten.

After finishing his apprenticeship Zurbaran seems to have gone to Llerena, a prosperous town in Estremadura not far from his birthplace, and there, according to Doña Maria Luisa Caturla, who has spent laborious years in a study of the artist's life and works, he married a certain Maria Paez. Her father had a large family and was by calling a gelder. Zurbaran was then eighteen and his wife some years older. Since the marriage brought him neither cash nor credit it must be supposed that it was a love match. A son was born to the couple in 1620 and a daughter in 1623. Maria Paez appears to have died about then, perhaps in childbirth, and in 1625 Zurbaran married Beatriz de Morales, a widow, who was a native of Llerena, and, again according to Dona Maria Luisa Caturla, hard on forty years of age. It is curious that he should twice have married women much older than himself. Beatriz de Morales bore him a daughter. She died in 1639 and five years later he married Doña Leonor de Tordesas, a widow of twenty-eight and the daughter of a goldsmith. By her he had no less than six children.

Strangely enough, with the exception of the two pictures I have mentioned, there is no trace of any of Zurbaran's paintings for something like eight years after he went to Llerena; yet he must have been slowly acquiring a reputation, for in 1624 he was commissioned to execute nine large compositions dealing with the life of St. Peter for the cathedral of Seville. This done, he went back to Llerena and is supposed to have spent two or three years more there; he was then invited by the monks of a convent in Seville to return to the city to paint for their new cloister a series of pictures concerned with the life of St. Peter Nolasco. He agreed to do this and after finishing his task he painted a Crucifixion for the convent of St. Paul. These works excited so much admiration that a petition was presented to the town council by certain gentlemen praying that 'in view of the consummate art he had shown in these productions, and taking for granted that painting is not the least ornament of the state,' he should be solicited to take up his residence in Seville, 'if not on a salary or with a contribution to his expenses, at least in language that would gratify him, since such an approach would effect the purpose.' The town council, having considered the matter, charged the author of the petition, Don Rodrigo Suarez, to inform Zurbaran 'how much the city desired that he should dwell there on account of the favourable opinions they had formed of him, and the city would take care to favour him, and to assist him on all occasions that presented themselves.' Zurbaran accepted the flattering invitation and, as a statement he made later indicates, sent to Llerena for his wife and children.

But this was not the end of the matter. The local painters were incensed that one whom, since he came from Estremadura, they looked upon as a foreigner should be settled among them in such an honourable way. Since for the most part the only commissions to be secured were to paint for churches and convents, the market was limited, and the competition of a stranger was resented. Alonso Cano presented another petition to the council protesting against the resolution they had passed and calling upon them to have Zurbaran interrogated to determine his qualifications. The town council seem to have been strangely amenable to petitions, for they agreed that what Alonso Cano asked was reasonable, and to Zurbaran's indignation the heads of the painters' union (for so I translate *alcaldes pintores*), supported by other members of the craft, with a scrivener and a policeman to accredit their authority, forthwith went to inform him that he must within three days submit to examination. He immediately called the council's attention to the fact that they themselves had invited him to stay in Seville on account of his eminence as a painter and for the glory of the city, whereupon at great personal inconvenience he had transferred his residence from Llerena to Seville, and he requested them therefore to declare that he was under no obligation to comply with so insulting a demand. It may be presumed that the town council saw the justice of his claim, for he remained in Seville, and continued to execute the numerous commissions he received from all parts of the peninsula.

In 1634 he was bidden to Madrid by Velasquez at the order of Philip IV to paint pictures for the palace called El Buen Retiro which the favourite, the Count-Duke of Olivares, was building to divert the King's attention from the unhappy condition of the country and the disastrous wars with Holland, France and England, for all of which the obstinate folly of the

Count-Duke was responsible. Velasquez had been settled in Madrid for some years. At that time if an artist did not paint religious pictures he could only make a living by painting portraits, and since such money as there was in Spain was to be found at Court, it was by repairing thither that the portrait-painter was most likely to meet with patrons. It is possible that Velasquez was unable to get commissions for religious pictures in his birthplace, where, as is shown by the efforts made by the painters of Seville to drive Zurbaran from the city, the competition was keen, or it may be that his astute father-in-law, Pacheco, saw that his great gifts would better serve him in Madrid; the fact remains that he went there, and there, as we know, he soon gained the King's favour and so entered upon his triumphal career. The commission offered to Zurbaran was to paint a series of canvases illustrating the labours of Hercules. I shall have something to say about them later; here I will only relate a charming anecdote that has come down to us. He had been given the honorary title of the King's Painter, either for the work he was then engaged on or for the decoration of a boat which the nobles of Seville had presented to Philip so that he might take his ease in it on the placid waters of the pleasure-grounds which surrounded his new palace. One day, having finished one of these pictures, he affixed his signature: Francisco de Zurbaran, the King's Painter. Someone touched him on the shoulder. He turned round and saw a gentleman in black standing behind him, a gentleman with long fair hair, a long pale face, pale blue eyes, and a long chin. It was the King. With a smile His Majesty of Spain, with the courtesy for which he was famous, pointed to the signature and said: 'The King's Painter and the Painters' King.'

The compliment was gracious, but does not appear to have been followed by the offer of further employment, for when Zurbaran had executed this commission he returned to Seville. He painted then for the Charterhouse at Jerez de la Frontera the fine pictures which are now in the museum at Cadiz. In 1638 he went to Guadalupe. Of the work he did there I shall also have something to say presently.

Zurbaran was paid small sums for his paintings and with a large family to support he can have had little chance to save money. Merely to pay his way he needed constant orders. The artist depends on the favour of the public. He spends years learning his craft and developing the personality which will give the peculiar tang to his work which is his originality; and it may be long then before he assembles a sufficient number of patrons to provide him with means adequate to his needs. But too often it happens that though he is still in full possession of his talent a younger man appears on the scene who has something new to offer which, even if inferior in quality, by the attraction of its novelty captures the fickle fancy of the public. What pleased before pleases no longer. This is what befell Zurbaran. People grew tired of the sort of pictures he painted and turned eagerly to the productions of a man still in his twenties who was supplying them with something that appealed to their emotions as perhaps the honest, sober work of Zurbaran had never done— Murillo. He was facile and graceful, his colour was rich and harmonious, and about the time of Zurbaran's third marriage, when he had adopted what is known as his 'warm' style, he was the most popular painter in Seville. He combined realism with sentimentality and so responded to two marked traits of the Spanish character. Zurbaran received fewer and fewer commissions. He does not seem to have signed a single picture between 1639 and 1659, and one can only suppose that if he painted any he did not think them important enough to affix his signature to them. In 1651 he went once more to Madrid, perhaps to see Velasquez, who had just returned from his second visit to Italy, and through whose influence, it may be, he hoped to get another commission from the King; but if this was his object, he failed, and shortly afterwards he went back to Seville. Things seem to have gone from bad to worse, for in 1656, because he had not paid the rent of his house for a year, his effects were seized and put up at auction; but so wretched were they that not a single bid was made.

Two years later he went to Madrid again, but this time for good, and so far as anyone knows he spent the rest of his life there. He was then sixty. He was old to attempt a new manner. Such communication as an artist has to make is primarily to his contemporaries. He may have curious and unusual things to tell them, but he speaks to them in the idiom of his day. Another generation adopts another idiom. There is one thing that is fairly certain, an artist can only develop on the lines which nature has marked out for him, his mode of expression is of the essence of his personality and the attempt to assume a new one is futile. If the language he speaks is no longer understood he must be content to remain silent and trust to the amends which time may have in store for him. Time sifts the significant from the trivial. Posterity is unconcerned with the fashions of a bygone era; it chooses from the mass of material that has come down it what responds to its immediate needs.

But Zurbaran had to live, and to live he had to paint the sort of pictures people wanted. They wanted the sort of pictures that Murillo painted. This is what Zurbaran set himself to do. It was an unfortunate experiment. The pictures he painted had little of his own strength and none of Murillo's charm.

He was still alive in 1664, for in that year he was engaged as an expert to decide the value of a collection of pictures, fifty-five in all, after the death of their owner, a certain Don Francisco Jacinto de Salcedo. It is perhaps significant of the conditions which then prevailed that on the list that has come down to us the names of the painters are not given, but only the subjects and the dimensions of the canvases. The highest value was put upon the largest. It represented the Adoration of the Kings and was ten foot long and just under eight foot high. It was valued at fifteen hundred reals. The real, according to Cotgrave, was equivalent to the English sixpence; so that, including the frame, which was then apt to be elaborate, highly decorated and costly, the picture was estimated to be worth thirty-seven pounds, ten shillings. The average value of full-length portraits of saints and monks seems to have been about five hundred reals, which was fifteen pounds. It is no wonder, if such were the prices paid, that Zurbaran was reduced to penury, and Murillo, his successful rival, died without leaving enough money for his burial.

III

Velasquez died before Zurbaran and in his place other artists were officially created Painters to the King, Mazo first and then Carreño. The dynasty of the Hapsburgs came to an end, and with the Bourbons the eighteenth century entered Spain. Zurbaran's art had nothing to say to a public that admired Van Loo and his sons, Rafael Mengs and Tiepolo. The nineteenth century knew nothing of him, and it was not till certain historical events occurred that his own countrymen thought to remember him. After the disasters of the Spanish-American war in which Spain lost the last remnants of the great empire upon which, Charles V could boast, the sun never set, the Spaniards, humiliated by the crushing defeat, sought by looking back on the glories of their Golden Age to find something in which they could still take pride. Cuba and the Philippines had gone, but nothing could rob them of the magnificence of their cathedrals and palaces, the genius of their writers Cervantes, Lope de Vega, Calderon, Quevedo, and the splendour of their painters.

Velasquez was already world-famous, and the discerning throughout Europe after some hesitation were succumbing to the enigmatic lure of El Greco, but it was left to the Spaniards themselves to rescue Zurbaran from oblivion. And when at last they took cognisance of him I think they must have felt, as we may all feel now, that he was the most Spanish of the three. He lacked the dazzling, air-fraught brilliance of Velasquez, the passionate intensity of El Greco, but he was of the soil as was neither of the others. He had the qualities which the Spaniards recognised in themselves. He had the honesty, the sobriety, the deep religious feeling, the self-respect, the hardihood, which, notwithstanding the misrule of three centuries, the profligacy of courts, the amiable frivolity of the eighteenth century, the dull stupidity of the nineteenth, they felt were deep-rooted in their being. His want of imagination did not offend them, for they were not creatures of ardent imagination, and his realism was agreeable to them, for they were inveterately realistic. They were not romantic, for romance is more at home in the misty north and thrives ill under a southern sun, but they were passionate, and in Zurbaran's pictures they dimly felt a passion held in check by force of will and by self-respect.

In 1905 the Spaniards collected as many of his pictures as they could procure and gave an exhibition of them in the Prado. I do not know what impression it made on the public; I cannot discover that it made any on the rest of Europe.

The paintings Zurbaran did for the Buen Retiro have been an embarrassment to his admirers, and for long they threw doubt on their authenticity, but that persevering searcher of the archives, Doña Maria Luisa Caturla, has within the last few years discovered a receipt for them signed by Zurbaran. They are poor. The subject doubtless was ungrateful, and it may be that it could only have been treated, as for example Piero da Cosimo might have treated it, with fantasy, as a decoration enlivened by little fauns disporting on the green, gaily coloured birds and mythological animals; but such a treatment could scarcely have occurred to Zurbaran. He was of a literal disposition. There was no place in his earnest realism for caprice. There is nothing heroic in his Hercules, nothing to remind you that he was the son of a god and of a princess of Mycenæ; he is but a Spanish peasant, naked but for a loin-cloth, muscular, coarse and ill-favoured; he might be no more than a professional strong man in a fair. The industrious lady performed an equivocal service to Zurbaran when she proved beyond question that he was their author.

But an artist has the right to be judged by his best work. This he generally produces within a comparatively few years; with Zurbaran this seems to have lasted from 1626 to 1639. Now, the *Labours of Hercules* were painted in 1634, when he was at the height of his powers. What is the explanation? The only one I can suggest is that like every other artist Zurbaran had his limitations, and when he attempted something out of their compass he could fail worse than one with lesser gifts would have done. I think he was a modest, sensible man, and he was accustomed to carry out the wishes of his patrons; one cannot suppose that, even if he had been able to afford it, the thought of refusing a royal commission crossed his mind. He was given a job to do, and he did it to the best of his ability. In this case he made a mess of it. There can be little doubt that the instructions which his ecclesiastical patrons gave him were precise, and he was obliged to follow them. Though they ordered pictures to adorn chapels, churches and sacristies, their aim primarily was not to acquire a work of art, but a work of edification, and also, and this frequently, one that should serve to glorify the community that had commissioned it by portraying for the devout and generous public its eminent members, the miracles they had performed, the graces of which they had been the recipients, and even the martyrdom one or other of them had suffered. On occasion their demands rendered it impossible for the painter to contrive a satisfactory composition. There is in the Prado a picture of Zurbaran's representing the Vision of St. Peter Nolasco. The Heavenly City, which an angel points out, is inset in the upper left-hand corner with a very disturbing effect. The angel reminds you of a lecturer delivering a travelogue, and you expect him at any moment to give the operator a nod, on which with a jerk the slide will display another aspect of the city.

Zurbaran had no great skill in composition and little ingenuity of invention; he is at his best in single figures or, if he has to deal with more, in very simple arrangements.

What he could do in favourable circumstances one may judge for oneself from the eight huge pictures he painted for the sacristy at Guadalupe. They may be seen in the place they were painted for, and therefore to their best advantage, and one may accept the tradition in the convent that he designed the polychrome frames and advised upon the decoration, somewhat fussy to the taste of today, of the walls and ceiling.

They represent notable events in the lives of certain monks of the order. Four are signed by Zurbaran, and four, of less importance, are not, so it has been supposed that, though begun by Zurbaran, they were finished by another hand. It was while he was engaged on this task that his wife contracted the illness from which she died, and it may be that he left it incomplete to be with her at her death.

Common opinion holds that Zurbaran's masterpiece is the *Apotheosis of St. Thomas Aquinas* which is now in the museum at Seville; I should have said rather that his masterpiece was the eight pictures, taken collectively, which I am now considering. They exhibit all his merits and none of his defects. In some of his paintings, in those at Grenoble for instance, his personages are distressingly wooden; they are lay figures, not human beings. The personages of the pictures at Guadalupe are of flesh and blood. They have the animation of life. They are convincingly real. Zurbaran was a very good draughtsman, and he seems to have had something of a dramatic sense which enabled him to arrange the set and choose the properties so as to give verisimilitude to the scene he was depicting. The backgrounds are pleasing, but conventional, and it is evident that his main interest was in the characterisation of his sitter. His models, I may add, were the monks who happened to be in the convent when he was there. One of the most impressive of these productions is the portrait of Father Gonzalo de Illescas, who was prior of the monastery about the middle of the fifteenth century. He is shown at his desk, a pen in his raised hand, looking up as though there had been a knock on the door and he were waiting for someone to come in. The face might be that of any business man of today, thoughtful, able and guarded. As I tried to explain to the reader at the beginning of this essay, such an establishment as Santa Maria de Guadalupe, with its widespread estates, its feudatory towns, its immense herds, with its hospitals and hostels, was a great business undertaking, and the prior, who was during his term of office in absolute control, had to be, though certainly of a piety sufficient to command respect, a very active man of affairs. Zurbaran's colour, though sober, hard, harsh even, and a trifle cold, was sumptuous. Such of the pictures in the sacristy as face the windows have been exposed to the violent light of the Spanish summer for three hundred years and the colour has faded to the soft tints of pastel. This has deprived them something of their force, but for all that there is a nobility about them which is imposing. There is in them the easy power of a craftsman who knows his business.

The *Apotheosis of St. Thomas Aquinas* is of vast dimensions and the figures are more than life-size. St. Thomas is standing on a cloud, with a pen in one hand and an open book in the other, and on each side of him, seated on clouds presumably, are four doctors of the Church magnificently attired. Below, on each side of a column behind which is a charming view of a street, are two kneeling groups, in one of which is the Emperor Charles V with three of his courtiers, and in the other, accompanied by three monks, the archbishop who built the church for the altarpiece of which this huge production was designed. Above, in the clouds, are

78

Zurbaran's 'Apotheosis of St. Thomas Aquinas',
now in the museum at Seville

Jesus Christ, carrying the Cross like a gun, the Blessed Virgin and two other inhabitants of the celestial region who have been identified as St. Paul and St. Dominic. The picture is impressive by its size, the vigour of its execution, the proficiency of its draughtsmanship and the brilliance of its colour; but you cannot fail to notice the awkwardness of its composition. It is divided into three sections so that the eye cannot survey it comfortably as a whole, and the lowest part, which should surely be the least important, is the most attractive. The name of the model who sat for St. Thomas has come down to us. He was a canon of the Cathedral of Seville, Don Augustin Abreu de Escobar, and a friend of Zurbaran's. In portraiture, when the sitter is a person of eminence, it is less necessary that a portrait should resemble him than that people who know him only by hearsay or through his works should feel that that is exactly how he must look. This is even more so when a painter sets out to represent someone who is long since dead. But in his portrayal of St. Thomas Aquinas, Zurbaran has painted a man who can scarcely have resembled him. You cannot persuade yourself that the Seraphic Doctor was a spry, plump young man of undistinguished appearance.

Zurbaran seldom made mistakes like this. There is in the museum at Seville a large picture of Pope Urban II in conference with St. Bruno. St. Bruno was the founder of the Carthusian order and was come to Rome from his retreat in the valley of the Chartreuse at the request of Urban II. Zurbaran has caught with his accustomed skill the characteristics of the Pope, who was a temporal as well as a spiritual ruler, and of the ascetic monk. Bruno is looking down, his hands modestly concealed in the sleeves of his habit. His face is emaciated, and there is in the expression, notwithstanding the humility of his bearing, the strength of purpose, the obstinacy with which according to history he fought simony and corruption in the Church. The Pope looks out at the spectator with a hard, shrewd look, a man accustomed to command and accustomed to be obeyed, but yet with a certain anxiety in his expression, as though, face to face with this austere, obdurate monk, whose pupil he had been, he did not, for all his great station, feel quite sure of himself.

At about the same time that Zurbaran painted this fine picture he painted for the same convent a picture representing St. Hugo, Bishop of Grenoble, visiting the convent which with his assistance St. Bruno had founded. The seven monks who constituted the new order are seated at their meal in the refectory. The white habits, which Zurbaran painted so admirably, have a curious stiffness. This is said to be due to the fact that whereas Zurbaran painted the heads from nature, he painted the clothes from lay figures. It is an old tradition; but I cannot see why, though he disposed the habits on a lay figure, they should not have hung in natural folds; it seems more plausible that if in many of his pictures the habits hang in folds that no material could assume, so that they appear to be of cardboard (as for example in the St. Antony with the Infant Jesus), it is owing to his early training as a wood-carver with the *imaginero* who was his master. He never quite lost his fondness for the stylised folds of material. It is, indeed, a fine simplification which gave him opportunity for the chiaroscuro in which he delighted, and to my mind it gives a dramatic value to the figures of many of the innumerable monks he painted.

When I said that Zurbaran lacked imagination I exaggerated; it would have been more accurate to say that he lacked fancy. Portraiture, and Zurbaran was pre-eminently a painter of portraits, is to some extent a collaboration between the painter and his sitter; the sitter must give something; there must be something in him which excites the painter's sensibility sufficiently to enable him to portray somewhat more than his model's outward seeming. The painter must have a faculty resembling the novelist's by virtue of which he can slip into the skin of the characters he creates and think their thoughts and feel their feelings. This faculty is imagination and this Zurbaran possessed. His sitters are so sharply individualised that it requires little perspicacity to discern their dispositions and idiosyncrasies. In the great array of his monkish portraits Zurbaran has depicted most of the humours to which men are prone. In this array you may recognise in turn the idealist, the mystic, the saint; the fanatic, the stoic, the autocrat, the precisian; the self-seeker, the sensualist, the glutton and the clown. For it was not only the love of God that induced these men to adopt the life of a religious. Sometimes it was frustrated ambition or a disappointment in love, sometimes a longing for peace and security and sometimes a desire, natural enough, to rise in the world, since if he was not inclined to seek fortune in America or in the wars, the Church offered the only means whereby a poor but clever boy of humble origins could hope to achieve distinction.

Zurbaran painted few secular portraits of men, but on the other hand many of young women, mostly beautiful, and dressed in the handsome clothes of the period. Since the young do not in the general cast of their features often display character he was unable to exhibit his peculiar gift for characterisation, and since the young women of his day, like those of ours, smothered their faces with paint and powder, thereby making themselves look as much like one another as they could, he satisfied himself with giving them good looks, and painting with a wealth of colour the silks and satins of their dress, their pearls and jewelled brooches. Of those I have seen the most striking is that of Santa Casilda. It is in the Prado. She has little of the youthful charm that marks the others, but a face in which there is, with a certain homeliness, an air of the somewhat severe distinction which we are apt to call aristocratic.

The interesting thing about these female portraits is that they purport to represent saints, but if you trouble to look into the lives of the various persons named you discover that, saintly as they were, they could never have worn such gorgeous clothes nor possessed such costly ornaments. There is evidence that at the period during which Zurbaran was active a fashion arose in Spain to have portraits painted either of the daughters or wives of noblemen, or by gentlemen of the objects of their affection, with the attributes of certain saints. Lope de Vega had a lady, with whom, from what we know of him, we may guess his relations were far from continent, painted as the Chaste Susanna, and it is recorded that a Prince of Esquilache caused his mistress to be portrayed with the insignia and in the costume of St. Helena. These saints of Zurbaran were the ladies of Seville. Spanish women of position, owing to the Moorish influence still in some respects prevalent, lived in seclusion, and it seems to have been thought unbecoming, unless they were of the blood royal, that they should allow themselves to be painted as themselves; but by the exercise of this ingenious subterfuge they managed without offence to their delicacy to gratify a natural desire and by presenting their likeness to church or convent at the same time perform an act of piety. It can hardly have failed to be a source of satisfaction when they attended Mass in the chapel of their predilection to see a picture of themselves hanging on a wall or decorating an altarpiece. There were no private views of the Royal Academy nor *vernissages* at the Salon, to which they could go to hear the comments of all and sundry on the portrait that hung on the line; but we may surmise that it was with just such a mingling of pride and apprehension as obtains today that these ladies listened to the congratulations of their friends who came to the chapel to see, to admire, to criticise, to decry the picture of their intimate acquaintance as St. Agnes, St. Rufina or St. Marina.

In speaking of the paintings of Zurbaran I have mentioned his masterly draughtsmanship, the felicity, the variety, the depth of tone with which he represented the white of his monks' habits, the opulence of colour in the habiliments of princes of the Church and the dresses of great ladies; I have dwelt on the sincerity of his workmanship, his honest craftsmanship, his dignity, his sobriety; and I have laid stress on his convincing portraiture, his keen appreciation of character and the persuasiveness of his representation of persons long since dead; I have pointed out how impressive these huge canvases are and how on occasion they have a striking nobility. I cannot expect the reader to have noticed that I have not claimed that any of the pictures I have spoken of had beauty. Beauty is a grave word. It is a word of high import. It is used lightly now—of the weather, of a smile, of a frock or the fit of a shoe, of a bracelet, of a garden, of a syllogism; beautiful serves as a synonym for good or pretty or pleasing or nice or engaging or interesting. But beauty is none of these. It is much more. It is very rare. It is a force. It is an enravishment. It is not a figure of speech when people say it takes their breath away; in certain cases it may give you the same suffocating shock as when you dive into ice-cold water. And after that first shock your heart throbs like a prisoner's when the jail gate clangs behind him and he breathes again the clean air of freedom. The impact of beauty is to make you feel greater than you are, so that for a moment you seem to walk on air; and the exhilaration and the release are such that nothing in the world matters any more. You are wrenched out of yourself into a world of pure spirit. It is like falling in love. It *is* falling in love. It is an ecstasy matching the ecstasy of the mystics. When I think of the works of art that have filled me with this intense emotion I think of the first glance at the Taj Mahal, the St. Maurice of El Greco, seen again after long years, the Adam with his outstretched arm

84

in the Sistine Chapel, Night and Day and the brooding figure of Giuliano on the tombs of the Medici and Titian's *Entombment of Christ*. Such an emotion I, for my part, have never received from the highly competent, well-painted, well-drawn, dignified, thoughtful canvases which Zurbaran painted for the altars of churches and the sacristies of convents. They have great qualities, but they appeal to the mind, to the intelligent appreciation, rather than to the heart and nerves which are thrilled and shattered by the rapture of pure beauty.

Yet he did paint a few pictures, in size or importance of subject of no great consequence, which to my mind have a rare and moving beauty, and of these I propose presently to speak. But before I do this I must deal with another topic.

When the Spaniards re-discovered Zurbaran and hailed him as one of the glories of their country they claimed that he was a mystical painter. Nothing could be further from the truth, and it is to the great credit of Don Bernardino de Pantorba, author of a very sensible, though too brief, essay on Zurbaran, that he has pointed out how mistaken they were. It is true that for the most part he painted pictures of religious subjects; as I have pointed out, Churchmen were his chief patrons, and there can be little doubt that this serious, simple-minded man was a good Catholic. The Spaniards have always been of a religious turn—after their fashion, and in the seventeenth century they were intensely devout. The Council of Trent was still fresh in their minds and the Inquisition was alert to punish any suspicion of heresy. But it was a devotion at once

fervid, sentimental, grim and brutal. To see to what
extravagance it could be carried one need only read
Calderon's play, *La Devocion de la Cruz*. We may be
pretty sure that Zurbaran performed his religious duties
with unction. It has seemed to me that one can get
some inkling of the nature of his religion from one of
the pictures he painted for the convent at Guadalupe.
It represents St. Jerome being chastised by two angels
because of his excessive predilection for secular literature. He is on his knees, naked but for a loin-cloth,
and the two angels with whips in their hands are
belabouring him with might and main, while Jesus
Christ sitting on a cloud a little way off, with one hand
upraised as though he were counting the strokes, wears
an expression of mild complacency. Since it is stated
that the Saint's particular transgression was to read
the works of Cicero to the neglect of the inspired Word
of God, an irreverent person might suggest that he
owed this castigation to a rival author's annoyance
that another author's works should be read as well as,
or in competition with, his own. But the significant
thing is that the Saint is evidently deeply conscious of
his sin, and his attitude of supplication indicates not
only that he prays for forgiveness, but looks upon the
hiding he receives as well-deserved. I think we may
hazard the surmise that Zurbaran thought so too.

In his various representations of Christ Zurbaran
surrendered to a sentimentality that was alien to his
temperament. He gives him the offensive smugness of
the self-satisfied rector of a fashionable church. This
is not the compassionate yet stern and virile teacher
who delivered the Sermon on the Mount. But on the

other hand his Crucifixions display a sombre power that was all his own. He does nothing to palliate the horror of the tragic scene. A dark and stormy background emphasises the solitude of the sufferer. In one, with the head downcast, the face in deep shadow, there is, strangely, a moving expression of despair. The body has already the cold greyness of a corpse. In another the agony of the uplifted face, appealing, you would have said in vain, to a deaf God has a harrowing intensity. It could hardly have failed to exacerbate the emotions of a people who found such a dreadful fascination in the spectacle of their Saviour's anguish.

It may be that Zurbaran's religious pictures accorded with the religious conception of the Spaniards of his day and aroused the feelings of devotion which they were designed to do. I don't think they can do that now. I have a notion that by his time faith had been rendered too formal, too rigid, too chartered for a painter to feel, and so portray, the artless emotion which makes the works of the early Sienese painters so simply and naïvely religious. The observances of religion were a method by which you escaped the tortures of hell and won the reward of eternal bliss, and your spiritual advisers were there with their cut-and-dried rules to point out your way for you and, if necessary, to indicate a short cut.

And of course it is a mistake to suppose that mysticism is necessarily religious in character. The mystic experience is a specific thing. It is true that it may arise from the practice of religion, and then it is generally the reward of prayer and mortification, but it may also arise through the influence of a drug, opium, for instance, or the mescal bean, and in rare instances from the hypnotic suggestion of running water (as with St. Ignatius Loyola), and sometimes from the impact of beauty on a soul of peculiar sensibility. So many people have described in terms so similar the ecstasy of illumination that there can be little doubt of its reality. I do not know that they who experience it through the effects of a drug or the impact of beauty draw the same inferences as do they who experience it through the practice of religion, but the sensations are the same, a sense of liberation, a sense that they are united with something larger than themselves, a sense of exhilaration, a sense of awe and of detachment from all that is base, idle and transitory.

Is it rash to suggest that when the artist, poet or painter, is mysteriously seized with that curious humour which is known as inspiration, so that notions come to him he cannot tell whence and he finds himself aware of things he never knew he knew, he enjoys a condition indistinguishable from that of the mystic in rapture?

It is absurd to call Zurbaran a mystic. He was, as a matter of fact, a downright, literal fellow, who was given a job to do and did it as well as he could. It is true that, like other painters of religious subjects, he painted various saints and monks in ecstasy. But he used the common formula. He painted them with their mouths gaping and their eyes turned up towards heaven so that little is seen but their whites. You are disconcertingly reminded of a dead codfish on a fish-monger's marble slab. The mystical state is probably something that the painter cannot represent, and it is not by attempting to do so that he can arouse in the spectator the mystical emotion which art can sometimes induce. I have seemed myself to feel it when I have contemplated the painting of the flesh in El Greco's *Crucifixion* in the Louvre and in one or two of Chardin's still-lifes. It is quite a different feeling from that which you get from the ingenuous and heart-felt pictures of the Sienese Primitives. Kant, as we all know, claimed that the sublime does not exist in nature, but is introduced into it by the sensibility of men of a considerable degree of culture. So it may be that mysticity does not reside in pictures, but that some pictures have in them a potentiality which enables a beholder of a peculiar disposition, of some æsthetic training, to infuse them with a magic which excites in him the mystical experience. They have then a beauty deeper than the beauty which takes your breath away, they have a beauty which is tremulous and animating so that for a brief moment you experience the same ecstasy as the saints experience in communion with Divine Reality.

I have spoken of Zurbaran as though he were a plodding, industrious, competent painter who painted pictures as a cabinet-maker might make a *bargueño* or a potter turn out an Hispano-Moorish plate. And so he was. He was no genius. And yet, perhaps because he was so honest, so sincere, because he had the sensibility which enabled him to paint the white of his monks' habits with such an admirable subtlety, sometimes, very rarely, he was able to surpass his limitations. Sometimes he excelled himself. Not in those huge canvases with their figures life-size or over, not in those representations of miracles or in those portraits of noble ladies masquerading as saints, but in certain small pictures which, when you survey his many works, you may easily overlook. There are in the museum at Cadiz pictures of Carthusian monks, one of St. Bruno, another of the Blessed John Houghton, which are of such beauty, which have in them so much emotion, that you feel that here at all events he was inspired. Of these to my mind the most moving is that of the English Carthusian. I have written about this picture before and I can only repeat what I have already written. I cannot but believe that it was an English monk and not a Spanish one who served Zurbaran as a model, and I have asked myself idly who was this unknown compatriot of mine who sat to the painter for a portrait of another Englishman. There is here the well-bred refinement, the clean-cut, shapely features that you sometimes find in a certain sort of Englishman of gentle birth. The hair, the little of it that is left round the shaven skull, appears to be of a reddish-brown; the face, emaciated from long fasting, has a tension that is restless and eager. A hectic flush mantles the cheek. The skin is darker than ivory, though with the warmly supple hue of ivory, and paler than olive, yet with something of that colour's morbid delicacy. Round his neck, fastened by a knot, is a rope. One wasted hand is clasped to his breast and in the other he holds a bleeding heart.

I have had the curiosity to learn who this beatified monk was, and this is what I have found out. He was born of an ancient family in Essex about 1488. After his education had run its course his parents arranged a marriage for him suitable to his condition, but, determined to embrace a state of celibacy and to dedicate himself to the service of God alone, he secretly left his father's house and hid himself in the house of a devout cleric. There he stayed till he was ordained. For four years after this he exercised the functions of a parish priest. But at the age of twenty-eight, aspiring to a way of life still more perfect, he entered the Carthusian order. In 1530 he was chosen to be prior of the Charterhouse in London. Three years later Anne Boleyn was crowned Queen of England, and John Houghton was required by the Royal Commissioners to declare that Henry's marriage with Catherine of Aragon was invalid. He refused and was sent to the Tower. A somewhat casuistical compromise was effected and he was released; but in the following year a subservient parliament enacted that the King was supreme head on earth of the Church of England, and pronounced every person who repudiated the statute to be a traitor. John Houghton, with two of his brother-priors, refused to take the oath which acknowledged its validity and the three of them were indicted for high treason. The jury hesitated to condemn such holy men as malefactors, but were compelled by Cromwell, the King's Vicar, to bring in a verdict of guilty. They were sentenced to be hanged and quartered. John Houghton ascended the scaffold first. A thick rope was placed round his neck which it was thought would not produce strangulation so quickly as a thin one. He addressed the populace and the ladder was dragged from under him. The rope was cut while he was still alive, and he fell to the ground. They dragged him away from the scaffold, stripped him of his clothes, and his heart and entrails were torn from his body and thrown into the fire.

No one can know whether Zurbaran was unwontedly moved by the pathos of this story or whether there was some characteristic in the model he chose that peculiarly appealed to him: when he painted this young monk, by some happy accident he achieved beauty. On this occasion he was no longer the sensible, level-headed, practical craftsman, but a great painter. On this occasion, inspired, he painted a picture in which there is the mystical exaltation which throbs through the lovely verse of St. John of the Cross.

But it was not alone then that he reached a height you would never have expected him to attain. I mentioned earlier that in his student days Zurbaran, forbidden to work from the nude, is presumed to have painted a number of still-lifes. They have disappeared. But it is plain that throughout he held in peculiar affection the inanimate objects which constitute the subject-matter of still-life. In the picture of St. Hugo visiting the Carthusian monks in their refectory, for instance, the loaves of bread on the table, the bowls containing their food, the earthenware jars for the water are painted with an intimacy so sensitive, with an insight so penetrating, that they appear to symbolise something other than themselves. Now and then, perhaps as a change or a rest, Zurbaran painted a still-life. There is one in the Prado. It shows two bowls and two pitchers in a row on a table against a dark background. The two bowls stand on plates. That is all. It is as simple and straightforward as all Zurbaran's work; yet it is of a staggering beauty. It is as beautiful as the picture of the blessed John Houghton and it fills you with an emotion as intense. One of the things that must strike the sojourner in Spain is the tenderness with which the Spaniards use children. However tiresome they are, however intrusive, wilful, noisy, they seem never to lose patience with them. Well, it seems to me that it is with just this tenderness that Zurbaran painted these modest household utensils. It renders them wonderfully touching. It gives them indeed the same mystical quality which, if you but have the temper to see it, pervades the pictures of those monks at Cadiz. It is for these pictures, for this still-life, for the Christ Crucified, with the painter, old, worn and haggard, looking up at his Saviour that I think one can claim Zurbaran to be a master.

Perhaps that is not very much when you think of his vast production. It is enough. The artist has no need to carry heavy baggage to find his way to posterity. A few pictures, a book or two, suffice. The artist's function is to create beauty, though not, I believe, the mainspring of his productiveness, and not, as some think, to reveal truth: if it were, a syllogism would be more significant than a sonnet. But it is not often that the artist can do more than suggest it or approximate to it, and the layman should be satisfied if he can attain the agreeable. It is only by a rare combination of technique, deep feeling and good fortune that the artist, be he painter or poet, can achieve that beauty which in its effects is akin to the ecstasy which the saints won to by prayer and mortification. Then his poems or his pictures give the sense of deliverance, the exaltation, the happiness, the liberality of spirit which the mystics enjoy in union with the Infinite. To me it is wonderfully moving that Zurbaran, this laborious, honest, matter-of-fact man, should on a few occasions in his long life have been, none can tell why, so transported out of himself as to have done just this. It is as though the grace of God had descended upon him.

THE DECLINE AND FALL OF THE
DETECTIVE STORY

I

WHEN, after a hard day's work, you are spending the evening alone and you look at your bookshelves for something to read, do you take down *War and Peace*, *L'Education Sentimentale*, *Middlemarch* or *Du Coté de chez Swann*? If you do I admire you. Or if, wishing to keep up with modern fiction, you take up a novel the publisher has sent you, a harrowing story of displaced persons in Central Europe, or one that a review has induced you to buy, a ruthless picture of the lives of poor white trash in Louisiana, you have my hearty approval. But that is not the sort of person I am. For one thing, I have read all the great novels three or four times already and they have nothing more to tell me; for another, when I look at the four hundred and fifty closely printed pages which according to the jacket are going to lay bare to me the secrets of a woman's soul or wring my withers with the horrors of life in the slums of Glasgow (all the characters speaking broad Scots) my heart sinks; and I choose a detective story.

At the outbreak of the last war I found myself imprisoned at Bandol, a seaside resort on the Riviera, imprisoned, I should add, not by the police but by circumstances. I was in fact in a sailing-boat. She was in peace-time berthed at Villefranche, but the naval authorities ordered us to leave, so we set sail for Marseilles. We were caught in a storm and took refuge at Bandol, where there was something of a harbour. The movements of private individuals were restricted and one could not even go as far as Toulon, but a few miles away, without a permit which could only be obtained after an intolerable delay by filling in a number of forms and producing a number of photographs. I was obliged to stay put.

The summer visitors had fled incontinently and the resort had a surprised and forlorn look. The casino, most of the hotels and many of the shops were closed. The days, however, passed pleasantly enough. There were the *Petit Marseillais* and the *Petit Var* to buy at the stationer's every morning, one's *café au lait* to drink and the marketing to do. I learnt where you could get the best butter for the money and which baker made the best bread. I exerted all my charm to wheedle an old peasant-woman to keep me half a dozen fresh eggs. I found out to my shame that a huge, an enormous mass of spinach had when cooked a very stingy look. I was confounded once more by my ignorance of human nature when I discovered that the keeper of a stall in the market whose honest face attracted my custom had sold me a melon which was too ripe to eat or a camembert (though in a voice tremulous with sincerity she had assured me it was *à point*) which was as hard as a brick. There was always a sporting chance that at ten the English papers would come in, and though they were a week old it was no matter; I read them with eagerness.

At twelve there was the wireless news from Marseilles. Then luncheon and a nap. In the afternoon I walked for exercise up and down the front or stood watching the boys and old men (all the rest had gone) playing their interminable games of *boule*. At five there was the *Soleil* from Marseilles and I read once more what I had read in the morning in the *Petit Marseillais* and the *Petit Var*. After that there was nothing but the wireless news again at half-past seven. At dusk we had to shut ourselves in, and if a chink of light showed, menacing shouts came from the air-wardens who patrolled the quay and we were sternly bidden to screen it. There was nothing to do then but to read detective stories.

With so much leisure it would have been fitting if I had improved my mind by reading one of the great monuments of English literature. I have never read more than a chapter here and there of the *Decline and Fall*, and I have always promised myself that some day I would read it right through from the first page of the first volume to the last page of the last. Here was a heaven-sent opportunity. But life in a forty-five-ton sailing-boat, though sufficiently comfortable, lacks quiet. Next door to the cabin is the galley and there the sailors are cooking their evening meal, with a rattle of pots and pans, and vociferously discussing their private affairs. One of them comes in to fetch a tin of soup or a box of sardines; then he remembers that the motor must be set going or the electricity will fail. Presently the cabin boy clatters down the companion to say he has caught a fish, and will you have it for dinner. Then he comes in to lay the table. The skipper of the boat next to yours gives a hail and a

97

sailor tramps over your head to find out what he wants. The pair have an animated conversation which you cannot help listening to because they both shout at the top of their voices. It is difficult to read with attention. I think it would have been doing an injustice to Gibbon's great work to set about it in such conditions and I must admit that my aloofness of spirit did not extend so far as to have enabled me just then to read it with interest. In fact I should have had difficulty to think of a book I less wanted to read at that time than *The Decline and Fall of the Roman Empire*, and this was lucky because I hadn't got it. On the other hand I had a number of detective stories, which I could always exchange for others belonging to the owners of other boats similarly swinging to their anchors, and there were any number for sale at the stationer's where I bought my papers. During the four weeks I spent at Bandol I read two a day.

This, of course, was not the first occasion on which I had read this class of fiction, but it is the first on which I read it in the mass. Part of the First World War I spent in a sanatorium for the tuberculous in the North of Scotland and there I learnt how pleasant it is to lie in bed, what a delicious sense of liberation it affords from the responsibilities of life and how conducive it is to profitable reflection and aimless reverie. Since then whenever I can square it with my conscience I go to bed. A cold in the head is a distressing ailment for which you get no sympathy. The persons with whom you are brought in contact regard you with anxiety, not because they fear it may turn to pneumonia and result in your demise, but because they fear they will catch it. They scarcely trouble to conceal their irritation that you should expose them to this danger. For my part when thus afflicted I promptly take to my bed. With aspirin, a hot-water bottle, rum toddy at night and half a dozen detective stories I am prepared to make an ambiguous virtue of an equivocal necessity.

I have read hundreds of detective stories, good and bad, and they have to be very bad indeed for me to cast them aside unfinished, but I do not pretend to be more than a dilettante. If I present the reader with the reflections that have occurred to me on this variety of fiction it is with a proper sense of my fallibility.

First of all I should like to distinguish between the shocker and the detective story. I read shockers only by accident, when I have been misled by the title or the wrapper into believing that I was about to engage in a story of crime. They are the bastard descendants of the boys' books, Henty and Ballantyne, which amused our youth, and their vogue is due, one can only suppose, to the fact that there is a large class of adult readers whose minds have remained puerile. I have no patience with these gallant heroes who perform acts of derring-do and those dauntless heroines who after incurring incredible adventures are united to them on the last page. I hate the stiff upper lip of the first and I shudder at the archness of the second. I sometimes wonder idly about their writers. Are they seized with a divine afflatus and do they write because they must with the anguish of spirit with which Flaubert wrote *Madame Bovary*? I refuse to believe that they sit down deliberately to write, tongue in cheek, something that will bring them in a tidy sum of money.

If they did I would not blame them, for evidently this is a pleasanter way of earning a living than by selling matches in the street, which exposes you to the inclemency of the weather, or being an attendant in a public lavatory, which affords but a narrow view of human nature. I prefer to think that they are lovers of their species who are deeply moved by the thought of this vast mass of readers that has been created by compulsory education, and by their tales of fire and shipwreck, train accidents, forced landings in the Sahara, smugglers' caves, opium dens, sinister orientals, hope to win their readers to an appreciation of Jane Austen.

It is with the stories of crime that I wish to concern myself, and especially with that of murder. Theft and fraud are crimes too, and they may give rise to some pretty work in detection, but they arouse in me an interest which is no more than languid. From the standpoint of the Absolute, which is the proper standpoint from which to consider this kind of fiction, it does not matter whether the string of pearls that has been stolen is worth twenty thousand pounds or was bought at Woolworth's for a few shillings; and fraud, whether it entails a cool million or three pounds seven and six, is an equally sordid business. The writer of crime stories cannot say like that rather tiresome old Roman that nothing human is alien to him; everything human is alien to him but murder. It is, of course, the most human of crimes, for I suppose we have all at one time or another contemplated it and have been held back from it either from dread of the penalty or from the fear (probably groundless) of our own remorse. But the murderer has taken the risk at which we hesitated and the prospect of the gallows invests his action with a grim impressiveness.

I think authors should be chary of their murders. One is the perfect number, two are permissible, especially when the second is a direct consequence of the first, but it is an unpardonable error to introduce a second murder to enliven an investigation which the author fears is growing tedious. When you have more than two it becomes a massacre and as one violent death follows another you are more inclined to laugh than to quiver. It is a fault of the American authors of crime stories that they are seldom satisfied with one, or even two murders; they shoot, stab, poison or black-jack *en masse*; they are apt to turn their pages into a shambles and the reader is left with the uncomfortable feeling that they have been playing the fool with him. It is a pity, for America with its mixed population and the multifarious cross-currents of its life, with its vitality, ruthlessness and adventurous temper, offers the novelist a far more diverse and inspiring field of action than our own settled, humdrum and on the whole law-abiding country.

II

The theory of the detective story of deduction is simple. Someone is murdered, there is an investigation, suspicion falls on a number of persons, the culprit is discovered and pays the penalty of his crime. This is the classic formula and it contains in itself all the elements of a good story, for it has a beginning, a middle and an end. It was laid down by Edgar Allan Poe in *The Murders in the Rue Morgue* and for many years was scrupulously followed. For long *Trent's Last Case* has been considered the perfect story constructed on these lines. It is written in a more leisurely manner than is now usual, but it is written with an agreeable lightness in good English. The characters are well-drawn and plausible. The humour is unobtrusive. It is a bit of bad luck for Mr. E. C. Bentley that finger-prints, about which at the time he wrote little was known, have now become part of the usual police procedure. They have since then been used by innumerable writers and the elaboration with which Mr. Bentley describes the process has lost its point. Readers of detective stories have now grown crafty, and when a gentle, kindly old man who has apparently no motive to commit a murder is presented to them, they have no hesitation in deciding that it was he who committed it. You cannot read many pages of *Trent's Last Case* without being sure that Mr. Cupples is the guilty party. But you can still read the book with interest to find out why he should have killed Manderson. Mr. Bentley has deliberately neglected to conform to the canon that the crime should be brought home to the culprit by the detective. The mystery would never have been solved if Mr. Cupples had not obligingly revealed the truth. It must be admitted that it is by a most improbable coincidence that he found himself concealed in a place in circumstances which obliged him to shoot Manderson in self-defence. Nor are these circumstances credible. It is asking us to believe too much that a hard-headed business man will plot his own suicide to get his secretary hanged and it is futile to adduce the well-known Campden Case in which John Perry accused his mother, brother and himself of murdering a man, afterwards discovered to be alive, in order to get them hanged even though, as happened, it meant that he would be hanged himself. That something has occurred in real life does not make it a fitting subject of fiction. Life is full of improbabilities which fiction does not admit of.

To me the greatest mystery, never explained, of *Trent's Last Case* is why a man of enormous wealth, with a country house of at least fourteen rooms and an indoor staff of six servants, should have had a garden so small that it needed no more attention than could be given it on two days a week by a man from the village.

But though, as I have said, the theory of the detective story is simple, it is astonishing how many pitfalls beset the author. His aim is to prevent you from discovering who the murderer is till you have reached the end of his book, and he is justified in using every wile he can think of to achieve it. But he must play fair with you. The murderer must be a person who takes a prominent part in the story, and it will not do to make him a shadowy character or one who has figured so slightly that your attention has never been drawn to him. But if he has loomed large in your narrative there is the danger that he will have excited your interest and perhaps your sympathy, so that you will be displeased if he is arrested and put to death. Sympathy is a very ticklish thing. It often attaches itself to a character contrary to the author's intention. (I believe Jane Austen meant Henry and Mary Crawford to be trashy creatures whom the reader was to condemn for their levity and heartlessness, but she has made them so gay and so charming that you like them much better than prim Fanny Price and pompous Edmund Bertram.) There is one curious thing about sympathy which I do not think everyone is aware of. The reader's sympathy goes to those characters who are first presented to him; and not only in crime stories, but in other stories as well, he will be left with the feeling that he has been imposed upon if the persons for whom his interest has been aroused during the first ten pages do not turn out to be those with whom he is afterwards to concern himself. I think it would be worth the while of the writers of detective stories to remember this law and introduce their murderer only after several other characters.

It is evident that if the murderer is from the beginning made odious, with whatever red herrings the ingenious author strews your path, your suspicions will fall on him and the story will be finished before it is begun. Authors sometimes try to evade the quandary by making all or most of the characters odious, so that you have a choice among them. I am not convinced that this is successful. For one thing, it is hard to believe now, as the Victorians did, in unrelieved villainy. We know that people are a mixture of good and bad; we do not believe in them when they are represented as all good or all bad, and as soon as we no longer do that, the author has lost us. We do not care what happens to his puppets. He has got then to make his murderer that same mixture of good and bad that we know human beings are, but he has so to load the dice that when his guilt is brought home to him we are content to see him hanged. One way of loading the dice is to make the crime a very mean and brutal one. Of course we may jib at the notion that such a crime can have been committed by someone who has at least certain engaging traits; but that is the least of the difficulties that here confront the author. No one (in a detective story) has any sympathy for the victim. Either he has been killed before the book starts, or is killed so soon after that, since you know little about him, you can take no interest in him on his own account, his death means no more to you than a chicken's, and however barbarous the method, his decease leaves you cold. Moreover, if suspicion is to be thrown on a number of persons, there must be a number of motives for his murder. He must, by his own crimes, follies, bad temper, brutality, avarice or what not, have made himself so objectionable that his death perturbs you but little. He would presumably not have been killed without good reason, and if we come to the conclusion that he is just as well out of the way we are not too well pleased to see his murderer hanged. Some authors avoid the dilemma by making the murderer commit suicide when he is discovered. This justifies the canon that a life should be paid for a life, but spares the susceptibilities of the reader to whom the circumstances of the hangman's rope are repellent. The murderer then should be bad, but not too bad to be obvious and not too bad to be incredible; his motive should be compelling and he should be sufficiently unsympathetic so that when his crime is brought home to him we should feel that he richly deserves the gallows.

I should like to dwell for a little on this matter of motive. I once visited the penal colony of French Guiana. I have told elsewhere of this experience, but I do not expect anyone to have read all I have written, and since it is to the point I make no apology for repeating myself. There were then at least three establishments to which convicts were sent according to the nature of their crimes and at St. Laurent de Maroni all were murderers. Since the jury had in their verdict allowed that there were extenuating circumstances they had been sentenced not to death, but to a long term of imprisonment. I spent one whole day enquiring into the reasons that had led them to commit their crime. They were quite willing to talk. On the surface many of them seemed to have murdered for love's sake or from jealousy. They had killed their wives, or their wife's lover, or their mistress. But I didn't have to ask much further to discover that the ulterior motive was financial. One man killed his wife because she was spending his money on a lover, another killed his mistress because she stood in the way of his making a rich marriage, a third because she blackmailed him into giving her money by threatening to divulge their relations to his wife. Even when sex had nothing to do with the murder money was still the compelling incentive. One man killed to rob, another killed his brother in a quarrel over the division of an inheritance, a third killed his partner because he did not receive his proper share on the sale of stolen motorcars. One *apache* killed the woman he was living with because she had betrayed him to the police, another killed a member of a rival gang in revenge for the killing in a drunken brawl of a member of his own gang.

I came across no murder that could justly be described as a crime of passion. Perhaps of course those who had committed one were acquitted by a lenient jury or sentenced to so short a term of imprisonment that they were not sent to Guiana. Another common motive was fear. There was a young shepherd boy who had raped a little girl in a field and when she screamed grew frightened and strangled her. One man, in a good position, killed a woman who discovered that he had once been in prison for fraud and he was afraid that she would tell his employers.

It looks then as though the most plausible motives for murder that the detective-story writer can use are money, fear and revenge. Murder is a horrible thing and the murderer takes a great risk. It is hard to make your reader believe that he will take it because the girl he loves has given her affection to somebody else or because a colleague in a bank has been promoted over his head. The stakes he plays for must be high. The author's business is to persuade you that they are worth playing for.

III

At least equal in importance with the murderer is the detective. Every assiduous reader of crime stories

THE MURDERS IN THE
RUE MORGUE
AND OTHER
TALES OF MYSTERY

By EDGAR ALLAN POE

LONDON
SAMPSON LOW, MARSTON & CO. LTD.,
St. Dunstan's House, Fetter Lane, E.C.
WILLIAM DAWSON & SONS, LTD.,
Cannon House, Bream's Buildings, E.C.
1895

PENGUIN
BOOKS

MYSTERY AND CRIME

**THE LADY IN
THE LAKE**

RAYMOND
CHANDLER

MYSTERY AND CRIME

COMPLETE · UNABRIDGED

2/-

E. C. BENTLEY

Trent's Last Case

MURDER
OF
SIGSBEE
MANDERSON

The
famous
classic
detective story

6s net *An Aldine Paperback* 6s net

PAN-Books

**CALL FOR THE
SAINT**
Leslie Charteris

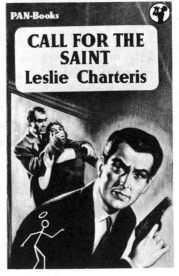

Landmarks in the development of the detective story

can trip off a list of eminent sleuths, but the most famous is certainly Sherlock Holmes. For an anthology of short stories that I was preparing several years ago I re-read the collected stories of Conan Doyle. I was surprised to find how poor they were. The introduction is effective, the scene well set, but the anecdote is thin and you finish the tale with a sense of dissatisfaction. Great cry and little wool. I thought it necessary, however, to have one of these stories in an anthology that purported to be representative, but I had difficulty in finding even one that I thought the intelligent reader would be content to read. The fact remains that Sherlock Holmes caught and has held the public fancy. His name is a household word in every country in the civilised world. People know it who have never heard of Sir Willoughby Patterne, Monsieur Bergeret or Madame Verdurin. He was drawn in broad and telling lines, a melodramatic figure, with marked idiosyncrasies which Conan Doyle hammered into the minds of his readers with the same pertinacity as the great advertisers use to proclaim the merits of their soap, beer or cigarettes, and the results were as remunerative. You know no more of Sherlock Holmes after you have read fifty stories than you did after reading one, but the constant reiteration has broken down your resistance; and this lay figure, decked out with theatrical properties, has acquired the same sort of life in your imagination as is held by Vautrin or Mr. Micawber. No detective stories have had the popularity of Conan Doyle's, and because of the invention of Sherlock Holmes I think it may be admitted that none has so well deserved it.

Detectives are of three kinds. There is the police officer, the 'private eye', known also, I believe, as a shamus, and the amateur. The amateur has for long been very popular and the writers of this class of fiction have exerted their invention to devise a character that they could use again and again. The police officer is generally a conventional figure with little individuality; at best he is astute, painstaking and logical; but for the most part he is unimaginative and obtuse. Then of course he serves as a convenient foil to the amateur's brilliance. The amateur may be endowed with a number of distinctive features which give him some semblance of a human being. By discovering things that had escaped the inspector from Scotland Yard he can prove that the amateur is more intelligent and more competent than the professional, and this is naturally gratifying to the readers of a country in which the expert is always regarded with suspicion. The conflict between the two has a dramatic quality and, law-abiding as we may be, it does not displease us to see authority in the end made ridiculous. The most important of the traits which the writer takes care to attribute to his amateur detective is humour; and this not, as you might suppose, because by making your reader laugh you induce in him an emotional instability which will make him react more violently to your thrills; but for a much more important reason. It is very necessary that your amateur detective should by his wit or some absurd mannerism of speech arouse laughter, for if you can laugh at or with a character you cannot but have a certain sympathy with him; and to enlist your sympathy is here essential to the writer.

For he has to use every means he can think of to conceal from you the patent fact that the amateur detective is a dirty dog.

He makes some show of working disinterestedly in the cause of justice, or if that is too much even for the readers of detective stories to swallow, that he is possessed by a passion for the chase; but the truth is that he is a busybody and a nosey-parker who from sheer love of interfering in what does not concern him engages in work which any decent person would leave to the officers of the law whose duty it is to do it. It is only by endowing him with engaging manners, an agreeable physique and lovable eccentricities that he can be made palatable to the reader. Above all he must have a line of amusing chatter. Unfortunately few of the writers of detective stories count a very delicate sense of humour among their accomplishments. Too many of them suppose that a joke can be repeated a hundred times and still amuse. Is it enough to make a character use English which is a literal, and often inaccurate, translation from the French to cause laughter? Is it enough to make him constantly quote or misquote hackneyed lines of verse or express himself in language of extravagant pomposity? Is it enough to use a Yorkshire dialect or reproduce an Irish brogue to make you split your sides? If it were, humorists would be two a penny, and neither Mr. P. G. Wodehouse nor Mr. S. J. Perelman would earn a living. I am still waiting for the story in which the amateur detective is shown as the despicable creature he really is and in the end gets his deserts.

I look upon the introduction of humour in a detective

story as mistaken, but I see the reason for it and with a sigh accept it; on the other hand I have no patience with love interest. It may be that love makes the world go round, but not the world of detective stories; it makes it go very much askew. I do not care if it is the gentleman-like sleuth, the chief inspector or the wrongly accused hero who wins the girl in the end. In a detective story I want detection. The line is indicated —murder, inquiry, suspicion, discovery and punishment; and the philandering of young women, however charming, with young gentlemen, however lantern-jawed, is a tiresome diversion from the theme. Love of course is one of the springs of human action, and when it gives rise to jealousy, fear or wounded vanity may well serve the author's purpose, but it narrows the field of investigation; for presumably not more than two or three of the persons in your story are affected by its power; and when it is indeed the motive for murder this becomes a *crime passionnel* and the murderer ceases to be an object of unmitigated horror. But to introduce a pretty little love story in the unravelling of a mystery is an error of taste for which there is no excuse. Marriage bells have no place in a detective story.

I think another error that these writers often commit is to make the method of murder too far-fetched. Considering how vast is the output of these stories it is natural enough that they should seek to tempt the reader's jaded appetite by murders of an extraordinary character. I remember reading one in which several murders were perpetrated by means of poisonous fish introduced into a swimming pool. To my mind such ingenuities are mistaken. The probable, as we know, is relative, and only the fact that we accept it as such is the test of it. In detective fiction we will accept a great deal; we will accept it that the murderer should leave on the scene of the crime a cigarette-end of an unusual make, muddy his shoes with a particular mould or scatter his finger-prints on my lady's chamber. We may all have our roof burnt over our heads and perish in the flames, be run over by an enemy's car, or pushed over a precipice; but we cannot believe that we shall ever be torn to pieces by a crocodile cunningly introduced into our sitting-room at the Dorchester or that when we are visiting the Louvre a villain by some fiendish machination will cause the Venus of Milo to fall and crush us as flat as a Dover sole. I think the classical methods still remain the best; the knife, the fire-arm, poison retain the advantages of probability. We may all fall victim to them or have occasion to use them.

The best writers of detective stories are those who give you the facts and the inferences to be drawn from them in readable English, but without any graces of style. Fine writing is here out of place. We do not want a purple passage to distract us when we hanker to know the meaning of that bruise on the butler's chin, nor do we want a description of scenery when the only thing that matters to us is to decide exactly how long it takes us to walk from the boat-house above the mill-race to the gamekeeper's cottage on the other side of the coppice. Nothing to us is the primrose by the river's brim. And in passing I may remark that I find it tedious to be asked by the aid of a map or a plan to make myself acquainted with the topography of the district or the lay-out of a house. Nor do we want erudition. The display of this has to my mind caused a sad falling off in one of the most ingenious and inventive of our contemporary masters of the detective story. She is a woman, I am told, of academic distinction and she has a remarkable knowledge of matters about which most of us are ignorant; but she would do better to keep it to herself. Of course it is galling to the writers of these clever books, which are read by everybody, high-brows, middle-brows and low-brows, that they should bring them so little credit. Are they invited to luncheon parties in Chelsea, or in Bloomsbury, or even in Mayfair? When publishers give their literary soirées do excited guests point them out to one another? Not more than a few of them are even known by name. The rest are enveloped in a vast anonymity of indifference.

It is natural that they should resent the patronising attitude which the very people who voraciously read their books adopt towards them, and should not be averse, when they have the chance, from drawing your attention to the fact that they are more refined and more cultivated than you appear to think. It is only human that they should wish to show the supercilious that they can be as learned as any Fellow of the Royal Society of Literature and as lyrical as any member of the Council of the Authors' Society. But it is a mistake. Let them be as strong as their own inspectors. It is very well that they should have wide information on all sorts of subjects, indeed they need it, but let them remark that the well-dressed man is he whose clothes you never notice; the culture of the detective-story writer should never distract attention from his proper business, which is to elucidate the mystery of a murder.

But let them have patience. It may well be that when the historians of literature come to discourse upon the fiction produced by the English-speaking peoples during the first half of this century they will pass somewhat lightly over the compositions of the 'serious' novelists and turn their attention to the immense and varied achievement of the detective writers. They will have to account first for the enormous popularity of this particular variety of fiction. They will be mistaken if they ascribe it to the increase of literacy which has created a huge body of avid but uneducated readers, for the 'whodunit', they will have to admit, was read also by men of learning and women of taste. My explanation is simple. The detective writers have a story to tell and they tell it briefly. They must capture and hold the reader's attention and so must get into their story with dispatch. They must arouse curiosity, excite suspense and by the invention of incident maintain the reader's interest. They must enlist his sympathy for the right characters, and the ingenuity with which they do this is not the least of their accomplishments. Finally they must work up to a satisfactory climax. They must in short follow the natural rules of story-telling that have been followed ever since some nimble-witted fellow told the story of Joseph in the tents of Israel.

Now, the 'serious' novelists of today have often little or no story to tell; indeed they have allowed themselves to be persuaded that to tell a story is a negligible element in the art they practise. Thus they throw

114

away their strongest appeal to our common human nature, for the desire to listen to stories is surely as old as the human race; and they have only themselves to blame if the writers of detective stories have stolen their readers from them. Moreover, they are often intolerably long-winded. They too seldom understand that a theme will only allow of a certain development and so will take four hundred pages to tell you what could be told in a hundred. They are encouraged to do this by the contemporary fashion for psychological analysis. To my mind the abuse of this is as harmful to the 'serious' fiction of today as was the abuse of the description of scenery in the novels of the nineteenth century. We have learnt now that descriptions of scenery should be short and should be used with the one and only purpose of getting on with the story. So should psychological analysis. In short, the detective writers are read because of their merits notwithstanding their often obvious defects: the 'serious' novelists remain in comparison little read because of their defects notwithstanding their often conspicuous merits.

IV

Hitherto I have dealt with the simple story of detection founded on the principles laid down by Poe in *The Murders in the Rue Morgue*. During the last half-century such stories have been written by the thousand and their authors have used every possible expedient to give them a specious novelty. I have already referred to murder by unusual means. Authors have been quick to make use of every new scientific and medical discovery. They have stabbed their victims with sharp icicles, electrocuted them by telephone, injected air bubbles into their blood vessels, infected their shaving brushes with anthrax bacilli, killed them by making them lick poisoned stamps, shot them with guns concealed in cameras and polished them off by invisible death rays. These extravagant methods are too improbable to carry conviction.

Sometimes of course authors have shown remarkable ingenuity. One of their cleverest inventions has been what is known as the locked room puzzle: a dead man, obviously murdered, is found in a room locked from the inside so that the murderer could apparently neither have got in or out. Poe used the idea in *The Murders in the Rue Morgue*. It is surprising that the critics have never noticed that his explanation of the mystery is demonstrably false. When, as the reader will remember, the neighbours, roused by terrific shrieks, broke into the house inhabited by the two women, mother and daughter, whom they found murdered, the daughter was found in a room locked from the inside with the windows securely fastened also from within. Monsieur Dupin proves that the giant ape which had killed them had got in by an open window and this had closed by its own weight after the beast's escape. Any policeman would have informed him that two Frenchwomen, one old and the other middle-aged, would *never* have left a window open to let in the noxious airs of night. However the ape got into the house it was not through an open window. The device has since then been most ably used by Carter

Dickson, but his success has produced so many imitators that it has by now lost its savour.

Every background has been utilised—the country house party in Sussex, Long Island or Florida, the quiet village in which nothing has happened since the Battle of Waterloo, the castle in the Hebrides isolated by a storm. So have clues—finger-prints, foot-prints, cigarette-ends, perfume, powder. So have unbreakable alibis which the detective breaks, the dog that does not bark, thus pointing to the fact that it was familiar with the murderer (this was first used, I think, by Conan Doyle), the code letter which the detective deciphers, the identical twins and secret passages. Readers no longer have patience with the girl who wanders about deserted corridors for no adequate reason and gets knocked on the head by a hooded, masked figure; nor with the girl who insists on accompanying the detective on a dangerous errand and by so doing makes a mess of his plans. All these settings, all these clues, all these puzzles have been worked to death. Of this, of course, the authors have grown well aware and they have sought to give interest to stories that have been told a hundred times already by inventions more and more extravagant. All in vain. Every method of murder, every finesse of detection, every guile to throw the reader off the scent, every scene of action in every class of life, has been used again and again. The story of pure deduction has run to seed.

It has been replaced in the public favour by the 'hard-boiled' story. This is said to have been invented by Dashiell Hammett, but Erle Stanley Gardner claims that the first to write it was a certain John Daly. In any case it was Hammett's *The Maltese Falcon* that created the vogue. The hard-boiled story purports to be realistic. Duchesses, cabinet ministers, wealthy industrialists seldom get murdered. Murders seldom take place in great country houses, on golf links or at race meetings. They are seldom committed by elderly maiden ladies or retired diplomatists. Raymond Chandler, the most brilliant author now writing this kind of story, in his sensible and amusing essay, *The Simple Art of Murder*, specifies the constituents of the genre. 'The realist in murder,' he says, 'writes of a world in which gangsters can rule nations and almost rule cities, in which hotels and apartment houses and celebrated restaurants are owned by men who made their money out of brothels, in which a screen star can be the fingerman for a mob, and a nice man down the hall is a boss of the numbers racket; a world where a judge with a cellar full of bootleg liquor can send a man to jail for having a pint in his pocket, where the mayor of your town may have condoned murder as an instrument of money-making, where no man can walk down a dark alley in safety because law and order are things we talk about but refrain from practising, a world where you may witness a hold-up in broad daylight and see who did it, but you will quickly fade back into the crowd rather than tell anyone, because the hold-up man may have friends with long guns or the police may not like your testimony, and in any case the shyster for the defence will be allowed to abuse and vilify you in open court, before a jury of selected morons, without any but the most perfunctory interference from a political judge.'

All this is very well put and it is evident that such a state of society offers the realistic author suitable matter for a story of crime. The reader is willing to believe that the incidents related actually happened; indeed, he has only to read the newspapers to know that such things are happening far from seldom.

'Dashiell Hammett,' as Raymond Chandler says, 'gave murder back to the kind of people that commit it for reasons, not just to provide a corpse, and with the means at hand, not with hand-wrought duelling pistols, curare and tropical fish. He put these people down on paper as they are, and he made them talk and think in the language they customarily used for their purposes.' This is high praise and it is justified. Hammett had been for eight years a Pinkerton detective and he knew the world of which he wrote. It enabled him to give a plausibility to his stories which has been equalled only by Raymond Chandler himself.

In the novels of this school actual detection takes a relatively minor place. No great secret is made of the murderer's identity and the interest of the story depends on the detective's efforts to fasten the guilt on him and the dangers he incurs while doing so. A consequence of this is that the writers have discarded the tiresome use of clues. In fact, in *The Maltese Falcon*, Sam Spade, the detective, pins the murder of Archer on Brigid O'Shaughnessy by pointing out to her that she is the only person who *could* have committed it, whereupon she loses her presence of mind and admits it. If she hadn't done this, but had coolly answered 'Prove it', he would have been nonplussed; and in any case had she got Perry Mason, Erle Stanley Gardner's astute

119

lawyer, to defend her, no jury would have convicted her on the flimsy evidence which was all that Spade had to produce.

The authors who specialise in the hard-boiled story have been at pains to give their detectives character and personality, but have mercifully refrained from giving them the extravagant oddities with which in imitation of Conan Doyle many of the writers of 'pure' detective stories have thought fit to endow their sleuths.

Dashiell Hammett is an inventive and original writer. Unlike the authors who use the same detective over and over again, he has created a different one for every story. The detective in *The Dane Curse* appears to be a fat, middle-aged man who depends on his wits and his nerve rather than upon his brawn; Nick Charles in *The Thin Man* has married a wife with money and retired from the business, which he resumes only on pressure; he is a pleasant fellow, with a sense of humour; Ned Beaumont in *The Glass Key*, a professional gambler and only a detective by accident, is a curious, intriguing character whom any novelist would have been proud to conceive; Sam Spade, in *The Maltese Falcon*, is the best of them all and the most convincing. He is an unscrupulous rogue and a heartless crook. He is himself so nearly a criminal that there is little to choose between him and the criminals he is dealing with. He is a nasty bit of goods, but he is admirably depicted.

Sherlock Holmes was a private detective, but the authors who came after Conan Doyle seem to have preferred to solve their mysteries by means of a police inspector or a brilliant amateur. Dashiell Hammett, having been himself a private detective, very naturally used private detectives when he came to write stories, and his successors in the hard-boiled school have very wisely followed his good example. The 'private eye' is at once a romantic and a sinister figure. Like the amateur he can be cleverer than members of the force and he can do things, mostly shady, which they are by law forbidden to do. He has the further advantage that, since the District Attorney and the police regard his unorthodox methods with suspicion, he has to fight them as well as the criminal. It adds tension and dramatic conflict to the story. Finally he has the advantage over the amateur detective that as it is his business to deal with crime he cannot be regarded as a busybody who pokes his nose into what is no concern of his. But why he has adopted this unsavoury profession we are not told. It does not appear to be a lucrative one, for he is always short of money, and his office is small and poorly furnished. We are told little about his antecedents. He seems to have neither father, mother, uncles, aunts, brothers or sisters. On the other hand he is fortunate in having a secretary who is blonde, beautiful and loving. He treats her with kindly affection and now and again rewards her devotion with a kiss, but so far as I can remember is never so far carried away as to make her a proposal of marriage. Though (with the exception of Chandler's Philip Marlow) we are not told where he comes from nor how he acquired the knowledge to pursue his avocation, we are told a good deal about his person and his habits. He is irresistible to women. He is tall and strong and tough, and can knock a man out as easily as we can swat a fly. He can take any amount of punishment without permanent injury, for he has more courage than prudence, and will put himself, often unarmed, in the power of dangerous criminals who beat him up so brutally that you are astonished to find him up and about in a day or so apparently none the worse for it, and he will take risks so hazardous that you hold your breath. The suspense, indeed, would be unbearable if you did not know that the gangsters, crooks and blackmailers who have him at their mercy dare not riddle him with bullets or your novel would come to an untimely end. He has remarkable power of absorbing hard liquor. In the drawer of his desk there is always a bottle of rye or bourbon which he gets out whenever he has a caller and whenever he has nothing else to do. He keeps a flask in his hip-pocket and a pint in the glove-compartment of his car. The first thing he does when he arrives at an hotel is to send the bell-boy for a bottle. His staple diet, like that of most Americans, has a certain monotony about it and consists for the most part of bacon and eggs or steak and 'French fried'. The only 'private eye' that I can remember who cares what he eats is Nero Wolf, but he is a mid-European and his un-American addiction to succulent victuals, like his passion for orchids, must be ascribed to his foreign birth.

The social historian of the future may notice with surprise what is plainly a difference in American habits between the time when Dashiell Hammett wrote his stories and the time when Raymond Chandler wrote his. After an exhausting day passed in heavy drinking and hair-breadth escapes from violent death Ned

Beaumont changes his collar and washes his hands and face, but Raymond Chandler's Marlow, unless my memory deceives me, has a shower and puts on a clean shirt. It is evident that the habit of cleanliness had in the interval gained an increasing hold on the American male. Marlow, unlike Sam Spade, is an honest man. He wants to make money, but will only earn it by lawful means, and he will not touch divorce. Marlow is himself the narrator of the too few stories Raymond Chandler has written. Usually the narrator and protagonist of a novel remains a shadowy character, as for instance is David Copperfield, but Raymond Chandler has succeeded in making Marlow a vivid human being. He is a hard, fierce, fearless man and a very likeable fellow.

To my mind the two best novelists of the hard-boiled school are Dashiell Hammett and Raymond Chandler. Raymond Chandler is the more accomplished. Sometimes Hammett's story is so complicated that you are not a trifle confused: Raymond Chandler maintains an unswerving line. His pace is swifter. He deals with a more varied assortment of persons. He has a greater sense of probability and his motivation is more plausible. Both write a nervous, colloquial English racy of the American soil. Raymond Chandler's dialogue seems to me better than Hammett's. He has an admirable aptitude for that typical product of the quick American mind, the wisecrack, and his sardonic humour has an engaging spontaneity.

The hard-boiled novel, as I have said, lays little stress on the detection of crime. It is concerned with the people, crooks, gamblers, thieves, blackmailers, corrupt policemen, dishonest politicians, who commit crimes. Incidents occur, but incidents derive their interest from the individuals who are concerned in them. If they are merely lay-figures you do not care what they do or what happens to them. The result of this is that the writers of this school have had to pay more attention to characterisation than the old writers of the story of deduction found necessary. They have had to make their people not only credible, but convincing. Most of the older detectives were creatures of farce and the extravagant oddities their authors gave them succeeded only in making them grotesque. Such persons never existed but in their begetters' wrong-headedness. The other actors in their stories were stock characters without individuality. Dashiell Hammett and Raymond Chandler have created characters that we can believe in. They are only a little more heightened, a little more vivid, than people we have all come across.

Having been at one time a novelist myself I have been interested in the way both these authors describe the appearance of the various persons they deal with. It is always difficult to give the reader an exact impression of what someone looks like and novelists have tried various methods to achieve it. Hammett and Raymond Chandler specify the appearance of their characters and the clothes they wear, though briefly, as exactly as do the police when they send to the papers a description of a wanted man. Raymond Chandler has effectively pursued the method further. When Marlow, his detective, enters a room or an office we are told concisely, but in detail, precisely what furniture is in it, what pictures hang on the walls and what rugs lie on the floor. We are impressed by the detective's power of observation. It is done as neatly as a playwright (if he is not as verbose as Bernard Shaw) describes for his director the scene and the furnishings of each act of his play. The device cleverly gives the perspicacious reader an indication of the sort of person and the circumstances the detective is likely to encounter. When you know a man's surroundings you already know something about the man.

But I think the enormous success these two writers have had, not only financial, for their books have sold by the million, but critical, has killed the genre. Dozens of imitators have sprung up. Like all imitators they have thought by exaggeration to improve upon their models. They have been more slangy, so slangy that you need a glossary to know what they are talking about; their criminals have been more brutal, more violent, more sadistic; their female characters have been more blonde and more man-crazy; their detectives have been more unscrupulous and more alcoholic; and their policemen have been more inept and more corrupt. In fact they have been so outrageous that they have become preposterous. In their frantic search for sensationalism they have numbed their readers and instead of horrifying them have caused them to laugh with derision. There is only one of the many merits of the two authors I have been discussing that they do not seem to have thought worth copying. They have made no attempt to write good English.

I do not see who can succeed Raymond Chandler. I believe the detective story, both the story of pure deduction and the hard-boiled story, is dead. But that will not prevent a multitude of authors from continuing to write such stories, nor will it prevent me from continuing to read them.

AFTER READING BURKE

I

I AM the happy possessor of the complete works of
Hazlitt and from time to time I take a volume from my
shelves and read an essay here, an essay there, as my
inclination prompts. I am seldom disappointed. Like
every writer he is not always at his best, which is very
good indeed, but even at his worst he is readable. He
is amusing, bitter, keen-witted, violent, sympathetic,
unjust, generous; he scarcely ever wrote a page in which
he does not give you himself, with his faults and his
virtues; and that in the end is all an author has to give.
The assiduous reader of Hazlitt cannot fail to notice how
often the name of Edmund Burke appears in his pages.
It never ceases to give me a little thrill when I find him
referred to as 'the late Mr. Burke'; the hundred and fifty
years that have passed since his death seem then to be
no great matter and I feel that he was, if not a contemporary of my own, someone whom if I had been
fortunate I might have known in my youth as, for
example, I might have known George Meredith or
Swinburne. Hazlitt was of opinion that Burke was the
first prose writer of his time and in one of his essays
states that at one period of his life his three favourite
writers were Burke, Junius and Rousseau. 'I was never

weary,' he says, 'of admiring and wondering at the felicities of the style, the turns of expression, the refinements of thought and sentiment: I laid the book down to find out the secret of so much strength and beauty, and took it up again in despair, to read on and admire.' In passage after passage Hazlitt praises Burke's style and it is evident that his own owes a good deal to his study of it. He describes him as, with the exception of Jeremy Taylor, the most poetical of prose writers. 'It has always appeared to me,' he says, 'that the most perfect prose-style, the most powerful, the most dazzling, the most daring, that which went the nearest to the verge of poetry and yet never fell over, was Burke's. It has the solidity and the sparkling effect of the diamond . . . Burke's style is airy, flighty, adventurous, but it never loses sight of the subject; nay, is always in contact with, and derives its increased and varying impulse from it.' And again: 'His style has all the familiarity of conversation, and all the research of the most elaborate conversation. He says what he wants to say, by any means, nearer or more remote within his reach. He makes use of the most common or scientific terms, of the longest or shortest sentences, of the plainest and most downright, or of the most figurative modes of speech. . . . He everywhere gives the image he wishes to give, in its true and appropriate colouring; and it is the very crowd and variety of these images that have given his language its peculiar tone of animation and even of passion. It is his impatience to transfer his conceptions entire, living, in all their rapidity, strength and glancing variety—to the minds of others, that constantly pushes him to the verge of extravagance, and yet supports him there in dignified security.'

This, and other passages too numerous or too long to cite, so much impressed me that I thought I should like to see for myself what justification there was for praise so unqualified. I had not read Burke since I was very young; I read then *On Conciliation with the Colonies* and *On the Affairs with America*; perhaps owing to my youth I did not find the matter very interesting, but I was deeply affected by the manner and I retained the recollection, vivid though vague, of a splendid magniloquence. I have now read these speeches once more, and the more important writings of Burke besides, and in the following pages I wish to submit to the reader the reflections that have occurred to me. I hasten, however, to tell him that I do not propose to deal with Burke's thought; for that it would be necessary to have a much greater knowledge of the eighteenth century than I can claim and an interest in, and a familiarity with, the principles of politics which I must admit (and it may be I should admit with shame) I am far from possessing. I desire to treat only of the manner in which Burke wrote without paying any more attention than can be helped to the matter of which he wrote. It is evident that the two can never be entirely separated, for style must be conditioned by the subject of discourse; a grave, balanced and deliberate manner befits an important theme, but has a grotesque effect when it is applied to a trivial one: contrariwise a gay, sparkling way of writing is ill-suited to those great topics of which Dr. Johnson remarked that you could no longer say anything new about them that was true or anything true about them that was new. But if writers must continue to speak of them they err when they try to excite our interest by jumping through verbal hoops and turning paradoxical somersaults. One of the difficulties that the novelist has to cope with is that his style must change with his matter and if he tries to keep it uniform he will find it hard to avoid an impression of artificiality; for he must be colloquial when he reports dialogue, rapid when he narrates action, and restrained or impassioned (according to his idiosyncrasy) when he describes emotion. But perhaps it is enough if the novelist contents himself with avoiding the grosser errors of grammar, for no one can have considered this matter without being struck by the significant and surprising fact that the four greatest novelists the world has seen, Tolstoi, Balzac, Dostoevsky and Dickens, wrote their respective languages very carelessly; and Dickens, as we know, did not even take the trouble to write tolerable grammar. It is for the historian, the divine and the essayist to acquire and maintain a settled style and it is no accident that in this country the most splendid monuments of the English language have been produced by such essayists as Sir Thomas Browne, Dryden, Addison and Johnson (for *Rasselas*, though purposing to be a work of fiction, is in effect an essay on the vanity of human wishes), by such divines as Jeremy Taylor and William Law, and by such historians as Gibbon. Among these Edmund Burke holds an eminent place.

Hazlitt says that he had tried half a dozen times to describe Burke's style without succeeding, and it may seem presumptuous in me to attempt something that

Hazlitt failed to do; but, in fact, in various of his essays he has given so good a description of it that there is really nothing left to add. He takes note of its severe extravagance; its literal boldness; its matter-of-fact hyperbole; its running away with a subject, and from it at the same time; and then he adds, 'but there is no making it out, for there is no example of the same thing anywhere else. We have no common measure to refer to; and his qualities contradict even themselves.' My object is not to describe Burke's style, but to examine its texture and to discover, if I can, the methods he employed by means of words to produce his effects. Hazlitt has set forth the rich succulence of the dish; my aim is to ferret out the ingredients that give it savour. I am concerned to find out how he constructed his sentences and how he ordered his paragraphs, what use he made of abstract and concrete words, of image and metaphor, and of what rhetorical devices he availed himself to serve his turn; and if this seems a dull subject, after all no one is under an obligation to read the following pages. To me, a writer, it is an interesting one. But I am confronted with two difficulties: the first is that I am none too confident of my capacity to deal with this somewhat ambitious task; the second is that I can only hope to achieve a measure of success by giving quotations, and these I believe only the most conscientious readers can resist the temptation to skip. Yet it is only by example that I can indicate practice. English is a difficult language to write, and few authors have written it consistently with accuracy and distinction. The best way of learning to do this is to study the great masters of the past. Much of what Burke wrote has no longer, except perhaps to the politician, a pressing interest; indeed, I believe that almost all that he has to say of value to the average reader now could be put into one volume of elegant extracts; and for my part I must confess that I could never have brought myself to read his voluminous works with such care if I had not hoped to gain something from them that would enable me to write more nearly as I wish to. The manner of writing changes with the fleeting generations and it would be absurd to try to write now like one of the great stylists of the eighteenth century, but I see no reason to suppose that they have not something to teach us that may be to our purpose. The language of literature maintains its vitality by absorbing the current speech of the people; this gives it colour, vividness and actuality; but if it is to avoid shapelessness and incoherence it must be founded on, and determined by, the standards of the period when English prose attained the highest degree of perfection of which it seems capable.

I think there are few writers who write well by nature. Burke was a man of prodigious industry and it is certain that he took pains not only over the matter of his discourse, but over the manner. 'With respect to his facility of composition,' says Hazlitt, 'there are contrary accounts. It has been stated by some that he wrote out a plain sketch first, like a sort of dead colouring, and added the ornaments and tropes afterwards. I have been assured by a person who had the best means of knowing, that the *Letter to a Noble Lord* (the most rapid, impetuous, glancing and sportive of all his works) was printed off, and the proof sent to him: and that it was returned to the printing-office with so many alterations and passages inter-lined, that the compositors refused to correct it as it was—took the whole matter in pieces, and re-set the copy. This looks like elaboration and afterthought.' And we learn from Dodsley that more than a dozen revises of the *Reflections on the French Revolution* were taken off and destroyed before the author could satisfy himself. A glance at the *Origin of Our Ideas of the Sublime and Beautiful* is enough to show that Burke's style was the result of labour. Though this work, praised by Johnson, turned to account by Lessing and esteemed by Kant, cannot now be read with great profit it may still afford entertainment. In arguing that perfection is not the cause of beauty, he asserts: 'Women are very sensible of this; for which reason they learn to lisp, to totter in their walk, to counterfeit weakness, and even sickness. In all this they are guided by nature. Beauty in distress is much the most affecting beauty. Blushing has little less power; and modesty in general, which is a tacit allowance of imperfection, is itself considered as an amiable quality, and certainly heightens every other that is so. I know it is in everybody's mouth, that we ought to love perfection. This is to me a sufficient proof that it is not the proper object of love.' Here is another quotation: 'When we have before us such objects as excite love and complacency, the body is affected so far as I could observe, much in the following manner: The head reclines something on one side, the eyelids are more closed than usual, and the eyes roll gently with an inclination to the object; the mouth is a little opened, and the breath drawn slowly, with now and then a long sigh; the whole body is composed, and the hands fall idly to the sides.' This book is supposed to have been first written when Burke was nineteen and it was published when he was twenty-six. I have given these quotations to show the style in which he wrote before he submitted to the influence which enabled him to become one of the masters of English prose. It is the general manner of the middle of the eighteenth century and I doubt whether anyone who read these passages would know who was the author. It is correct, easy and flowing; it shows that Burke had by nature a good ear. English is a language of harsh consonants, and skill is needed to avoid the juxtaposition of sounds that offend the hearing. Some authors are insensible to this and will use a word ending with a consonant, or even a pair of them, and put beside it a word beginning with the same one or the same pair (a fast stream); they will use alliteration (always dangerous in prose) and will write words that rhyme (thus producing an unpleasant jingle) without any feeling of discomfort. Of course the sense is the first thing, but the riches of the English language are such that it is seldom a sufficiently exact synonym cannot be found for the word that comes first to mind. It is seldom that an author is obliged to let something stand that grates upon his ear because only so can he say precisely what he wants to. One of the most valuable things that can be learnt from Burke is that, however unmanageable certain words may appear, it is possible by proper placing, the judicious admixture of long ones with short, by alternation of consonants and vowels and by alternation of accent, to secure euphony. Of course no one could write at all if he bore these considerations in his conscious mind; the ear does the work. In Burke's case I think it evident that the natural sensibility of the organ was infinitely developed by the exigencies of public speech: even when he wrote only to be read the sound of the spoken phrase was present to him. He was not a melodious writer as Jeremy Taylor was in the seventeenth century or Newman in the nineteenth; his prose has force, vitality and speed rather than beauty; but notwithstanding the intricate complication of many of his sentences they remain easy to say and good to hear. I have no doubt that at times Burke wrote a string of words that was neither and in the tumult of his passion broke the simple rules of euphony which I have indicated. An author has the right to be judged by his best.

I have read somewhere that Burke learnt to write by studying Spenser and it appears that many of his gorgeous sentences and poetical allusions can be traced to the poet. He himself said that: 'Whoever relishes and reads Spenser as he ought to be read, will have a strong hold of the English language.' I do not see what he can have acquired from that mellifluous but (to my mind) tedious bard other than that sense of splendid sound of which I have just been speaking. He was certainly never influenced by the excessive use of alliteration which (again to my mind) makes the *Faerie Queene* cloying and sometimes even absurd. It has been said, among others by Charles James Fox, who should have known, that Burke founded his style on Milton's. I cannot believe it. It is true that he often quoted him and it would be strange indeed if with his appreciation of fine language Burke had failed to be impressed by the magnificence of vocabulary and grandeur of phrase in *Paradise Lost*; but the *Letters on a Regicide Peace*, on which, such as it is, the evidence for the statement rests, were written in old age: it seems improbable that if Burke had really studied Milton's prose for the purpose of forming his own its influence should not have been apparent till he had one foot in the grave. Nor can I believe, as the *Dictionary of National Biography* asserts, that he founded it on Dryden's. I see in Burke's deliberate, ordered and resonant prose no trace of Dryden's charming grace and happy-go-lucky facility. There is all the difference that there is between a French garden of trim walks and ordered parterres and a Thames-side park with its coppices and its green meadows. For my part I think it more likely that the special character of Burke's settled manner must be ascribed to the robust and irresistible example of Dr. Johnson. I think it was from him that Burke learnt the value of a long intricate sentence, the potent force of polysyllabic words, the rhetorical effect of balance and the epigrammatic elegance of antithesis. He avoided Johnson's faults (small faults to those who like myself have a peculiar fondness for Johnson's style) by virtue of his affluent and impetuous fancy and his practice of public speaking.

II

We all know Buffon's dictum that *Le style c'est l'homme même*. If it is true, then by making yourself acquainted with the man it should be possible to come to a better

Edmund Burke (1729-1797)

understanding of his style. But is it true? I think Buffon thought men more of a piece than they really are. They are for the most part an amalgam of virtues and vices, of strengths and weaknesses so incompatible that it is only because they are manifest that you can believe it possible for them to co-exist in one and the same person. Burke was much discussed in his day, passionately praised by some, violently decried by others, and from the various reports that have come down to us, from Hazlitt's essays and the excellent *Life* of Sir Philip Magnus, it is possible, I think, to get a fairly accurate impression of the kind of man he was. But it is not a plausible one. It is with difficulty that you can persuade yourself to believe that merits so rare can go hand-in-hand with defects so deplorable. You are left utterly perplexed.

Edmund Burke was born in Ireland, in 1729, the son of an attorney, a profession then held in small respect: Johnson once remarked of someone who had quitted the company that 'he did not care to speak ill of any man behind his back, but he believed the gentleman was an *attorney*.' When just over twenty Burke went to London to study law and soon after his arrival formed a close friendship with a certain William Burke who, if a relation at all, was a very distant one. He soon abandoned the law for literature and for some years made his living as best he could by writing for the booksellers. He published a couple of books which appear to have attracted sufficient attention to secure him the acquaintance of Horace Walpole and the warm friendship of Dr. Johnson. He married in 1757 and the same year his younger brother Richard joined him in

London. The three Burkes were devoted to one another; William and Richard lived with Edmund and his wife, and they shared a common purse. Richard was a noisy, exuberant, disreputable fellow without, as far as one can tell, any redeeming qualities; but William was able and pushing. He had made useful friends at Oxford and when in 1765 Lord Rockingham was called upon by the King to form a ministry he persuaded him to offer Edmund the post of his private secretary and got Lord Verney to give him one of the pocket boroughs at his disposal.

Burke immediately made his mark in the House of Commons. Dr. Johnson wrote to Bennet Langton that he had 'gained more reputation than perhaps any man at his first appearance ever gained before. He made two speeches in the House for repealing the Stamp Act, which were publicly commended by Mr. Pitt, and have filled the town with wonder.' The ministry fell in 1766 and two years later Burke bought a house called Gregories with an estate of six hundred acres at Beaconsfield. It is natural enough that he should have wished to do this. His reputation was great and he had a well-justified confidence in his ability. We may suppose that his lofty spirit, his boisterous exuberance, made it irksome to him to live meanly. He was a sociable creature and loved to entertain his friends. It was a pleasure to him to succour deserving (and often undeserving) talent and to relieve the necessities of the needy. His origins were modest and such were the manners of the time it may be that he was often twitted with them. He lived in the company of the great; he was used by his party and knew himself to be invaluable, but he could not be unaware that he was regarded with suspicion; he was with them, but not of them, and there hung about him the taint of the Irish adventurer. And that of course is exactly what he was; he happened to be also a man of high principle, brilliant gifts, social and intellectual, and wide knowledge. He may well have thought that the acquisition of Gregories, by giving him a stake in the country, would add to his prestige and, by enabling him to meet these lords and gentlemen on a more equal footing, increase the influence on them which till then he had owed only to his talents.

The estate cost twenty thousand pounds and twenty-five hundred a year to keep up. It seemed strange that a man who a few years before had been glad to accept from Dodsley, the bookseller, a hundred pounds a year to do hackwork could think of disbursing so large a sum and be prepared to burden himself with an expense so great. The Burkes, with Lord Verney to back them, were engaged in vast gambling transactions in East India Stock and they seem to have bought Gregories on the profits they had made; but then, unfortunately for them, the stock fell heavily, they were unable to meet their differences, and in the end Lord Verney was ruined and William Burke fled the country. Edmund, involved in financial difficulties which harassed him to the end of his life, was obliged to mortgage the property 'up to the hilt' and borrow money from his friends. The year he bought Gregories he borrowed a thousand pounds from David Garrick, and at some later date two thousand more from Sir Joshua Reynolds. During the seventeen years of his connection with Rockingham he received from him loans amounting to thirty thousand pounds. Now it is a common experience that when sums of money of any extent have passed from one person to another there arises a constraint between them that often results in coldness. In Burke's case, such was the esteem in which his friends held him, nothing of the sort happened. They revered his 'private virtues and transcendent worth', and it may be supposed that, like Dr. Brocklesby who made him a present of a thousand pounds, they gave him the money he so badly needed as proof of their devotion. When Rockingham died he left instructions that Burke's bonds should be destroyed. Reynolds did the same thing and left him a couple of thousand pounds besides.

Burke was a proud man, sensitive of his honour, and one asks oneself if he did not feel it a humiliation to apply to his friends for money. It seems never to have occurred to him that he could very well sell Gregories and by paying his debts extricate himself from a situation that was not only mortifying but damaging to his reputation. One can only suppose that he looked upon it as an asset of such consequence that it must be retained at whatever cost to his dignity. And of course it is only a surmise that he looked upon the situation as mortifying. Borrowing, as we know, is a habit easy to contract, hard to break, and the habitual borrower soon finds a way to satisfy his need and retain his self-respect.

Burke had the insouciance which is generally considered a characteristic of the Irish in money matters, and he had also their generous warm-heartedness.

However hard pressed, he continued to give financial aid to those who enlisted his sympathies. There was an Irish painter, James Barry by name, whom he mistakenly thought a genius and to whom he gave an income so that he might study in Italy. Crabbe, the poet, was destitute; the applications he had made to one distinguished person and another for help went unanswered and as a last resource he applied to Burke. Burke installed him at Gregories and never rested till he saw him comfortably settled for life. These are only two instances of his constant benefactions. Few people came in contact with him without growing conscious of his greatness. It is remarkable how often one comes across references to the veneration with which he was regarded; so frequent are they that I have asked myself whether the word had then a slightly different connotation from what it has now. I have respect and admiration for the statesmen, generals and admirals who conducted affairs during the last war. I esteem the great gifts of the poets and novelists with whom it has been my good fortune to be acquainted, but it has never occurred to me, nor, I imagine, to anybody else, to look upon them with veneration. Perhaps we no longer possess the faculty of doing so. Burke had charm, and until worry and disappointment soured him a genial temper. He was a great talker and, as we know, Dr. Johnson valued him for the 'affluence of his conversation'. I have asked myself how this would please us at the present day. It is hard to avoid the impression that we should find it a trifle heavy, for it appears to have been devastatingly informative, and we are inclined to be impatient of being told what we can read for ourselves, if not in a book, in the news-papers. We are no better listeners than was Burke himself (Johnson complained that: 'So desirous is he to talk that if one is speaking at one end of the table, he'll speak to somebody at the other end'), and we are restless of a talker who monopolises the conversation. And Burke had neither wit nor humour. It is possible that we should think him something of a bore, and I am afraid that, notwithstanding the commanding air and fine presence that impressed Fanny Burney, we should prefer to his eloquence the playful flippancy of Miss Austen's Henry Tilney.

After the crash of East India Stock, Richard Burke, who by Edmund's influence had some years before been appointed Receiver-General of His Majesty's revenues in the West India island of Granada, returned to his post. He bought for next-door to nothing from the Red Caribbees, descendants of the indigenous inhabitants of the neighbouring island of St. Vincent, a great tract of land which was estimated to be worth a hundred thousand pounds. The transaction was so disreputable that the Council of St. Vincent refused to admit its legality. The Burkes were by this time in desperate straits and Edmund made every effort to have his brother's claim substantiated. He offered Fox, himself badly in need of money, a share of the swag if he could induce Lord North, then in office, to rule that the purchase was valid. Fox tried, and Lord North was apparently prepared to oblige, but he bungled the matter and Richard, defeated, returned to England. He was then charged with misappropriating ten thousand pounds of His Majesty's revenues, tried and found guilty. He appealed. Burke used his influence to have the appeal indefinitely postponed. One would think that had he been convinced of his brother's innocence he would have been glad to see it proved. William Burke, on leaving England to escape being arrested for debt, went to India, and there, again by Edmund's interest, was appointed Paymaster of the King's Troops. He engaged in a variety of shady enterprises, from one of which he expected to net a hundred and fifty thousand pounds and which Sir Philip Magnus describes as flagrantly dishonest. When, utterly discredited, he was obliged to return to England he was in danger of being arrested for embezzlement. A pretty pair!

Much of this dirty business was not known till Sir Philip examined the papers at Wentworth Woodhouse, but enough leaked out gravely to discredit Edmund. Dr. Johnson was a shrewd judge of character and he retained his affection for him till his death. He valued Burke's intelligence, his knowledge, his amiability and his benevolence, but there are passages in Boswell which suggest that even he doubted his honesty. It is true that during the eighteenth century it was an understood thing that they who served the State had the right to live on it. But Burke was a moralist and a reformer. He prided himself on his high principles, and yet could use his power to get men appointed to lucrative offices for which they were notoriously unfitted. He prided himself on his veracity, and yet could untruthfully make a public declaration that he had never had dealings in East India Stock. He consistently fought injustice and corruption, and yet strained every nerve to further the corrupt and unjust chicaneries of William and Richard. Burke was a great orator; it was difficult to reconcile his admirable precepts with his reprehensible practice and it is no wonder that people said he was a humbug and a hypocrite. I don't think he was. He had to an extreme degree the failing, common to most men, and one to which politicians are not immune, of believing what it was to his interest to believe. He would not look at what he did not want to see. I don't know what name to give to this failing, but neither hypocrisy nor humbug is the right one. When Burke's affections were engaged his judgment was vitiated. It was the misfortune of his life that his most engaging trait, his power of affection, should have had such unhappy consequences. William and Richard were a pair of crooks, and not even clever crooks, for not one of their nefarious schemes succeeded; yet Edmund could write: 'Looking back to the course of my life I remember no one considerable merit in the whole course of it which I did not, mediately or immediately, derive from William Burke.' And of Richard he wrote that his integrity was such that no temptation could corrupt it. He loved them both to the end and, incredible as it may seem, respected them. In his eyes they could do no wrong and so, no matter how damning was the evidence against them, he disbelieved it.

'If a man were to go by chance at the same time with Burke under a shed, to shun a shower,' said Dr. Johnson, 'he would say—"this is an extraordinary man".' Burke was extraordinary in more ways than Johnson knew. It is not often that you come across a man the features of whose personality are so incompatible as was the case with Burke. He was upright and abject, straightforward and shifty, disinterested and corrupt. How is one to reconcile characteristics so discordant? I don't know. But let us not be censorious. Did not Becky Sharp say that it was easy to be good on five thousand a year? If Burke had been born a gentleman with a fine estate and an ample income his conduct would doubtless have been as irreproachable as he was invariably convinced it was. About that, the propriety of his conduct, he never had a doubt and he looked upon the obloquy (his own word) with which he was pursued as a shameful injustice. Machiavelli has told us that when he retired to his study to write he discarded his country clothes and donned the damask robe in which as Secretary of the Republic he was wont to appear before the Signoria. So, in spirit, did Burke. In his study he was no longer the reckless punter, the shameless sponge, the unscrupulous place-hunter (not for himself, but for others), the dishonest advocate who attacked measures introduced to correct scandalous abuses because his pocket would be affected by their passage. In his study he was the high-minded man whom his friends loved and honoured for his nobility of spirit, his greatness and his magnanimity. In his study he was the honest man he was assured he was. Then, but only then, you can say of Burke: *Le style c'est l'homme même.*

III

His style, it must be obvious, is solidly based on balance. Hazlitt stated that it was Dryden who first used balance in the formation of his sentences. That seems an odd thing to say since one would have thought that balance came naturally to anyone who added two sentences together by a copulative: there is balance of a sort when you say: 'He went out for a walk and came home wet through'. Dr. Johnson on the other hand, speaking of Dryden's prose, said: 'The clauses are never balanced, nor the periods modelled: every word seems to drop by chance, though it falls in its proper place.' Thus do authorities disagree. Burke was much addicted to what for want of a better word I will call the triad; by this I mean the juxtaposition of three nouns, three adjectives, three clauses to reinforce a point. Here are some examples: 'Never was cause supported with more constancy, more activity, more spirit.'—'Shall there be no reserve power in the Empire, to supply a deficiency which may weaken, divide or dissipate the whole?'—'Their wishes ought to have great weight with him; their opinion, high respect; their business, unremitted attention.'—'I really think that for wise men this is not judicious; for sober men, not decent; for minds tinctured with humanity, not mild or merciful.' Burke had recourse to this pattern so often that in the end it falls somewhat monotonously on the ear. It has another disadvantage, more noticeable perhaps when read than when heard, that one member of the triad may be so nearly synonymous with another that you cannot but realise that it has been introduced for its sound rather than for its sense.

Burke made frequent use of the antithesis, which of course is merely a variety of balance. Hazlitt says it is first found in *The Tatler*. I have discovered no marked proof of this in an examination which I admit was cursory; there are traces of it, maybe, but adumbrations rather than definite instances. You can find more striking examples in the *Book of Proverbs*. I hazard the guess that it was from this and from his reading of the Latin writers that Johnson developed a device which he made his own. He perfected the form and by his authority gave it a long-continued vogue. The grammars tell us that the antithesis is a mode of structure in which two clauses of a compound sentence are made similar in form, but if this is correct then we must allow two forms of antithesis, the open and the disguised. The open emphasises a contrast, the disguised a balance. Here is an example of an open antithesis: 'The doctor recollected that he had a place to preserve, though he forgot that he had a reputation to lose'; and here is what might be described as a disguised one: 'But if fortune should be as powerful over fame, as she has been prevalent over virtue, at least our conscience is beyond her jurisdiction.'

The antithetical style is vastly effective, and if it has gone out of common use it is doubtless for a reason that Johnson himself suggested. Its purpose is by the balance of words to accentuate the balance of thought, and when it serves merely to tickle the ear it is tiresome. Oddly enough it is just on this account that

Coleridge, comparing Johnson's use of it with that of Junius, condemned Johnson: 'the antithesis of Junius,' he said, 'is a real antithesis of images or thought; but the antithesis of Johnson is rarely more than verbal.' It became a trick of phraseology, and with Macaulay, who was the last writer of eminence to practise it, an exasperating trick. It is perhaps a pity that it has gone so completely out of fashion, for it had vigour and cogency. It hit the nail on the head with precision.

The master of the antithesis is the author of the *Letters of Junius*. He wrote admirably. Coleridge, it is true, claimed that when he wrote a sentence of five or six lines long nothing could exceed the slovenliness of his style, a fact which I must confess I have not noticed, but Hazlitt not only admired it, he learnt from it. I will quote the last passage of the letter he addressed to the Duke of Bedford. It is a very good sample of his manner.

'It is in vain therefore to shift the scene. You can no more fly from your enemies than from yourself. Persecuted abroad, you look into your own heart for consolation, and find nothing but reproaches and despair. But, my Lord, you may quit the field of business, though not the field of danger; and though you cannot be safe, you may cease to be ridiculous. I fear you have listened too long to the advice of those pernicious friends, with whose interests you have sordidly united your own, and for whom you have sacrificed everything that ought to be dear to a man of honour. They are still base enough to encourage the follies of your age, as they once did the vices of your youth. As little acquainted with the rules of decorum, as with the laws of morality, they will not suffer you to profit by experience, nor even to consult the propriety of a bad character. Even now they tell you that life is no more than a dramatic scene, in which the hero should preserve his constancy to the last, and that as you lived without virtue you should die without repentance.'

Now, the vogue of the antithesis had a marked effect on sentence structure, as anyone can see for himself by comparing the prose of Dryden, for example, with that of Burke. It brought into prominence the value of the period. I may remind the reader that a period is a sentence in which the sense is held up until the end: when a clause is added after a natural close the sentence is described as loose. The English language does not allow of the inversions which make it possible to suspend the meaning, and so the loose sentence is common. To this is largely due the diffusiveness of our prose. When once the unity of a sentence is abandoned there is little to prevent the writer from adding clause to clause. The antithetical structure was advantageous to the cultivation of the classical period, for it is obvious that its verbal merit depends on its compact and rounded form. I will quote a sentence of Burke's.

'Indeed, when I consider the face of the kingdom of France; the multitude and opulence of her cities; the useful magnificence of her spacious high roads and bridges; the opportunity of her artificial canals and navigations opening the conveniences of maritime communication through a solid continent of so immense an extent; when I turn my eyes to the stupendous works of her ports and harbours, and to her whole naval apparatus, whether for war or trade; when I bring before my view the number of her fortifications, constructed with so bold and masterly a skill, and made and maintained at so prodigious a charge, presenting an armed front and impenetrable barrier to her enemies upon every side; when I recollect how very small a part of that extensive region is without cultivation, and to what complete perfection the culture of many of the best productions of the earth have been brought in France; when I reflect on the excellence of her manufactures and fabrics, second to none but ours, and in some particulars not second; when I contemplate the grand foundations of charity public and private; when I survey the state of all the arts that beautify and polish life; when I reckon the men she has bred for extending her fame in war, her able statesmen, the multitude of her profound lawyers and theologians, her philosophers, her critics, her historians and antiquaries, her poets and her orators, sacred and profane; I behold in all this something which awes and commands the imagination, which checks the mind on the brink of precipitate and indiscriminate censure, and which demands that we should very seriously examine, what and how great are the latent vices that could authorise us at once to level so spacious a fabric with the ground.'

The paragraph ends with three short sentences.

I should like to point out with what skill Burke has given a 'loose' structure to his string of subordinate clauses, thus further suspending the meaning till he brings his period to a close. Johnson, as we know, was apt to make periods of his subordinate clauses, writing what, I think, the grammarians call an extended complex, and so lost the flowing urgency which is characteristic of Burke. I should like to point out also what a happy effect Burke has secured in this compound sentence by forming his different clauses on the same plan and yet by varying cadence and arrangement avoiding monotony. He used the method of starting successive clauses with the same word, in this case with the word *when*, frequently and with effectiveness. It is of course a rhetorical device, which when delivered in a speech must have had a cumulative force, and shows once more how much his style was influenced by the practice of public speaking. I do not know that there is anyone in England who is capable now of writing such a sentence; perhaps there is no one who wants to; for, perhaps from an instinctive desire to avoid the 'loose' sentences which the idiosyncrasy of the language renders so inviting, it is the fashion these days to write short sentences. Indeed not long ago I read that the editor of an important newspaper had insisted that none of his contributors should write a sentence of more than fourteen words. Yet the long sentence has advantages. It gives you room to develop your meaning, opportunity to constitute your cadence and material to achieve your climax. Its disadvantages are that it may be diffuse, flaccid, crabbed or inapprehensible. The stylists of the seventeenth century wrote sentences of great length and did not always escape these defects. Burke seldom failed, however long his sentence, however elaborate its clauses and opulent his 'tropes', to make its fundamental structure so solid that you seem to be led to the safety of the full stop by a guide who knows his business and will permit you neither to take a side-turning nor to loiter by the way. Burke was careful to vary the length of his sentences. He does not tire you with a succession of long ones,.nor, unless with a definitely rhetorical intention, does he exasperate you with a long string of short ones.

He has a lively sense of rhythm. His prose has the eighteenth-century tune, like any symphony of Haydn's, though with a truly English accent, and you hear the drums and fifes in it, but an individual note rings through it. It is a virile prose and I can think of no one who wrote with so much force combined with so much elegance. If it seems now a trifle formal, I think that is due to the fact that, like most of the eighteenth-century writers, he used general and abstract terms when we are now more inclined to use special and concrete ones. This gives a greater vividness to modern writing, though at the cost perhaps of concision. It is an amusing exercise to try to translate one of Burke's sentences into such English as the average writer would now write. I have taken one almost at random: 'The tenderest minds, confounded with the dreadful exigence in which morality submits to the suspension of its own rules in favour of its own principles, might turn aside whilst fraud and violence were accomplishing the destruction of a pretended nobility, which disgraced whilst it persecuted, human nature.' It is a fine, rounded period, its meaning is clear and there is not a single word, except perhaps *exigence*, which is not in common use today; yet it is one that smacks of its time, no one would express the thought in such a way now, and in passing I may remark that it is a thought which not a few at the present moment may have had. Perhaps a modern writer would put it somewhat as follows: 'There are times when people even of the most sensitive conscience must put the spirit of the law before the letter, and can do no more than stand aside when an effete plutocracy which has disgraced human nature by its persecutions is destroyed, even though by violence and double dealing.' I do not claim that this is good, it is the best I can do after several attempts and I would not deny that it has neither the balance, the nobility nor the compactness of the original.

Burke was an Irishman, and the Irish, as we know, are inclined to verbosity. With them enough is not as good as a feast. They load their table with sumptuous viands, so that sometimes the mere sight surfeits you, and on occasion even, when you come to attack these game pasties, these boars' heads, these lordly peacocks, you discover to your dismay that like the victuals at a banquet in Italian opera they are of papier mâché. English is a rich language. Very generally you have a choice between a plain word and a literary one, a concrete and an abstract word; you can say a thing directly or you can use a periphrase. The greatness, the stateliness of Burke's nature led him to express himself with grandiloquence. His subjects were important and I suppose he would have thought it unbecoming to them and to himself to deliver himself with simplicity. 'It is very well for Burke to express himself in that figurative way,' said Fox. 'It is natural to him; he talks so to his wife, to his servants, to his children.' It must be admitted that it is sometimes fatiguing. It was not the least of the reasons for his failure in the House of Commons. The greatest speech he ever made there was that on conciliation with the Thirteen States. Lord Morley describes it as 'the wisest in temper, the most closely logical in its reasoning, the amplest in appropriate topics, the most generous and conciliatory in the substance of its appeals.' It drove everybody away.

Dr. Johnson has told us that in his day nobody talked much of style, since everybody wrote pretty well. 'There is an elegance of style universally diffused,' he said. Burke was outstanding. His contemporaries were impressed, as well they might be, by his command of words, his brilliant similes, his hyperboles and fertile imagination, but did not invariably approve. Hazlitt relates a conversation between Fox and Lord Holland on the subject of his style. It appears that this 'Noble Person objected to it as too gaudy and meretricious, and said that it was more profuse of flowers than fruit. On which Mr. Fox observed, that though this was a common objection, it appeared to him altogether an unfounded one; that on the contrary the flowers often concealed the fruit beneath them; and the ornaments of style were rather an hindrance than an advantage to the sentiments they were meant to set off. In confirmation of this remark, he offered to take down the book and translate a page anywhere into his own plain, natural style; and by his doing so, Lord Holland was convinced that he had often missed the thought from having his attention drawn off to the dazzling imagery.' It is instructive to learn that Noble Persons and Eminent Politicians were interested in such questions in those bygone days and with such amiable exercises beguiled their leisure. But of course if his lordship's attention was really drawn off the matter of Burke's discourse by the brillancy of the manner, it is a reflection on his style. For the purpose of imagery is not to divert the reader, but to make the meaning clearer to him; the purpose of simile and metaphor is to impress it on his mind and by engaging his fancy make it more acceptable. An illustration is otiose unless it illustrates. Burke had a romantic and a poetic mind such as no other of the eighteenth-century masters of prose possessed, and it is this that gives his prose its variegated colour; but his aim was to convince rather than to please, to overpower rather than to persuade, and by all the resources of his imagination not only to make his point more obvious, but by an appeal to sentiment or passion to compel acquiescence. I don't know when Mr. Fox held his conversation with the Noble Lord, but if the *Reflections on the French Revolution* had then appeared he might well have pointed to it to refute his lordship's contention. For in that work the decoration so interpenetrates the texture of the writing that it becomes part and parcel of the argument. Here imagery, metaphor and simile fulfil their function. The one passage that leaves me doubtful is the most celebrated of all, that in which Burke tells how he saw Marie Antoinette at Versailles: 'and surely never lighted on this orb, which she hardly seemed to touch, a more delightful vision.' It is to be found in anthologies, so I will not quote it, but it is somewhat high flown to my taste. But if it is not perfect prose it is magnificent rhetoric; magnificent even when it is slightly absurd: 'I thought ten thousand swords must have leapt from their scabbards to avenge even a look that threatened her with insult'; and the cadence with which the paragraph ends is lovely: 'The unbought grace of life, the cheap defence of nations, the nurse of manly sentiment and heroic enterprise is gone! It is gone, that sensibility of principle, that chastity of honour, which felt a stain like a wound, which inspired courage whilst it mitigated ferocity, which ennobled whatever it touched, and under which vice itself lost half its evil, by losing all its grossness.'

Sir Philip Francis, who was perhaps the author of the *Letters of Junius*, condemned this passage as 'downright foppery' and somewhat surprisingly went on to write: 'Once for all I wish you would let me teach you to write English. To me, who aim to read everything you write, it would be a great comfort, and to you, no sort of disparagement. Why will you not allow yourself to be persuaded that polish is material to preservation?'

As the quotations I have given plainly show, Burke made abundant use of metaphor. It is interwoven in the substance of his prose as the weavers of Lyons thread one colour with another to give a fabric the shimmer of shot silk. Of course like every other writer he uses what Fowler calls the natural metaphor, for common speech is largely composed of them, but he uses freely what Fowler calls the artificial metaphor. It gave concrete substance to his generalisations. He used it to enforce a statement by means of a physical image; but unlike some modern writers, who will pursue the implications of a metaphor like a spider scurrying along every filament of its web, he took care never to run it to death. Here is a good example of his practice: 'Your constitution, it is true, whilst you were out of possession, suffered waste and dilapidation; but you possessed in some parts the walls, and, in all, the foundations, of a noble and venerable castle. You might have repaired those walls; you might have built on those foundations.'

On the other hand Burke used the simile somewhat sparingly. Modern writers might well follow his example. For of late a dreadful epidemic has broken out. Similes are clustered on the pages of our young authors as thickly as pimples on a young man's face, and they are as unsightly. A simile has use. By reminding you of a familiar thing it enables you to see the subject of the comparison more clearly or by mentioning an unfamiliar one it focuses your attention on it. It is dangerous to use it merely as an ornament; it is detestable to use it to display your cleverness; it is preposterous to use it when it neither decorates nor impresses. (Example: 'The moon like a huge blanc-mange wobbled over the tree-tops.') When Burke used a simile it was generally, as might be expected, with elaboration. Here is the most celebrated one: 'But as to *our* country and *our* race, as long as the well-compacted structure of our church and state, the sanctuary, the holy of holies of that ancient law, defended by reverence, defended by power—a fortress at once and a temple—shall stand inviolate on the brow of the British Sion, as long as the British Monarchy —not more limited than fenced by the orders of the state—shall, like the proud Keep of Windsor, rising in the majesty of proportion, and girt with the double belt of its kindred coeval towers; as long as this awful structure shall oversee and guard the subjected land, so long the mounds and dykes of the low, fat, Bedford level will have nothing to fear from all the pick-axes of all the levellers of France.'

Few of us writers pay much attention to the paragraph; we are apt, regardless of the sense, to make a break when we feel the reader deserves the slight rest it gives him. But the extent of a paragraph should be determined not by its length, but by its burden. A paragraph is a collection of sentences with unity of purpose. It should be concerned with a single topic and contain nothing irrelevant to this. Just as in a 'loose' sentence qualifying statements should not over-weight the statement qualified, so in the paragraph statements which are of less import should be sub-ordinate to the statement which is essential. Such are the counsels of perfection given by the grammarian. Burke followed them with considerable fidelity. In his best paragraphs he begins with a statement of his subject in short sentences that arrest attention; goes on with a series of sentences of medium length or with a great, majestic period; the phrases grow ampler and more emphatic till he reaches his climax about the middle of the paragraph, or a little later; then he slows down, the sentences grow shorter, sometimes even abrupt, and he concludes.

I have harped upon the fact that Burke's style owed many of its merits to his practice of speaking in public; to this it owed also such defects as a carping critic might find in it. There is more than one passage in the famous speech on the Nabob of Arcot's Debts when he asks a long series of rhetorical questions. It may have been effective in the House of Commons, but on the printed page it is restless and fatiguing. To this may be ascribed his too frequent recourse to the exclamatory sentence. 'Happy if they had all continued to know their indissoluble union, and their proper place! Happy if learning, not debauched by ambition, had been satisfied to continue the instructor, and not aspired to be the master.' Something of an old-fashioned air he has by his frequent use of an inverted construction, a mode now seldom met with; he employs it to vary the monotony of the simple order —subject, verb, object—and also to emphasise the significant member of the sentence by placing it first; but such a phrase as 'Personal offence I have given them none' needs the emphasis of the living voice to appear natural. On the other hand it is to his public speaking, I think, that Burke owed his skill in giving to a series of quite short sentences as musical a cadence and as noble a ring as when he set himself to compose an elaborate period with its pompous train of subordinate clauses; and this is shown nowhere to greater advantage than in the *Letter to a Noble Lord*. Here a true instinct made him see that when he was appealing for compassion on account of his age and infirmities and by reminding his readers of the death of his beloved and only son, he must aim at simplicity. The passage is deeply moving:

'The storm has gone over me; and I lie like one of those old oaks which the late hurricane has scattered about me. I am stripped of all my honours, I am torn up by the roots, and lie prostrate on the earth . . . I am alone. I have none to meet my enemies in the gate. Indeed, my lord, I greatly deceive myself, if in this hard season I would give a peck of refuse wheat for all that is called fame and honour in the world. This is the appetite but of a few. It is a luxury, it is a privilege, it is an indulgence for those who are at their ease. But we are all of us made to shun disgrace, as we are made to shrink from pain, and poverty, and disease. It is an instinct; and under the direction of reason, instinct is always in the right. I live in an inverted order. They who ought to have succeeded me have gone before me. They who should have been to me as posterity are in the place of ancestors. I owe to the dearest relation (which ever must subsist in memory) that act of piety, which he would have performed to me; I owe it to him to show that he was not descended, as the Duke of Bedford would have it, from an unworthy parent.'

Here the best words are indeed put in the best places. This piece owes little to picturesque imagery, nothing to romantic metaphor, and proves with what justification Hazlitt described him as, with the exception of Jeremy Taylor, the most poetical of prose-writers. I hope it will not be considered a literary conceit (a trifling, tedious business) when I suggest that in the tender melody of these cadences, in this exquisite choice of simple words, there is a foretaste of Wordsworth at his admirable best. If these pages should persuade anyone to see for himself how great a writer Burke was I cannot do better than advise him to read this *Letter to a Noble Lord*. It is the finest piece of invective in the English language and so short that it can be read in an hour. It offers in its brief compass a survey of all Burke's dazzling gifts, his formal as well as his conversational style, his gift for epigram and for irony, his wisdom, his sense, his pathos, his indignation and his nobility.

REFLECTIONS ON A CERTAIN BOOK

I

PUNCTUALLY at five minutes to five Lampe, his servant, waked Professor Kant and by five, in his slippers, dressing-gown and night-cap, over which he wore his three-cornered hat, he seated himself in his study ready for breakfast. This consisted of a cup of weak tea and a pipe of tobacco. The next two hours he spent thinking over the lecture he was to deliver that morning. Then he dressed. The lecture room was on the ground floor of his house. He lectured from seven till nine and so popular were his lectures that if you wanted a good seat you had to be there by six-thirty. Kant, seated behind a little desk, spoke in a conversational tone, in a low voice, and very rarely indulged in gesture, but he enlivened his discourse with humour and abundant illustrations. His aim was to teach his students to think for themselves and he did not like it when they busied themselves with their quills to write down his every word.

'Gentlemen, do not scratch so,' he said once. 'I am no oracle.'

It was his custom to fix his eyes on a student who sat close to him and judge by the look on his face whether or no he understood what he said. But a very small

162

thing distracted him. On one occasion he lost the thread of his discourse because a button was wanting on the coat of one of the students, and on another when a sleepy youth persistently yawned he broke off to say:

'If one cannot avoid yawning, good manners require that the hand should be placed before the mouth.'

At nine o'clock Kant returned to his room, once more put on his dressing-gown, his night-cap, his three-cornered hat and his slippers and studied till exactly a quarter to one. Then he called down to his cook, told her the hour, dressed and went back to his study to await the guests he expected to dinner. There were never less than two nor more than five. He could not bear to eat alone and it is related that once when it happened that he had no one to bear him company he told his servant to go out into the street and bring in anyone he could find. He expected his cook to be ready and his guests to arrive punctually. He was in the habit of inviting them on the day he wished them to come so that they might not, to dine with him, be tempted to break a previous engagement; and though a certain Professor Kraus for some time dined with him every day but Sunday he never failed to send him an invitation every morning.

As soon as the guests were assembled Kant told his servant to bring the dinner and himself went to fetch the silver spoons which he kept locked up with his money in a bureau in the parlour. The party seated themselves in the dining-room and with the words: 'Now, gentlemen,' Kant set to. The meal was substantial. It was the only one he ate in the day, and consisted of soup, dried pulse with fish, a roast, cheese to end with and fruit when in season. Before each guest was placed a pint bottle of red wine and a pint bottle of white so that he could drink whichever he liked.

Kant was fond of talking, but preferred to talk alone, and if interrupted or contradicted was apt to show displeasure; his conversation, however, was so agreeable that none minded if he monopolised it. In one of his books he wrote: 'If a young, inexperienced man enters a company (especially when ladies are present) surpassing in brilliance his expectations, he is easily embarrassed when he is to begin to speak. Now, it would be awkward to begin with an item of news reported in the paper, for one does not see what led him to speak of that. But as he has just come from the street, the bad weather is the best introduction to conversation.' Though at his own table ladies were never present, Kant made it a rule to start the conversation with this convenient topic; then he turned to the news of the day, home news and foreign, and from this went on to discourse of travellers' tales, and peculiarities of foreign peoples, general literature and food. Finally he told humorous stories, of which he had a rich supply and which he told uncommonly well, so, he said, 'that the repast may end with laughter, which is calculated to promote digestion.' He liked to linger over dinner and the guests did not rise from table till late. He would not sit down after they had left in case he fell asleep and this he would not permit himself to do since he was of opinion that sleep should be enjoyed sparingly, for thus time was saved and so life lengthened. He set out on his afternoon walk.

He was a little man, barely five feet tall, with a

narrow chest and one shoulder higher than the other, and he was thin almost to emaciation. He had a crooked nose, but a fine brow and his colour was fresh. His eyes, though small, were blue, lively and penetrating. He was natty in his dress. He wore a small blond wig, a black tie, and a shirt with ruffles round the throat and wrists; a coat, breeches and waistcoat of fine cloth, grey silk stockings and shoes with silver buckles. He carried his three-cornered hat under his arm and in his hand a gold-headed cane. He walked every day, rain or fine, for exactly one hour, but if the weather was threatening, his servant walked behind him with a big umbrella. The only occasion on which he is known to have omitted his walk is when he received Rousseau's *Emile*, and then, unable to tear himself away from it, he remained indoors for three days. He walked very slowly because he thought it was bad for him to sweat, and alone because he had formed the habit of breathing through his nostrils, since thus he thought to avoid catching cold and, had he had a companion with whom courtesy would oblige him to speak, he would have been constrained to breathe through his mouth. He invariably took the same walk, along the Linden Allee, and this, according to Heine, he strolled up and down eight times. He issued from his house at precisely the same hour, so that the people of the town could set their clocks by it. When he came home he returned to his study and read and wrote letters till the light failed. Then, as was his habit, fixing his eyes on the tower of a neighbouring church, he pondered over the problems that just then occupied him. A story is attached to this: it appears that one evening he noticed that he could no longer see the tower, for some poplars had grown so tall that they hid it. It completely upset him, but fortunately the owners of the poplars consented to cut off their tops so that he could continue to reflect in comfort. At a quarter to ten he suspended his arduous labour and by ten was safely tucked up in bed.

But one day somewhere between the middle and the end of July, in the year 1789, when Kant stepped out of his house to take his afternoon walk, instead of turning towards the Linden Allee he took another direction. The inhabitants of Königsberg were astounded and they said to one another that something must have happened in the world of shattering consequence. They were right. He had just received the news that on the fourteenth of July the Paris mob had stormed the Bastille and released the prisoners. It was the beginning of the French Revolution.

Kant was born in very humble circumstances. His father, a harness maker, was a man of high character, and his mother a deeply religious woman. Of them he said: 'They gave me a training which in a moral point of view could not have been better, and for which, at every remembrance of them, I am moved with the most grateful emotions.' He might have gone further and said that the rigid pietism of his mother had no small influence on the system of philosophy he eventually developed. He went to school when he was eight and at sixteen entered the University of Königsberg. By then his mother was dead. His father was too poor to provide him with more than board and lodging, and he got through the six years he spent at the university with some financial help from his uncle, a shoemaker, by taking pupils and, unexpectedly enough, by making a certain amount of money through his skill at billiards and at the card game of ombre. When his father died, Kant being then twenty-two, the home, such as it was, broke up. Of the eleven children Frau Kant had borne her husband, five remained alive: the immediate subject of this narrative, a much younger brother and three girls. The girls went into domestic service and two of them eventually married in their own class of life. The boy was taken care of by his uncle, the shoemaker, and Kant, having failed in his application for an assistant's place at a local school, got a succession of jobs as tutor in the families of the provincial gentry. It was by mixing in a society more polite than that in which he was born and brought up that he acquired the good manners and the social grace for which he was afterwards distinguished. He spent nine years thus occupied, and then, having taken his degree, started upon his career as a lecturer at Königsberg. He lived in lodgings and took his meals at eating-houses which he selected on the chance of meeting agreeable company. But he was pernickety. In one of the lodging-houses he was disturbed in his meditations by the crowing of a cock, and though he tried to buy it the owner would not sell and so he had to move elsewhere. He left one eating-house because a fellow guest talked boringly and another because he found himself expected to hold forth on learned subjects, which was the very thing he did not want to do. It was not till after many years that he was well enough off to have a house of his own and a servant to look after him. The house was sparsely furnished and the only picture in it was a portrait of Rousseau which had been given him by a friend. The walls had been whitewashed, but in time had grown so black from smoke and soot that you could write your name on them; when, however, a visitor once proceeded to do something like this, Kant mildly rebuked him.

'Friend, why will you disturb the ancient rust?' he asked. 'Is not such a hanging, which arose of its own accord, better than one which is purchased?'

Though he lived to be eighty, he never went more than sixty miles away from the town in which he was born. He suffered from frequent indispositions and was seldom free from pain, but he was able by the exertion of his will to turn his attention away from his feelings just as though they did not concern him. 'He was accustomed to say that one should know how to adapt oneself to one's body.' He was of a cheerful disposition, amiable to all, and considerate; but he was punctilious. He expected the same deference to be paid to him as he paid to others. So when his celebrity made people eager to meet him and a common acquaintance tried to arrange that they should do so by inviting him to his own house he would not consent to go till, however distinguished they were, they had paid him a visit of courtesy.

II

I have given this brief account of what sort of a man Kant was, and what sort of life he led, in the hope of sufficiently whetting the readers' interest in this great philosopher to induce him to have patience with me while I submit to him the reflections that have occurred to me during the reading of a book of his with the somewhat forbidding title of the *Critique of the Power of Judgment*. It deals with two subjects, æsthetics and teleology, but I hasten to add that it is only with the first of these, æsthetics, that I propose to concern myself; and that only with diffidence, for I am well aware that it may be thought presumptuous in a writer of fiction to concern himself with such a matter. I do not pretend to be a philosopher, but merely a man who has throughout his life been profoundly interested in art. All I venture to claim is that I know from experience something of the process of creation and as a writer of fiction can look upon the question of beauty, which is of course the subject matter of æsthetics, with impartiality. Fiction is an art, but an imperfect one. The great novels of the world may deal with all the passions to which man is subject, discover the depths of his variable and disconsolate soul, analyse human relations, describe a civilisation or create immortal characters; it is only by a misuse of the word that beauty can be ascribed to them. We writers of fiction must leave beauty to the poets.

But before I begin to speak of Kant's æsthetic ideas I must tell the reader one very odd thing: he appears to have been entirely devoid of æsthetic sensibility. One of his biographers writes as follows: 'He never seemed to pay much attention to paintings and engravings, even of a superior kind. In galleries and rooms containing much admired and highly praised collections,

I never noticed that he specially directed his attention to the pictures, or in any way gave evidence of his appreciation of the artist's skill.' He was not what was called in the eighteenth century a man of feeling. Twice he thought seriously of marrying, but he took so long to consider the advantages and disadvantages of the step he had in mind that in the interval one of the young women he had his eye on married somebody else and the other left Königsberg before he reached a decision. I think this argues that he was not in love, for when you are, even if you are a philosopher, you have no difficulty in finding very good reasons for doing what your inclinations prompt. His two married sisters lived in Königsberg. Kant never spoke to them for twenty-five years. The reason he gave for this was that he had nothing to say to them. This seems sensible enough, and though we may deplore his lack of heart, when we remember how often our pusillanimity has led us to rack our brains in the effort to make conversation with persons with whom we have nothing in common but a tie of blood, we cannot but admire his strength of mind. He had intimate acquaintances rather than friends. When they were ill, he did not care to go to see them, but sent every day to enquire after them, and when they died he put them out of his mind with the words: 'Let the dead rest with the dead.' He was neither impulsive nor demonstrative, but he was kindly, within his scanty means generous, and obliging. His intelligence was great, his power of reasoning impressive, but his emotional nature was meagre.

It is all the more remarkable then that, writing on a

subject which depends on feeling, he should have said so much that was wise and even profound. He saw, of course, that beauty does not reside in the object. It is the name we give to the specific feeling of pleasure which the object gives us. He saw also that art can give beauty to things which are in nature ugly or displeasing, but he made the reservation, which certain modern painters might well bear in mind, that some things may be so ugly in their representation as to excite disgust. And in suggesting that when experience proves too commonplace the artist by means of his imagination may work up the material he borrows from nature into something that surpasses nature, Kant may almost be supposed to have foreseen the non-representational art of our own day.

Now, the ideas of a philosopher are largely conditioned by his personal characteristics, and, as one might have expected, Kant's approach to the problems of æsthetics is rigidly intellectual. His aim is to prove that the delight we take in beauty is one of mere reflection. It is interesting to see how he sets about doing this. He starts by making a distinction between the agreeable and the beautiful. The pleasure which the beautiful occasions is independent of all interest. The agreeable is what the senses find pleasing in sensation. The agreeable arouses inclination, and inclination is bound up with desire, and so with interest. A trivial illustration may make Kant's point clear: when I look at the Doric temples at Pæstum the pleasure they afford me is quite obviously independent of all interest and so I may safely call them beautiful; but when I look at a ripe peach the pleasure it causes me is

171

not disinterested, for it excites in me a desire to eat it and therefore I am bound to call it no more than agreeable. The senses of men differ and what causes me pleasure may leave you indifferent. Each of us may judge the agreeable according to his own taste and there is no disputing that. The satisfaction it gives is mere enjoyment, and so, states Kant, has no worth. That is a hard saying, which, I think, can only be explained by his conviction that the faculties of the mind alone have real value. But now, since beauty has no connection with sensation (which is bound up with interest) colour, charm and emotion, which are mere matters of sensation and so only cause enjoyment, have nothing to do with it. This of course is rather startling, but why Kant makes a statement at first sight so outrageous is plain. Since the senses of men differ, if the beautiful depends on the senses your judgment and mine are as good as that of anybody else, and æsthetics will not exist. If a judgment of taste, or what, I think, we would now more conveniently call appreciation of the beautiful, is to have any validity it must depend not on anything so capricious as feeling, but on a mental process. When you come to consider an object with a view to deciding its æsthetic value, you must discard everything, its colour, such charm as it has, the emotion it excites in you, and attend only to its form; and if then you become aware of a harmony between your imagination and your understanding (both faculties of the mind) you will receive a sensation of pleasure and be justified in calling the object beautiful.

But then, having performed this singular operation,

you may demand that everyone else should agree with you. The judgment that a thing is beautiful, though a subjective judgment since it is based not on a concept, but on the feeling of pleasure it arouses, has universal validity, and you have the right to claim that everyone *ought* to find beautiful what you find beautiful. In fact it is in a way the duty of others to fall in with your judgment. Kant justifies this contention thus: 'For where anyone is conscious that his delight in an object is with him independent of interest, it is inevitable that he should look on the object as one containing a ground of delight for all men. For, since the delight is not based on any inclination of the subject (or on any other deliberate interest), but the subject feels himself completely free in respect of the liking which he accords to the object, he can find as the reason for his delight no personal conditions to which his own subjective self might alone be party. Hence he must regard it as resting on what he may also presuppose in every other person; and therefore he must believe that he has reason for demanding a similar delight from everyone.'

Yet it looks as though Kant had an inkling that this was rather thin. It may even have occurred to him that the imagination and the understanding were in no better case than the senses, for it is obvious that these two faculties of the mind are not the same in all men. There must have been many people in Königsberg who had more imagination than our philosopher, but none who had so solid an understanding. Kant is forced to presuppose that we can only exact from others agreement with our estimate of what is beautiful by a sense common to all men. But since he admits almost in the same breath that people are often mistaken in judging that an object is beautiful it does not seem to get us much further. And in another place he remarks that an interest in the beautiful is not common: one would have thought that if there were a sense common to all men, all men should be interested in the beautiful. Indeed in the section of his treatise called *Dialectic of Æsthetic Judgment* he states that the only means of saving the claim of the judgment of taste, that is the appreciation of beauty, to universal validity is by supposing a concept of the supersensible lying at the basis of the object and of the judging subject; if I understand aright he means by this that the object of beauty and the person who considers it are both appearances of reality, and reality is one. They are, as it were, a coat and a pair of trousers made out of a bolt of the same fabric. I find this unconvincing. The assumption that in the appreciation of beauty there is a sense common to all men looks to me like nothing more than a futile attempt to prove something that all experience refutes. If the pleasure that is afforded by a beautiful object is subjective, and that of course Kant insists upon, it must depend on the idiosyncrasies of the observer, idiosyncrasies of the mind as well as idiosyncrasies of the senses; and though we, inheritors of Hebraic, Greek and Roman civilisation, have many traits in common we are none of us alike as two peas. Though we may agree more or less on the beauty of certain familiar things, and then perhaps only because they are familiar, it is only natural that our judgments of the beautiful should be as diverse as those of the agreeable admittedly are.

Kant then claimed that when you have decided that an object is beautiful by the process I have just described, you can not only impute the pleasure (a feeling) you experience to everyone else, but also suppose that your pleasure (a feeling, I repeat) is universally communicable. This seems very strange. I should have thought the peculiarity of feeling is that it is not communicable. If I am looking at Giorgione's *Virgin Enthroned* at Castel Franco, I can, if I have any gift of expression, *tell* you what I feel about it, but I cannot make you *feel* my feeling. I can tell you I am in love; I can even describe the feelings that my love excites in me; but I cannot communicate my love, a feeling, to you. If I could you would be in love with the object of my affections, and that might be highly embarrassing to me. Our feelings are surely conditioned by our dispositions. So much is this so that I do not think it an exaggeration to say that no two persons see exactly the same picture or read exactly the same poem. I can only suppose that Kant came by this notion of the universal communicability of feeling owing to his conviction that feeling was negligible except in so far as by means of the imagination and the understanding it gave rise to ideas; and since ideas by the nature of our cognitive faculties *are* universally communicable, the feeling that occasioned them must be so too. He was not, as I ventured at the beginning of this essay to point out, a man who felt with intensity. That may, perhaps, be the reason why he insisted that the appreciation of beauty is merely contemplative.

But contemplation is a passive state. It does not suggest the thrill, the excitement, the breathlessness, the agitation with which the sight of a beautiful picture, the reading of a beautiful poem, must affect a person of æsthetic sensibility. It may well describe his reaction to the agreeable, but surely not to the beautiful. It is difficult for me to believe that any such person can read certain passages of Shakespeare or Milton, listen to certain pieces by Mozart or Beethoven, see certain pictures by El Greco or Chardin with so tepid a feeling that it can be justly called contemplation.

III

Kant's doctrine of the communicability of feeling leads not unnaturally to a consideration of the question of communication. It is obvious that the artist, be he poet, painter or composer, makes a communication, but from this the writers on æsthetics infer that this is his intention. There I think they are mistaken. They have not sufficiently examined the process of creation. I don't believe the artist who sets to work to create a work of art has any such purpose as they ascribe to him. If he has he is a didactic or a propagandist, and as such not an artist. I know what happens to a writer of fiction. An idea comes to him, he knows not whence, and so he gives it the rather grand name of inspiration. It is as slight a thing as the tiny foreign body that finds its way into the oyster's shell and so creates the disturbance that will result in the creation of a pearl. For some reason the idea excites him, his imagination goes to work, out of his unconscious arise thoughts and feelings, characters crowd upon him and events suggest

Immanuel Kant (1724-1804)

themselves that will express them, for character is expressed by action, not by description, till at length he is possessed of a shapeless mass of material. This sometimes, but not always, falls into a pattern that enables him to see a path, as it were, which he can follow through the jungle of this confused medley of feelings and ideas till he is so obsessed by the muddle of it that to liberate his soul from a burden that has grown intolerable he is constrained to put it all down on paper. Having done this he regains his freedom. What communication the reader gets from it is not his affair.

So it is, I surmise, with the landscape painter, the young Monet for instance or Pissarro; he cannot tell you why some scene, the bend of a river, say, or a road under the snow, bordered by leafless trees, gives him a peculiar thrill so that the creative instinct is stirred in him and he has the feeling that here is something that he can deal with, and because nature has made him a painter he is able to transmute his emotion into an arrangement of colour and form that does not satisfy his sensibility, for I think it doubtful whether the artist, whatever art he practises, ever achieves the full result he saw in his mind's eye, yet allays the urge of creation which is at once his delight and his torment. But I do not believe it has ever entered his head that he was making a communication to the persons who afterwards see his picture.

So it is, I submit, with the poet and the composer of music, and if I have spoken of painting rather than of poetry or music it is, frankly, because it is not so difficult to deal with. A picture can be seen at once.

Not that I mean a glance will give you all that it has
to give. That you can get, if you get it at all, only by
giving it your continued and renewed attention. Poetry
deals with words and words have overwhelming associations, associations different in different countries and in
different cultures. Words affect by their meaning as
well as by their sound, and so are addressed to the mind
as well as to the sensibility. The only meaning of a
picture is the æsthetic delight it gives you. In any case
I would not venture to speak of music; the peculiar
gift which enables someone to invent it is to me the
most mysterious of the processes which produce a work
of art. One is taken aback at first to find that Kant
placed music (along with cooking) among the inferior
arts because, though perhaps the highest among the
arts which are valued for their agreeableness, it merely
plays with sensation. It was natural that he should do
this since he estimated the worth of the arts by the
culture they supply to the mind. He has, however, a
good word to say of poetry because it gives the imagination an impetus to bring more thought into play than
allows of being brought into the embrace of a concept,
or therefore being definitely formulated in language;
but 'among the formative arts,' he writes, 'I would give
the palm to painting because it can penetrate much
further into the region of ideas.'

IV

And now, since this does not pretend to be a philosophical dissertation, but merely a discourse on a subject that happens to interest me, I propose to permit myself a digression. The intellectual attitude towards æsthetic appreciation is that of pretty well all the writers on æsthetics. This is perhaps inevitable, for they are compelled to reason about what has little or nothing to do with reason, but almost only with feeling. It was certainly the attitude of Roger Fry. He was a charming man, a lucid writer and an indifferent painter. He rightly earned a high reputation as a critic of art, but, as all but few of us are, he was swayed by certain prejudices of his time. He claimed that a work of art should be conceived in response to a free æsthetic impulse and so condemned the patron unless he allowed the artist to go his own way regardless of the patron's wishes. He had little patience with portraiture because, according to him, people have their portraits painted for social prestige or for purposes of publicity. He regarded the painters who accept such commissions as useless, probably mischievous, parasites upon society. He divided works of art into two distinct classes—'one in which for some reason the artist can express his genuine æsthetic impulse, the other in which the artist uses his technical skill to gratify a public incapable of responding to æsthetic appeal.' This seems very high-handed. Because the Pharaohs had colossal statues made of themselves presumably with the same intention as Mussolini and Hitler had when they plastered walls with portraits of themselves, namely to impress themselves on the imagination of their subjects, there are Bellini's Doge, Titian's *Man with a Glove*, Velasquez' Pope Innocent, to prove that a portrait can be a work of art and a thing of beauty. We can only suppose that they satisfied their patrons. It is unlikely that had Philip IV been displeased with the portraits Velasquez painted of him, he would have sat to him so often.

The flaw in Roger Fry's argument lies in the presumption that the motives which have led the artist to create a work of art are any business of the critic's or of the layman's. He may, if he is a novelist, start writing a novel to ridicule another novelist, as Fielding started to write *Joseph Andrews* to mock at Richardson, and then, the creative instinct moving him, go on writing for his own enjoyment. Dickens, as we know, was asked to write a book on a subject which did not appeal to him to serve as letterpress for the illustrations of a popular draughtsman and he accepted the commission only because he needed the fourteen pounds a month he was offered for the work. Since he had immense vitality, an exuberant sense of the comic, the power of creating characters as alive as they were fantastic, he produced in *The Pickwick Papers* the greatest work of humour in the English language. It may well be that it was the irksome conditions that he felt bound to accept which gave rise to the flash of genius by means of which, without rhyme or reason, out of the blue, came Sam Weller and Sam Weller's father. It is news to me that the artist who knows his business is hampered by the limitations that are imposed upon him. When the donor of an altarpiece wanted portraits of himself and his wife kneeling at the foot of the Cross with Christ Crucified, perhaps for publicity or for social prestige, but perhaps also because his piety was sincere, in either case the painter had no difficulty in complying with his patron's wish. I cannot believe that it ever entered his head that he looked upon this as an infringement of his æsthetic freedom: on the contrary I am more inclined to believe that the difficulty he was asked to cope with excited and inspired him. Every art has its limitations and the better the artist the more comfortably does he exercise his creative instincts within them.

A generation or two ago a claim was made that painting was an esoteric business that only painters could adequately appreciate since they alone knew its technique. This claim, probably first made in France, where during the last hundred years most æsthetic ideas have arisen, was launched in England, I believe, by Whistler. He asserted that the layman was by his nature a Philistine, and his duty was to accept what the artist oracularly told him. His only function was to buy the painter's picture in order to provide him with bread and butter, but his appreciation was as impertinent as his censure. That was a farrago of nonsense. There is nothing mystical about technique; it is merely the name given to the processes by means of which the artist achieves the effects he aims at. Every art has its technique. It has nothing to do with the layman. He is only concerned with the result. When you look at a picture, if you are of a curious turn of mind it may interest you to examine the way in which the painter has achieved integration through relations of colour,

light, line and space; but that is not the æsthetic communication which it has to give you. You do not look
at a picture only with your eyes, you look at it with
your experience of life, your instinctive likes and dis-
likes, your habits and feelings, your associations, in
fact with the whole of your personality. And the
richer your personality the richer is the communication
the picture has to give you. The notion, foolish to my
mind, that painting is a mystery accessible only to the
initiated, is flattering to the painters. It has led them
to be scornful of the writers on art who see in pictures
what from their professional standpoint is of no interest.
I think they are wrong. Leonardo's *Mona Lisa* is not
a picture that everyone can care for now, but we know
the communication it had to make to Walter Pater;
it was not a purely æsthetic communication, but it is
surely not the least of this particular picture's merits
that it had it to make to a man of peculiar sensibility.

There is a painting by Degas in the Louvre which is
popularly known as *L'Absinthe*, but in fact represents
an engraver well-known in his day and an actress
called Ellen André. There is no reason to suppose that
they were more disreputable than other persons of
their calling. They are seated side by side at a marble-
topped table in a shabby *bistro*. The surroundings are
sordid and vulgar. A glass of absinthe stands before
the actress. Their dress is slovenly and you can almost
smell the stench of their unwashed bodies and grubby
clothes. They are slumped down on the *banquette* in an
alcoholic stupor. Their faces are heavy and sullen.
There is an air of apathetic hopelessness in their listless
attitude and you would say that they were dully

resigned to sink deeper and deeper into shameless degradation. It is not a pretty picture, nor a pleasing one, and yet it is surely one of the great pictures of the world. It offers the authentic thrill of beauty. Of course I can see how admirable the composition is, how pleasing the colour and how solid the drawing, but to me there is much more in it than that. As I stand before it, my sensibilities quickened, at the back of my mind, somewhere between the conscious and the subconscious, I become aware of Verlaine's poems, and of Rimbaud's, of *Manette Salomon*, of the *quais* along the Seine with their second-hand book-stalls, of the Boulevard St. Michel and the cafés and *bistros* in old mean streets. I dare say that from the standpoint of æsthetic appreciation, which should be occupied only with æsthetic values, this is reprehensible. Why should I care? My delight in the picture is enormously increased. Is it possible that a picture which gives one so much can have been painted, as the distinguished critic, Camille Mauclair, says it was, because Degas was fascinated by the paradoxical perspective of the marble-topped tables in the foreground?

But now I must break off to make a confession to the reader. I have glibly used the word *Beauty* as though I knew just what it meant. I'm not at all sure that I do. It obviously means something, but exactly what? When we say that something is beautiful can we really say why we say it? Do we mean anything more than that it happens to give us a peculiar feeling? I have noticed that the word has bothered the writers on æsthetics not a little; some indeed have sought to avoid it altogether. Some have claimed that it resides in harmony, symmetry and formal relations. Others have identified it with truth and goodness; others again have held that it is merely that which is pleasant. Kant has given several definitions of it, but they all tend to substantiate his claim that the pleasure which beauty affords us is a pleasure of reflection. For all I have been able to discover to the contrary he seems to have believed that beauty was immutable, a belief, I think, generally shared by the writers on æsthetics. Keats expressed the same idea in the first line of *Endymion*: 'A thing of beauty is a joy for ever.' By this he may have meant one of two things: one, that so long as an object retains its beauty it is a pleasure; but that is what I believe philosophers call an analytical proposition, and tells us nothing that we didn't know before, since the characteristic of beauty is that it affords pleasure. Keats was too intelligent to make a statement so trite and I can only think he meant that a thing of beauty is a joy for ever because it retains its beauty for ever. And there he was wrong. For beauty is as transitory as all other things in this world. Sometimes it has a long life, as Greek sculpture has had owing to the prestige of Greek culture and owing to its representations of the human form which have provided us with an ideal of human beauty; but even Greek sculpture, owing to the acquaintance we have now made with Chinese and Negro art, has with the artists themselves lost much of its appeal. It is no longer a source of inspiration. Its beauty is dying. An indication of this may be seen in the movies. Directors no longer choose their heroes as they did twenty years ago for their classical beauty, but for their expression and such evidence as their outward seeming offers of character and personality. They would not do this unless they had discovered that classical beauty had lost its allure. Sometimes the life of beauty is short. We can all remember pictures and poems which gave us the authentic thrill of beauty in our youth, but from which beauty has now seeped out as water seeps out of a porous jar. Beauty depends on the climate of sensibility and this changes with the passing years. A different generation has different needs and demands a different satisfaction. We grow tired of something we know too well and ask for something new. The eighteenth century saw nothing in the paintings of the Italian Primitives but the fumblings of immature, unskilful artists. Were those pictures beautiful then? No. It is we who have given them their beauty and it is likely enough that the qualities we find in them are not the qualities which appealed to the lovers of art, long since dead, who saw them when they were first painted. Sir Joshua Reynolds, in his *Second Discourse*, recommended Ludovico Caracci as a model for style in painting, in which he thought he approached the nearest to perfection. 'His unaffected breadth of light and shadow,' he said, 'the simplicity of colouring, which, holding its proper rank, does not draw aside the least part of the attention from the subject, and the solemn effect of that twilight which seems diffused over his pictures, appear to me to correspond with grave and dignified subjects, better than the more artificial brilliancy of sunshine which enlightens the pictures of Titian.' Hazlitt was a great critic and enough of a painter to paint a tolerable portrait of Charles Lamb. Of Correggio he wrote that he 'possessed a greater variety of excellence in the different departments of his art than any other painter.' 'Who can think of him,' he asks rhetorically, 'without a swimming of the head?' We can. Hazlitt considered Guercino's *Endymion* one of the finest pictures in Florence. I doubt whether anyone today would give it more than a passing glance. Now, it is no good saying that these eminent persons didn't know what they were talking about; they expressed the cultivated æsthetic opinions of their time. Beauty in fact is only that which produces the specific pleasure which leads us to describe an object as beautiful during a certain period of the world's history, and it does so because it responds to certain needs of the period. It would be foolish to suppose that our opinions are any more definitive than those of our fathers, and we may be pretty sure that our descendants will look upon them with the same perplexity as we look upon Sir Joshua's high praise of Pellegrino Tibaldi and Hazlitt's passionate admiration for Guido Reni.

V

I have suggested that there is between the creation of beauty and the appreciation of it a disjunction which no bridge can span, and from what I have said the reader will have gathered that I think the appreciation is enhanced by, if not actually dependent upon, the culture of the individual. That is what the connoisseurs of art and the lovers of beauty claim, and they claim also that the gift of æsthetic appreciation is a rare one. If they are right it demolishes Tolstoi's contention that real beauty is accessible to everyone. Perhaps the most interesting part of Kant's *Critique of Æsthetic Judgment* is the long section he devotes to the sublime. I need only trouble the reader with his conclusions. He points out that the peasant who lives among mountains merely looks upon them as horrible and dangerous (as we know the ancient travellers did) and the sea-faring man looks upon the sea as a treacherous and uncertain element which it is his business to contend with. To receive from the snow-clad mountains and the storm-tossed sea the specific pleasure which we call the sublime demands a susceptibility to ideas and a certain degree of culture. That has an air of truth. Is the farmer conscious of the beauty of the landscape in the sight of which he earns his daily bread? I should say not; and that is natural, for the appreciation of beauty, it is agreed, must not be affected by practical considerations, and he is concerned to plough a field or to dig a ditch. The appreciation of the beauty of nature is a recent acquisition of the human race. It was created by the painters and writers of the Romantic Era. It needs leisure and sophistication. In order to appreciate it, then, not only disinterestedness is needed, but culture and a susceptibility to ideas. Unwelcome as the idea may be, I don't see how one can escape admitting that beauty is accessible but to the chosen few.

But to admit that excites in me a feeling of deep discomfort. More than twenty-five years ago I bought an abstract picture by Fernand Léger. It was an arrangement of squares, oblongs and spheres in black, white, grey and red, and for some reason he had called it *Les Toits de Paris*. I did not think it beautiful, but I found it ingenious and decorative. I had a cook then, a bad-tempered and quarrelsome woman, who would stand looking at this picture for quite long periods in a state of something that looked very like rapture. I asked her what she saw in it. 'I don't know,' she answered, '*mais ça me plait, ça me dit quelque chose.*' It seemed to me that she was receiving as genuine an æsthetic emotion as I flattered myself I received from El Greco's *Crucifixion* in the Louvre. I am led by this (a single instance, of course) to suggest that it is a very narrow point of view which claims that the specific pleasure of artistic appreciation can only be felt by the privileged few. It may well be that the pleasure is subtler, richer and more discriminating in someone whose personality is cultivated, whose experience is wide, but why should we suppose that someone else, less fortunately circumstanced, cannot feel a pleasure as intense and as fruitful? The object that in the latter gives rise to the pleasure may be what the æsthete considers no great shakes. Does that matter? It appears that the urn which inspired Keats to write his great ode was a mediocre piece of Greco-Roman sculpture, yet it gave him the æsthetic thrill which, being what he was, occasioned one of the most beautiful poems in the English language. Kant put the matter succinctly when he said that beauty does not reside in the object. It is the name we give to the specific pleasure which the object gives us. Pleasure is a feeling.

I can see no reason why there should not be as many people capable of enjoying the specific pleasure of beauty as there are who are capable of feeling grief or joy, love, tenderness and compassion. I am inclined to say that Tolstoi was right when he said that real beauty is accessible to everyone if you leave out the word *real*. There is no such thing as real beauty. Beauty is what gives you and me and everyone else that sense of exultation and liberation which I have already spoken of. But in discourse it is more convenient to use the word as if it were a material entity, like a chair or a table, existing in its own right, independent of the observer, and that I shall continue to do.

VI

Now, after this long digression from my subject, which is Kant's æsthetic ideas, I must attempt to cope with what I have found the most difficult part of his treatise, and that is his discussion of purposiveness and purpose in relation to beauty. And what makes it more difficult is that he seems sometimes to use the two words as though they were synonymous. (The German words are *Zweck* and *Zweckmässigkeit*.) In this essay, designed to interest the general reader, I have been at pains to avoid the technical terms of philosophy, but now I must ask his indulgence while I give him Kant's definition of purpose and purposiveness. It runs as follows: 'Purpose is the object of a concept in so far as this concept is regarded as the cause of the object, that is to say as the real ground of its possibility. The causality of a concept in respect of its object is its purposiveness.' Kant gives an illustration which makes the matter clear: A man builds a house in order to rent it. That is his purpose in building it. But the house would not have been built at all unless he had conceived the idea that he would receive rent from it. This concept is the purposiveness of building the house. There is a certain humour, probably unconscious, in one example which our philosopher gives of purposiveness in nature: 'The vermin that torment men in their clothes, their hair, or their bed may be according to a wise appointment of nature a motive of cleanliness which is in itself an important means for the preservation of health.' But that these vermin have been created for this purpose cannot be a conviction, but at most a persuasion. It may be no more than a wholesome illusion. The purposiveness which we seem to find in nature may be occasioned only by the peculiar constitution of our cognitive faculties. It is a principle we make use of to provide ourselves with concepts in the vast multiplicity of nature, so that we may take our bearings in it and enable our understanding to feel itself at home in it.

Fortunately for myself I am only concerned with this principle in so far as it is related to Kant's æsthetic ideas. Beauty, he states, is the form of purposiveness in an object so far as it is perceived in it apart from the representation of a purpose. This purposiveness, however, is not real; we are forced by the subjective needs of our nature to ascribe it to the object which we call beautiful. Since I am more at ease with the concrete than with the abstract I have tried to think of an object of beauty which has purposiveness apart from purpose, and that is not so easy since the simplest definition of purposiveness is that it is characterised by purpose. I offer an illustration with diffidence. A rice bowl of the Yung Lo period, of the porcelain known as egg-shell, is so wafer-thin, so fragile, so delicate in texture that its purpose is evidently not to contain rice. Such a purpose would be of practical interest and the appreciation of beauty is essentially disinterested. Furthermore, there is an admirably drawn design under the glaze which can only be seen when you hold the bowl, empty, up to the light. What other purposiveness can it have but to please the eye? But if by the purposiveness of an object of beauty Kant had merely meant that it affords pleasure he would surely have said so. I have an inkling that at the back of his great mind was a disinclination to admit that pleasure was the only effect to be obtained from the consideration of a great work of art.

Pleasure has always had a bad name. Philosophers and moralists have been unwilling to own that it is good and only to be eschewed when its consequences are harmful. Plato, as we know, condemned art unless it led to right action. Christianity with its contempt of the body and its obsession with sin viewed pleasure with apprehension and its pursuit unworthy of a human being with an immortal soul. I suppose that the disapproval with which pleasure is regarded arises from the fact that when people think of it, it is in connection with the pleasures of the body. That is not fair. There are spiritual pleasures as well as physical pleasures, and if we must allow that sexual intercourse, as St. Augustine (who knew something about it) declared, is the greatest of physical pleasures, we may admit that æsthetic appreciation is the greatest of spiritual pleasures.

Kant says that the artist produces a work of art with no other purpose than to make it beautiful. I do not believe that is so; I believe that the artist produces a work of art to exercise his creative faculty, and whether what he creates is beautiful is a fortuitous result in which he may well be uninterested. We know from Vasari that Titian was a fashionable and prolific portrait painter. His experience was wide and he knew his business, so that when he came to paint the *Man with a Glove* it is probable enough that he was concerned only to get a good likeness and satisfy his client. It was a happy accident that, owing to his own great gifts and the natural grace of his sitter, he achieved beauty. Milton has concisely told us what his purpose was in writing *Paradise Lost*, it was a didactic purpose, and if in passage after passage he achieved beauty I cannot but think that this too was a happy accident. It may be that beauty, like happiness and originality, is more likely to be obtained when it is not deliberately attempted.

I have not thought it necessary in this discourse to touch upon Kant's discussion of the sublime, though, as he insists, our judgments about the beautiful and the sublime are akin, since both are æsthetic judgments. The purposiveness we are obliged to ascribe to both (unfortunately Kant does not tell us why) is entirely subjective. 'We call things sublime', he says, 'on the ground that they make us feel the sublimity of our own minds.' Our imagination cannot cope with the feeling that arises in us when we contemplate the raging, storm-tossed sea and the massed immensities of the Himalayas, with their eternal snows. We are made to feel our insignificance, but at the same time we are exalted, since, awe-struck as we may be, we are conscious that we are not limited to the world of sense, but can raise ourselves above it. 'Nature may deprive us of everything, but it has no power over our moral personality.' So Pascal said: "*L'homme n'est qu'un roseau, le plus foible de la nature, mais c'est un roseau pensant, il ne faut pas que l'Univers entier s'arme pour l'écraser, une vapeur, une goutte d'eau suffit pour le tuer. Mais quand l'Univers l'écraserait, l'homme serait encore plus noble que ce qui le tue, parce qu'il scait qu'il meurt et l'avantage que l'Univers a sur lui, L'Univers n'en scait rien.*" If Kant had had the æsthetic sensibility which, as I remarked early in this essay, he seems singularly to have lacked, it might perhaps have occurred to him that the emotions we feel, and the ideas that spring from them, when we contemplate a supreme work of art, the ceiling of the Sistine Chapel or El Greco's *Crucifixion* in the Louvre, are not so very different from those we have when we are confronted with the objects we describe as sublime. They are moral emotions and moral ideas.

Kant, as we know, was a moralist. 'Reason,' he says, 'can never be persuaded that the existence of a man who merely lives for enjoyment has worth in itself.' That we may all agree to. Then he says: 'If the beautiful arts are not brought into more or less combination with moral ideas . . . they serve only as a distraction, of which we are the more in need the more we avail ourselves of them to disperse the discontent of the mind with itself, so that we render ourselves ever more useless and more discontented.' He goes even further when at the very end of his treatise he says that the true introduction to the appreciation of beauty is the development of the moral ideas and the culture of moral feeling. It is not for me who am no philosopher to suggest that by his difficult proposition that beauty is the form of the purposiveness of an object so far as this is perceived without any presentation of a purpose, Kant may have meant something other than what he said, but, I must confess, it seems to me that if the purposiveness which we are apparently forced to ascribe to the work of art lies only in the artist's intention these scattered observations of his are somewhat pointless; for what has the artist's intention to do with us? We, I repeat, are only concerned with what he has done.

Jeremy Bentham startled the world many years ago by stating in effect that if the amount of pleasure obtained from each be equal there is nothing to choose between poetry and push-pin. Since few people now know what push-pin is, I may explain that it is a child's game in which one player tries to push his pin across that of another player, and if he succeeds and then is able by pressing down on the two pins with the ball of his thumb to lift them off the table he wins possession of his opponent's pin. When I was a small boy at a preparatory school we used to play it with steel nibs till the headmaster discovered that we had somehow turned it into a gambling game, whereupon he forbade us to play it, and when he caught us still

194

doing so, soundly beat us. The indignant retort to Bentham's statement was that spiritual pleasures are obviously higher than physical pleasures. But who say so? Those who prefer spiritual pleasures. They are in a miserable minority, as they acknowledge when they declare that the gift of æsthetic appreciation is a very rare one. The vast majority of men are, as we know, both by necessity and choice preoccupied with material considerations. Their pleasures are material. They look askance at those who spend their lives in the pursuit of art. That is why they have attached a depreciatory sense to the word æsthete, which means merely one who has a special appreciation of beauty. How are we going to show that they are wrong? How are we going to show that there *is* something to choose between poetry and push-pin? I surmise that Bentham chose push-pin for its pleasant alliteration with poetry. Let us speak of lawn tennis. It is a popular game which many of us can play with pleasure. It needs skill and judgment, a good eye and a cool head. If I get the same amount of pleasure out of playing it as you get by looking at Titian's *Entombment of Christ* in the Louvre, by listening to Beethoven's *Eroica* or by reading Eliot's *Ash Wednesday*, how are you going to prove that your pleasure is better and more refined than mine? Only, I should say, by manifesting that this gift you have of æsthetic appreciation has a moral effect on your character.

In one place Kant makes the significant remark that 'connoisseurs in taste, not only often, but generally are given up to idle, capricious and mischievous passions' and that 'they could perhaps make less claims than others to any superiority of attachment to moral principles.' This was doubtless true then: it is true now. Human nature changes little. No one can have lived much in the society of those whom Kant calls connoisseurs of taste, and whom we may more conveniently call æsthetes, without noticing how seldom it is that you find in them the modesty, the tolerance, the loving-kindness and liberality, in short the goodness with which you might have expected their addiction to spiritual pleasures to inform them. If the delight in æsthetic appreciation is no more than the opium of an intelligentsia it is no more than, as Kant says, a mischievous distraction. If it is more it should enable its possessor to acquire virtue. Kant finely says that beauty is the symbol of morality. Unless the love of beauty ennobles the character, and that is the only purposiveness of beauty that seems, as far as I can see, important enough to give it value, then I can't tell how we can escape from Bentham's affirmation that if the amount of pleasure obtained from each be equal there is nothing to choose between poetry and push-pin.

SOME NOVELISTS I HAVE KNOWN

I

ONE of Hazlitt's most enchanting essays is *My First Acquaintance with Poets*, in which he relates how he came to know Coleridge and Wordsworth. Coleridge had come to Shrewsbury to take charge of its Unitarian Congregation, and Mr. Rowe, whom he was succeeding, went down to the coach to meet him; but though he saw a round-faced man in a short black coat who seemed to be talking at a great rate to his fellow-passengers he could find no one answering the description of the man he was expecting. He went home, but had scarcely got there when the round-faced man in the black coat entered and 'dissipated all doubts on the subject, by beginning to talk. He did not cease while he stayed; nor has he since, that I know of.' Hazlitt's father, a dissenting minister, lived ten miles from Shrewsbury and a few days later Coleridge walked over to see him. Hazlitt, then twenty years old, was presented to him. The poet found the young man an enthusiastic and intelligent listener and invited him to come to Nether-Stowey in the spring. This Hazlitt did, and after he had been there a day or two Wordsworth arrived. 'He instantly began to make havoc of the half of a Cheshire cheese on the table, and said triumphantly that his marriage with experience had not been so unproductive as Mr. Southey's in teaching him a knowledge of the good things of this life.' Next day Coleridge and Hazlitt accompanied Wordsworth to Alfoxden, where he read in the open air the story of Peter Bell. 'There is a charm in the recitation both of Coleridge and Wordsworth,' says Hazlitt, 'which acts as a spell upon the heart, and disarms the judgment. Perhaps they have deceived themselves by making use of this ambiguous accompaniment.' Hazlitt, though excited and admiring, relinquished neither his critical acumen nor his sense of humour.

It is the delight I take in this essay that has prompted me to write the following pages. Alas, I have no such great figures to write about as Coleridge and Wordsworth. *The Ancient Mariner, Kubla Khan,* the great ode and *The Solitary Reaper* will be read as long as English poetry is read; but who can tell whether any of the authors with whom I propose to deal in this essay will be remembered by posterity. Brahma, the Indian monists think, created the world for sport, thus exercising in this little bit of fun the infinite activity which is one of his attributes; and it is with just such sardonic and unscrupulous humour that posterity orders literary fame. Its wilfulness is beyond reason. It takes no account of virtue and little of industry; it is indifferent to high endeavour and sincerity of purpose. How unjust it is that Mrs. Humphry Ward, with her well-stored mind and her command of language, with her solid gifts, her conscientiousness and her seriousness, should be so forgotten that even her name will be unknown to most readers of today, whereas a dissipated French abbé, a hack-writer of the eighteenth century who wrote interminable and unreadable novels, should have achieved immortality because in the long course of one of them he wrote the story of a little baggage called Manon Lescaut.

Before I begin I should like to make it quite clear that though I knew the authors I am going to speak of over a long period I was not really intimate with any of them. One reason of this is that until I made a success as a writer of light comedies I knew very few authors, and for the most part those I knew, and only casually, were like myself very small fry. One's intimate friends are those one makes in one's teens or early twenties. I was thirty-four when I became a popular playwright, and though after that I came in contact with many of the literary figures of the day they were a good deal older than me and they were by then too much occupied with their own activities and the friends these had brought them for me to become anything more than a random acquaintance. I have been a wanderer all my life and when I was not wanted in London for the rehearsals of a play I spent long periods out of England so that I lost touch with the people my success had enabled me to meet.

French authors live for the greater part of the year in Paris. They form cliques and the members of a clique meet constantly, in cafés, in newspaper offices, in their apartments; they dine together and talk and criticise one another's books; they write to one another (with a view to future publication) immense letters. They defend one another; they attack one another. English authors are different. On the whole they are not much interested in their fellow-writers. They are apt to live in the country and only go to London when they need to. They are more indiscriminately social than the French and mix freely in circles other than literary. Their close friends are, as with Henry James, a little group of fervent admirers or, as with H. G. Wells, the persons who share their particular interests. If you are not numbered among one or other of these classes you have little chance of admittance into their intimacy. But the chief reason why I have never become easily familiar with the men of letters I propose to write about is owing to some fault in my own character. I am either too self-centred, or too diffident, or too reserved, or too shy to be able to be on confidential terms with anyone I know at all well, and when on occasion a friend in trouble has opened his heart to me I have been too embarrassed to be of much help to him. Most people like to talk about themselves and when they tell me things I should have thought they would prefer to keep to themselves I am abashed. I prefer to guess at the secrets of their hearts. It is not in me to take people at their face value and I am not easily impressed. I have no power of veneration. It is more in my humour to be amused by people than to respect them.

Many have been on terms of much closer friendship with the more or less illustrious persons my recollections of whom I am now offering to the reader, and I have written the above only to impress upon him that they (my recollections) can suggest no more than a partial portrait of my subjects.

I saw Henry James long before I knew him. Somehow or other I was allotted two seats in the dress circle for the first night of *Guy Domville*. I can't think why, because I was still a medical student and one of George Alexander's first nights was a fashionable affair and seats in the better parts of the house were distributed among critics, regular first-nighters, friends of the management and persons of consequence. The play was a dreadful failure. The dialogue was graceful, but perhaps not quite direct enough to be taken in by an audience and there was a certain monotony in its rhythm. Henry James was fifty when he wrote the play and it is hard to understand how such a practised writer could have invented such a tissue of absurdities as was that night presented to the public. There was in the second act a distressing scene of pretended drunkenness which gave one goose-flesh. One blushed for the author. The play reached its tedious end and Henry James was very unwisely brought on the stage to take a bow, as was the undignified custom of the time. He was greeted with such an outburst of boos and catcalls as only then have I heard in the theatre. From my seat in the dress circle he seemed oddly foreshortened. A stout man on stumpy legs, and owing to his baldness, notwithstanding his beard, a vast expanse of naked face. He confronted the hostile audience, his jaw fallen so that his mouth was slightly open and on his countenance a look of complete bewilderment. He was paralysed. I don't know why the curtain wasn't immediately brought down. He seemed to stand there interminably while the gallery and the pit continued to bawl. There was clapping in the stalls and dress circle, and he said afterwards that it was enthusiastic, but there he was mistaken. It was half-hearted. People clapped in protest at the rudeness of pit and gallery, and out of pity because they could not bear to see the wretched man's humiliation. At last George Alexander came out and led him, crushed and cowed, away.

In a letter he wrote to his brother William after that disastrous evening Henry James, like many another dramatist who has had a failure, said that his play was 'over the heads of the usual vulgar theatre-going London public'. That was not the fact. It was a bad play. It is possible that the outcry would have been less violent if the audience had not been exasperated by the incredible conduct of the characters. Their motives were, as in so much of Henry James's work, not the motives of normal human beings, and though in his fiction he was persuasive enough very often to conceal the fact from the reader, presented on the stage they glaringly lacked plausibility. The audience felt instinctively that people did not behave with the lack of common sense with which he made them behave and, so feeling, felt that they had been made fools of. In their boos there was more than irritation because they had been bored, there was resentment.

One can see the play Henry James wanted to write and perhaps thought he had written, but it is wretchedly evident that he fell very far short of his intention. He despised the English theatre and was convinced that he could write much better plays himself. Years before in Paris he wrote that he had 'mastered Dumas, Augier and Sardou', and claimed that he knew 'all they knew

and a great deal more besides.' Why he failed as a
dramatist is obvious enough. He was like a man who
because he can ride a bicycle thinks he can ride a horse.
If under that impression he goes out for a day with the
Pytchley he will come a cropper at the first fence. One
unfortunate result of Henry James's misadventure was
that it confirmed managers in the belief that no novelist
could write a play.

II

It was not till many years later, when I had myself
written successful plays, that I met Henry James. It
was at a luncheon party given by Lady Russell, the
author of *Elizabeth and her German Garden*, in a flat she
then had, if I remember rightly, near Buckingham Gate.
It was by way of being a literary party and Henry
James was of course the lion of the occasion. He said
a few polite words to me, but I received the impression
that they meant very little. I forget how long it was
after this that I happened to go to an afternoon performance of *The Cherry Orchard* given by the Stage
Society and found myself sitting next to Henry James
and Mrs. W. K. Clifford, the widow of the mathematician, and herself the author of two good novels,
Mrs. Keith's Crime and *Aunt Anne*. The intervals were
long and we had ample time to talk. Henry James was
perplexed by *The Cherry Orchard*, as well he might be
when his dramatic values were founded on the plays
of Alexander Dumas and Sardou, and in the second
interval he set out to explain to us how antagonistic to

his French sympathies was this Russian incoherence. Lumbering through his tortuous phrases, he hesitated now and again in search of the exact word to express his dismay; but Mrs. Clifford had a quick and agile mind; she knew the word he was looking for and every time he paused immediately supplied it. This was the last thing he wanted. He was too well-mannered to protest, but an almost imperceptible expression on his face betrayed his irritation and, obstinately refusing the word she offered, he laboriously sought another, and again Mrs. Clifford suggested it only to have it again turned down. It was a scene of high comedy.

Ethel Irving was playing the part of Chekov's feckless heroine. She was herself moody, neurotic and emotional, which suited the character, and her performance was excellent. She had made a great success in a play of mine and Henry James was curious to know about her. I told him what I could. Then he put me a very simple question, but he felt it would be crude and perhaps a trifle snobbish to put it simply. Both Mrs. Clifford and I knew exactly what he wanted to say. He led up to his enquiry like a big-game hunter stalking an antelope. He approached stealthily and drew back when he suspected that the shy creature winded him. He wrapped up his meaning in an increasingly embarrassed maze of circumlocution till at last Mrs. Clifford could stand it no longer and blurted out: 'Do you mean, is she a lady?' A look of real suffering crossed his face. Put so, the question had a vulgarity that outraged him. He pretended not to hear. He made a little gesture of desperation and said:

'Is she, *enfin*, what you'd call if you were asked point-blank, if so to speak you were put with your back to the wall, is she a *femme du monde*?'

In 1910 I went to America for the first time and in due course paid a visit to Boston. Henry James, his brother having recently died, was staying at Cambridge, Massachusetts, with his sister-in-law and Mrs. James asked me to dinner. There were but the three of us. I can remember nothing of the conversation, but I could not help noticing that Henry James was troubled in spirit, and after dinner, when the widow had left us alone in the dining-room, he told me that he had promised his brother to remain at Cambridge for, I think, six months after his death, so that if he found himself able to make a communication from beyond the grave there would be two sympathetic witnesses on the spot ready to receive it. I could not but reflect that Henry James was in so nervous a state that it would be difficult to place implicit confidence in any report he might make. His sensibility was so exacerbated that he was capable of imagining anything. But hitherto no message had come and the six months were drawing to their end.

When it was time for me to go Henry James insisted on accompanying me to the corner where I could take the street-car back to Boston. I protested that I was perfectly capable of getting there by myself, but he would not hear of it, not only on account of the kindness and the great courtesy which were natural to him, but also because America seemed to him a strange and terrifying labyrinth in which without his guidance I was bound to get hopelessly lost.

As we walked along, he told me what his good manners had prevented him from saying before Mrs. James, that he was counting the days that must elapse before, having fulfilled his promise, he could sail for the blessed shores of England. He yearned for it. There, in Cambridge, he felt himself forlorn. He was determined never to set foot again on that bewildering and unknown country that America was to him. It was then that he uttered the phrase which seemed to me so fantastic that I have never forgotten it. 'I wander about these great empty streets of Boston,' he said, 'and I never see a soul. I could not be more alone in the Sahara.' The street-car hove in sight and Henry James was seized with agitation. He began waving frantically when it was still a quarter of a mile away. He was afraid it wouldn't stop, and he besought me to jump on with the greatest agility of which I was capable, for it would not pause more than an instant, and if I were not very careful I might be dragged along and if not killed, at least mangled and dismembered. I assured him I was quite accustomed to getting on street-cars. Not American street-cars, he told me, they were of a savagery, an inhumanity, a ruthlessness beyond any conception. I was so infected by his anxiety that when the car pulled up and I leapt on, I had almost the sensation that I had had a miraculous escape from certain death. I saw him standing on his short legs in the middle of the road, looking after the car, and I felt that he was trembling still at my narrow shave.

But homesick as he was for England I don't believe that he ever felt himself quite at home there. He remained a friendly, but critical alien. He did not know the English as an Englishman instinctively knows them and so his English characters never to my mind ring quite true. His American characters, at least to an Englishman, on the whole do. He had certain remarkable gifts, but he lacked the quality of empathy which enables a novelist to feel himself into his characters, think their thoughts and suffer their emotions. Flaubert vomited as though he too had swallowed arsenic when he was describing the suicide of Emma Bovary. It is impossible to imagine Henry James being similarly affected if he had had to narrate a similar episode. Take *The Author of Beltraffio*. In that a mother lets her only child, a little boy, die of diphtheria so that he should not be corrupted by his father's books, of which she profoundly disapproves. No one could have conceived such a monstrous episode who could imagine a mother's love for her son and in his nerves feel the anguish of the child tossing restlessly on his bed and the pitiful, agonising struggle for breath. That is what the French call *littérature*. There is no precise English equivalent. On the pattern of writer's cramp you might call it writer's hokum. It signifies the sort of writing produced purely for literary effect without a relation to truth or probability. A novelist may ask himself what it feels like to commit a murder and then may invent a character who commits one to know what it feels like. That is *littérature*. People commit murders for reasons that seem good to them, not in order to enjoy a curious experience. The great novelists, even in seclusion, have lived life passionately. Henry James was content to observe it from a window.

But you cannot describe life convincingly unless you have partaken of it; nor, should your object be different, can you fantasticate upon it (as Balzac and Dickens did) unless you know it first. Something escapes you unless you have been an actor in the tragi-comedy. However realistic he tries to be, the novelist cannot hope to give a representation of life as exactly as a lithograph can give a representation of a drawing. With his characters and the experiences he causes them to undergo he draws a pattern, but he is more likely to convince his readers that the pattern is acceptable if the people he depicts have the same sort of motives, foibles and passions as they know they have themselves and if the experiences of the persons in question are such as their characters render plausible.

Henry James regarded his relations and friends with deep affection, but this is no indication that he was capable of love. Indeed he showed a singular obtuseness in his stories and novels when he came to deal with the most deeply seated of human emotions; so that, interested and amused as you are, (often amused at him rather than with him,) you are constantly jolted back to reality by your feeling that human beings simply do not behave as he makes them do. You cannot take Henry James's fiction quite seriously as, for instance, you take *Anna Karenina* or *Madame Bovary*; you read it with a smile, and with the suspension of disbelief with which you read the Restoration dramatists. (This notion is not so far-fetched as it may seem at first sight: if Congreve had been a novelist he might well have written the bawdy narrative of promiscuous fornication which Henry James entitled *What Maisie*

Knew.) There is all the difference between his novels and those of Flaubert and Tolstoi as there is between the paintings of Daumier and the drawings of Constantin Guys. The draughtsman's pretty women drive in the Bois in their smart carriages, luxurious and fashionable, but they have no bodies in their elegant clothes. They amuse, they charm; but they are as unsubstantial as the stuff that dreams are made of. Henry James's fictions are like the cobwebs which a spider may spin in the attic of some old house, intricate, delicate and even beautiful, but which at any moment the housemaid's broom with brutal common sense may sweep away.

It is not my purpose to criticise Henry James's work, yet it is impossible in his case to write of the man rather than of the author. They are in fact inseparable. The author absorbed the man. To him it was art that made life significant, but he cared little for any of the arts except the one he practised. He was little interested in music or painting. When Gosse was going to Venice he conjured him without fail to see Tintoretto's *Crucifixion* at San Cassiano. It is odd that he should have picked out this fine but stagey picture to commend rather than Titian's grand *Presentation of the Virgin* or Veronese's *Jesus in the House of Levi*. No one who knew Henry James in the flesh can read his stories dispassionately. He got the sound of his voice into every line he wrote, and you accept (not willingly, but with indulgence) the abominable style of his later work, with its ugly Gallicisms, its abuse of adverbs, its too elaborate metaphors, the tortuosity of its long sentences, because they are part and parcel of the charm, benignity and amusing pomposity of the man you remember.

I am not sure that Henry James was fortunate in his friends. They were disposed to be possessive, and they regarded one another's claim to be in the inner circle of his confidence with no conspicuous amiability. Like a dog with a bone, each was inclined to growl when another showed an inclination to dispute his exclusive right to the precious object of his devotion. The reverence with which they treated him was of no great service to him. They seemed to me, indeed, sometimes a trifle silly: they whispered to one another with delighted giggles that Henry James privately stated that the article in *The Ambassadors* on the manufacture of which the fortune of the widow Newsome was founded, and the nature of which he had left in polite obscurity, was in fact a chamber pot. I did not find this so amusing as they did. I think it would be unfair to say that Henry James demanded the admiration of his friends, but he certainly enjoyed it. English authors, unlike their fellows in France and Germany, are chary of assuming an attitude. The pose of *Cher Maire* makes them feel faintly ridiculous. Perhaps because Henry James had first come to know distinguished writers in France he took the pedestal on which his admirers placed him as a natural prerogative. He was touchy and could be cross when he was not treated with what he thought proper respect. On one occasion a young Irish friend of mine was staying at Hill for the week-end in company with Henry James. Mrs. Hunter, their hostess, told him that he was a talented young man and Henry James on the Saturday afternoon engaged him in conversation. My friend was petulant and impatient, and at length, driven to desperation by James's interminable struggle to find the one word that would express exactly what he wanted to say, blurted out: 'Oh, Mr. James, I'm not of any importance. Don't bother about rooting around for the right word. Any old word is good enough for me.' Henry James was deeply affronted and complained to Mrs. Hunter that the young man had been very rude to him, whereupon Mrs. Hunter gave him a severe scolding and insisted that he should apologise to her distinguished guest. This he accordingly did.

Once Jane Wells inveigled Henry James and me to go with her to a subscription dance in aid of some worthy object in which H. G. was interested. Mrs. Wells, Henry James and I were chatting in a kind of ante-room adjoining the ballroom when a brash young man bounced in, interrupting Henry James in his discourse, and seizing Jane Wells's hands said: 'Come on and dance, Mrs. Wells, you don't want to sit there listening to that old man talking his head off.' It wasn't very polite. Jane Wells gave Henry James an anxious glance and then with a strained smile went off with the brash young man. Henry James was too little accustomed to be treated like that to take it, as he might sensibly have done, with a good-natured laugh, and he was much offended. When Mrs. Wells came back he got up and a little too formally bade her goodnight.

When someone transplants himself from one country to another he is more likely to assimilate the defects of its inhabitants than their virtues. The England in

211

which Henry James lived was excessively class-conscious, and I think it is to this that must be ascribed the somewhat disconcerting attitude he adopted in his fiction to those who were so unfortunate as to be of humble origin. Unless he were an artist, by choice a writer, it seemed to him more than a little ridiculous that anyone should be under the necessity of earning a living. The death of a member of the lower orders could be trusted to give him a mild chuckle. I think this attitude was emphasised by the fact that, himself of good family, he could not have dwelt long in England without becoming aware that to the English one American was very like another. He saw compatriots on the strength of a fortune acquired in Michigan or Ohio received with as great cordiality as though they belonged to the eminent families of Boston and New York, and in self-defence somewhat exaggerated his native fastidiousness in social relations. Sometimes he made rather ludicrous mistakes and would attribute to some young man who had taken his fancy a distinction which he obviously did not possess.

If in these pages I have made Henry James, I hope not unkindly, a trifle absurd it is because that is what I found him. I think he took himself a good deal too seriously. We look askance at a man who keeps on telling you he is a gentleman; I think it would have been more becoming in Henry James if he had not insisted so often on his being an artist. It is better to leave others to say that. But he was gracious, hospitable and when in the mood uncommonly amusing. He had uncommon gifts and if I think they were too often ill-directed that is only what I think and I ask no one to agree with me. The fact remains that those last novels of his, notwithstanding their unreality, make all other novels, except the very best, unreadable.

III

I met H. G. Wells for the first time at a flat which Reggie Turner had near Berkeley Square. I was living then in Mount Street and sometimes I would drop in to see him. Reggie Turner was on the whole the most amusing man I have known. I will not attempt to describe his humour, since Max Beerbohm has done it to perfection in the essay called *Laughter*. Reggie was not so well pleased as he might have been with this flattering tribute because Max had added that he was not very responsive to the humour of others. He asked me if it was true, and I was bound to admit that it was. Reggie liked an audience, though he was quite content with one of three or four, and then he would take a theme and embroider upon it with such drollery that he made your sides so ache with laughter that at last you had to beg him to stop. He was by way of being a novelist, but somehow, when he took up his pen his gaiety, his extravagant invention, his lightness deserted him, and his novels were dull. They were unsuccessful. He said of them: 'With most novelists it's their first edition that is valuable, but with mine it's the second. It doesn't exist.' I will set down here a quip of his because I do not think it is well known. He was one of the few of Oscar Wilde's friends who remained faithful to him after his disgrace. Reggie was in Paris when Wilde, living in a cheap, dingy hotel on the left bank of the Seine, was dying. Reggie went to see him every day. One morning he found him distraught. He asked him what was the matter. 'I had a terrible dream last night,' said Oscar, 'I dreamt I was supping with the dead.' 'Well,' said Reggie, 'I'm sure you were the life and soul of the party, Oscar.' Wilde burst into a roar of laughter and regained his spirits. It was not only witty, but kind.

On the day on which I was first introduced to H. G. he had been lunching with Reggie and they had gone back to his flat to continue their conversation. H. G. was then, I suppose, at the height of his fame. I had not expected to find him there and was slightly disconcerted. I had recently made a success as a dramatist which the newspapers described as spectacular, but I was well aware that I had thereby lost caste with the intelligentsia. H. G. was cordial enough, but, perhaps because I was sensitive, I received the impression that he looked upon me with a sort of off-hand amusement as he might have looked upon Arthur Roberts or Dan Leno. He was busy reconstructing the world according to his own notions of how it should be shaped, and he had no time for anyone who was not with him, so that he could be enlisted to serve his ideas, or against him, so that he could be reasoned with, argued with, and if not brought round ignominiously discarded.

Though after that I saw him now and then, it was not till a number of years later, when I had settled down on the Riviera and H. G. had a house there too at which he spent a considerable part of the year, that our slight acquaintance ripened into friendship. Later still, when he had parted with the companion who shared the house with him (carved on the chimney-piece in the sitting-room was the phrase: This house was built by two lovers), and abandoned it to her, he would from time to time come to stay with me. He was very good company. He was not a wit as Max Beerbohm or Reggie Turner was, but he had a lively sense of humour and could laugh at himself as well as at others. Once he asked me to lunch to meet Barbusse, the author of a novel called *Le Feu* that had made a great stir It is a long time ago and I can only remember that Barbusse was a long, thin, hirsute man dressed in shabby black like a mute at a French funeral. He had dark angry eyes and a restless manner. He was an ardent, violent socialist and his speech was torrential. Though H. G. understood French well enough he spoke it haltingly, so that Barbusse had the conversation pretty much to himself. He treated us as though we were a public meeting. When he left, H. G. turned to me with a wry smile and said: 'How silly our own ideas sound when we hear them out of somebody else's mouth.' He was sharp-witted and, though apt to find persons who didn't agree with him stupid and so objects of ridicule, the humour he exercised at their expense was devoid of malice.

H. G. had strong sexual instincts and he said to me more than once that the need to satisfy these instincts had nothing to do with love. It was a purely physio-logical matter. If humour, as some say, is incom-patible with love, then H. G. was never in love, for he was keenly alive to what was rather absurd in the objects of his unstable affections and sometimes seemed almost to look upon them as creatures of farce. He was incapable of the idealisation of the desired person which most of us experience when we fall in love. If his companion was not intelligent he soon grew bored with her, and if she was her intelligence sooner or later palled on him. He did not like his cake unsweetened and if it was sweet it cloyed. He loved his liberty and when he found that a woman wished to restrict it he became exasperated and somewhat ruthlessly broke off the connection. Sometimes this was not so easily done and he had to put up with scenes and recriminations that he even found difficult to treat with levity. He was of course like most creative persons self-centred. That to sever a tie that had lasted for years might cause the other party pain and humiliation appeared to him merely silly. I was somewhat closely concerned in one of these upheavals in his life, and speaking of the trouble it was causing him he said: 'You know, women often mistake possessiveness for passion and when they are left, it is not so much that their heart is broken as that their claim to property is repudiated.' He thought it unreasonable that what on his side was merely the relaxation from what he regarded as his life's work on the other might be enduring passion. This he aroused. It surprised me since his physical appearance was not particularly pleasing. He was fat and homely. I once asked one of his mistresses what especially attracted her in him. I expected her to say his acute mind and his sense of fun; not at all; she said that his body smelt of honey.

Notwithstanding H. G.'s immense reputation and the

great influence he had had on his contemporaries he was devoid of conceit. There was nothing of the stuffed shirt in him. He never put on airs. He had naturally good manners and he would treat some unknown scribbler, the assistant librarian, for instance, of a provincial library, with the same charming civility as if he were as important as himself. It was only later that by a grin and a quip you could tell what a donkey he had thought him. I remember attending a dinner of the P.E.N., of which H. G. was then president. There were a great many people present and after H. G. had read a report a number of them got up to ask questions. Most of them were silly, but H. G. replied to them all with great courtesy. One thickly bearded man, which marked him out as a conscious intellectual, leapt to his feet time time and again to make short speeches of a singular ineptitude and it was only too obvious that he was trying merely to attract attention to himself. H. G. could have crushed him with a retort, but he listened to him attentively and then reasoned with him as if he had been talking sense. After the proceedings were over I told H. G. how much I admired the wonderful patience with which he had dealt with the silly fellow. He chuckled and said: 'When I was a member of the Fabian Society I got a lot of practice in dealing with fools.'

He had no illusions about himself as an author. He always insisted that he made no pretension to be an artist. That was, indeed, something he despised rather than admired, and when he spoke of Henry James, an old friend, who claimed, as I have hinted, perhaps a little too often that he was an artist and nothing else, it was good-humouredly to ridicule him. 'I'm not an author,' H. G. would say, 'I'm a publicist. My work is just high-class journalism.' On one occasion, after he had been staying with me, he sent me a complete edition of his works and next time he came he saw them displayed in an imposing row on my shelves. They were well printed on good paper and handsomely bound in red. He ran his finger along them and with a cheerful grin said: 'They're as dead as mutton, you know. They all dealt with matters of topical interest and now that the matters aren't topical any more they're unreadable.' There is a good deal of truth in what he said. He had a fluent pen and too often it ran away with him. I have never seen any of his manuscripts, but I surmise that he wrote with facility and corrected little. He had a way of repeating in one sentence, but in other words, exactly what he said in the previous one. I suppose it was because he was so full of the idea he wanted to express that he was not satisfied to say it only once. It made him unnecessarily verbose.

H. G.'s theory of the short story was a sensible one. It enabled him to write a number that were very good and several that were masterly. His theory of the novel was different. His early novels, which he had written to earn a living, did not accord with it and he spoke of them slightingly. His notion was that the function of the novelist was to deal with the pressing problems of the day and to persuade the reader to adopt the views for the betterment of the world which he, H. G., held. He was fond of likening the novel to a woven tapestry of varied interest, and he would not accept my objec-

Top left :
Henry James (1843-1916)

Top right :
H. G. Wells (1866-1946)

Bottom right :
Arnold Bennett (1867-1931)

tion that after all a tapestry has unity. The artist who designed it has given it form, balance, coherence and arrangement. It is not a jumble of unrelated items.

His later novels are, if not, as he said, unreadable, at least difficult to read with delight. You begin to read them with interest, but as you go on you find your interest dwindle and it is only by an effort of will that you continue to read. I think *Tono Bungay* is generally considered his best novel. It is written with his usual liveliness, though perhaps the style is better suited to a treatise than to a novel, and the characters are well presented. He has deliberately avoided the suspense which most novelists attempt to create and he tells you more or less early on what is going to happen. His theory of the novelist's function allows him to digress abundantly, which, if you are interested in the characters and their behaviour, can hardly fail to arouse in you some impatience.

One day when he was staying with me in the course of conversation he made the remark: 'I'm only interested in people in the mass, I'm indifferent to the individual.' Then with a smile: 'I like you, in fact I've got a real affection for you, but I'm not interested in you.' I laughed. I knew it was true. 'I'm afraid I can't multiply myself by ten thousand to arouse your interest, old boy,' I said. 'Ten thousand?' he cried. 'That's nothing. Ten million.' During the course of his life he came in contact with a great many people, but with rare exceptions, though consistently pleasant and courteous, they made no more impression on him than the 'extras' who compose the crowd in a moving picture.

I think that is why his novels are less satisfactory than one would have liked them to be. The people he puts before you are not individuals, but lively and talkative marionettes whose function it is to express the ideas he was out to attack or to defend. They do not develop according to their dispositions, but change for the purposes of the theme. It is as though a tadpole did not become a frog, but a squirrel—because you had a cage that you wanted to pop him into. H. G. seems often to have grown tired of his characters before he was half-way through and then, frankly discarding any attempt at characterisation, he becomes an out-and-out pamphleteer. One curious thing that you can hardly help noticing if you have read most of H. G.'s novels is that he deals with very much the same people in book after book. He appears to have been content to use with little variation the few persons who had played an intimate part in his own life. He was always a little impatient with his heroines. He regarded his heroes with greater indulgence. He had of course put more of himself in them; most of them in fact are merely himself in a different guise. Trafford in *Marriage* is indeed the portrait of the man H. G. thought he was, added to the man he would have liked to be.

IV

In the last twenty-five years I have had a lot of people staying with me, and sometimes I am tempted to write an essay on guests. There are the guests who never shut a door after them and never turn out the light when they leave their room. There are the guests who throw themselves on their bed in muddy boots to have a nap after lunch, so that the counterpane has to be cleaned on their departure. There are the guests who smoke in bed and burn holes in your sheets. There are the guests who are on a régime and have to have special food cooked for them and there are the guests who wait till their glass is filled with a vintage claret and then say: 'I won't have any, thank you.' There are the guests who never put back a book in the place from which they took it and there are the guests who take away a volume from a set and never return it. There are the guests who borrow money from you when they are leaving and do not pay it back. There are the guests who can never be alone for a minute and there are the guests who are seized with a desire to talk the moment they see you glancing at a paper. There are the guests who, wherever they are, want to be somewhere else and there are the guests who want to be doing something from the time they get up in the morning till the time they go to bed at night. There are the guests who treat you as though they were gauleiters in a conquered province. There are the guests who bring three weeks laundry with them to have washed at your expense and there are the guests who send their clothes to the cleaners and leave you to pay the bill. There are the guests who take all they can get and offer nothing in return.

There are also the guests who are happy just to be with you, who seek to please, who have resources of their own, who amuse you, whose conversation is delightful, whose interests are varied, who exhilarate

221

and excite you, who in short give you far more than you can ever hope to give them and whose visits are only too brief. Such a guest was H. G. He had a social sense. When there was a party he wanted to make it go. Now and then there were neighbours who had to be asked to lunch or dine and sometimes they were dull. H. G. would talk to them as entertainingly as if they had the wits to understand him. One such occasion stands out in my memory because it is the only time I saw him defeated. One of my neighbours, hearing that he was staying with me, called me up and told me that she had a great admiration for him and that she'd always been told that he was a marvellous talker and would so much like to meet him. I asked her to lunch. We sat down and H. G., who liked to talk, began to do so. He had just got into his stride when the lady interrupted him with a remark which showed that she hadn't listened to a word he said. He stopped, and when she had finished went on. Again she interrupted him and again he stopped. When she paused he started once more and again she interrupted. It was evident that her wish was not to hear H. G. talk, but to have him listen to her talk. He gave me one of his funny grins and relapsed into silence. For the rest of lunch he sat mute while she cheerfully gave utterance to a stream of shattering platitudes. When she went away she said she'd had a wonderful time.

I saw H. G. for the last time during the war. I was in New York and he had come to America to deliver a series of lectures. He came to lunch with me just before his return to England. He looked old, tired and shrivelled. He was as perky as ever, but with something of an effort. His lectures were a dismal failure. He was not a good speaker. It was odd that after so much public speaking he had never been able to deliver a discourse, but was obliged to read it. His voice was thin and squeaky and he read with his nose in his manuscript. People couldn't hear what he said and they left in droves. He had also seen a number of highly influential persons, but though they listened to him politely he could not but see that they paid little attention to what he said. He was hurt and disappointed. 'I've been saying the same things to people for the last thirty years,' he said to me with exasperation, 'and they won't listen.' That was the trouble. He had said the same things too often. Many of his ideas were sensible, none of them was complicated; but, like Goethe, he thought that one must always repeat truth: *Man muss das Wahre immer wiederholen.* He was so constituted that never a doubt entered his mind that he was definitely possessed of *das Wahre*. Naturally people grew impatient when they were asked once more to listen to views they knew only too well. He had had an immense influence on a whole generation and had done a great deal to alter the climate of opinion. But he had had his say. He was mortified to find that people looked upon him as a has-been. They agreed with him or they didn't. When they listened to him it was no longer with the old thrill of excitement, but with the indulgence you accord to an old man who has outlived his interest.

He died a disappointed man.

V

H. G. set little store on the pure novelist. I think he
would have segregated the novelists who seek primarily
to entertain on an island next to the one on which in
A New Utopia he settled the drunkards, where, well-
fed and comfortably housed, they could spend their
leisure in reading one another's works. The only
straight novelist with whom he was on terms of real
intimacy was Arnold Bennett. A woman I knew told
me how once standing next to Henry James at a very
grand party at Londonderry House, one of those
parties graced by royalty, where decorations were
worn, stars and impressive ribbons, and the women
blazed with diamonds, she had perhaps flippantly said
to him: 'Fun, isn't it, for middle-class people like you
and me to find ourselves hobnobbing with all these
swells.' She saw at once by the look on his face that
she had said the wrong thing. He didn't at all like
being called middle class, and the look of amusement
in her eyes when she noticed his annoyance increased
his displeasure. Henry James was wrong to take
offence, for after all it is the middle class that has
created the wealth of English literature. That is
natural enough. The boy of poor parents has received
a scanty education and is forced to go to work at an
early age. He has had little opportunity to read. The
boy born in the upper ranks of society is seduced by
the amusements his circumstances put within his easy
reach, and his ambition, if he has any, is more likely
to lead him to seek distinction in the way approved of

by the people among whom his happy lot is cast. In either case his urge to create must be very strong to overcome the hindrances, though very different in character, which combine to thwart him. The nobility and gentry, so far as I know, have only produced two poets whose work is definitely a part of English literature, Shelley and Byron, and only one novelist, Fielding. The youth of middle-class parentage who has an irresistible impulse to write has received an education which is at least adequate; he has had access to something of a library; he has probably come in contact with a greater variety of people than either the son of an artisan or the son of a country squire; and though his family may deplore his taking to the hazardous profession of literature the idea is not quite foreign to their prepossessions and may even make a certain appeal to their pride. The English middle class is never without the desire to rise in the social scale and to have a writer in the family is to the clergyman, the solicitor, the Civil Servant something of a prestige item.

I think H. G. and Arnold were drawn together because both were of modest origin and both had had an arduous struggle to win recognition. After they had achieved success both felt that, though for somewhat different reasons, they stood slightly apart from the rest of the literary world, and that again was a bond between them. But the chief cause of H. G.'s genuine attachment to Arnold was that Arnold was a very lovable man.

I first knew him in 1904 when we were both living in Paris. I had taken a tiny apartment near the Lion de Belfort, on the fifth floor, from which I had a spacious view of the cemetery of Montparnasse. I used to dine at a restaurant in the rue d'Odessa. A number of painters, illustrators, sculptors and writers were in the habit of dining there and we had a little room to ourselves. We got a very good dinner, *vin compris*, for two francs fifty, and it was usual to give four sous to Marie, the good-humoured and sharp-tongued maid who waited on us. We were of various nationalities and the conversation was carried on indifferently in English and French. On occasion someone would bring his mistress and her mother, whom he introduced politely to the company as *ma belle mère*, but for the most part we were all men. We discussed every subject under the sun, generally with heat, and by the time we came to coffee (with which, I seem to remember, a *fine* was thrown in) and lit our cigars, *demi londrès* at three sous apiece, the air was heady. We differed with extreme acrimony. Arnold used to come there once a week. He reminded me years later that the first time we met, which was at this restaurant, I was white with passion. The conversation was upon the merits of Hérédia. I asserted that there was no sense in him, and a painter scornfully replied that you didn't want sense in poetry, you wanted sound. Someone contributed an anecdote about Mallarmé and Degas. Degas arrived late at one of Mallarmé's celebrated Tuesdays and said he'd been trying all day to write a sonnet and couldn't get an idea. To this Mallarmé replied: 'But, my dear Degas, one doesn't write a sonnet with ideas, one writes it with words.' From this an argument arose upon the objects and limitations of poetry which soon enlivened the whole company. I exercised such powers as I had of sarcasm, invective and vituperation, and my antagonist, Roderic O'Connor by name, a taciturn Irishman, than whom there is no man more difficult to cope with, was coldly and bitingly virulent. The entire table took up the dispute and I have still a dim recollection of Arnold, smiling a little, calm and a trifle Olympian, putting in now and then a brief, dogmatic, but, I am certain, judicious remark. He was older than most of us. He was then a thin man, with dark hair very smoothly done in a fashion that suggested the private soldier of the day. He was much more neatly dressed than we were and more conventionally. He looked like a managing clerk in a city office. At that time the only book he had written that we knew of was *The Grand Babylon Hotel* and our attitude towards him was somewhat patronising. We were arrogantly high-brow. Some of us had read the book and enjoyed it, which was enough for us to decide that there was nothing in it, but the rest shrugged their shoulders and declined to waste their time over such trash. Had you read *Marie Donadieu*? That was the stuff to give the troops.

Arnold was living at that time in Montmartre, I think in the Rue de Calais, in a small dark apartment which he had filled with Empire furniture. It was certainly not genuine, but this he did not know, and he was exceedingly proud of it. Arnold was a tidy man and his apartment was very neat, with every article in an appointed place, but it was not very comfortable and you could not imagine anyone making a home of it. It gave you the impression of a 'set' arranged for a man who saw himself in a certain rôle which he was playing conscientiously, but into the skin of which he hadn't quite got. On deciding to live in Paris Arnold had given up the editorship of a magazine called *Woman* and was settled down to train himself for the profession of literature. Through Marcel Schwob he had got to know several of the French writers of the day, and I seem to remember his telling me that Schwob had taken him to see Anatole France, who was then the high priest of French letters. Arnold diligently read the French literary reviews, of which at that time the *Mercure de France* was the most distinguished; he read Stendhal and Flaubert, but chiefly Balzac, and I think he told me that he had read through the whole of the *Comédie Humaine* in a year. When I first knew him he was starting on the Russians and talked with enthusiasm of *Anna Karenina*. He thought it the greatest of all novels. I am under the impression that he did not discover Chekov till somewhat later. When he did, he began to admire Tolstoi less.

Arnold's plan of campaign to achieve success in his calling was cut-and-dried. He proposed to make his annual expenditure by writing novels, and by writing plays to make provision for his old age. He meant to write two or three books to get his hand in and then write a masterpiece. When I asked him what sort of book this was going to be he said, something on the lines of *A Great Man*; but that, he added, had brought him in nothing at all and he couldn't afford to go on in that style till he was properly established. I listened, but attached no importance to what he said. I did not think him capable of writing anything of consequence. Because I had lately had my first play produced by the Stage Society he asked me to read one of his. The characters were plausible and the dialogue natural, but in his determination to be realistic he had allowed none of them to make a witty or even a clever remark and had, so it seemed to me, gone out of his way to eschew anything in the nature of dramatic action. As a picture of middle-class life the play had verisimilitude, but I found it dull. Perhaps only it was before its time.

Like everyone else who lives in Paris Arnold had come across a particular little restaurant where you could get a better dinner for less money than anywhere else. This one was on the first floor, somewhere in Montmartre, and now and then I used to go over to dine, Dutch Treat, with him. After dinner we went back to his apartment and he would play Beethoven on a cottage piano. He was nothing if not thorough, and it was obvious that if you were living in Montmartre as a man of letters and a Bohemian (though a clean, respectable one) to complete the picture you must have a mistress. But that costs money and Arnold, who had come to Paris for a definite purpose and had only a certain sum to dispose of, was too cagey to squander on luxuries what he needed for necessities. He was not a son of the Five Towns for nothing and he solved the problem in a characteristic fashion. One night after we had been dining together and were sitting amid the Empire furniture of his apartment, he said:

'Look here, I have a proposal to make to you.'

'Oh?'

'I have a mistress with whom I spend two nights a week. She has another gentleman with whom she spends two other nights. She likes to have her Sundays to herself and she's looking for someone who'll take the two nights she has free. I've told her about you. She likes writers. I'd like to see her nicely fixed up and I thought it would be a good plan if you took the two nights that she has vacant.'

The suggestion startled me.

'It sounds rather cold-blooded to me,' I said.

'She's not an ignorant woman, you know,' Arnold insisted. 'Not by any manner of means. She reads a great deal, Madame de Sévigné and all that, and she can talk very intelligently.'

But even that didn't tempt me.

Arnold was good company, and I always enjoyed spending an evening with him, but I didn't very much like him. He was cocksure and bumptious, and he was rather common. I don't say this depreciatingly, but as I might say that someone was short and fat. I left Paris after a year and so lost touch with him. He wrote one or two books which I did not read. The Stage Society produced a play of his which I liked. I wrote and told him so and he wrote to thank me and in the course of his letter laid out the critics who had not thought so well of the play as I had. I can't remember whether it was before or after this that *The Old Wives' Tale* was published. I began reading it with misgiving, but this quickly changed to astonishment. I had never supposed that Arnold could write anything so good. I was deeply impressed. I thought it a great book. I have read many appreciations of it, and I think everything has been said but one thing, which is that it is eminently readable. I should not mention a merit that is so obvious except that many great books do not possess it. It is the novelist's most precious gift, and it is one that Arnold had even in his slightest and most trivial pieces. I have of late read *The Old Wives' Tale* again. Though written in rather a drab style, with an occasional use of 'literatese' which gives you a jolt, and without elegance, it is still extremely readable. The characters ring true: they are not intrinsically interesting, it was not to Arnold's purpose to make them brilliant, and it is a mark of his skill that notwithstanding you follow their fortunes with interest and sympathy. Their motives are plausible and they behave as from what you know of them you would expect them to behave. The incidents are completely probable: Sophia is in Paris during the siege and the Commune; an author less determined to avoid the sensational would have looked upon it as an opportunity, by describing scenes of terror, anguish and bloodshed, to give his narrative a lift. Not Arnold. Sophia goes about her business unperturbed; she looks after her lodgers, buys and hoards food, makes money when she can, and in fact conducts herself precisely as of course the great mass of the people did.

The Old Wives' Tale was slow to make its way. I think I am right in saying that it was received favourably, but not with frantic eulogy, and that its circulation was inconsiderable. For a time it looked as though it would have no more than the sort of *succès d'estime* that *Maurice Guest* had and be forgotten as all but one novel out of a thousand is forgotten. By a happy chance, however, it was brought to the attention of George Doran, an American publisher, and he bought sheets; he then acquired the American rights, set it up and launched it on its triumphal course. It was not until after its great success in America that it was taken over by another publisher in England and won favour with the British public.

For many years, what with one thing and another, I do not think I met Arnold, or if I did it was only at a party, literary or otherwise, at which I had the opportunity to say no more than a few words to him; but after the First World War and until his death I saw him frequently. By this time he had become a 'character'. He was very different from the thin, rather insignificant man that I had known in Paris. He had grown stout. His hair, very grey, was worn long and he had cultivated the amusing cock's comb that the caricaturists made famous. He walked with an arrogant strut, his back arched and his head thrown back. He had always been neat in his dress, disconcertingly even, but now he was grand. He wore a fob and frilled shirts in the evening and took an immense pride in his white waistcoats. At one time he had a yacht and he dressed the part of the owner in style. Yachting cap, blue coat with brass buttons, white trousers: no actor playing the rôle in a musical comedy could have arrayed himself more perfectly in character. In one of his diaries he has related the story of a picnic I took him on while he was staying with me in the

South of France. I had a motor-boat then and after picking up the rest of my guests in Cannes we went over to the Isle Sainte Marguerite to bathe, eat *bouillabaisse* and gossip. The women wore pyjamas and the men tennis shirts, ducks and espadrilles, but Arnold, refusing to permit himself such *sans gène*, was dressed in a check suit of a sort of mustard colour, fancy socks and fancy shoes, a striped shirt, a starched collar and a foulard tie. After lunch a violent mistral sprang up which prevented us from leaving the island. Some of the persons present took the prospect without amenity of being marooned for an indefinite period and when twelve hours later the sea had sufficiently calmed down to allow us to risk the crossing more than one of them faced the slight danger we were in with a good deal of anxiety. Arnold throughout remained dignified, self-possessed, good-tempered and interested. When at six in the morning, bedraggled and unshaven, we at last got home, he, in his smart shirt and neat suit, looked as dapper and well-groomed as he had looked eighteen hours before.

But it was not only in appearance that Arnold differed from the man I had known before. Life had changed him. I think it possible that when I first knew him he was hampered by a certain diffidence and his bumptiousness was assumed to conceal it. Success had given him confidence. It had certainly mellowed him. He had acquired a proper assurance of his own merit. He told me once that there were only two novels written during the first twenty years of the century that he was confident would survive and one of them was *The Old Wives' Tale*. It may be that he was right. That depends on the whirligig of taste. Realism is a fashion that comes and goes. When readers ask their novels to give them fantasy, romance, excitement, suspense, surprise, they will find Arnold's masterpiece pedestrian and rather dull. When the pendulum swings back and they want homely truth, verisimilitude, good sense and sympathetic delineation of character they will find it in *The Old Wives' Tale*.

I have said before that Arnold was a lovable man. His very oddities were endearing. Indeed it was to them that the great affection in which he was held was largely owing, for people laughed at foibles in him of which they believed themselves exempt and thus mitigated the oppression which his talent must otherwise have made them feel. They liked him all the better for the absurdities which gave them a comfortable sense of superiority. He was never what in England is technically known as a gentleman, but he was never vulgar any more than the traffic surging up Ludgate Hill is vulgar. He was devoid of envy. He was generous. He was courageous. He always said with perfect frankness what he thought and because it never struck him that he could offend he seldom did; but if, with his quick sensitiveness, he imagined that he had hurt somebody's feelings, he did everything in reason to salve the wound. But only in reason. If the affronted person continued to bear a grudge he dismissed him with a shrug of the shoulders and a 'silly ass'. He retained to the end an engaging naïvety. He was convinced that there were two things he knew all about—money and women. His friends were unanimous in agreeing that this was an illusion. It got him now and then into trouble. With all his common sense, and he had more common sense than most of us, he made the mistake to which many novelists are prone, of ordering his life after the pattern of one of the novels he might very well have written. In a work of fiction the author can pull the strings and with sufficient skill on the whole get his characters to act as he wants them to. In real life people are more difficult to cope with.

I was surprised to see how patronising in general were the obituary notices written at Arnold's death. A good deal of fun was made of his obsession with grandeur and luxury, and the pleasure he took in *trains de luxe* and first-class hotels. He never grew quite accustomed to the appurtenances of wealth. Once he said to me: 'If you've ever really been poor you remain poor at heart all your life. I've often walked,' he added, 'when I could very well afford to take a taxi because I simply couldn't bring myself to waste the shilling it would cost.' He admired and disapproved of extravagance.

The criticism to which he devoted much time during his later years came in for a good deal of adverse comment. He loved his position on the *Evening Standard*. He liked the power it gave him and enjoyed the interest his articles aroused. The immediate response, like the applause an actor receives after an effective scene, gratified his appetite for actuality. It gave him the illusion, peculiarly pleasant to the author whose avocation necessarily entails a sense of apartness, that he was in the midst of things. Whatever he thought, he said without fear or favour. He had no patience with the precious, the affected or the pompous. If he thought little of writers who are now more praised than read it is not certain that he thought wrongly. He was more interested in life than in art. In criticism he was an amateur. The professional critic is probably somewhat shy of life, for otherwise it is unlikely that he will devote himself to the reading and judging of books rather than to the stress and turmoil of living. He is more at ease with it when the sweat has dried and the acrid odour of humanity has ceased to offend the nostrils. He can be sympathetic enough to the realism of Defoe and the tumultuous vitality of Balzac, but when it comes to the productions of his own day he feels more comfortable with works in which a deliberately literary attitude has softened the asperities of reality.

That is why, I suppose, the praise that was accorded to Arnold for *The Old Wives' Tale* after his death was cooler than one would have expected. Some of the critics said that notwithstanding everything he had a sense of beauty, and they quoted passages to show his poetic power and his feeling for the mystery of existence. I do not see the point of making out that he had something of what you would have liked him to have a great deal more of and ignoring that in which his power and value lay. He was neither mystic nor poet. He was interested in material things and in the humours of common men in general and he described life, as every writer does, in the terms of his own temperament.

Arnold was afflicted with a very bad stammer; it was painful to watch the struggle he sometimes had to get the words out. It was torture to him. Few realised the exhaustion it caused him to speak. What to most men is as easy as breathing was to him a constant strain. It tore his nerves to pieces. Few knew the humiliations it exposed him to, the ridicule it excited in many, the impatience it aroused, the awkwardness of feeling that it made people find him tiresome, the minor exasperation of thinking of a good, amusing or apt remark and not venturing to say it in case the stammer ruined it. Few knew the distressing sense it gave rise to of a bar to complete contact with other men. It may be that except for the stammer which forced him to introspection Arnold would never have become a writer. But I think it is no small proof of his strong and sane character that notwithstanding this impediment he was able to retain his splendid balance and regard the normal life of man from a normal point of view.

The Old Wives' Tale is certainly the best book he wrote. He never lost the desire to write another as good and because it was written by an effort of will he thought he could repeat it. He tried in *Clayhanger*, and for a time it looked as though he might succeed. I think he failed only because his material fizzled out. After *The Old Wives' Tale* he had not enough left to complete the vast structure he had designed. No writer can get more than a certain amount of ore out of one seam; when he has got that, though it remains, miraculously, as rich as before, it is only others who can profitably work it. Arnold tried again in *Lord Raingo*, and he tried for the last time in *Imperial Palace*. In this I think the subject was at fault. Because it profoundly interested him he thought it was of universal interest. He gathered his data systematically, but they were jotted down in note-books and not garnered (as were those of *The Old Wives' Tale*) unconsciously, and preserved, not in black and white, but as old memories in his bones, in his nerves, in his heart. But that Arnold should have spent the last of his energy and determination on the description of an hotel seems to me to have symbolic significance. For I feel that he was never quite at home in the world. It was to him perhaps a sumptuous hotel, with marble bathrooms and a perfect cuisine, in which he was a transient guest. I feel that he was, here among men, impressed, delighted, but a little afraid of doing the wrong thing and never entirely at his ease. Just as his little apartment in the rue de Calais years before had suggested to me a part played carefully, but from the outside, I feel that to him life was a rôle that he played conscientiously, and with ability, but into the skin of which he never quite got.

I remember that once, beating his knee with his clenched fist to force the words from his writhing lips, he said: 'I am a nice man.' He was.

VI

I mentioned early in this essay that I was introduced to Henry James by Elizabeth Russell. I knew her slightly over a number of years, but when she built herself a house near Mougins, which is an easy hour's drive from my own, I saw her fairly often, and so came to know her much better. She made her reputation with three books, starting with *Elizabeth and her German Garden*, when she was still Countess von Arnim, but later on wrote a number of novels in a style in which the English have never had much success. This is the light, amusing novel which is not an outrage to the intelligence. I think the English are apt to be suspicious of books that are so entertaining and so easy to read. Farce they wallow in, but high comedy causes them a vague discomfort. Perhaps it makes them feel that the author is poking fun at them. And it is true that Elizabeth was inclined to be flippant about matters that we are more inclined to take seriously. She was a little, rather plump woman, not pretty, but with a pleasant, open, frank face, which was a very fallacious indication of her character. In one of his aphorisms Pearsall Smith said: 'Hearts that are delicate and kind and tongues that are neither—these make the finest company in the world.' I do not know whether Elizabeth's heart, except where dogs were concerned, was delicate and kind, but her tongue was neither and she was very good company. She regarded her fellow-creatures with a robust common sense which some thought verged on the cynical. It was typical of her that over her writing-room she should have affixed the quotation: 'Peace, perfect peace, with loved ones far away.' She had a low voice and an innocent manner which added to the effect of the devastating things she said. She could be very malicious. I remember one occasion when I asked her to lunch because H. G., a very old friend of hers, was staying with me. He had recently published his autobiography and in the course of conversation he mentioned that he had gone down to see again the house, Up Park, where in his boyhood he had spent his holidays. His mother had been lady's maid to the owner and much later had returned as housekeeper. From time to time H. G. spent considerable periods there and as was natural enough lived, as the phrase goes, 'below stairs'.

'And this time, H. G.,' asked Elizabeth with her most ingenuous air, 'did you go in by the front door?'

It was said of course to embarrass him and for a moment succeeded. He flushed a little, grinned and did not answer. Afterwards another of my guests asked Elizabeth why she had put that awkward question to him. She opened her eyes wide and with a wonderful assumption of innocence answered: 'I wanted to know.'

I asked Elizabeth once whether the story I had often heard was true that when her husband was very ill she read to him as he lay in bed the book in which she had drawn a caustic portrait of him. When she reached the last page, so the story ran, shattered by what he had been made to listen to, he turned his face to the wall and died. She looked at me blandly and said:

'He was very ill. He would have died in any case.'

Elizabeth lived to a ripe old age and retained to the end the complacent air of a woman who knows she is attractive to men. Before I leave her I will recount a story she told which is not only characteristic, but so diverting that I think it would be a pity if it were forgotten. I don't know whether she told it to anybody else. She was living with her second husband, Lord Russell, on Telegraph Hill. When she went into the kitchen one morning she found the cook gasping; she asked what was the matter, and the cook told her that she had just cut off the head of the chicken they were to have for dinner that night, and then the headless chicken had laid an egg.

'Show it me,' said Elizabeth.

She looked at it pensively for a moment and then said:

'Give it to his lordship for breakfast tomorrow.'

Next morning, sitting at table opposite her husband, she watched him as he ate the boiled egg. When he had finished she asked him:

'Did you notice anything funny about that egg, Frank?'

'No,' he answered. 'Was there anything peculiar about it?'

'No, nothing,' she said, 'except that it was laid by a dead hen.'

He gave her a startled look, sprang to the window and vomited. With a demure smile she added to me:

'And d'you know, I don't believe he ever really loved me after that.'

I will end this essay with an account of my one and only meeting with Mrs. Wharton. She was then a well-known and highly esteemed novelist. Her short stories are ingenious and well-contrived, and in *Ethan Frome* she wrote a remarkably able novel about the country folk of New England; but her main interests lay with the rich and fashionable people who lived on Fifth Avenue and had sumptuous palaces at Newport. She described a phase of American civilisation which has long since passed away, and the manners and customs of her characters, their attitude towards the problems and

241

difficulties that confront them, are so different from those of today that we can only believe what she tells us because we know that she wrote of what she knew. Her novels have now the same sort of charm that time gives to certain pictures regardless of their artistic merit. The crinolines, the bustles that women wore, as fashion changed made them absurd, but today, with the passing of the years, they have become 'costume' and give us an amused delight. Mrs. Wharton's style was easy, pleasant and not undistinguished. She deserves a place, even though but a minor one, in American literature.

Mrs. Wharton lived in Paris, but sometimes came to England, chiefly, I think, to see Henry James, who was an intimate and revered friend; and on these visits she spent a few days in London. On one of these occasions Lady St. Helier asked her to lunch and asked me too. She had a large house in Portland Place and she entertained a great deal. People were inclined to laugh at her because she was something of a lion-hunter, but they accepted her invitations with alacrity since they were pretty sure to find themselves in company with persons who were either eminent, amusing or notorious. When a certain man was being tried for what looked like a peculiarly callous murder and his birth and antecedents made the case the talk of high society one bright young spark asked another if he knew the accused. 'No,' he answered, 'but if he isn't hanged I shall certainly meet him at Lady St. Helier's next week.' The party to which I was bidden was choice and rather select, and because besides Mrs. Wharton I was the only author present, when lunch was over my

hostess took me up to her so that we could have a chat.
She was seated in the middle of a small French sofa
in such a way as to give it the appearance of a throne,
and since she gave no indication that she wished to
share it with me I took a chair and sat down in front
of her. She was a smallish woman, with fine eyes,
regular features and a pale clear skin drawn rather
tightly over the bones of her face. She was dressed with
the sober magnificence suitable to a woman of birth,
of wealth and of letters. She made the other ladies
there, all of exalted rank, look dowdy and provincial.
She talked and I listened. She talked very well. She
talked for twenty minutes. In that time, with a light
touch and well-chosen words, she traversed the fields of
painting, music and literature. Nothing she said was
commonplace, everything she said was just. She said
exactly the right things about Maurice Barrès, André
Gide and Paul Valéry; it was impossible not to concur
with her admirable remarks upon Debussy and
Stravinsky; and of course what she had to say about
Rodin and Maioll, about Cézanne, Degas and Renoir
was just what one would have wished her to say. I
have never met anyone whose perceptions were so
sensitive, whose opinions so sound and whose artistic
sentiments so exemplary.

Though my literary friends do not, I am sorry to say,
look upon me as a member of the intelligentsia, I very
much enjoy the conversation of cultured persons and
I think (perhaps mistakenly) that I can adequately
hold my own with them. Indeed sometimes I gently
lead them down the garden path of mysticism and when
I talk to them of Denis the Areopagite and Fray Luis

de Leon, throwing in Samkaracharia for good measure,
I often have them gasping for breath like speckled
trout on a river bank. But Mrs. Wharton got me down.
Most people have a blind spot; many suffer from
vagaries of taste. I was once sitting at the opera behind
a distinguished and talented woman. The opera was
Tristan and Isolde. At the end of the second act she
gathered her ermine cloak around her shoulders and,
turning to her companion, said: 'Let's go. There's
not enough action in this play.' Of course she was
right, but perhaps that wasn't quite the point. There
are persons of intelligence and susceptibility who prefer
Verdi to Wagner, Charlotte Brontë to Jane Austen
and cold mutton to cold grouse. Mrs. Wharton was
devoid of frailty. Her taste was faultless. She admired
only what was admirable. But such is the frowardness
of human nature (of mine at all events), in the end I
began to grow a trifle restive. It would have been a
comfort to me if I could have found a chink in the
shining armour of her impeccable refinement, if she
had unaccountably expressed a sneaking tenderness for
something that was downright vulgar; if, for instance,
she had admitted to a secret passion for Marie Lloyd,
or, though it had not yet burst on an enraptured world,
had confided in me that she went to the Victoria Palace
every night to hear *The Lambeth Walk.* But no. She
said nothing but the right thing about the right
person. The worst of it was that I could not but agree
with everything she said. I could not bring myself to
affirm that I thought Maioll boring and André Gide
silly. She said about everyone that she so lightly
touched upon, for there was nothing pedantic in her

discourse, precisely what I thought myself and what every right-minded person should think. I cannot imagine anything more exasperating.

At last I said to her: 'And what do you think of Edgar Wallace?'

'Who is Edgar Wallace?' she replied.

'Do you never read thrillers?' I asked.

'No.'

Never has a monosyllable contained more frigid displeasure, more shocked disapproval nor more wounded surprise. I will not say she blenched, for she was a woman of the world and she knew instinctively how to deal with a solecism, but her eyes wandered away and a little forced smile slightly curled her lips. The moment was embarrassing for both of us. Her manner was that of a woman to whom a man has made proposals offensive to her modesty, but which her good breeding tells her it will be more dignified to ignore than to make a scene about.

'I'm afraid it's getting very late,' said Mrs. Wharton.

I knew that my audience was at an end. I never saw her again. She was an admirable creature, but not my cup of tea.

TEN NOVELS
AND THEIR AUTHORS

CONTENTS

J'ai toujours aimé les correspondances, les conversations, les pensées, tous les détails du caractère, des mœurs, de la biographie en un mot, des grands écrivains . . .
                                        SAINTE-BEUVE

La première condition d'un roman est d'intéresser. Or, pour cela, il faut illusionner le lecteur à tel point qu'il puisse croire que ce qu'on lui raconte est réellement arrivé.

                                        BALZAC

CHAPTER ONE

The Art of Fiction

I

I SHOULD like to tell the reader of this book how the essays in it first came to be written. One day, while I was in the United States, the Editor of *Redbook* asked me to make a list of what in my opinion were the ten best novels in the world. I did so, and thought no more about it. Of course my list was arbitrary. I could have made one of ten other novels, just as good in their different ways as those I chose, and give just as sound reasons for selecting them. If a hundred persons, well read and of adequate culture, were asked to produce such a list, in all probability at least two or three hundred novels would be mentioned, but I think that in all the lists most of those I have chosen would find a place. That there should be a diversity of opinion in this matter is understandable. There are various reasons that make a particular novel so much appeal to a person, even of sound judgment, that he is led to ascribe outstanding merit to it. It may be that he has read it at a time of life when, or in circumstances in which, he was peculiarly liable to be moved by it; or it may be that its theme, or its setting, has a more than ordinary significance for him owing to his own predilections or personal associations. I can imagine that a passionate lover of music might place Henry Handel Richardson's *Maurice Guest* among the ten best novels, and a native of the Five Towns, delighted with the fidelity with which Arnold Bennett described their character and their inhabitants, might in his list place *The Old Wives' Tale*. Both are good novels, but I do not think an unbiassed judgment would put either of them among the best ten. The nationality of a reader lends to certain works an interest that inclines him to attribute a greater excellence to them than would generally be admitted. During the eighteenth century, English literature was widely

251

read in France, but since then, till fairly recently, the French have not taken much interest in anything that was written beyond their own frontiers, and I don't suppose it would occur to a Frenchman to mention *Moby Dick* in such a list as I myself made, and *Pride and Prejudice* only if he were of quite unusual culture; he would certainly, however, include Madame de Lafayette's *La Princesse de Clèves*; and rightly, for it has outstanding merits. It is a novel of sentiment, a psychological novel, perhaps the first that was ever written: the story is touching; the characters are soundly drawn; it is written with distinction, and it is commendably brief. It deals with a state of society which is well known to every schoolboy in France; its moral atmosphere is familiar to him from his reading of Corneille and Racine; it has the glamour of association with the most splendid period of French history, and it is a worthy contribution to the golden age of French literature. But the English reader may think the magnanimity of the protagonists inhuman, their discourse with one another stilted, and their behaviour incredible. I do not say he is right to think this; but, thinking it, he will never class this admirable novel among the ten best in the world.

In a brief commentary to accompany the list of books I made for *Redbook*, I wrote: "The wise reader will get the greatest enjoyment out of reading them if he learns the useful art of skipping." A sensible person does not read a novel as a task. He reads it as a diversion. He is prepared to interest himself in the characters and is concerned to see how they act in given circumstances, and what happens to them; he sympathizes with their troubles and is gladdened by their joys; he puts himself in their place and, to an extent, lives their lives. Their view of life, their attitude to the great subjects of human speculation, whether stated in words or shown in action, call forth in him a reaction of surprise, of pleasure or of indignation. But he knows instinctively where his interest lies and he follows it as surely as a hound follows the scent of a fox. Sometimes, through the author's failure, he loses the scent. Then he flounders about till he finds it again. He skips.

Everybody skips, but to skip without loss is not easy. It may be, for all I know, a gift of nature, or it may be something that has to be acquired by experience. Dr. Johnson skipped ferociously, and Boswell tells us that "he had a peculiar facility in seizing at once what was valuable in any book without submitting to the labour of perusing it from beginning to end". Boswell was doubtless referring to books of information or of edification; if it is a labour to read a novel it is better not to read it at all. Unfortunately, for reasons I shall go into presently, there are few novels which it is possible to read from beginning to end with unfailing interest. Though skipping may be a bad habit, it is one that is forced upon the reader. But when the reader once begins to skip, he finds it hard to stop, and so may miss much that it would have been to his advantage to read.

Now it so happened that some time after the list I had made for *Redbook* appeared, an American publisher put before me the suggestion of reissuing the ten novels I had mentioned in an abridged form, with a preface to each one written by me. His idea was to omit everything but what told the story the author had to tell, expose his relevant ideas and display the characters he had created so that readers might read these fine novels, which they would not have done unless what might not unfairly be described as a lot of dead wood had been cut away from them; and thus, since nothing but what was valuable was left in them, enjoy to the full a great intellectual pleasure. I was at first taken aback; but then I reflected that though some of us have acquired the knack of skipping to our profit, most people have not, and it would surely be a good thing if they could have their skipping done for them by a person of tact and discrimination. I welcomed the notion of writing the prefaces to the novels in question, and presently set to work. Some students of literature, some professors and critics, will exclaim that it is a shocking thing to mutilate a masterpiece, and that it should be read as the author wrote it. That depends on the masterpiece. I cannot think that a single page could be omitted from so enchanting a novel as *Pride and Prejudice*, or from one so tightly constructed as *Madame Bovary*; but that very sensible critic George Saintsbury wrote that "there is very little fiction that will stand concentration and condensation as well as that of Dickens". There is nothing reprehensible in cutting. Few plays have ever been produced that were not to their advantage more or less drastically cut in rehearsal. One day, many years ago, when we were lunching together, Bernard Shaw told me that his plays were much more successful in Germany than they were in England. He ascribed this to the stupidity of the British public and to the greater intelligence of the German. He was wrong. In England he insisted that every word he had written should be spoken. I had seen his plays in Germany; there the directors had ruthlessly pruned them of verbiage unnecessary to the dramatic action, and so provided the public with an entertainment that was thoroughly enjoyable. I did not, however, think it well to tell him this. I know no reason why a novel should not be subjected to a similar process.

Coleridge said of *Don Quixote* that it is a book to read through once and then only to dip into, by which he may well have meant that parts of it are so tedious, and even absurd, that it is time ill-spent, when you have once discovered this, to read them again. It is a great and important book, and a professed student of literature should certainly read it once through (I have myself read it from cover to cover twice in English and three times in Spanish), yet I cannot but think that the ordinary reader, the reader who reads for delight, would lose nothing if he did not read the dull parts at all. He would surely enjoy all the more the passages in which the narrative is directly concerned with the adventures and conversations, so amusing and so touching, of the gentle knight and his earthy squire. A Spanish publisher has, in point of fact, collected these in a single volume. It makes very good reading. There is another novel, certainly important, but to be called great only with hesitation, Samuel Richardson's *Clarissa*, which is of a length to defeat all but the most obstinate of novel readers. I do not believe I could ever have brought myself to read it if I had not come across a copy in an abridged form. The abridgment had been so well done that I had no feeling that anything was lost.

I suppose most people would admit that Marcel Proust's

À la Recherche du Temps Perdu is the greatest novel that has been produced in this century. Proust's fanatical admirers, of whom I am one, can read every word of it with interest; in a moment of extravagance, I stated once that I would sooner be bored by Proust than amused by any other writer; but I am prepared now, after a third reading, to admit that the various parts of his book are of unequal merit. I suspect that the future will cease to be interested in those long sections of desultory reflection which Proust wrote under the influence of ideas current in his day, but now in part discarded and in part commonplace. I think then it will be more evident than it is now that he was a great humorist and that his power to create characters, original, various and lifelike, places him on an equality with Balzac, Dickens and Tolstoy. It may be that some day an abridged version of his immense work will be issued from which will be omitted those passages that time has stripped of their value and only those retained which, because they are of the essence of a novel, remain of enduring interest. *À la Recherche du Temps Perdu* will still be a very long novel, but it will be a superb one. So far as I can make out from the somewhat complicated account in André Maurois' admirable book, *À la Recherche de Marcel Proust*, the author's intention was to publish his novel in three volumes of about four hundred pages each. The second and third volumes were in print when the First World War broke out, and publication was postponed. Proust's health was too poor to allow him to serve in the war and he used the ample leisure thus at his disposal to add to the third volume an immense amount of material "Many of the additions," says Maurois, "are psychological and philosophical dissertations, in which the intelligence" (by which I take him to mean the author in person) "comments on the actions of the characters." And he adds: "One could compile from them a series of essays after the manner of Montaigne: on the role of music, novelty in the arts, beauty of style, on the small number of human types, on flair in medicine, etc." That is true, but whether they add to the value of the novel as a novel depends, I suppose, on what opinions you hold on the essential function of the form.

255

On this, different people have different opinions. H. G. Wells wrote an interesting essay which he called *The Contemporary Novel*: "So far as I can see," he says, "it is the only medium through which we can discuss the great majority of the problems which are being raised in such a bristling multitude by our contemporary social development." The novel of the future "is to be the social mediator, the vehicle of understanding, the instrument of self-examination, the parade of morals and the exchange of manners, the factory of customs, the criticism of laws and institutions and of social dogmas and ideas." "We are going to deal with political questions and religious questions and social questions." Wells had little patience with the idea that it was merely a means of relaxation, and he stated categorically that he could not bring himself to look upon it as an art-form. Strangely enough, he resented having his own novels described as propaganda, "because it seems to me that the word propaganda should be confined to the definite service of some organised party, church or doctrine." The word, at all events now, has a larger meaning than that; it indicates the method through which by word of mouth, through the written word, by advertisement, by constant repetition, you seek to persuade others that your views of what is right and proper, good and bad, just and unjust, are the correct views, and should be accepted and acted upon by all and sundry. Wells's principal novels were designed to diffuse certain doctrines and principles; and that is propaganda.

What it all comes down to is the question whether the novel is a form of art or not. Is its aim to instruct or to please? If its aim is to instruct, then it is not a form of art. For the aim of art is to please. On this poets, painters and philosophers are agreed. But it is a truth that shocks a good many people, since Christianity has taught them to look upon pleasure with misgiving as a snare to entangle the immortal soul. It seems more reasonable to look upon pleasure as a good, but to remember that certain pleasures have mischievous consequence and so may more wisely be eschewed. There is a general disposition to look upon pleasure as merely sensual, and that is natural since the sensual pleasures are more vivid than the intellectual; but that is surely an error, for there are pleasures of the mind as well as of the body, and if they are not so keen, they are more enduring. The Oxford Dictionary gives as one of the meanings of art: "The application of skill to subjects of taste, as poetry, music, dancing, the drama, oratory, literary composition, and the like." That is very well, but then it adds: "Especially in modern use skill displaying itself in perfection of workmanship, perfection of execution as an object in itself." I suppose that is what every novelist aims at, but, as we know, he never achieves it. I think we may claim that the novel is a form of art, perhaps not a very exalted one, but a form of art nevertheless. It is, however, an essentially imperfect form. Since I have dealt with this subject in lectures which I have delivered here and there, and can put what I have to say now no better than I did in them, I am going to permit myself briefly to quote from them.

I think it an abuse to use the novel as a pulpit or a platform, and I believe readers are misguided when they suppose they can thus easily acquire knowledge. It is a great nuisance that knowledge can only be acquired by hard work. It would be fine if we could swallow the powder of profitable information made palatable by the jam of fiction. But the truth is that, so made palatable, we can't be sure that the powder will be profitable, for the knowledge the novelist imparts is biassed and thus unreliable; and it is better not to know a thing at all than to know it in a distorted fashion. There is no reason why a novelist should be anything but a novelist. It is enough if he is a good novelist. He should know a little about a great many things, but it is unnecessary, and sometimes even harmful, for him to be a specialist in any particular subject. He need not eat a whole sheep to know what mutton tastes like; it is enough if he eats a chop. Then, by applying his imagination and his creative faculty to the chop he has eaten, he can give you a pretty good idea of an Irish stew; but when he goes on from this to broach his views on sheep-raising, the wool industry and the political situation in Australia, it is wise to accept them with reserve.

The novelist is at the mercy of his bias. The subjects he

257

chooses, the characters he invents and his attitude towards them are conditioned by it. Whatever he writes is the expression of his personality and it is the manifestation of his innate instincts, his feelings and his experience. However hard he tries to be objective, he remains the slave of his idiosyncrasies. However hard he tries to be impartial, he cannot help taking sides. He loads his dice. By the mere fact of introducing a character to your notice early in his novel, he enlists your interest and your sympathy in that character. Henry James insisted again and again that the novelist must dramatize. That is a telling, though perhaps not very lucid, way of saying that he must arrange his facts in such a manner as to capture and hold your attention. So, if need be, he will sacrifice verisimilitude and credibility to the effect he wants to get. That, as we know, is not the way a work of scientific or informative value is written. The aim of the writer of fiction is not to instruct, but to please.

2

There are two main ways in which a novel may be written. Each has its advantages, and each its disadvantages. One way is to write it in the first person, and the other is to write it from the standpoint of omniscience. In the latter, the author can tell you all that he thinks is needful to enable you to follow his story and understand his characters. He can describe their emotions and motives from the inside. If one of them crosses the street, he can tell you why he does so and what will come of it. He can concern himself with one set of persons and series of events, and then, putting them aside for a period, can concern himself with another set of events and another set of persons, so reviving a flagging interest and, by complicating his story, give an impression of the multifariousness, complexity and diversity of life. The danger of this is that one set of characters may be so much more interesting than the other, as, to take a famous example, happens in *Middlemarch*, that the reader may find it irksome when he is asked to occupy himself with the fortunes of persons he doesn't in the least care about. The novel written from the standpoint of omniscience runs the risk of being unwieldy, verbose and diffuse. No one has written it better than Tolstoy, but even he is not free from these imperfections. The method makes demands on the author which he cannot always meet. He has to get into the skin of every one of his characters, feel his feelings, think his thoughts; but he has his limitations and he can only do this when there is in himself something of the character he has created. When there isn't, he can only see him from the outside, and then the character lacks the persuasiveness which causes the reader to believe in him.

I suppose it was because Henry James, with his solicitude for form in the novel, became conscious of these disadvantages that he devised what may be described as a sub-variety of the method of omniscience. In this the author is still omniscient, but his omniscience is concentrated on a single character, and since the character is fallible the omniscience is not complete. The author wraps himself in omniscience when he writes: "He saw her smile"; but not when he writes: "He saw the irony of her smile"; for irony is something he ascribes to her smile, and, it may be, without justification. The usefulness of the device, as Henry James without doubt very well saw, is that since this particular character, in *The Ambassadors*, Strether, is all-important, and it is through what he sees, hears, feels, thinks, surmises that the story is told and the characters of the other persons concerned in it are unfolded, the author finds it easy to resist the irrelevant. The construction of his novel is necessarily compact. The device, besides, gives an air of verisimilitude to what he writes. Because you are asked to concern yourself primarily with one person, you are insensibly led to believe what he tells you. The facts that the reader should know are imparted to him as the person through whom the story is told gradually learns them; and so the reader enjoys the pleasure of the elucidation, step by step, of what was puzzling, obscure and uncertain. The method thus gives the novel something of the mystery of a detective story, and so that dramatic quality which Henry James was always eager to obtain. The danger, however, of divulging little by little a string of facts is that the reader may be more quick-witted than the character through whom the revelations are made and so guess the answers long before the author wishes him to. I don't suppose anyone can read *The Ambassadors* without growing impatient with Strether's obtuseness. He does not see what is staring him in the face, and what everyone he comes in contact with is fully aware of. It was a *secret de Polichinelle* and that Strether should not have guessed it points to some defect in the method. It is unsafe to take your reader for more of a fool than he is.

Since novels have for the most part been written from the standpoint of omniscience, it must be supposed that novelists have found it on the whole the most satisfactory way of dealing with their difficulties; but to tell a story in the first person has also certain advantages. Like the method adopted by Henry James, it lends verisimilitude to the narrative and obliges the author to stick to his point; for he can tell you only what he has himself seen, heard or done. To use this method more often would have served the great English novelists of the nine-teenth century well, since, partly owing to methods of publica-tion, partly owing to a national idiosyncrasy, their novels have tended to be shapeless and discursive. Another advantage of using the first person is that it enlists your sympathy with the narrator. You may disapprove of him, but he concentrates your attention on himself and so compels your sympathy. A disadvantage of the method, however, is that the narrator, when, as in *David Copperfield*, he is also the hero, cannot without impropriety tell you that he is handsome and attractive; he is apt to seem vainglorious when he relates his doughty deeds and stupid when he fails to see, what is obvious to the reader, that the heroine loves him. But a greater disadvantage still, and one that no authors of this kind of novel have managed entirely to surmount, is that the hero-narrator, the central character, is likely to appear pallid in comparison with the persons he is concerned with. I have asked myself why this should be, and the only explanation I can suggest is that the author, since he sees himself in the hero, sees him from the inside, subjectively, and, telling what he sees, gives him the confusions, the weak-nesses, the indecisions he feels in himself; whereas he sees the other characters from the outside, objectively, through his imagination and his intuition; and if he is an author with, say, Dickens's brilliant gifts, he sees them with a dramatic intensity, with a boisterous sense of fun, with a keen delight in their oddity, and so makes them stand out with a vividness that overshadows his portrait of himself.

There is a variety of the novel written on these lines which for a time had an immense vogue. This is the novel written in letters; each letter, of course, is written in the first person, but the letters are by different hands. The method had the advantage of extreme verisimilitude. The reader might easily believe that they were real letters, written by the persons they purported to have been written by, and come into his hands by a betrayal of confidence. Now, verisimilitude is what the novelist strives to achieve above all else; he wants you to believe that what he tells you actually happened, even if it is as improbable as the tales of Baron Münchausen or as horrifying as Kafka's *The Castle*. But the genre had grave defects. It was a roundabout, complicated way of telling a story, and it told it with intolerable deliberation. The letters were too often verbose and contained irrelevant matter. Readers grew bored with the method and it died out. It produced three books which may be accounted among the masterpieces of fiction: *Clarissa*, *La Nouvelle Héloise* and *Les Liaisons Dangereuses*.

There is, however, a variety of the novel written in the first person which, to my mind, avoids the defects of the method and yet makes handsome use of its merits. It is, perhaps, the most convenient and effective way in which a novel can be written. To what good use it can be put may be seen in Herman Melville's *Moby Dick*. In this variety, the author tells the story himself, but he is not the hero and it is not his story that he tells. He is a character in it, and is more or less closely connected with the persons who take part in it. His role is not to determine the action, but to be the confidant, the mediator, the observer of those who do take part in it. Like the chorus in a Greek tragedy, he reflects on the circumstances which he witnesses; he may lament, he may advise, he has no power to influence the course of events. He takes the reader into his

261

confidence, tells him what he knows, hopes or fears, and when he is non-plussed frankly tells him so. There is no need to make him stupid, so that he should not divulge to the reader what the author wishes to hold back, as happens when the story is told through such a character as Henry James's Strether. On the contrary, he can be as keen-witted and clear-sighted as the author can make him. The narrator and the reader are united in their common interest in the persons of the story, their characters, motives and conduct; and the narrator begets in the reader the same sort of familiarity with the creatures of his invention as he has himself. He gets an effect of verisimilitude as persuasive as that which the author obtains who is himself the hero of his novel. He can so build up his protagonist as to arouse your sympathy and show him in an heroic light, which the hero-narrator cannot do without somewhat exciting your antagonism. A method of writing a novel which conduces to the reader's intimacy with the characters, and adds to its verisimilitude, has obviously much to recommend it.

I will venture now to state what in my opinion are the qualities that a good novel should have. It should have a widely interesting theme, by which I mean a theme interesting not only to a clique, whether of critics, professors, highbrows, bus-conductors or bar-tenders, but so broadly human that its appeal is to men and women in general; and the theme should be of enduring interest: the novelist is rash who elects to write on subjects whose interest is merely topical. When they cease to be so, his novel will be as unreadable as last week's news-paper. The story the author has to tell should be coherent and persuasive; it should have a beginning, a middle and an end, and the end should be the natural consequence of the beginning. The episodes should have probability and should not only develop the theme, but grow out of the story. The creatures of the novelist's invention should be observed with individuality, and their actions should proceed from their characters; the reader must never be allowed to say: "So and so would never behave like that"; on the contrary, he should be obliged to say: "That's exactly how I should have expected so and so to behave." I think it is all the better if the characters are in themselves interesting. In Flaubert's *L'Éducation Sentimentale* he wrote a novel which has a great reputation among many excellent critics, but he chose for his hero a man so null, so featureless, so vapid that it is impossible to care what he does or what happens to him; and in consequence, for all its merits, the book is hard to read. I think I should explain why I say that characters should be observed with individuality: it is too much to expect the novelist to create characters that are quite new; his material is human nature, and although there are all sorts and conditions of men, the sorts are not infinite, and novels, stories, plays, epics have been written for so many hundreds of years that the chance is small that an author will create an entirely new character. Casting my mind's eye over the whole of fiction, the only absolutely original creation I can think of is Don Quixote, and I should not be surprised to learn that some learned critic had found a remote ancestry for him also. The author is fortunate if he can see his characters through his own individuality, and if his individuality is sufficiently out of the common to give them an illusive air of originality.

And just as behaviour should proceed from character, so should speech. A woman of fashion should talk like a woman of fashion, a street-walker like a street-walker, a racing tout like a racing tout and an attorney like an attorney. (It is surely a fault in Meredith and Henry James that their characters invariably talk like Henry James and Meredith respectively.) The dialogue should be neither desultory nor should it be an occasion for the author to air his views; it should serve to characterize the speakers and advance the story. The narrative passages should be vivid, to the point, and no longer than is necessary to make the motives of the persons concerned, and the situations in which they are placed, clear and convincing. The writing should be simple enough for anyone of fair education to read with ease, and the manner should fit the matter as a well-cut shoe fits a shapely foot. Finally, a novel should be entertaining. I have put this last, but it is the essential quality, without which no other quality avails. And the more intelligent the entertainment a novel offers, the better it is. Entertainment is a word that has a good many meanings. One item is that which affords interest or amusement. It is a common error to suppose that in this sense amusement is the only one of importance. There is as much entertainment to be obtained from *Wuthering Heights* or *The Brothers Karamazov* as from *Tristram Shandy* or *Candide*. The appeal is different, but equally legitimate. Of course, the novelist has the right to deal with those great topics which are of concern to every human being, the existence of God, the immortality of the soul, the meaning and value of life; though he is prudent to remember that wise saying of Dr. Johnson's that of these topics one can no longer say anything new about them that is true, or anything true about them that is new. The novelist can only hope to interest his reader in what he has to say about them if they are an integral element of the story he has to tell, are essential to the characterization of the persons of his novel and affect their conduct—that is, if they result in action which otherwise would not have taken place.

But even if the novel has all the qualities that I have mentioned, and that is asking a lot, there is, like a flaw in a precious stone, a faultiness in the form that renders perfection impossible to attain. That is why no novel is perfect. A short story is a piece of fiction that can be read, according to its length, in anything between ten minutes and an hour, and it deals with a single, well-defined subject, an incident or a closely related series of incidents, spiritual or material, which is complete. It should be impossible to add to it or to take away from it. Here, I believe, perfection can be reached, and I do not think it would be difficult to collect a number of short stories in which this has in fact been done. But a novel is a narrative of indefinite length; it may be as long as *War and Peace*, in which a succession of events is related and a vast number of characters are displayed through a period of time, or as short as *Carmen*. Now, in order to give probability to his story, the author has to narrate a series of facts that are relevant to it, but that are not in themselves interesting. Events often require to be separated by a lapse of time, and the author for the balance of his work has to insert, as best he can, matter that will fill up this lapse. These passages are known as bridges. Most writers resign themselves to crossing them, and they cross them with more or less skill, but it is only too likely that in the process they will be tedious. The novelist is human and it is inevitable that he should be susceptible to the fashions of his day, since after all he has an unusual affectivity, and so is often led to write what, as the fashion passes, loses its attractiveness. Let me give an instance: until the nineteenth century novelists paid little attention to scenery, a word or two sufficed to enable them to say all they wanted to about it; but when the romantic school, and the example of Chateaubriand, captivated the public fancy, it grew modish to write descriptions for their own sake. A man could not go down a street to buy a tooth-brush at the chemist's without the author telling you what the houses he passed looked like and what articles were for sale in the shops. Dawn and the setting sun, the starry night, the cloudless sky, the snow-capped mountains, the dark forests—all gave occasion to interminable descriptions. Many were in themselves beautiful; but they were irrelevant: it took writers a long time to discover that a description of scenery, however poetically observed and admirably expressed, was futile unless it was necessary—that is, unless it helped the author to get on with his story or told the reader something it behoved him to know about the persons who take part in it. This is an adventitious imperfection in the novel, but there is yet another that seems inherent. Since it is a work of considerable length, it must take some time to write, weeks at least, generally months and occasionally even years. It is only too likely that the author's inventiveness will sometimes fail him. Then he can only fall back on dogged industry and his general competence. It will be a marvel if by these means he can hold his readers' attention.

In the past, readers, preferring quantity to quality, to get their money's worth wanted their novels long, and the author was often hard put to it to provide more matter for the printer than the story he had to tell required. He hit upon an easy way to do this. He inserted into his novel stories, sometimes long enough to be called novelettes, which had nothing to do

265

with his theme or, at best, were tacked on to it with little plausibility. No writer did this with greater nonchalance than Cervantes in *Don Quixote*. These interpolations have always been regarded as a blot on an immortal work, and can only be read now with impatience. Contemporary criticism attacked him on this account, and in the second part of the book we know he eschewed the bad practice, so producing what is generally thought to be impossible, a sequel that was better than its forerunner; but this did not prevent succeeding writers (who doubtless had not read the criticisms) from using so convenient a device to enable them to deliver to the booksellers a quantity of copy sufficient to make a saleable volume. In the nineteenth century new methods of publication exposed novelists to new temptations. Monthly magazines that devoted much of their space to what is somewhat depreciatingly known as light literature achieved great success, and so provided authors with the opportunity to bring their work before the public in serial form with profit to themselves. At about the same time, the publishers found it to their advantage to issue the novels of popular authors in monthly numbers. The authors contracted to provide a certain amount of material to fill a certain number of pages. The system encouraged them to be leisurely and long-winded. We know from their own admissions how from time to time the authors of these serials, even the best of them, Dickens, Thackeray, Trollope, found it a hateful burden to be obliged to deliver an instalment by a given date. No wonder they padded! No wonder they burdened their stories with irrelevant episodes! When I consider how many obstacles the novelist has to contend with, how many pitfalls to avoid, I am not surprised that even the greatest novels are imperfect; I am only surprised that they are not more imperfect than they are.

3

I have in my time, hoping to improve myself, read several books on the novel. Their writers are, on the whole, as disinclined as was H. G. Wells to look upon it as a means of relaxation. One point they are pretty unanimous on is that the story is of little consequence. Indeed, they are inclined to regard it as a hindrance to the reader's capacity to occupy himself with what in their opinion are the novel's significant elements. It does not seem to have occurred to them that the story, the plot, is as it were a lifeline which the author throws to the reader in order to hold his interest. They consider the telling of a story for its own sake as a debased form of fiction. That seems strange to me, since the desire to listen to stories appears to be as deeply rooted in the human animal as the sense of property. From the beginning of history men have gathered round the camp-fire, or in a group in the market place, to listen to the telling of a story. That the desire is as strong as ever is shown by the amazing popularity of detective stories in our own day. The fact remains that to describe a novelist as a mere storyteller is to dismiss him with contumely. I venture to suggest that there is no such creature. By the incidents he chooses to relate, the characters he selects and his attitude towards them, the author offers you a criticism of life. It may not be a very original one, or very profound, but it is there; and consequently, though he may not know it, he is in his own modest way a moralist. But morals, unlike mathematics, are not a precise science. Morals cannot be inflexible for they deal with the behaviour of human beings, and human beings, as we know, are vain, changeable and vacillating.

We live in a troubled world, and it is doubtless the novelist's business to deal with it. The future is uncertain. Our freedom is menaced. We are in the grip of anxieties, fears and frustrations. Values that were long unquestioned now seem dubious. But these are serious matters, and it has not escaped the writers of fiction that the reader may find a novel that is concerned with them somewhat heavy going. Now, owing to the invention of contraceptives, the high value that was once placed on chastity no longer obtains. Novelists have not been slow to notice the difference this has made in the relations of the sexes and so, whenever they feel that something must be done to sustain the reader's flagging interest, they cause their characters to indulge in copulation. I am not sure they are well-advised. Of

267

sexual intercourse Lord Chesterfield said that the pleasure was momentary, the position ridiculous and the expense damnable: if he had lived to read modern fiction he might have added that there is a monotony about the act which renders the reiterated narration of it excessively tedious.

At present there is a tendency to dwell on characterization rather than on incident and, of course, characterization is important; for unless you come to know intimately the persons of a novel, and so can sympathize with them, you are unlikely to care what happens to them. But to concentrate on your characters, rather than on what happens to them, is merely one way of writing a novel like another. The tale of pure incident, in which the characterization is perfunctory or commonplace, has just as much right to exist as the other. Indeed, some very good novels of this kind have been written, *Gil Blas*, for instance, and *Monte Cristo*. Scheherazade would have lost her head very soon if she had dwelt on the characters of the persons she was dealing with, rather than on the adventures that befell them.

In the chapters that follow I have given in each case some account of the life and character of the author I am writing about. This I have done partly to please myself, but also for the reader's sake, since I think that to know what sort of a person the author was adds to one's understanding and appreciation of his work. To know something about Flaubert explains a good deal that would otherwise be disturbing in *Madame Bovary*, and to know the little there is to know about Emily Brontë gives a greater poignancy to her strange and wonderful book. A novelist, I have written these essays from my own standpoint. The danger of this is that the novelist is very apt to like best the sort of thing he does himself, and he will judge the work of others by how nearly they approach his own practice. In order to do full justice to works with which he has no natural sympathy, he needs a dispassionate integrity, a liberality of spirit, of which the members of an irritable race are seldom possessed. On the other hand, the critic who is not himself a creator is likely to know little about the technique of the novel, and so in his criticism he gives you either his personal impressions, which may well be of no great value, unless like

Desmond MacCarthy he is not only a man of letters but also a man of the world; or else he proffers a judgment founded on hard and fast rules which must be followed to gain his approbation. It is as though a shoemaker made shoes only in two sizes and if neither of them fitted your foot, you could for all he cared go shoeless.

The essays which are contained in this volume were written in the first place to induce readers to read the novels with which they are concerned, but in order not to spoil their pleasure it seemed to me that I had to take care not to reveal more of the story than I could help. That made it difficult to discuss the book adequately. In re-writing these pieces I have taken it for granted that the reader already knows the novels I treat of, and so it cannot matter to him if I divulge facts which the author has for obvious reasons delayed to the end to tell him. I have not hesitated to point out the defects as well as the merits that I see in these various novels, for nothing is of greater disservice to the general reader than the indiscriminate praise that is sometimes bestowed on certain works that are rightly accepted as classics. He reads and finds that such and such a motive is unconvincing, a certain character unreal, such and such an episode irrelevant and a certain description tedious. If he is of an impatient temper, he will cry that the critics who tell him that the novel he is reading is a masterpiece are a set of fools, and if he is of a modest one, he will blame himself and think that it is above his head and not for the likes of him; if, on the other hand, he is by nature dogged and persistent he will read on conscientiously, though without enjoyment. But a novel is to be read *with* enjoyment. If it doesn't give the reader that, it is, so far as he is concerned, valueless. In this respect every reader is his own best critic, for he alone knows what he enjoys and what he doesn't. I think, however, that the novelist may claim that you do not do him justice unless you admit that he has the right to demand something of his readers. He has the right to demand that they should possess the small amount of application that is needed to read a book of three or four hundred pages. He has the right to demand that they should have sufficient imagination to be able to interest themselves in the lives, joys and sorrows, tribulations, dangers and adventures of the characters of his invention. Unless a reader is able to give something of himself, he cannot get from a novel the best it has to give. And if he isn't able to do that, he had better not read it at all. There is no obligation to read a work of fiction.

CHAPTER TWO

Henry Fielding and *Tom Jones*

I

THE difficulty of writing about Henry Fielding, the man, is that very little is known about him. Arthur Murphy, who wrote a short life of him in 1762, only eight years after his death, as an introduction to an edition of his works, seems to have known him, if he knew him at all, only in his later years, and had so little material to work with that, presumably to fill the eighty pages of his essay, he indulged in long and tedious digressions. The facts he tells are few, and subsequent research has shown that they are not always accurate. The last author to deal at length with Fielding is Dr. Homes Dudden, Master of Pembroke. The two stout volumes of his work are a monument of painstaking industry. By giving a lively picture of the political circumstances of the times, and a vivid account of the Young Pretender's disastrous adventure in 1745, he has added colour, depth and substance to the narrative of his hero's checkered career. I don't believe that there is anything to be said about Henry Fielding that the eminent Master of Pembroke has left unsaid.

Fielding was a gentleman born. His father was the third son of John Fielding, a Canon of Salisbury, and he in turn was the fifth son of an Earl of Desmond. The Desmonds were a younger branch of the family of Denbigh, who flattered themselves that they were descended from the Habsburgs. Gibbon, the Gibbon of *The Decline and Fall*, wrote in his autobiography: "The successors of Charles the Fifth may disclaim their brethren of England; but the romance of *Tom Jones*, that exquisite picture of human manners, will outlive the palace of the Escorial, and the imperial eagle of the House of Austria." The phrase has a fine resonance, and it is a pity that the claim of these noble lords has been shown to have no foundation. They spelt their

271

name Feilding, and there is a well-known story that on one occasion the then Earl asked Henry Fielding how this came about; whereupon he answered: "I can only suppose it is because my branch of the family learnt to spell before your lordship's."

Fielding's father entered the army and served in the wars under Marlborough "with much bravery and reputation". He married Sarah, the daughter of Sir Henry Gould, a Judge of the King's Bench; and at his country seat, Sharpham Park, near Glastonbury, our author was born in 1707. Two or three years later the Fieldings, who by this time had had two more children, daughters, moved to East Stour in Dorsetshire, a property which the judge had settled on his daughter, and there three more girls and a boy were born. Mrs. Fielding died in 1718, and in the following year Henry went to Eton. Here he made some valuable friends and, if he did not leave, as Arthur Murphy states, "uncommonly well versed in the Greek authors and an early master of the Latin classics," he certainly acquired a real love for classical learning. Later in life, when he was ill and poverty-stricken, he found comfort in reading Cicero's *De Consolatione*; and when, dying, he set out in the ship that took him to Lisbon, he carried with him a volume of Plato.

On leaving Eton, instead of going up to a university, he lived for a while at Salisbury with his grandmother, Lady Gould, the judge being dead; and there, according to Dr. Dudden, read some law and a good deal of miscellaneous literature. He was then a handsome youth, over six feet tall, strong and active, with deep-set eyes, a Roman nose, a short upper lip with an ironical curl to it, and a stubborn, prominent chin. His hair was brown and curly, his teeth white and even. By the time he was eighteen, he gave promise of the sort of man he was going to be. He happened to be staying at Lyme Regis with a trusty servant, ready to "beat, maim or kill" for his master, and there fell in love with a Miss Sarah Andrews, whose considerable fortune added to the charm of her beauty, and he concocted a scheme to carry her off, by main force if necessary, and marry her. It was discovered, and the young woman was hurried away and safely married to a more eligible suitor. For all one knows to the contrary, Fielding spent the next two or three years in London, with an allowance from his grandmother, engaging in the gaieties of the town as agreeably as a well-connected young man can do when he has good looks and charm of manner. In 1728, by the influence of his cousin, Lady Mary Wortley-Montagu, and with the help of the charming, but not particularly chaste, actress, Anne Oldfield, a play of Fielding's was put on by Colley Cibber at Drury Lane. It was called *Love in Several Masques* and was given four performances. Shortly after this he entered the University of Leyden with an allowance from his father of two hundred pounds a year. But his father had married again and either could not, or would not, continue to pay him the allowance he had promised, so after about a year Fielding was obliged to return to England. He was in such straits then that, as in his light-hearted way he put it himself, he had no choice but to be a hackney coachman or a hackney writer.

Austin Dobson, who wrote his life for the English Men of Letters Series, says that "his inclinations as well as his opportunities led him to the stage". He had the high spirits, the humour, the keen-witted observation of the contemporary scene, which are needed by the playwright; and he seems to have had, besides, some ingenuity and a sense of construction. The "inclinations" of which Austin Dobson speaks may very well mean that he had the vicarious exhibitionism which is part of the playwright's make-up, and that he looked upon writing plays as an easy way to make quick money; the "opportunities" may be a delicate way of saying that he was a handsome fellow of exuberant virility and had taken the fancy of a popular actress. To please a leading lady has ever been the surest way for a young dramatist to get his play produced. Between 1729 and 1737 Fielding composed or adapted twenty-six plays, of which at least three greatly pleased the town; and one of which made Swift laugh, a thing that to the best of the Dean's recollection he had only done twice in his life before. Fielding did not do very well when he attempted pure comedy; his great successes seem to have been in a genre which, so far as I know, he devised himself, an entertainment in which there were singing and dancing, brief topical sketches, parodies and

273

allusions to public figures: in fact, something indistinguishable from the revues popular in our own day. According to Arthur Murphy, Fielding's farces "were generally the production of two or three mornings, so great was his facility in writing". Dr. Dudden looks upon this as an exaggeration. I don't think it is. Some of these pieces were very short, and I have myself heard of light comedies that were written over a week-end and were none the worse for that. The last two plays Fielding wrote were attacks on the political corruption of the times, and the attacks were effective enough to cause the Ministry to pass a Licensing Act which obliged managers to obtain the Lord Chamberlain's licence to produce a play. This act still obtains, to torment British authors. After this, Fielding wrote only rarely for the theatre and, when he did, presumably for no other reason than that he was more than usually hard up.

I will not pretend that I have read his plays, but I have flipped through the pages, reading a scene here and there, and the dialogue seems natural and sprightly. The most amusing bit I have come across is the description which, after the fashion of the day, he gives in the list of Dramatis Personæ in *Tom Thumb the Great*: "A woman entirely faultless, save that she is a little given to drink." It is usual to dismiss Fielding's plays as of no account, and doubtless no one would give them a thought if he were not the author of *Tom Jones*. They lack the literary distinction (such as Congreve's plays have) which the critic, reading them in his library two hundred years later, would like them to have. But plays are written to be acted, not to be read; it is certainly well for them to have literary distinction; but it is not that which makes them good plays, it may (and often does) make them less actable. Fielding's plays have by now lost what merit they had, for the drama depends very much on actuality and so is ephemeral, almost as ephemeral as a newspaper, and Fielding's plays, as I have said, owed their success to the fact that they were topical; but light as they were, they must have had merit, for neither a young man's wish to write plays, nor pressure brought to bear by a favourite actress, will induce managers to put on play after play unless they please the public. For in this matter the public is the final

274

judge. Unless the manager can gauge their taste, he will go bankrupt. Fielding's plays had at least the merit that the public liked to go to see them. *Tom Thumb the Great* ran for "upwards of forty nights", and *Pasquin* for sixty, which was as long as *The Beggar's Opera* had run.

Fielding had no illusions about the worth of his plays, and himself said that he left off writing for the stage when he should have begun. He wrote for money, and had no great respect for the understanding of an audience. "When he had contracted to bring on a play, or a farce," says Murphy, "it is well known by many of his friends now living, that he would go home rather late from a tavern and would, the next morning, deliver a scene to the players, written upon the papers which had wrapped the tobacco, in which he so much delighted." During the rehearsals of a comedy called *The Wedding Day*, Garrick, who was playing in it, objected to a scene and asked Fielding to cut it. "No, damn 'em," said Fielding, "if the scene isn't a good one let them find it out." The scene was played, the audience noisily expressed their displeasure, and Garrick retired to the green-room, where his author was "indulging his genius and solacing himself with a bottle of champagne. He had by this time drunk pretty plentifully; and cocking his eye at the actor, with streams of tobacco trickling down from the corner of his mouth, 'What's the matter, Garrick,' says he, 'what are they hissing now?'

"'Why, the scene that I begged you to retrench; I knew it would not do; and they have so frightened me, that I shall not be able to collect myself the whole night.'

"'Oh, damn 'em,' replies the author, 'they *have* found it out, have they?'"

This story is told by Arthur Murphy, and I am bound to say that I doubt its truth. I have known and had dealings with actor-managers, which is what Garrick was, and it does seem to me very unlikely that he would have consented to play a scene which he thought would wreck the play; but the anecdote wouldn't have been invented unless it had been plausible. It at least indicates how Fielding's friends and boon-companions regarded him.

If I have dwelt on his activity as a playwright, though it was after all not much more than an episode in his career, it is because I think it was important to his development as a novelist. Quite a number of eminent novelists have tried their hands at playwriting, but I cannot think of any that have conspicuously succeeded. The fact is that the techniques are very different, and to have learnt how to write a novel is of no help when it comes to writing a play. The novelist has all the time he wants to develop his theme, he can describe his characters as minutely as he chooses and make their behaviour plain to the reader by relating their motives; if he is skilful, he can give verisimilitude to improbabilities; if he has a gift for narrative, he can gradually work up to a climax which a long preparation makes more striking (a supreme example of this is Clarissa's letter in which she announces her seduction); he does not have to show action, but only to tell it; he can make the persons explain themselves in dialogue for as many pages as he likes. But a play depends on action, and by action, of course, I don't mean violent action like falling off a precipice or being run over by a bus; such an action as handing a person a glass of water may be of the highest dramatic intensity. The power of attention that an audience has is very limited, and it must be held by a constant succession of incidents; something fresh must be doing all the time; the theme must be presented at once and its development must follow a definite line, without digression into irrelevant bypaths; the dialogue must be crisp and to the point, and it must be so put that the listener can catch its meaning without having to stop and think; the characters must be all of a piece, easily grasped by the eye and the understanding, and however complex, their complexity must be plausible. A play cannot afford loose ends; however slight, its foundation must be secure and its structure solid.

When the playwright, who has acquired the qualities which I have suggested are essential to writing a play which audiences will sit through with pleasure, starts writing novels, he is at an advantage. He has learnt to be brief; he has learnt the value of rapid incident; he has learnt not to linger on the way, but to stick to his point and get on with his story; he has learnt to make his characters display themselves by their words and actions, without the help of description; and so, when he comes to work on the larger canvas which the novel allows, he can not only profit by the advantages peculiar to the form of the novel, but his training as a playwright will enable him to make his novel lively, swift-moving and dramatic. These are excellent qualities, and some very good novelists, whatever their other merits, have not possessed them. I cannot look upon the years Fielding spent writing plays as wasted; I think, on the contrary, the experience he gained then was of value to him when he came to writing novels.

In 1734 Fielding married Charlotte Cradock. She was one of the two daughters of a widow who lived in Salisbury, and nothing is known of her but that she was beautiful and charming. Mrs. Cradock was a worldly, strong-minded woman, who apparently did not approve of Fielding's attentions to her daughter, and she can hardly be blamed for that, since his means of livelihood were uncertain and his connection with the theatre can hardly have inspired a prudent mother with confidence; anyhow, the lovers eloped, and though Mrs. Cradock pursued, "she did not catch up with them in time to stop the marriage." Fielding has described Charlotte as Sophia in *Tom Jones* and again as Amelia in the novel of that name, so that the reader of those books can gain a very exact notion of what she looked like in the eyes of her lover and husband. Mrs. Cradock died a year later and left Charlotte fifteen hundred pounds. It came at a fortunate moment, since a play that Fielding had produced early in the year was a disastrous failure, and he was very short of cash. He had been in the habit of staying from time to time on the small estate which had been his mother's, and he went there now with his young wife. He spent the next nine months lavishly entertaining his friends and enjoying the various pursuits which the country offered, and on his return to London with what, it may be supposed, remained of Charlotte's legacy he took the Little Theatre in the Haymarket, and there presently produced the best (they say) and the most successful of his plays—*Pasquin; a Dramatic Satire on the Times.*

When the Licensing Act became law, and so put an end to his theatrical career, Fielding had a wife and two children and precious little money to support them on. He had to find a means of livelihood. He was thirty-one. He entered the Middle Temple, and though, according to Arthur Murphy, "it happened that the early taste he had taken of pleasure would occasionally return upon him; and conspire with his spirit and vivacity to carry him into the wild enjoyments of the town", he worked hard, and he was in due course called to the Bar. He was ready to follow his profession with assiduity, but he seems to have had few briefs; and it may well be that the attorneys were suspicious of a man who was known only as a writer of light comedies and political satires. Moreover, within three years of being called, he began to suffer from frequent attacks of gout which prevented him from regularly attending the courts. In order to make money he was obliged to do hack work for the papers. He found time, meanwhile, to write *Joseph Andrews*, his first novel. Two years later his wife died. Her death left him distracted with grief. Lady Louisa Stuart wrote: "He loved her passionately, and she returned his affection; yet led no happy life, for they were almost always miserably poor, and seldom in a state of quiet and safety. All the world knows what was his imprudence; if ever he possessed a score of pounds nothing could keep him from lavishing it idly, or make him think of tomorrow. Sometimes they were living in decent lodgings with tolerable comfort; sometimes in a wretched garret without necessaries, not to speak of the sponging-houses and hiding places where he was occasionally to be found. His elastic gaiety of spirit carried him through it all; but, meanwhile, care and anxiety were preying upon her more delicate mind, and undermining her constitution. She gradually declined, caught a fever, and died in his arms." This has an air of truth, and is in part confirmed by Fielding's *Amelia*. We know that novelists habitually make use of any little experience that they have had, and when Fielding created the character of Billy Booth, he not only drew a portrait of himself and of his wife as Amelia, but utilized various incidents in their married life. Four years after his wife's death he married her maid,

Mary Daniel. She was at the time three months' pregnant. The marriage shocked his friends, and his sister, who had lived with him since Charlotte's death, left the house. His cousin Lady Mary Wortley-Montagu was haughtily scornful because he could "feel rapture with his cook-maid". Mary Daniel had few personal charms, but she was an excellent creature and he never spoke of her but with affection and respect. She was a very decent woman, who looked after him well, a good wife and a good mother. She bore him two boys and a girl.

When still a struggling dramatist, Fielding had made advances to Sir Robert Walpole, then all-powerful; but though he dedicated to him with effusive compliments his play, *The Modern Husband*, the ungrateful Minister seems to have been disinclined to do anything for him. He therefore decided that he could do better with the party opposed to Walpole, and forthwith made overtures to Lord Chesterfield, one of its leaders. As Dr. Dudden puts it: "He could hardly have given a broader hint that he was ready to place his wit and humour at the disposal of the opposition, should they be willing to employ him." Eventually they showed themselves willing, and Fielding was made editor of a paper called *The Champion*, founded to attack and ridicule Sir Robert and his Ministry. Walpole fell in 1742 and, after a brief interlude, was succeeded by Henry Pelham. The party Fielding worked for was now in power, and for some years he edited and wrote for the papers which supported and defended the Government. He naturally expected that his services should be rewarded. Among the friends he had made at Eton, and whose friendship he had retained, was George Lyttelton, a member of a distinguished political family (distinguished to the present day) and a generous patron of literature. Lyttelton was made a Lord of the Treasury in Henry Pelham's Government, and in 1784 by his influence Fielding was made Justice of the Peace for Westminster. Presently, so that he might discharge his duties more effectively, his jurisdiction was extended over Middlesex, and he established himself with his family in the official residence in Bow Street. He was well fitted for the post by his training as a lawyer, his knowledge of life and his natural gifts. Fielding says

279

that before his accession the job was worth five hundred pounds a year of dirty money, but that he made no more than three hundred a year of clean. Through the Duke of Bedford he was granted a pension out of the public-service money. It is supposed that this was either one or two hundred pounds a year. In 1749 he published *Tom Jones*, which he must have been writing when he was still editing a paper on behalf of the Government. He received altogether seven hundred pounds for it, and since money at that period was worth five or six times at least what it is worth now, this sum was equivalent to something like four thousand pounds. That would be good payment for a novel to-day.

Fielding's health by now was poor. His attacks of gout were frequent, and he had often to go to Bath to recuperate, or to a cottage he had near London. But he did not cease to write. He wrote pamphlets concerning his office; one, an *Enquiry into the Causes of the Late Menace of Robbers* is said to have caused the famous Gin Act to be passed; and he wrote *Amelia*. His industry was indeed amazing. *Amelia* was published in 1751 and in the same year Fielding undertook to edit still another paper, *The Covent Garden Journal*. His health grew worse. It was evident that he could no longer perform his duties at Bow Street, and in 1754, after breaking up "a gang of villains and cut-throats" who had become the terror of London, he resigned his office to his half-brother, John Fielding. It looked as though his only chance of life was to seek a milder climate than that of England, and so, in the June of that year, 1754, he left his native country in *The Queen of Portugal*, Richard Veal, master, for Lisbon. He arrived in August, and two months later died. He was forty-seven years old.

2

When I consider Fielding's life, which from inadequate material I have briefly sketched, I am seized with a singular emotion. He was a man. As you read his novels, and few novelists have put more of themselves into their books than he, you feel the same sort of affection as you feel for someone with whom you have been for years intimate. There is something contemporary about him. There is a sort of Englishman that till recently was far from uncommon. You might meet him in London, at Newmarket, in Leicestershire during the hunting season, at Cowes in August, at Cannes or Monte Carlo in mid-winter. He is a gentleman, and he has good manners. He is good-looking, good-natured, friendly and easy to get on with. He is not particularly cultured, but he is tolerant of those who are. He is fond of the girls and is apt to find himself cited as a co-respondent. He is not one of the world's workers, but he sees no reason why he should be. Though he does nothing, he is far from idle. He has an adequate income and is free with his money. If war breaks out, he joins up and his gallantry is conspicuous. There is absolutely no harm in him and everyone likes him. The years pass and youth is over, he is not so well-off any more and life is not so easy as it was. He has had to give up hunting, but he still plays a good game of golf and you are always glad to see him in the card-room of your club. He marries an old flame, a widow with money, and, settling down to middle age, makes her a very good husband. The world to-day has no room for him and in a few years his type will be extinct. Such a man, I fancy, was Fielding. But he happened to have the great gift which made him the writer he was and, when he wanted to, he could work hard. He was fond of the bottle and he liked women. When people speak of virtue, it is generally sex they have in mind, but chastity is only a small part of virtue, and perhaps not the chief one. Fielding had strong passions, and he had no hesitation in yielding to them. He was capable of loving tenderly. Now love, not affection, which is a different thing, is rooted in sex, but there can be sexual desire without love. It is only hypocrisy or ignorance that denies it. Sexual desire is an animal instinct, and there is nothing more shameful in it than in thirst or hunger, and no more reason not to satisfy it. If Fielding enjoyed, somewhat promiscuously, the pleasures of sex, he was not worse than most men. Like most of us, he regretted his sins, if sins they are, but when opportunity occurred, committed them again. He was hot-tempered, but kind-hearted, generous and, in a corrupt age, honest; an affectionate husband and father; courageous and truthful, and a good friend to his friends, who till his death remained faithful to him. Though tolerant to the faults of others, he hated brutality and double-dealing. He was not puffed up by success and, with the help of a brace of partridges and a bottle of claret, bore adversity with fortitude. He took life as it came, with high spirits and good humour, and enjoyed it to the full. In fact he was very like his own Tom Jones, and not unlike his own Billy Booth. He was a very proper man.

I should, however, tell the reader that the picture I have drawn of Henry Fielding does not at all accord with that drawn by the Master of Pembroke in the monumental work to which I have often referred, and to which I owe much useful information. "Until comparatively recently," he writes, "the conception of Fielding which prevailed in the popular imagination was that of a man of brilliant genius, endowed with what is called 'a good heart' and many amiable qualities, but dissipated and irresponsible, guilty of regrettable follies, and not wholly unstained even by graver vices." And he has done his best to persuade his readers that Fielding has been grossly maligned.

But this conception, which Dr. Dudden tries to refute, is that which prevailed in Fielding's lifetime. It was held by persons who knew him well. It is true that he was violently attacked in his own day by his political and literary enemies, and it is very likely that the charges that were brought against him were exaggerated; but if charges are to be damaging they must be plausible. For example: the late Sir Stafford Cripps had many bitter enemies who were only too anxious to throw mud at him; they said that he was a turncoat and a traitor to his class; but it would never have occurred to them to say that he was a lecher and a drunkard, since he was well-known to be a man of high moral character and fiercely abstemious. It would only have made them absurd. In the same way, the legends that gather round a famous man may not be true, but they could not be believed unless they are specious. Arthur Murphy relates that on one occasion Fielding, in order to pay the tax-collector, got his publisher to give him an advance and, while taking the money home, met a friend who was in even worse case than himself; so he gave him the money and, when the tax-collector called, sent him the message: "Friendship has called for the money and had it; let the collector call again." Dr. Dudden shows that there can be no truth in the anecdote; but if it was invented, it is because it was credible. Fielding was accused of being a spendthrift; he probably was; it went with his insouciance, his high spirits, his friendliness, conviviality and indifference to money. He was thus often in debt and probably on occasion haunted by "duns and bumbailiffs"; there is little doubt that when he was at his wits' end for money he applied to his friends for help and they gave it. So did the noble-minded Edmund Burke. As a playwright, Fielding had lived for years in theatrical circles, and the theatre has in no country, either in the past or the present, been regarded as a favourable place to teach the young a rigid continence. Anne Oldfield, by whose influence Fielding had his first play produced, was buried in Westminster Abbey; but since she had been kept by two gentlemen, and had had two illegitimate children, permission to honour her with a monument was refused. It would be strange if she did not grant her favours to the handsome youth that Fielding then was; and, since he was pretty well penniless, it would not be surprising if she had helped him with some of the funds she received from her protectors. It may be that his poverty, but not his will, consented. If in his youth he was much given to wenching, he was no different from most young men in his day (and ours) who had his opportunities and advantages. And, doubtless, he spent "many a night drinking deep in taverns". Whatever philosophers may aver, common sense is pretty well agreed that there is a different morality for youth and age, and a different one according to the station in life. It would be reprehensible for a doctor of divinity to engage in promiscuous fornication, but natural for a young man to do so; and it would be unpardonable for the master of a college to get drunk, but to be expected on occasion, and not really disapproved, in an undergraduate.

Fielding's enemies accused him of being a political hireling.

He was. He was quite ready to put his great gifts at the service of Sir Robert Walpole and, when he found they were not wanted, he was equally ready to put them at the service of his enemies. That demanded no particular sacrifice of principle, since at that time the only real difference between the Government and the Opposition was that the Government enjoyed the emoluments of office and the Opposition did not. Corruption was universal, and great lords were as willing to change sides when it was to their advantage as was Fielding when it was a question of bread and butter. It should be said to his credit that when Walpole discovered he was dangerous, and offered to give him his own terms if he would desert the Opposition, he refused. It was also intelligent of him, for not so long afterwards Walpole fell! Fielding had a number of friends in the higher ranks of society, and friends eminent in the arts, but from his writings it seems certain that he enjoyed the company of the low and disreputable. He was severely censured for this, but it seems to me that he could not have described with such wonderful vivacity scenes of what is called low life unless he had himself taken part in them, and enjoyed it. Common opinion in his own day decided that Fielding was licentious and profligate. The evidence that he was is too great to be ignored. If he had been the respectable, chaste, abstemious creature that the Master of Pembroke would have us believe, it is surely very unlikely that he would have written *Tom Jones*. I think what has misled Dr. Dudden, in his perhaps meritorious attempt to whitewash Fielding, is that it has not occurred to him that contradictory, and even mutually exclusive, qualities may exist in the same man and somehow or other form a tolerably plausible harmony. That is natural enough in one who has led a sheltered, academic life. Because Fielding was generous, goodhearted, upright, kindly, affectionate and honest, it has seemed to the Master impossible that he should have been at the same time a spendthrift who would cadge a dinner and a guinea from his rich friends, who would haunt taverns and drink to the ruin of his health, and who would engage in sexual congress whenever he had the chance. Dr. Dudden states that, as long as his first wife lived, Fielding was absolutely faithful to her.

How does he know? Certainly Fielding loved her, he loved her passionately, but he would not have been the first loving husband who, when the circumstances were propitious, had a flutter on the side; and it is very probable that after such an occurrence, like his own Captain Booth in similar circumstances, he bitterly regretted it; but that did not prevent him from transgressing again when the opportunity offered.

In one of her letters Lady Mary Wortley-Montagu wrote: "I am sorry for H. Fielding's death, not only as I shall read no more of his writings, but I believe he lost more than others, as no man enjoyed life more than he did, though few had less reason to do so, the highest of his preferment being raking in the lowest sinks of vice and misery. I should think it a nobler and less nauseous employment to be one of the staff officers that conduct the nocturnal weddings. His happy constitution (even when he had, with great pains, half demolished it) made him forget everything when he was before a venison pasty, or over a flask of champagne; and I am persuaded he has known more happy moments than any prince upon earth."

3

There are people who cannot read *Tom Jones*. I am not thinking of those who never read anything but the newspapers and the illustrated weeklies, or of those who never read anything but detective stories; I am thinking of those who would not demur if you classed them as members of the intelligentsia, of those who read and re-read *Pride and Prejudice* with delight, *Middlemarch* with self-complacency, and *The Golden Bowl* with reverence. The chances are that it has never even occurred to them to read *Tom Jones*; but, sometimes, they have tried and not been able to get on with it. It bores them. Now it is no good saying that they ought to like it. There is no 'ought' about the matter. You read a novel for its entertainment, and, I repeat, if it does not give you that, it has nothing to give you at all. No one has the right to blame you because you don't find it interesting, any more than anyone has the right to blame you because you don't like oysters. I cannot but ask myself, however, what it is that puts readers off a book which Gibbon described as an exquisite picture of human manners, which Walter Scott praised as truth and human nature itself, which Dickens admired and profited by, and of which Thackeray wrote: "The novel of *Tom Jones* is indeed exquisite; as a work of construction quite a wonder; the by-play of wisdom, the power of observation, the multiplied felicitous turns and thoughts, the varied character of the great comic epic, keep the reader in a perpetual admiration and curiosity." Is it that they cannot interest themselves in the way of life, the manners and customs, of persons who lived two hundred years ago? Is it the style? It is easy and natural. It has been said—I forget by whom, Fielding's friend, Lord Chesterfield, perhaps—that a good style should resemble the conversation of a cultivated man. That is precisely what Fielding's style does. He is talking to the reader and telling him the story of Tom Jones as he might tell it over the dinner-table with a bottle of wine to a number of friends. He does not mince his words. The beautiful and virtuous Sophia was apparently quite used to hearing such words as "whore", "bastard", "strumpet", and that which, for a reason hard to guess, Fielding writes "b..ch". In fact, there were moments when her father, Squire Western, applied them very freely to herself.

The conversational method of writing a novel, the method in which the author takes you into his confidence, telling you what he feels about the creatures of his invention and the situations in which he had placed them, has its dangers. The author is always at your elbow, and so hinders your immediate communication with the persons of his story. He is apt to irritate you sometimes by moralizing and once he starts to digress, is apt to be tedious. You do not want to hear what he has to say on some moral or social point; you want him to get on with his story. Fielding's digressions are nearly always sensible or amusing; they are brief, and he has the grace to apologize for them. His good nature shines through them. When Thackeray unwisely imitated him in this, he was priggish, sanctimonious and, you cannot but suspect, insincere.

Fielding prefaced each of the books into which *Tom Jones* is divided with an essay. Some critics have greatly admired them, and have looked upon them as adding to the excellence of the novel. I can only suppose that is because they were not interested in it as a novel. An essayist takes a subject and discusses it. If his subject is new to you, he may tell you something that you didn't know before, but new subjects are hard to find and, in general, he expects to interest you by his own attitude and the characteristic way in which he regards things. That is to say, he expects to interest you in himself. But that is not what you want to do when you read a novel. You don't care about the author; he is there to tell you a story and introduce you to a group of characters. The reader of a novel should want to know what happens next to the persons in whom the author has interested him and, if he doesn't, there is no reason for him to read the novel at all. For the novel, I can never repeat too often, is not to be looked upon as a medium of instruction or edification, but as a source of intelligent diversion. It appears that Fielding wrote the essays with which he introduced the successive books of *Tom Jones* after he had finished the novel. They have hardly anything to do with the books they introduce; they gave him, he admits, a lot of trouble, and one wonders why he wrote them at all. He cannot have been unaware that many readers would look upon his novel as low, none too moral, and possibly even bawdy; and it may be that by them he thought to give it a certain elevation. These essays are sensible, and sometimes uncommonly shrewd; and when you know the novel well, you can read them with a certain amount of pleasure; but anyone who is reading *Tom Jones* for the first time is well advised to skip them. The plot of *Tom Jones* has been much admired. I learn from Dr. Dudden that Coleridge exclaimed: "What a master of composition Fielding was!" Scott and Thackeray were equally enthusiastic. Dr. Dudden quotes the latter as follows: "Moral or immoral, let any man examine this romance as a work of art merely, and it must strike him as the most astonishing production of human ingenuity. There is not an incident ever so trifling but advances the story, grows out of former incidents, and is connected with the whole. Such a literary *providence*, if we may use such a word, is not to be seen in any other work of fiction. You might cut out half of *Don Quixote*, or add, transpose, or alter any given romance of Walter Scott, and neither would suffer. Roderick Random and heroes of that sort run through a series of adventures, at the end of which the fiddles are brought, and there is a marriage. But the history of *Tom Jones* connects the very first page with the very last, and it is marvellous to think how the author could have built and carried all the structure in his brain, as he must have done, before he put it on paper."

There is some exaggeration here. *Tom Jones* is fashioned on the model of the Spanish picaresque novels and of *Gil Blas*, and the simple structure depends on the nature of the genre: the hero for one reason or another leaves his home, has a variety of adventures on his travels, mixes with all sorts and conditions of men, has his ups and downs of fortune, and in the end achieves prosperity and marries a charming wife. Fielding, following his models, interrupted his narrative with stories that had nothing to do with it. This was an unhappy device that authors adopted not only, I think, for the reason I give in my first chapter, because they had to furnish a certain amount of matter to the bookseller and a story or two served to fill up; but partly, also, because they feared that a long string of adventures would prove tedious, and felt it would give the reader a fillip if they provided him here and there with a tale; and partly because if they were minded to write a short story, there was no other way to put it before the public. The critics chid, but the practice died hard, and, as we know, Dickens resorted to it in *The Pickwick Papers*. The reader of *Tom Jones* can without loss skip the story of 'The Man of the Hill' and Mrs. Fitzherbert's narrative. Nor is Thackeray quite accurate in saying that there is not an incident that does not advance the story and grow out of former incidents. Tom Jones's encounter with the gipsies leads to nothing; and the introduction of Mrs. Hunt, and her proposal of marriage to Tom, is very unnecessary. The incident of the hundred-pound bill has no use and is, besides, grossly, fantastically improbable. Thackeray marvelled that Fielding could have carried all the structure in his brain before he began to put it on paper. I don't believe that he did anything of the sort, any more than Thackeray did before he began to write *Vanity Fair*. I think it much more probable that, with the main lines of his novel in his mind, Fielding invented the incidents as he went along. For the most part they are happily devised. Fielding was as little concerned with probability as the picaresque novelists who wrote before him, and the most unlikely events occur, the most outrageous coincidences bring people together; yet he bustles you along with such gusto that you have hardly time, and in any case little inclination, to protest. The characters are painted in primary colours with a slap-dash bravura, and if they somewhat lack subtlety, they make up for it by animation. They are sharply individualized, and if they are drawn with some exaggeration, that was the fashion of the day, and perhaps their exaggeration is no greater than comedy allows. I am afraid Mr. Allworthy is a little too good to be true, but here Fielding failed, as every novelist since has failed who has attempted to depict a perfectly virtuous man. Experience seems to show that it is impossible not to make him a trifle stupid. One is impatient with a character who is so good that he lets himself be imposed upon by all and sundry. Mr. Allworthy is said to have been a portrait of Ralph Allen of Prior Park. If this is so, and the portrait is accurate, it only shows that a character taken straight from life is never quite convincing in a piece of fiction.

Blifil, on the other hand, has been thought too bad to be true. Fielding hated deceit and hypocrisy, and his detestation of Blifil was such that it may be he laid on his colours with too heavy a hand; but Blifil, a mean, sneaking, self-seeking, cold-blooded fish, is not an uncommon type. The fear of being found out is the only thing that keeps him from being an utter scoundrel. But I think we should have believed more in Blifil if he had not been so transparent. He is repellent. He is not alive, as Uriah Heep is alive, and I have asked myself whether Fielding did not deliberately under-write him from an instinctive feeling that if he gave him a more active and prominent role, he would make him so powerful and sinister a figure as to overshadow his hero.

On its appearance, *Tom Jones* was an immediate success with the public, but the critics were on the whole severe. Some of the objections were rather touchingly absurd: Lady Luxborough, for instance, complained that the characters were too like the persons "one meets with in the world". It was on its supposed immorality, however, that the novel was generally condemned. Hannah More in her memoirs relates that she never saw Dr. Johnson angry with her but once, and that was when she alluded to some witty passage in *Tom Jones*. "I am shocked to hear you quote from so vicious a book," he said. "I am sorry to hear you have read it: a confession which no modest lady should ever make. I scarcely know a more corrupt work." Now, I should say that a modest lady would do very well to read the book before marriage. It will tell her pretty well all she needs to know about the facts of life, and a lot about men which cannot fail to be useful to her before entering upon that difficult state. But no one has ever looked upon Dr. Johnson as devoid of prejudice. He would allow no literary merit to Fielding, and once described him as a blockhead. When Boswell demurred, he said: "What I mean by his being a blockhead is that he was a barren rascal." "Will you not allow, Sir, that he draws very natural pictures of human life?" answered Boswell. "Why, Sir, it is of very low life. Richardson used to say that had he not known who Fielding was he should have believed that he was an ostler." We are used to low life in fiction now, and there is nothing in *Tom Jones* that the novelists of our own day have not made us familiar with. Dr. Johnson might have remembered that in Sophia Western Fielding drew a charming and tender portrait of as delightful a young woman as ever enchanted a reader of fiction. She is simple but not silly, virtuous but no prude; she has character, determination and courage; she has a loving heart, and she is beautiful. Lady Mary Wortley-Montagu, who very properly thought that *Tom Jones* was Fielding's masterpiece, regretted that he did not perceive that he had made his hero a scoundrel. I suppose that she referred to the incident that has been looked upon as the most reprehensible in the career of Mr. Jones. Lady Bellaston took a fancy to him, and found him not unprepared to gratify her desires, for he regarded it as a part of good breeding to behave with "gallantry" with a woman who showed an inclination for sexual commerce; he hadn't a penny in his pocket, not even a shilling in his pocket to pay for a chair to convey him to her abode, and Lady Bellaston was rich. With a generosity unusual with women, who are apt to be lavish with the money of others but careful with their own, she handsomely relieved his necessities. Well, it is doubtless not a pretty thing for a man to accept money from a woman; it is also an unprofitable one, because rich ladies in these circumstances demand much more than their money's worth; but morally it is no more shocking than for a woman to accept money from a man, and it is only foolishness on the part of common opinion to regard it as such. Our own day has found it necessary to invent a term, gigolo, to describe the male who turns his personal attractiveness into a source of profit; so Tom's lack of delicacy, however reprehensible, can hardly be regarded as unique. I have no doubt that the gigolo flourished as hardily under the reign of George the Second as he did under that of George the Fifth. It was characteristic, and to Tom Jones's credit, that on the very day on which Lady Bellaston had given him fifty pounds for passing the night with her, he was so moved by a hard-luck story which his landlady told him about some relations of hers that he handed her his purse and told her to take what she thought needful to relieve their distress. Tom Jones was honestly, sincerely and deeply in love with the charming Sophia, and yet felt no qualms about indulging in the pleasures of the flesh with any woman who was attractive and facile. He loved Sophia none the less for these episodes. Fielding was much too sensible to make his hero more continent than the normal man. He knew we should all be more virtuous if we were as prudent at night as we are in the morning. Nor was Sophia unreasonably vexed when she heard of these adventures. That in this particular she showed common sense unusual to her sex is surely one of the most engaging of her traits. It was well said by Austin Dobson, though with no elegance of style, that Fielding "made no pretence to produce models of perfection, but pictures of ordinary humanity, rather perhaps in the rough than in the polished, the natural than the artificial, his desire is to do this with absolute truthfulness, neither extenuating nor disguising defects and shortcomings." That is what the realist strives to do and, throughout history he has always been more or less violently attacked for it. For this the two main reasons, so far as I know, are as follows: there is a vast number of people, especially among the elderly, the well-to-do, the privileged, who take up the attitude: "Of course we know that there is a lot of crime and immorality in the world, poverty and unhappiness, but we don't want to read about it. Why should we make ourselves uncomfortable? It is not as though we could do anything about it. After all, there always have been rich and poor in the world." Another sort of people have other reasons for condemning the realist. They admit that there are vice and wickedness in the world, cruelty and oppression; but, they ask, is this proper matter for fiction? Is it well that the young should read about things which their elders know, but deplore, and may they not be corrupted by reading stories which are suggestive if not actually obscene? Surely fiction is better employed in showing how much beauty, kindness, self-sacrifice, generosity and heroism there is in the world. The answer the realist makes is that he is interested in telling the truth, as he sees it, about the world he has come in contact with. He does not believe in the unalloyed goodness of human beings; he thinks them a mixture of good and bad; and he is tolerant to idiosyncrasies of human nature which conventional morality reprobates, but which he accepts as human, natural, and therefore to be palliated. He hopes that he depicts the good in his characters as faithfully as the bad in them, and it is not his fault if his readers are more interested in their vices than in their virtues. That is a curious trait in the human animal for which he cannot be held responsible. If, however, he is honest with himself, he will admit that vice can be painted in colours that glow, whereas virtue seems to bear a hue that is somewhat dun. If you asked him how he could defend himself against the charge of corrupting the young, he would answer that it is very well for the young to learn what sort of a world it is that they will have to cope with. The result may be disastrous if they expect too much. If the realist can teach them to expect little from others; to realize from the beginning that each one's main interest is in himself; if he can teach them that, in some way or other, they will have to pay for everything they get, be it place, fortune, honour, love, reputation; and that a great part of wisdom is not to pay for anything more than it is worth, he will have done more than all the pedagogues and preachers to enable them to make the best of this difficult business of living. He will add, however, that he is not a pedagogue or a preacher, but, he hopes, an artist.

CHAPTER THREE

Jane Austen and *Pride and Prejudice*

I

THE events of Jane Austen's life can be told very briefly. The Austens were an old family whose fortunes, like those of many of the greatest families in England, had been founded on the wool trade, which was at one time the country's staple industry; and having made money, again like others of greater importance, they had bought land and so, in course of time, joined the ranks of the landed gentry. But the branch of the family to which Jane Austen belonged seems to have inherited very little of such wealth as its other members possessed. It had come down in the world. Jane's father, George Austen, was the son of William Austen, a surgeon of Tonbridge, a profession which at the beginning of the eighteenth century was regarded no more highly than the attorney's; and, as we know from *Persuasion*, even in Jane Austen's day an attorney was a person of no social consequence. It shocks Lady Russell, "the widow only of a knight", that Miss Elliot, the daughter of a baronet, should have social relations with Mrs. Clay, daughter of an attorney, "who ought to have been nothing to her but the object of distant civility." William Austen, the surgeon, died early, and his brother, Francis Austen, sent the orphaned boy to Tonbridge School and afterwards to St. John's College, Oxford. These facts I learn from Dr. R. W. Chapman's Clark Lectures, which he has published under the title *Jane Austen Facts and Problems*. For all that follows I am indebted to this admirable book.

George Austen became a Fellow of his college and, on taking orders, was presented with the living of Steventon, in Hampshire, by a kinsman, Thomas Knight of Godmersham. Two years later, George Austen's uncle bought him the near-by living of Deane. Since we are told nothing of this generous

294

man, we may surmise that, like Mr. Gardner in *Pride and Prejudice*, he was in trade.

The Rev. George Austen married Cassandra Leigh, the daughter of Thomas Leigh, a Fellow of All Souls and incumbent of the living of Harpsden near Henley. She was what was known in my youth as well-connected; that is to say, like the Hares of Hurstmonceux, she was distantly related to members of the landed gentry and the aristocracy. It was a step up for the surgeon's son. Eight children were born of the marriage: two daughters, Cassandra and Jane, and six sons. To add to his income, the rector of Steventon took pupils, and his sons were educated at home. Two went to St. John's College, Oxford, because through their mother they were Founder's Kin; of one, George by name, nothing is known, and Dr. Chapman suggests that he was deaf and dumb; two others entered the Navy and had careers of distinction: the lucky one was Edward, who was adopted by Thomas Knight and inherited his estates in Kent and Hampshire.

Jane, Mrs. Austen's younger daughter, was born in 1775. When she was twenty-six, her father resigned his living in favour of his eldest son, who had taken orders, and moved to Bath. He died in 1805, and some months later his widow and daughters settled in Southampton. It was while there that, after paying a call with her mother, Jane wrote to her sister Cassandra: "We found only Mrs. Lance at home, and whether she boasts any offspring besides a grand pianoforte did not appear . . . They live in a handsome style and are rich, and she seems to like to be rich; we gave her to understand that we were far from being so; she will soon feel that we are not worth her acquaintance." Mrs. Austen was indeed left badly off, but her sons added enough to her income to enable her to live in tolerable comfort. Edward, after making the Grand Tour, married Elizabeth, daughter of Sir Brook Bridges, Bart., of Goodnestone; and three years after Thomas Knight's death in 1794, his widow made over to him Godmersham and Chawton and retired to Canterbury with an annuity. A good many years later, Edward offered his mother a house on either of his estates; she chose Chawton; and there, with occasional visits, sometimes lasting for many weeks, to friends and relations, Jane lived till illness obliged her to go to Winchester in order to put herself in the hands of better doctors than could be found in the country. At Winchester in 1817 she died. She was buried in the Cathedral.

2

Jane Austen is said to have been in person very attractive: "Her figure was rather tall and slender, her step light and firm, and her whole appearance expressive of health and animation. In complexion she was a clear brunette with a rich colour; she had full round cheeks with mouth and nose small and well-formed, bright hazel eyes, and brown hair forming natural curls close round her face." The only portrait of her I have seen shows a fat-faced young woman with undistinguished features, large round eyes and an obtrusive bust; but it may be that the artist did her less than justice.

Jane was greatly attached to her sister. As girls and women they were very much together and, indeed, shared the same bedroom till Jane's death. When Cassandra was sent to school, Jane went with her because, though too young to profit by such instruction as the seminary for young ladies provided, she would have been wretched without her. "If Cassandra were going to have her head cut off," said her mother, "Jane would insist on sharing her fate." "Cassandra was handsomer than Jane, of a colder and calmer disposition, less demonstrative and of a less sunny nature; but she had the merit of always having her temper under command, but Jane had the happiness of a temper that never required to be commanded." Most of Jane's letters that have remained were written to Cassandra when one or other of the sisters was staying away. Many of her warmest admirers have found them paltry, and have thought they showed that she was cold and unfeeling and that her interests were trivial. I am surprised. They are very natural. Jane Austen never imagined that anyone but Cassandra would read them, and she told her just the sort of things that she knew would interest her. She told her what people were wearing, and how much she had paid for the flowered muslin she had bought, what acquaintances she had made, what old friends she had met and what gossip she had heard.

Of late years, several collections of letters by eminent authors have been published, and for my part, when I read them, I am now and then disposed to suspect that the writers had at the back of their minds the notion that one day they might find their way into print. And when I learn that they had kept copies of their letters, the suspicion is changed into certainty. When André Gide wished to publish his correspondence with Claudel, and Claudel, who perhaps didn't wish it to be published, told him that Gide's letters had been destroyed, Gide answered that it was no matter as he had kept copies of them. André Gide has told us himself that when he discovered that his wife had burned his love letters to her, he cried for a week, since he had looked upon them as the summit of his literary achievement and his chief claim on the attention of posterity. Whenever Dickens went on a journey, he wrote long letters to his friends in which he described eloquently the sights he had seen; and which, as John Forster, his first biographer, justly observes, might well have been printed without the alteration of a single word. People were more patient in those days; still, one would have thought it a disappointment to receive a letter from your friend, who gave you word pictures of mountains and monuments when you would have been glad to know whether he had run across anyone of interest, what parties he had been to and whether he had been able to get you the books, neck-cloths or handkerchiefs you had asked him to bring home.

In one of her letters to Cassandra, Jane said: "I have now attained the true art of letter-writing, which we are always told is to express on paper exactly what one would say to the same person by word of mouth. I have been talking to you almost as fast as I could the whole of this letter." Of course she was quite right; that *is* the art of letter-writing. She attained it with consummate ease, and since she says that her conversation was exactly like her letters, and her letters are full of witty, ironical and malicious remarks, we may be pretty sure that her conversation was delightful. She hardly ever wrote a letter that had not a smile or a laugh in it, and for the delectation of the reader I will give some examples of her manner:

"Single women have a dreadful propensity for being poor, which is one very strong argument in favour of matrimony."

"Only think of Mrs. Holder being dead! Poor woman, she has done the only thing in the world she could possibly do to make one cease to abuse her."

"Mrs. Hale, of Sherborne, was brought to bed yesterday of a dead child, some weeks before she expected, owing to a fright. I suppose she happened unawares to look at her husband."

"The death of Mrs. W. K. we had seen. I had no idea that anybody liked her, and therefore felt nothing for any survivor, but I am now feeling away on her husband's account and think he had better marry Miss Sharpe."

"I respect Mrs. Chamberlayne for doing her hair well, but cannot feel a more tender sentiment. Miss Langley is like any other short girl with a broad nose and wide mouth, fashionable dress and exposed bosom. Admiral Stanhope is a gentleman-like man, but then his legs are too short and his tail too long."

"Eliza has seen Lord Craven at Barton, and probably by this time at Kentbury, where he was expected for one day this week. She found his manners very pleasing indeed. The little flaw of having a mistress now living with him at Ashdown Park seems to be the only unpleasing circumstance about him."

"Mr. W. is about five or six and twenty, not ill-looking and not agreeable. He is certainly no addition. A sort of cool, gentlemanlike manner, but very silent. They say his name is Henry, a proof how unequally the gifts of fortune are bestowed. I have seen many a John and Thomas much more agreeable."

"Mrs. Richard Harvey is going to be married, but as it is a great secret, and only known to half the neighbourhood, you must not mention it."

"Dr. Hale is in such very deep mourning that either his mother, his wife or himself must be dead."

Miss Austen was fond of dancing and she gave Cassandra an account of the balls she went to:

"There were only twelve dances, of which I danced nine,

and was merely prevented from dancing the rest by want of a partner."

"There was one gentleman, an officer of the Cheshire, a very good-looking young man, who, I was told, wanted very much to be introduced to me; but as he did not want it quite enough to take much trouble in effecting it, we never could bring it about."

"There were few beauties, and such as there were, were not very handsome. Miss Iremonger did not look well and Mrs. Blunt was the only one much admired. She appeared exactly as she did in September, with the same broad face, diamond bandeau, white shoes, pink husband and fat neck."

"Charles Powlett gave a dance on Thursday to the great disturbance of all his neighbours, of course, who you know take a most lively interest in the state of his finances, and live in hopes of his being soon ruined. His wife is discovered to be everything that the neighbourhood would wish her to be, silly and cross as well as extravagant."

A relation of the Austens seems to have given occasion to gossip owing to the behaviour of a certain Dr. Mant, behaviour such that his wife retired to her mother's, whereupon Jane wrote: "But as Dr. M. is a clergyman their attachment, however immoral, has a decorous air."

Miss Austen had a sharp tongue and a prodigious sense of humour. She liked to laugh, and she liked to make others laugh. It is asking too much of the humorist to expect him—or her— to keep a good thing to himself when he thinks of it. And, heaven knows, it is hard to be funny without being sometimes a little malicious. There is not much kick in the milk of human kindness. Jane had a keen appreciation of the absurdity of others, their pretensions, their affectations and their insincerities; and it is to her credit that they amused rather than annoyed her. She was too amiable to say things to people that would pain them, but she certainly saw no harm in amusing herself at their expense with Cassandra. I see no ill-nature even in the most biting of her remarks; her humour was based, as humour should be, on observation and mother-wit. But when there was occasion for it, Miss Austen could be serious. Though

Edward Austen inherited from Thomas Knight estates in Kent and in Hampshire, he lived for the most part at Godmersham Park, near Canterbury, and here Cassandra and Jane came in turn to stay, sometimes for as long as three months. His eldest daughter, Fanny, was Jane's favourite niece. She eventually married Sir Edward Knatchbull, whose son was raised to the peerage and assumed the title of Lord Brabourne. It was he who first published Jane Austen's letters. There are two which she wrote to Fanny, when that young person was considering how to cope with the attentions of a young man who wanted to marry her. They are admirable both for their cool sense and their tenderness.

It was a shock to Jane Austen's many admirers when, a few years ago, Mr. Peter Quennell published in *The Cornhill* a letter which Fanny, by this time Lady Knatchbull, many years later wrote to her younger sister, Mrs. Rice, in which she spoke of her famous aunt. It is so surprising, but so characteristic of the period, that, having received permission from the late Lord Brabourne to do so, I here reprint it. The italics mark the words the writer underlined. Since Edward Austen in 1812 changed his name to Knight, it may be worth while to point out that the Mrs. Knight Lady Knatchbull refers to is the widow of Thomas Knight. From the way the letter begins, it is evident that Mrs. Rice was uneasy about some things she had heard that reflected on her Aunt Jane's gentility, and had written to enquire whether they were by any frightful chance true. Lady Knatchbull replied as follows:

"Yes my love it is very true that Aunt Jane from various circumstances was not so refined as she ought to have been from her talent, and if she had lived fifty years later she would have been in many respects more suitable to our more refincd tastes. They were not rich & the people around with whom they chiefly mixed, were not at all high bred, or in short anything more than *mediocre* & they of course tho' superior in *mental powers & cultivation* were on the same level as far as *refinement goes*—but I think in later life their intercourse with Mrs. Knight (who was very fond & kind to them) improved them both & Aunt Jane was too clever not to put aside all possible signs of 'common-ness' (if such an expression is allowable) & teach herself to be more refined at least in intercourse with people in general. Both the aunts (Cassandra and Jane) were brought up in the most complete ignorance of the World & its ways (I mean as to fashion etc.) & if it had not been for Papa's marriage which brought them into Kent, & the kindness of Mrs. Knight, who used often to have one or other of the sisters staying with her, they would have been, tho' not less clever and agreeable in themselves, very much below par as to good society and its ways. If you hate all this I beg yr' pardon, but I felt it at my pen's end & it chose to come along & speak the truth. It is now nearly dressing time . . .

". . . I am ever beloved Sister yours most affec.

"F.C.K."

This letter has excited the indignation of Jane's devotees, and they have claimed that Lady Knatchbull was senile when she wrote it. There is nothing in the letter to suggest that; nor, surely, would Mrs. Rice have written to make the enquiry had she thought her sister in no condition to answer it. It has seemed to the devotees dreadfully ungrateful that Fanny, whom Jane doted on, should have expressed herself in such terms. There they show themselves ingenuous. It is regrettable, but it is a fact, that children do not look upon their parents, or their relations belonging to another generation, with the same degree of affection as their parents, or relations, look upon them. Parents and relations are very unwise to expect it. Jane, as we know, never married, and she gave Fanny something of the mother-love she would, had she married, have bestowed on her own children. She was fond of children, and was a favourite with them; they liked her playful ways and the long circumstantial stories she told them. She and Fanny became fast friends. Fanny could talk to her in a way that perhaps she couldn't with her father, occupied with the pursuits of the country squire that he had become, or with her mother, who was continuously giving birth to offspring. But children have sharp eyes, and are apt to judge cruelly. When Edward Austen inherited Godmersham and Chawton, he rose in the world, and his marriage allied him with the best families of the County. We know nothing of what Jane and Cassandra thought of his wife. Dr. Chapman tolerantly suggests that it was her loss which made Edward feel "that he ought to do more for his mother and sisters, and induced him to offer them a cottage on one or other of his estates". He had been in possession of them for twelve years. It seems to me more likely that his wife thought they did enough for the members of his family if they were asked at intervals to pay them visits, and did not welcome the notion of having them permanently settled on her doorstep; and it was her death that freed him to do what he liked with his own property. If this were so, it cannot have escaped Jane's sharp eyes, and may well have suggested those passages in *Sense and Sensibility* in which she describes John Dashwood's treatment of his stepmother and her daughters. Jane and Cassandra were poor relations. If they were asked to spend long periods with their rich brother and his wife, with Mrs. Knight at Canterbury, with Lady Bridges, Elizabeth Knight's mother, at Goodnestone, it was a kindness of which their hosts were not improbably conscious. Few of us are so well constituted that we can do others a good turn without taking some credit to ourselves. When Jane went to stay with the elder Mrs. Knight, she always gave her a 'tip' at the end of her visit, which Jane accepted with alacrity, and in one of her letters to Cassandra she tells her that her brother Edward had given Fanny and her a present of five pounds. Quite a nice little present to give to a young daughter, kindly to give to a governess, but only patronizing to give to a sister.

I am sure that Mrs. Knight, Lady Bridges, Edward and his wife, were very kind to Jane, and liked her, as how could they fail to, but it is not unreasonable to suppose that they thought the two sisters not quite up to the mark. They were provincial. There was still in the eighteenth century a good deal of difference between the people who lived for at least part of the year in London and those who never left the country. The difference provided the writers of comedy with their most fruitful material. Bingley's sisters in *Pride and Prejudice* despised the Misses Bennet for their want of style, and Elizabeth Bennet on the other hand had little patience for what she considered their affectations. The Misses Bennet were a step higher in the social scale than the Misses Austen, because Mr. Bennet was a landed proprietor, though not a rich one, whereas the Rev. George Austen was a poor country parson.

It would not be strange if, with her upbringing, Jane was a trifle wanting in the elegances valued by the ladies of Kent; and if that were so, and it had escaped the sharp eyes of Fanny, we may be sure that her mother would have remarked on it. Jane was frank and outspoken, and I daresay often indulged in a blunt humour which those humourless females failed to appreciate. We can imagine their embarrassment if she said to them what she wrote to Cassandra, that she had a good eye for an adultress. She was born in 1775. That is only twenty-five years after the publication of *Tom Jones*, and there is no reason to suppose that in the interval the manners of the country had greatly changed. Jane's may well have been such as Lady Knatchbull, fifty years later, considered, "below par as to good society and its ways." When Jane went to stay with Mrs. Knight at Canterbury, it is probable, from what Lady Knatchbull says, that the elder lady gave her hints on behaviour which made her more "refined". It may be on that account that in her novels she lays so much stress on good breeding. A novelist to-day, writing of the same class as she did, would take that for granted. For my part, I can see nothing to blame in Lady Knatchbull's letter. Her pen's end "chose to come along and speak the truth". And what of it? It does not offend me in the least to guess that Jane spoke with a Hampshire accent, that her manners lacked a certain polish, and that her home-made dresses were in bad taste. We know, indeed, from Caroline Austen's *Memoir*, that the family were agreed that the sisters, notwithstanding their interest in clothes, did not dress well; but whether dowdily or unsuitably is not stated. The members of the family who have written about Jane Austen have been at pains to give it greater social consequence than in point of fact belonged to it. This was unnecessary. The

303

Austens were nice, honest, worthy people, belonging to the fringe of the upper-middle class, and they were perhaps a little more conscious of their position than if it had been more assured. The sisters were at ease, as Lady Knatchbull observed, with the people with whom they chiefly consorted, and they, according to her, were not at all high-bred. When they were confronted with persons of somewhat higher station, like Bingley's sisters, women of fashion, they were apt to protect themselves by being critical. Of the Rev. George Austen we know nothing. His wife seems to have been a good, rather silly woman, who was constantly troubled with ailments which her daughters appear to have treated with kindness not unmingled with irony. She lived to hard upon ninety. The boys, till they went out into the world, presumably indulged in such sport as the country provided and, when they could borrow a horse, rode to hounds.

Austen Leigh was Jane's first biographer. There is a passage in his book from which, by the exercise of a little imagination, we can get some idea of the sort of life she led during the long quiet years she spent in Hampshire. "It may be asserted as a general truth," he writes, "that less was left to the charge and discretion of servants, and more was done, or superintended by the masters and mistresses. With regard to the mistresses, it is, I believe, generally understood that . . . they took a personal part in the higher branches of cookery, as well as in the concoction of home-made wines, and distilling of herbs for domestic medicine . . . Ladies did not disdain to spin thread out of which the household linen was woven. Some ladies liked to wash with their own hands their choice china after breakfast and tea." From the letters one gathers that sometimes the Austens were without a servant at all, and at others had to make do with a slip of a girl who knew nothing. Cassandra did the cooking, not because ladies "left less to the charge and discretion of servants", but because there was no servant to do it. The Austens were neither poor nor rich. Mrs. Austen and her daughters made most of their own clothes, and the girls made their brothers' shirts. They made their mead at home, and Mrs. Austen cured the household hams. Pleasures were simple and the great excitement was a ball given by one of the more affluent neighbours. There were in England, in that long-past time, hundreds of families who lived such quiet, humdrum and decent lives: is it not strange that one of them, without rhyme or reason, should have produced a greatly gifted novelist?

3

Jane was very human. In her youth she loved dancing and flirting and theatricals. She liked young men to be good-looking. She took a healthy interest in gowns, bonnets and scarves. She was a fine needlewoman, "both plain and orna-mental," and this must have stood her in good stead when she was making over an old gown and using part of a discarded skirt to fashion a new cap. Her brother Henry in his *Memoir* says: "Jane Austen was successful in everything that she attempted with her fingers. None of us could throw spilikins in so perfect a circle, or take them off with so steady a hand. Her performances with cup and ball were marvellous. The one used at Chawton was an easy one, and she has been known to catch it on the point a hundred times in succession, till her hand was weary. She sometimes found a resource in that simple game, when unable, from weakness in her eyes, to read or write long together."

It is a charming picture.

No one could describe Jane Austen as a blue-stocking, a type with which she had no sympathy, but it is plain that she was far from being an uncultivated woman. She was, in fact, as well instructed as any woman of her time and station. Dr. Chapman, the great authority on her novels, has made a list of the books she is known to have read. It is an imposing one. Of course she read novels, the novels of Fanny Burney, Miss Edgeworth and those of Mrs. Radcliffe (of *The Mysteries of Udolpho*); and she read novels translated from French and German (among others, Goethe's *Sorrows of Werther*); and whatever novels she could get from the circulating library at Bath or Southampton. But she was interested not only in fiction. She knew her Shakespeare well and, among the moderns, she read Scott and Byron, but her favourite poet seems to have been Cowper. It is natural that his cool, elegant and sensible verse should have appealed to her. She read Johnson and Boswell, and a good deal of history, besides miscellaneous literature of various kinds. She was fond of reading aloud, and is said to have had a pleasant voice.

She read sermons, and was particularly fond of Sherlock's, a divine born in the seventeenth century. That is not so surprising as at first sight appears. In my early youth I lived in a country vicarage, and in the study several shelves were closely packed with handsomely-bound collections of sermons. If they were published, it was presumably because they sold; and if they sold, it was because people read them. Jane Austen was pious without being devout. Of course she went to church on Sundays, and partook of communion; and doubtless both at Steventon and Godmersham family prayers were read morning and evening. But, as Dr. Chapman says: "It was admittedly not an age of religious ferment." Just as we take a bath every day and wash our teeth morning and evening, and only feel at ease if we have done so; so, I should think, Miss Austen, like most others of her generation, having with proper unction performed her religious duties, put away the matters with which religion is concerned, as one puts away an article of clothing one does not for the moment want, and, for the rest of the day and week, gave her whole mind with an untroubled conscience to secular affairs. "The evangelists were not yet." A gentleman's younger son was properly provided for by taking orders and being given a family living. It was unnecessary that he should have a vocation, but desirable that the house he was to live in should be commodious and the income adequate. But, taking orders, it was only right that he should perform the duties of his profession. Jane Austen certainly believed that a clergyman should "live among his parishioners and prove himself by constant attention their well-wisher and friend". That is what her brother Henry had done; he was witty and gay, the most brilliant of her brothers; he went into business and for some years greatly prospered; eventually, however, he went bankrupt. He then took orders, and was an exemplary parish priest.

Jane Austen shared the opinions common in her day and, so far as one can tell from her books and letters, was satisfied with the conditions that prevailed. She had no doubt that social distinctions were of importance, and she found it natural that there should be rich and poor. Young men, as was right and proper, obtained advancement in the service of the King by the influence of powerful friends. A woman's business was to marry, for love certainly, but in satisfactory conditions. This was in the order of things, and there is no sign that Miss Austen saw anything in it to object to. In one of her letters to Cassandra she remarks: "Carlo and his wife live in the most private manner imaginable at Portsmouth, without keeping a servant of any kind. What a prodigious amount of virtue she must have to marry under such circumstances." The vulgar squalor in which Fanny Price's family lived, owing to her mother's imprudent marriage, was an object-lesson to show how careful a young woman should be.

4

Jane Austen's novels are pure entertainment. If you happen to believe that to entertain should be the novelist's main endeavour, you must put her in a class by herself. Greater novels than hers have been written, *War and Peace*, for example, and the *Brothers Karamazov*; but you must be fresh and alert to read them with profit. No matter if you are tired and dispirited, Jane Austen's enchant.

At the time she wrote, it was thought far from lady-like for a woman to do so. Monk Lewis observed: "I have an aversion, a pity and contempt for all female scribblers. The needle, not the pen, is the instrument they should handle, and the only one they ever use dexterously." The novel was a form held in scant esteem, and Miss Austen was herself not a little perturbed that Sir Walter Scott, a poet, should write fiction. She was "careful that her occupation should not be suspected by servants, or visitors, or any person beyond her family party. She wrote upon small sheets of paper which could easily be put away, or covered with a piece of blotting paper. There was between the front door and the offices, a swing door which creaked when it was opened; but she objected to having this little inconvenience remedied, because it gave her notice when anyone was coming." Her eldest brother, James, never even told his son, then a boy at school, that the books he read with delight were by his Aunt Jane; and her brother Henry in his *Memoir* states: "No accumulation of fame would have induced her, had she lived, to affix her name to any productions of her pen." So her first book to be published, *Sense and Sensibility*, was described on the title page as "by a Lady".

It was not the first she completed. That was a novel called *First Impressions*. Her father wrote to a publisher offering for publication, at the author's expense or otherwise, a "manuscript novel, comprising three volumes; about the length of Miss Burney's *Evelina*". The offer was refused by return of post. *First Impressions* was begun during the winter of 1796 and finished in August 1797; it is generally supposed to have been substantially the same book as sixteen years later was issued as *Pride and Prejudice*. Then, in quick succession she wrote *Sense and Sensibility* and *Northanger Abbey*, but had no better luck with them, though after five years a Mr. Richard Crosby bought the latter, then called *Susan*, for ten pounds. He never published it, and eventually sold it back for what he had paid: since Miss Austen's novels were published anonymously, he had no notion that the book with which he had parted for so small a sum was by the successful and popular author of *Pride and Prejudice*. She seems to have written little but a fragment, *The Watsons*, between 1798, when she finished *Northanger Abbey*, and 1809. It is a long time for a writer of such creative power to remain silent, and it has been suggested that the cause was a love affair that occupied her to the exclusion of other interests. We are told that, when staying with her mother and sister at a seaside resort in Devonshire, "she became acquainted with a gentleman, whose charm of person, mind and manners was such that Cassandra thought him worthy to possess and likely to win her sister's love. When they parted he expressed his intention of soon seeing them again; and Cassandra felt no doubt as to his motives. But they never again met. Within a short time, they heard of his sudden death." The acquaintance was short, and the author of the *Memoir* adds that he is unable to say "whether her feelings were of such a nature as to affect her happiness". I do not for my part think they were. I do not believe that Miss Austen was capable of being very much in love. If she had been, she would surely have attributed to her heroines a greater warmth of emotion than in fact she did. There is no passion in their love. Their inclinations are tempered with prudence and controlled by common sense. Real love has no truck with these estimable qualities. Take *Persuasion*: Jane states that Anne Elliot and Wentworth fell deeply in love with one another. There, I think, she deceived herself and deceives her readers. On Wentworth's side it was certainly what Stendhal called *amour passion*, but on Anne's no more than what he called *amour goût*. They became engaged. Anne allows herself to be persuaded by that interfering snob, Lady Russell, that it would be imprudent to marry a poor man, a naval officer, who might be killed in the war. If she had been deeply in love with Wentworth, she would surely have taken the risk. It was not a very great one, for on her marriage she was to receive her share of her mother's fortune; this share amounted to rather more than three thousand pounds, equivalent now to over twelve thousand; so in any case she would not have been penniless. She might very well, like Captain Benwick and Miss Hargreaves, have remained engaged to Wentworth till he got his command and so was able to marry her. Anne Elliot broke off her engagement because Lady Russell persuaded her that she might make a better match if she waited, and it was not till no suitor, whom she was prepared to marry, presented himself that she discovered how much she loved Wentworth. We may be pretty sure that Jane Austen thought her behaviour natural and reasonable.

The most plausible explanation of her long silence is that she was discouraged by her inability to find a publisher. Her close relations, to whom she read her novels, were charmed by them, but she was as sensible as she was modest, and she may well have decided that their appeal was only to persons who were fond of her, and had, perhaps, a shrewd idea who the models of her characters were. The author of the *Memoir* rejects emphatically that she had such models, and Dr. Chapman seems to agree with him. They are claiming for Jane Austen a power of invention which is frankly incredible. All the greatest novelists, Stendhal and Balzac, Tolstoy and Turgenev, Dickens and Thackeray, have had models from whom they created their characters. It is true that Jane said: "I am too proud of my gentlemen to admit that they were only Mr. A, or Colonel B." There the significant word is *only*. As with every other novelist, by the time her imagination had worked on the person who had suggested the character, he was to all intents and purposes her own creation; but that is not to say that he was not evolved from an original Mr. A. or Colonel B.

Be that as it may, in 1809, in which year Jane settled with her mother and sister in the quiet of Chawton, she set about revising her old manuscripts, and in 1811 *Sense and Sensibility* at last appeared. By then it was no longer outrageous for a woman to write. Professor Spurgeon, in a lecture on Jane Austen delivered to the Royal Society of Literature, quotes a preface to *Original Letters from India* by Eliza Fay. This lady had been urged to publish them in 1782, but public opinion was so averse "to female authorship" that she declined. But writing in 1816, she said: "Since then a considerable change has gradually taken place in public sentiment, and its development; we have now not only as in former days a number of women who do honour to their sex as literary characters, but many unpretending females, who fearless of the critical perils that once attended the voyage, venture to launch their little barks on the vast ocean through which amusement or instruction is conveyed to a reading public."

Pride and Prejudice was published in 1813. Jane Austen sold the copyright for one hundred and ten pounds.

Besides the three novels already mentioned, she wrote three more, *Mansfield Park*, *Emma* and *Persuasion*. On these few books her fame rests, and her fame is secure. She had to wait a long time to get a book published, but she no sooner did than her charming gifts were recognized. Since then, the most eminent persons have agreed to praise her. I will only quote what Sir

310

Walter Scott had to say; it is characteristically generous: "That young lady had a talent for describing the involvements, feelings and characters of ordinary life which is to me the most wonderful I have ever met with. The big bow-wow I can do myself like anyone going; but the exquisite touch which renders commonplace things and characters interesting from the truth of the description and the sentiment is denied to me."

It is odd that Sir Walter should have omitted to make mention of the young lady's most precious talent: her observation was searching and her sentiment edifying, but it was her humour that gave point to her observation and a prim liveliness to her sentiment. Her range was narrow. She wrote very much the same sort of story in all her books, and there is no great variety in her characters. They are very much the same persons, seen from a somewhat different point of view. She had common sense in a high degree, and no one knew better than she her limitations. Her experience of life was confined to a small circle of provincial society, and that is what she was content to deal with. She wrote only of what she knew. As was first pointed out by Dr. Chapman, she never attempted to reproduce a conversation of men when by themselves, which in the nature of things she could never have heard.

It has been noticed that though she lived through some of the most stirring events of the world's history, the French Revolution, the Terror, the rise and fall of Napoleon, she made no reference to them in her novels. She has on this account been blamed for an undue detachment. It should be remembered that in her day it was not polite for women to occupy themselves with politics, that was a matter for men to deal with; few women even read the newspapers; but there is no reason to suppose that, because she did not write about these events, she was not affected by them. She was fond of her family, two of her brothers were in the Navy, often enough in danger, and her letters show that they were much on her mind. But did she not display her good sense in not writing about such matters? She was too modest to suppose that her novels would be read long after her death; but if that had been her aim, she could not have acted more wisely than she did in avoiding to deal with affairs

311

which from the literary standpoint were of passing interest. Already the novels concerned with the Second World War that have been written in the last few years are as dead as mutton. They were as ephemeral as the newspapers that day by day told us what was happening.

Most novelists have their ups and downs. Miss Austen is the only exception I know to prove the rule that only the mediocre maintain an equal level, a level of mediocrity. She is never more than a little below her best. Even in *Sense and Sensibility* and *Northanger Abbey*, in which there is much to cavil at, there is more to delight. Each of the others has its devoted, and even fanatic, admirers. Macaulay thought *Mansfield Park* her greatest achievement; other readers, equally illustrious, have preferred *Emma*; Disraeli read *Pride and Prejudice* seventeen times; to-day many look upon *Persuasion* as her most finished work. The great mass of readers, I believe, has accepted *Pride and Prejudice* as her masterpiece, and in such a case I think it well to accept their judgment. What makes a classic is not that it is praised by critics, expounded by professors and studied in schools, but that large numbers of readers, generation after generation, have found pleasure and spiritual profit in reading it.

I myself think that *Pride and Prejudice* is on the whole the most satisfactory of all the novels. Its first sentence puts you in good humour: "It is a truth universally acknowledged, that a single man in possession of a good fortune, must be in want of a wife." It sets the note, and the good humour it induces remains with you till, with regret, you have reached the last page. *Emma* is the only one of Miss Austen's novels that I find long-winded. I can take no great interest in the love affair of Frank Churchill and Jane Fairfax; and, though Miss Bates is immensely amusing, don't we get a little too much of her? The heroine is a snob, and the way she patronizes those whom she looks upon as her social inferiors is repulsive. But we must not blame Miss Austen for that: we must remember that we of to-day do not read the same novel that was read by the readers of *her* day. Changes in manners and customs have wrought changes in our outlook; in some ways we are narrower than our forebears, in others more liberal; an attitude which even a hundred years ago was general now affects us with malaise. We judge the books we read by our own prepossessions and our own standards of behaviour. That is unfair, but inevitable. In *Mansfield Park* the hero and heroine, Fanny and Edmund, are intolerable prigs; and all my sympathies go out to the unscrupulous, sprightly and charming Henry and Mary Crawford. I cannot understand why Sir Thomas Bertram should have been enraged when, on his return from overseas, he found his family amusing themselves with private theatricals. Since Jane herself thoroughly enjoyed them, one cannot see why she found his anger justifiable. *Persuasion* has a rare charm, and though one may wish that Anne were a little less matter-of-fact, a little more disinterested, a little more impulsive—in fact a little less old-maidish—except for the incident on the Cobb at Lyme Regis, I should be forced to look upon it as the most perfect of the six. Jane Austen had no particular gift for inventing incident of an unusual character, and this one seems to me a very clumsy contrivance. Louisa Musgrove runs up some steep steps, and is "jumped down" by her admirer, Captain Wentworth. He misses her, she falls on her head and is stunned. If he were going to give her his hands, as we are told he had been in the habit of doing in "jumping her off" a stile, even if the Cobb then were twice as high as it is now, she could not have been more than six feet from the ground and, as she was jumping down, it is impossible that she should have fallen on her head. In any case, she would have fallen against the stalwart sailor and, though perhaps shaken and frightened, could hardly have hurt herself. Anyhow, she was unconscious, and the fuss that ensued is unbelievable. Captain Wentworth, who has seen action and made a fortune from prize-money, is paralysed with horror. The immediately subsequent behaviour of all concerned is so idiotic that I find it hard to believe that Miss Austen, who was able to take the illnesses and death of her friends and relations with quiet fortitude, did not look upon it as uncommonly foolish.

Professor Garrod, a learned and witty critic, has said that Jane Austen was incapable of writing a story, by which, he explains, he means a sequence of happenings, either romantic or uncommon. But that is not what Jane Austen had a talent for, and not what she tried to do. She had too much sense, and too sprightly a humour, to be romantic, and she was interested not in the uncommon, but in the common. She *made* it uncommon by the keenness of her observation, her irony and her playful wit. By a story most of us mean a connected and coherent narrative with a beginning, a middle and an end. *Pride and Prejudice* begins in the right place, with the arrival on the scene of the two young men whose love for Elizabeth Bennet and her sister Jane provide the novel with its plot, and it ends in the right place with their marriage. It is the traditional happy ending. This kind of ending has excited the scorn of the sophisticated, and of course it is true that many, perhaps most, marriages are not happy, and, further, that marriage concludes nothing; it is merely an introduction to another order of experience. Many authors have in consequence started their novels with marriage and dealt with its outcome. It is their right. But there is something to be said for the simple people who look upon marriage as a satisfactory conclusion to a work of fiction. They do so because they have an instinctive feeling that, by mating, a man and a woman have fulfilled their biological function; the interest which it is natural to feel in the steps that have led to this consummation, the birth of love, the obstacles, the misunderstandings, the avowals, now yields to its result, their issue, which is the generation that will succeed them. To nature, each couple is but a link in a chain, and the only importance of the link is that another link may be added to it. This is the novelist's justification for the happy ending. In *Pride and Prejudice*, the reader's satisfaction is considerably enhanced by the knowledge that the bridegroom has a substantial income and will take his bride to a fine house, surrounded by a park, and furnished throughout with expensive and elegant furniture.

Pride and Prejudice is a very well-constructed book. The incidents follow one another naturally, and one's sense of probability is nowhere outraged. It is, perhaps, odd that Elizabeth and Jane should be well-bred and well-behaved, whereas their mother and their three younger sisters should be, as Lady Knatchbull put it, "very much below par as to good society and its ways"; but that this should be so was essential to the story. I have allowed myself to wonder that Miss Austen did not avoid this stumbling-block by making Elizabeth and Jane the daughters of a first marriage of Mr. Bennet and making the Mrs. Bennet of the novel his second wife and the mother of the three younger daughters. She liked Elizabeth best of all her heroines. "I must confess," she wrote, "that I think her as delightful a creature as ever appeared in print." If, as some have thought, she was herself the original for her portrait of Elizabeth—and she has certainly given her her own gaiety, high spirit and courage, wit and readiness, good sense and right feeling—it is perhaps not rash to suppose that when she drew the placid, kindly and beautiful Jane Bennet she had in mind her sister Cassandra. Darcy has been generally regarded as a fearful cad. His first offence was his disinclination to dance with people he didn't know, and didn't want to know, at a public ball to which he had gone with a party. Not a very heinous one. It was unfortunate that Elizabeth should overhear the derogatory terms in which he spoke of her to Bingley, but he could not know that she was listening, and his excuse might have been that his friend was badgering him to do what he had no wish to. It is true that when Darcy proposes to Elizabeth it is with an unpardonable insolence, but pride, pride of birth and position, was the predominant trait of his character, and without it there would have been no story to tell. The manner of his proposal, moreover, gave Jane Austen opportunity for the most dramatic scene in the book; it is conceivable that, with the experience she gained later, she might have been able to indicate Darcy's feelings, very natural and comprehensible feelings, in such a way as to antagonize Elizabeth, without putting into his mouth speeches so outrageous as to shock the reader. There is, perhaps, some exaggeration in the drawing of Lady Catherine and Mr. Collins, but to my mind little more than comedy allows. Comedy sees life in a light more sparkling, but colder, than that of common day, and a touch of exaggeration, that is, of farce, is often no disadvantage. A discreet admixture of farce, like a sprinkle of sugar on strawberries, may

315

well make comedy more palatable. With regard to Lady Catherine, one must remember that in Miss Austen's day rank gave its possessors a sense of immense superiority over persons of inferior station; and they not only expected to be treated by them with the utmost deference, but were. In my own youth I knew great ladies whose sense of importance, though not quite so blatant, was not far removed from Lady Catherine's. And as for Mr. Collins, who has not known, even to-day, men with that combination of obsequiousness and pomposity? That they have learnt to screen it with a front of geniality only makes it more odious.

Jane Austen was not a great stylist, but she wrote plainly and without affectation. I think the influence of Dr. Johnson may be discerned in the structure of her sentences. She is apt to use the word of Latin origin, rather than the homely English one. It gives her phrase a slight formality which is far from unpleasant; indeed, it often adds point to a witty remark, and a demure savour to a malicious one. Her dialogue is probably as natural as dialogue could then be. To us it may seem somewhat stilted. Jane Bennet, speaking of her lover's sisters, says: "They were certainly no friends to his acquaintance with me, which I cannot wonder at, since he might have chosen so much more advantageously in many respects." It may, of course, be that these were the very words she uttered; I think it unlikely. It is obviously not how a modern novelist would phrase the same remark. To set down on paper speech exactly as it is spoken is very tedious, and some arrangement of it is certainly necessary. It is only of late years, comparatively, that novelists, striving for verisimilitude, have been at pains to make their dialogue as colloquial as possible: I suspect that it was a convention of the past to cause persons of education to express themselves with a balance, and with a grammatical correctness, which cannot commonly have been at their command, and I presume readers accepted it as natural.

Allowing, then, for the slight formality of Miss Austen's dialogue, we must admit that she invariably made the person of her stories speak in character. I have only noticed one occasion upon which she slipped up: "Anne smiled and said,

316

'My idea of good company, Mr. Elliot, is the company of clever, well-informed people, who have a great deal of conversation; that is what I call good company.' 'You are mistaken,' said he gently, 'that is not good company that is the best.' "

Mr. Elliot had faults of character; but if he was capable of making so admirable a reply to Anne's remark, he must have had qualities with which his creator did not see fit to acquaint us. For my part, I am so charmed with it that I would have been content to see her marry him rather than the stodgy Captain Wentworth. It is true that Mr. Elliot had married a woman "of inferior station" for her money, and neglected her; and his treatment of Mrs. Smith was ungenerous; but, after all, we only have her side of the story, and it may be that, had we been given a chance to hear his, we should have found his conduct pardonable.

There is one merit which Miss Austen has and which I have almost omitted to mention. She is wonderfully readable— more readable than some greater and more famous novelists. She deals, as Walter Scott said, with commonplace things, "the involvements, feelings and characters of ordinary life"; nothing very much happens in her books, and yet, when you come to the bottom of a page, you eagerly turn it to learn what will happen next. Nothing very much does and again you eagerly turn the page. The novelist who has the power to achieve this has the most precious gift a novelist can possess.

CHAPTER FOUR

Stendhal and *Le Rouge et le Noir*

I

In 1826 a virtuous young Englishman, but of literary inclinations, stayed for a while in Paris on his way to Italy, and presented the letters of introduction he had brought with him. One of the persons whose acquaintance he thus made took him to see Madame Ancelot, wife of a well-known dramatist, who received her friends on Tuesday evenings. Looking about him, he presently noticed a very fat little man who was talking with animation to a small group of his fellow-guests. He had enormous whiskers and wore a wig, and he was dressed in tight violet-coloured trousers which emphasized his corpulence, a dark-green coat with full tails, a lilac waistcoat, with a frilled shirt and a great flowing cravat. So odd was his appearance that the young Englishman could not but ask who he was. His companion mentioned a name. It meant nothing to him.

"He makes us all nervous," the Frenchman went on. "He's a republican, although he served under Bonaparte, and, with conditions as they are now, it's dangerous to listen to the indiscreet things he says. At one time he had quite a good position, and he was on the Russian campaign with the Corsican. He's probably telling his anecdotes about him now. He has a collection of them, and never misses a chance to repeat them. If you're interested, I'll present you to him when I get the opportunity."

The opportunity came, and the little fat man greeted the stranger with amiability. After some desultory conversation, the young Englishman asked him whether he had ever been to England.

"Twice," he replied.

318

He said that in London he'd stayed with two friends of his at the Tavistock Hotel. Then, with a chuckle, he went on to say that he would tell him of a curious adventure he'd had there. He'd been bored to death in London, and one day he complained to the valet he'd engaged that there was no pleasant company to be had; whereupon the valet, thinking he wanted women, after making enquiries gave him an address in Westminster Road where he and his friends could go on the following night, without fear of unpleasantness. When they discovered that the Westminster Road was in a poverty-stricken suburb, where they might be robbed and murdered, one of the party refused to go; but the other two, having armed themselves with daggers and pistols, started off in a cab. They were set down at a tiny cottage, and three pale young working girls came out and invited them in. They sat down and had tea, and finally spent the night there. The girl had been very much alarmed when, before undressing, he had significantly put his pistols on the chest of drawers. The young Englishman listened with embarrassment to the detailed and frank account the funny fat little man gave of the experience, and when he returned to his companion told him how shocked, how embarrassed, he had been by the story which he, a perfect stranger, had been obliged to listen to.

"Don't believe a word of it," said his friend, laughing. "It's well known that he's impotent."

The youth blushed, and to change the conversation mentioned that the fat man had told him that he wrote for English reviews.

"Yes, he does a certain amount of hackwork like that. He's published one or two books at his own expense, but nobody reads them."

"What did you say his name was?"

"Beyle. Henri Beyle. But he isn't of any importance; he has no talent."

This episode, I must confess, is imaginary; but it may very well have taken place, and it reflects accurately enough the opinion in which Henri Beyle, better known to us now as Stendhal, was held by his contemporaries. He was at that time forty-three. He was writing his first novel. Owing to the vicissitudes of his life, he had acquired a variety of experience such as few novelists can boast of. He had been thrown, in a period of great change, with men of all kinds and all classes, and so had gained as wide a knowledge of human nature as his own limitations permitted. For even the most observant and acute student of his fellow-creatures can only know them through the medium of his own personality. He knows them not as they really are, but as they appear to him distorted by his peculiar idiosyncrasy.

Henri Beyle was born at Grenoble in 1783, the son of an attorney, a man of property and of some consequence in the city; his mother, the daughter of a distinguished and cultured doctor, died when he was seven. I cannot in these pages give more than a summary account of Stendhal's life, for it would need a book to describe it adequately, and I should have to go into the social and political history of the time: fortunately such a book has been written, and if the reader of *Le Rouge et le Noir* is sufficiently interested to want to know more about its author than I propose to tell him, he cannot do better than to read the lively and well-documented biography which Mr. Matthew Josephson has published under the title: *Stendhal, or The Pursuit of Happiness.*

2

Stendhal has described at length his life as child and boy, and it is interesting to study, because during this period he conceived prejudices which he maintained to his life's end. On the death of his mother, whom he loved, as he says, with a lover's love, he was left to the care of his father and his mother's sister. His father was a grave, conscientious man; his aunt strict and devout. He hated them. Though belonging to the middle class, the family had aristocratic leanings, and the Revolution, which broke out in 1789, filled them with dismay. Stendhal claims that his childhood was miserable, but it does not appear from his own account that he had much to complain of. He was clever, argumentative and very much of a handful. When the Terror reached Grenoble, Monsieur Beyle was placed on the list of suspects; he thought he owed this to a rival lawyer, named Amar, who wanted his practice. "But Amar," said the smart little boy, "has put you on the list of those suspected of not loving the republic, and it is certain that you do not love it." True, of course; but not very pleasant for a middle-aged gentleman who is in danger of losing his head to hear from the lips of his only son. Stendhal accused his father of a horrid stinginess, but he seems always to have been able to wheedle money out of him when he wanted it. He was forbidden to read certain books, but, as thousands upon thousands of children the world over have done since books were first printed, he read them on the sly. His chief complaint was that he was not permitted to mix freely with other children; but his life cannot have been so solitary as he liked to make out, since he had two sisters, and other little boys shared his lessons with the Jesuit priest who was his tutor. He was, in fact, brought up as children in the well-to-do middle class were brought up at the time. Like all children, he looked upon ordinary restraints as the exercise of outrageous tyranny; and when he was obliged to do lessons, when he was not allowed to do exactly as he chose, regarded himself as treated with monstrous cruelty.

In this he resembled most children, but most children, when they grow up, forget their grievances. Stendhal was unusual in that, at fifty-three, he harboured his old resentments. Because he hated his Jesuit tutor, he became violently anti-clerical, and to the end of his life could hardly bring himself to believe that a religious person might be sincere; and because his father and aunt were devoted royalists, he became ardently republican. But when one evening, being then eleven years old, he slipped out of the house to go to a revolutionary meeting, he had something of a shock. He found the proletariat dirty and smelly, vulgar and ill-spoken. "In short, I was then as I am today," he wrote, "I love the people, I hate their oppressors, but it would be a perpetual torture for me to live with the people . . . I had, and I have still, the most aristocratic tastes, I would do everything for the happiness of the people, but I would sooner, I believe, pass two weeks every month in prison than live with shop-keepers."

The boy was clever and a good mathematician, and at sixteen he persuaded his father to let him go to Paris to enter the Ecole Polytechnique to prepare himself for a career in the army But this was only an excuse to get away from home. When the day came for him to present himself for the entrance examination, he stayed away. His father had given him an introduction to a connection of his, a Monsieur Daru, whose two sons were in the War Office. Pierre, the elder, held an important position, and after some time, at the request of M. Daru, his father, he engaged the youth, who was at a loose end and for whom some occupation had to be found, as one of his many secretaries. Napoleon set out on his second campaign in Italy, the brothers Daru followed him, and a little later Stendhal joined them at Milan. After some months on the clerical staff, Pierre Daru got him a commission in a regiment of dragoons, but, enjoying the gaieties of Milan as he did, he made no attempt to join it and, taking advantage of his patron's absence, he wheedled a certain General Michaud into making him his A.D.C. When Pierre Daru came back, he ordered Stendhal to join his regiment; but this, on one pretext and another, he avoided doing for six months, and when at last he did, found himself so bored that on a plea of illness he got leave of absence to go to Grenoble, and there resigned his commission. He saw no action, but this did not prevent him from boasting in after years of his prowess as a combatant; and indeed in 1804, when he was looking for a job, he wrote a testimonial himself (which General Michaud signed) in which he certified to his gallantry in various battles in which it has been proved he could not possibly have been engaged.

After spending three months at home, Stendhal went to live in Paris on a small, but sufficient, allowance from his father. He had two objects in view. One was to become the greatest dramatic poet of the age. For this purpose, he studied a manual of playwriting and assiduously frequented the theatre. He seems, however, to have had little power of invention, since over and over again one finds him unscrupulously remarking in his diary how he could take a play he had just seen and work it over into one of his own; and he was certainly no poet. His other object was to become a great lover. For this nature had ill-equipped him. He was somewhat undersized, an ugly, plump young man with a big body and short legs, a large head and a mass of black hair; his mouth was thin, his nose thick and prominent; but his brown eyes were eager, his feet and hands small, and his skin as delicate as a woman's. He was proud to declare that to hold a sword raised blisters on his hand. He was, besides, shy and awkward. Through his cousin, Martial Daru, Pierre's younger brother, he was able to frequent the *salons* of some of the ladies whose husbands the Revolution had enriched; but he was sadly tongue-tied in company. He could think of clever things to say, but could never summon up the courage to say them. He never knew what to do with his hands, and he bought a cane so that by playing with it he should make some use of them. He was conscious of his provincial accent, and it may be that it was to cure himself of this that he entered a dramatic school. Here he met a small-part actress, Mélanie Guilbert by name, two or three years older than himself, and, after some hesitation, decided to fall in love with her. He hesitated partly because he was not sure whether she had a greatness of soul equal to his own and partly because he suspected that she was suffering from a venereal disease. Having presumably satisfied himself on both these points, he followed her to Marseilles, where she had an engagement, and where for some months he worked at a wholesale grocer's. He came to the conclusion that she was not, either spiritually or intellectually, the woman he had thought; and it was a relief to him when, her engagement having come to an end, lack of money obliged her to return to Paris.

Stendhal was highly sex-conscious, but not particularly sexual; indeed, until some very frank letters were discovered from one of his later mistresses, it was commonly suspected that he was impotent. That is what the hero of his first novel, *Armance*, was. It is not a good novel. André Gide, however, greatly admired it; for a reason, I think, which is not hard to guess: it corroborated his own conviction, derived of course from his peculiar relations with his wife, that it is possible to be deeply in love without sexual desire. But there is all the difference between loving and being in love. It is possible to love without desire, but without desire impossible to be in love. Stendhal was evidently not impotent. He made his condition clear in the chapter of *De l'Amour* which he entitled 'Fiasco'. To put it bluntly, his fear of not coming up to the scratch on occasion made him unable to do so, and thus gave rise to the rumours which mortified him. His passions were cerebral, and to possess a woman was chiefly a satisfaction to his vanity. It assured him of his own virility. Notwithstanding his high-flown phrases, there is no sign that he was capable of tenderness. He admits frankly that most of his love affairs were unfortunate, and it is not hard to see why. He was faint-hearted. When in Italy, he asked a brother officer how to go about it to win a woman's "favours", and solemnly wrote down the advice he received. He laid siege to women by rule, just as he had tried to write plays by rule; and he was affronted when he discovered that they thought him ridiculous, and surprised when they discerned his insincerity. Intelligent as he was, it seems never to have occurred to him that the language a woman understands is the language of the heart, and that the language of reason leaves her cold. He thought he could achieve by stratagem and chicanery what can only be achieved by feeling.

Some months after Mélanie left him, Stendhal once more found himself in Paris. This was in 1806. By this time Pierre, now Count Daru, was more important than ever. Stendhal's conduct in Italy had caused Pierre to form a poor opinion of his cousin, and it was only on his wife's persuasion that he was induced to give him another chance. After the battle of Jena his younger brother, Martial, was assigned to serve at Brunswick, and Stendhal accompanied him as deputy commissary of war. He performed his duties so capably that, when Martial Daru was called elsewhere, he succeeded him. Stendhal abandoned the idea of being a great dramatist and decided to make a career for himself in the bureaucracy. He saw himself as a Baron of the Empire, a Knight of the Legion of Honour and, finally, as Prefect of a department with a princely stipend. Ardent republican though he was, and looking upon Napoleon as a tyrant who had robbed France of her liberty, he wrote to his father asking him to buy him a title. He added the *particule* to his name, and called himself Henri de Beyle. But notwithstanding this foolishness, he was a competent and resourceful administrator; and in an uprising occasioned by a French officer who in a dispute with a German civilian drew his sword and killed him, he behaved with notable courage. In 1810, having gained promotion, he was once more in Paris, with an office in a superb suite in the Palais des Invalides and a handsome salary. He acquired a cabriolet with a pair of horses, a coachman and a man-servant. He took a chorus-girl to live with him. But this did not suffice: he felt that he owed it to himself to have a mistress he could love, and whose position would add to his prestige. He decided that Alexandrine Daru, Pierre's wife, would fill the bill. She was a handsome woman many years younger than her distinguished husband, and the mother of his four children. There is no sign that Stendhal gave a thought to the kindness and long-suffering tolerance with which Count Daru had treated him, nor that, since he owed his advancement to him and his career depended on his good graces, it was neither politic nor elegant to seduce his wife. Gratitude was a virtue unknown to him.

He set about the enterprise with a crop of amorous devices, but the unfortunate diffidence of which he could not rid himself still hampered him. He was by turns sprightly and sad, flirtatious and cold, ardent and indifferent: nothing served; and he could not tell whether the Countess cared for him or not. It was a mortification to him to suspect that, because of his bashfulness, she laughed at him behind his back. At length, he went to an old friend and, having exposed his dilemma, asked him what tactics to pursue. They discussed the matter. The friend asked pertinent questions, and wrote down Stendhal's answers. Here, as summarized by Matthew Josephson, are the replies to the question: "What are the advantages of seducing Madame de B.?" (Madame de B. was what they called Countess Daru.) "They are as follows: He would be following the inclinations of his character; he would win great social advantages; he would pursue further his study of human passions; he would satisfy honour and pride." A footnote to the document was written by Stendhal: "The best advice. Attack! Attack! Attack!" It was good advice, but not easy to follow by one who is cursed with an unsurmountable timidity. Some weeks later, however, Stendhal was asked to stay at Bècheville, the Darus' country house, and on the second morning, after a sleepless night, resolved to take the plunge, he put on his best striped trousers. Countess Daru complimented him on them. They walked in the garden, while a friend of hers with her mother and the children followed twenty yards behind. They strolled up and down, and Stendhal, trembling but determined, fixed upon a certain point, which he called B, at a little distance from the point A to which they had come, and swore that if he did not speak out when they reached it he would kill himself. He spoke, he seized her hand and sought to kiss it; he told her that he had loved her for eighteen months, had done his best to conceal it, and even tried not to see her, but could bear his agony no longer. The Countess replied, not unkindly, that she could look upon him as nothing but a friend, and had no intention of being unfaithful to her husband. She called the rest of the party to join them. Stendhal had lost what he called the Battle of Bècheville. It may be surmised that his vanity rather than his heart was hurt.

Two months after this, still smarting from his disappointment, he applied for leave of absence and went to Milan, with which he had been much taken on his first visit to Italy. There, ten years before, he had been attracted by a certain Gina Pietragrua, who was the mistress of a brother officer of his; but he was then an impecunious sub-lieutenant, and she paid little attention to him. On his return to Milan, however, Stendhal immediately sought her out. Her father kept a shop and, when quite young, she had married a government clerk; by this time she was thirty-four, and had a son of sixteen. On seeing her again, Stendhal found her "a tall and superb woman. She still had something of the majestic in her eyes, expression, brow and nose. I found her (he adds) cleverer, with more majesty and less of that full grace of voluptuousness." She was certainly clever enough on her husband's small salary to have an apartment in Milan, a house in the country, servants, a box at the Scala and a carriage.

Stendhal was highly conscious of his homeliness and, to overcome it, made a point of dressing with elegance and fashion. He had always been plump, but by now with good living he was grown portly; however, he had money in his pocket and fine clothes to his back. With these advantages, he must have thought that he had more chance of pleasing the majestic lady than when he was a poverty-stricken dragoon, and he decided to amuse himself with her during his short stay in Milan. But she was not so facile as he had expected. In fact, she led him a dance, and it was not till the eve of his departure for Rome that she consented to receive him in her apartment early one morning. One would have thought it an unpropitious hour for love. That day he wrote in his diary: "On the 21st September at half-past eleven, I won the victory I had so long desired." He also wrote the date on his braces. He had worn the same striped trousers as on the day of his declaration to Countess Daru.

His leave came to an end, and he returned to Paris. Somewhat to his dismay, he found Count Daru, who had witnessed his young cousin's attention to his wife with disfavour, more than cold; and when Napoleon started on his disastrous expedition to Russia, it was only with difficulty that Stendhal prevailed upon him to transfer him from his comfortable job at the Invalides to active service in the commissariat. He followed in the wake of the army to Moscow, and in the retreat proved himself as ever cool, enterprising and courageous. On one of the worst mornings, he turned up at Daru's headquarters for orders, carefully shaved and perfectly groomed in his only uniform. At the passage of the Beresina he saved his life, and that of a wounded officer whom he had taken into his carriage, by his presence of mind. He arrived at last at Königsberg, half starved, having lost his manuscripts and everything he possessed but the clothes he stood up in. "I saved myself by force of will," he wrote, "for I saw many around me give up hope and perish." A month later he was back in Paris.

3

In 1814 the Emperor abdicated, and Stendhal's official career came to an end. He claims to have refused the important posts that were offered him and exiled himself rather than serve under the Bourbons; but the facts are not quite like that; he took the oath of allegiance to the King and made attempts to get back into public service. They failed, and he returned to Milan. He still had enough money to live in a pleasant apartment and go to the opera as often as he chose; but he had neither the rank, the prestige nor the cash he had had before. Gina was cool. She told him that her husband had grown jealous on hearing of his arrival, and that her other admirers were suspicious. He could not conceal from himself that she had no further use for him, but her indifference only inflamed his passion, and at length it occurred to him that there was but one way to regain her love. He raised three thousand francs to give her. They went to Venice, accompanied by her mother, her son and a middle-aged banker. To save appearances, she insisted that Stendhal should live in a different hotel, and much to his annoyance the banker joined them when he and Gina dined together. Here is an extract, in his own English, from his diary: "She pretends that she makes me a great sacrifice in going to Venice. I was very foolish of giving her three thousand francs which were to pay for this tour." And ten days later: "I have had her . . . but she talked of our financial arrangements. There was no illusion possible yesterday morning. Politics kills all voluptuousness in me, apparently by drawing all the nervous fluid to the brain."

Notwithstanding this contretemps, Stendhal spent June 18, 1815, the day on which Napoleon was defeated at Waterloo, in the majestic Gina's arms.

In the autumn the party went back to Milan. For the sake of her reputation, she insisted on Stendhal's taking rooms in an obscure suburb. When she gave him an assignation, he went, disguised, in the dead of night, throwing spies off the scent by changing carriage several times, and then was admitted to the apartment by a chambermaid. But the chambermaid, having quarrelled with her mistress or won over by the money of Beyle, made on a sudden the startling revelation that Madame's husband was not jealous at all; she demanded all this mystery to prevent Monsieur Beyle from encountering a rival, several rivals, for there were many, and the maid offered to prove it to him. Next day she hid him in a small closet beside Gina's boudoir, and there he saw with his own eyes, through a hole in the wall, the treachery that was being done him, only three feet from his hiding place. "You may think perhaps," said Beyle, when relating the incident to Mérimée years afterward, "that I rushed out of the closet in order to poniard the two of them? Not at all . . . I left my dark closet as quietly as I went in, thinking only of the ridiculous side of the adventure, laughing to myself, and also full of scorn for the lady, and quite happy, after all, to have regained my liberty."

But he was deeply mortified. He claims that for eighteen months he was unable to write, to think or to speak. Gina tried to win him back. One day she waylaid him at the Brera, the great picture gallery, and going down on her knees begged him to forgive her. "I had the ridiculous pride," he told Mérimée, "to repulse her with disdain. I seem still to see her pursuing me, clinging to my coat tails and dragging herself on her knees the length of a great gallery. I was a fool not to forgive her, for certainly she never loved me so much as on that day."

In 1818, however, Stendhal met the beautiful Countess Dembrowski, and promptly fell in love with her. He was thirty-six and she ten years younger. This was the first time he had set his affections on a woman of distinction. The Countess, an Italian, was married in her teens to a Polish general, but had left him after some years and gone to Switzerland with her two children. The poet, Ugo Foscolo, was living there in exile, and public opinion wrongly believed that it was to live with him that she had left her husband. When she returned to Milan, she was under a cloud, not because she had had a lover, which, according to the manners of the time, was far from reprehensible, but because she had left her husband and lived by herself abroad. It was not till after five months of passionate admiration that Stendhal ventured to declare his love. She promptly showed him the door. He wrote humbly apologizing, and eventually she so far relented as to allow him to come to see her once a fortnight. She made it very obvious that his attentions were distasteful to her, but he persisted. One of the odd things about Stendhal is that though he was always on the watch lest anyone made a fool of him, he was constantly making a fool of himself. On one occasion the Countess went to Volterra to see her two sons, who were at school there, and Stendhal followed her; but, knowing it would anger her, disguised himself by wearing green spectacles. He took them off in the evening when he went for a stroll, and by chance met the Countess. She cut him dead and next day sent him a note "berating him for having followed her to Volterra and compromised her by hanging about the park where she walked every day". He answered, beseeching her to pardon him and a day or two later called on her. She sent him coldly away. He went to Florence and bombarded her with unhappy letters. She sent them back to him unopened, and wrote as follows: "Monsieur, I do not wish to receive any more letters from you and will not write to you. I am with perfect esteem, etc. . . ."

Stendhal, disconsolate, returned to Milan, only to learn that his father had died. He started at once for Grenoble. There he found that the attorney's affairs were in a bad way, and instead of inheriting the fortune he expected, he was left with little but debts to settle. He hurried back to Milan, and somehow, we are not told how, managed to persuade the Countess to let him once more see her again at stated intervals; but such was his vanity, he would not believe that she was perfectly indifferent to him, and later he wrote: "After three years of intimacy, I left a woman whom I loved and who loved me, and yet who never gave herself to me."

In 1821, on account of his relations with certain Italian patriots, the Austrian police requested him to leave Milan. He settled down in Paris and for the next nine years mostly lived there. He frequented the *salons* where wit was appreciated. He was no longer tongue-tied, but was become an amusing, caustic talker, at his best with eight or ten persons whom he liked; but, as many good talkers do, he was inclined to monopolize the conversation. He liked to lay down the law, and took no pains to conceal his contempt for anyone who did not agree with him. In his desire to shock, he indulged somewhat freely in the bawdy and the profane, and carping critics thought that, to entertain or to provoke, he often forced his humour. He could not suffer bores, and found it hard to believe that they were not scoundrels as well.

During this period he had the only love affair in which his love appears to have been requited. The Countess de Curial, née Clémentine Bougeot, was separated from an unfaithful, but jealous and irascible, husband. She was a handsome woman of thirty-six and Stendhal was over forty, a fat short man with a fat red nose, an enormous paunch and a huge behind. He wore a reddish-brown wig and great whiskers dyed to match. He dressed as grandly as his limited means allowed. Clémentine de Curial was attracted by Stendhal's wit and good humour, and when after a proper interval he "attacked", she received his proposals with the gratitude proper to her age. During the two years the affair lasted she wrote him two hundred and fifteen letters. It was all as romantic as Stendhal could have wished. Fearing her husband's rage, he would pay her secret visits. I quote from Matthew Josephson: "He would assume a disguise, would take a carriage from Paris and, in darkness, ride full tilt to her château, where he would arrive after midnight. And Madame de Curial proved herself as audacious as any heroine of a novel by Stendhal. Once, when unexpected guests arrived—perhaps her husband—interrupting their assignation, she hurriedly led him down to the cellar, removed the ladder by which he descended, and shut the trap door. There in a dark, romantic cavern the enraptured Stendhal remained for three whole days imprisoned, nay entombed, while the madly-devoted Clémentine prepared food for him, lowered and raised the ladder so that she might come to him secretly, and even, in order to provide for his wants, brought down and then emptied the close stool." "She was sublime," Stendhal wrote afterwards, "when she came to the cellar at night." But presently quarrels arose between the lovers which were as tempestuous as their passion, and eventually the lady threw Stendhal over for another, and perhaps less exacting or more exciting, lover.

Then came the revolution of 1830. Charles X went into exile, and Louis Philippe ascended the throne. Stendhal had, by this time, spent the little he had been able to save from his father's ruin, and his literary efforts, for he had reverted to his old ambition to become a famous writer, brought him neither money nor reputation. *De l'Amour* was published in 1822, and in eleven years only seventeen copies were sold. *Armance*, in 1827, succeeded neither with the critics nor the public. He had, as I have mentioned, tried in vain to get some government post, and at last, with the change of régime, he was appointed to the consulate at Trieste; but, owing to his liberal sympathies, the Austrian authorities refused to accept him, and he was transferred to Civita Vecchia in the Papal States.

He took his official duties lightly; he was a tireless sightseer and, whenever possible, went on a jaunt. He found in Rome friends who made much of him. But notwithstanding these distractions, he was hideously bored, and lonely; and, at the age of fifty-one, he made an offer of marriage to a young girl, the daughter of his laundress and of a minor employee at the consulate. To his mortification, the offer was refused, not, as one might have expected, because of his age and bad character, but because of his liberal opinions. In 1836 he persuaded his Minister to give him some small job that allowed him to live in Paris for three years, while someone else temporarily occupied his post. He was by then fatter than ever, and apoplectic, but this did not prevent him from dressing in the height of fashion, and a slighting remark on the cut of his coat or the style of his trousers deeply affronted him. He continued to make love, but with little success. He persuaded himself that he was still in love with Clémentine de Curial, and sought to resume some sort of relations with her. Ten years had passed since the break, and she very sensibly replied that one cannot light an extinct fire with embers. She told him that he must be content to be her first and best friend. Mérimée relates that he was shattered by the blow: "He could not pronounce her name without his voice changing . . . It was the only time I had seen him weep." But he seems to have recovered sufficiently within a month or two unsuccessfully to make advances to a certain Madame Gaulthier. At length, he was obliged to return to Civita Vecchia and there, two years later, he had a stroke. On his recovery he asked for leave of absence to consult a famous doctor at Geneva. He moved from there to Paris and resumed his old life. He went to parties and talked with undiminished vivacity. One day in March, 1842, he attended an official dinner at the Ministry of Foreign Affairs and that evening, while walking along the boulevard, had a second stroke. He was carried to his lodging and died next day. He had passed his life in the pursuit of happiness, and had never learnt that happiness is best attained when it is not sought; and, moreover, is only known when it is lost. It is doubtful whether anyone can say "I am happy"; but only "I was happy". For happiness is not well-being, content, heart's ease, pleasure, enjoyment: all these go to make happiness, but they are not happiness.

4

Stendhal was an eccentric. His character was even more incongruous than that of most men, and one is amazed that so many contradictory traits should co-exist in one and the same person. They do not form a harmony that is in any way plausible. He had great virtues and great defects. He was sensitive, emotional, diffident, talented, a hard worker when there was work to be done, cool and brave in danger, a good friend and of a remarkable originality. His prejudices were absurd, his aims unworthy. He was distrustful (and so an easy dupe), intolerant, uncharitable, none too conscientious, fatuously vain and vainglorious, sensual without delicacy, and licentious without passion. But if we know that he had these defects, it is because he has told us so himself. Stendhal was not a professional author, he was hardly even a man of letters, but he wrote incessantly, and he wrote almost entirely about himself. For years he kept a journal, of which great sections have come down to us, and it is plain that he wrote with no view to publication; but in his early fifties he wrote an autobiography in five hundred pages, which carried him to the age of seventeen, and this, though left unrevised at his death, he meant to be read. In it he sometimes makes himself out more important than he really was, and claims to have done things he did not do, but on the whole it is truthful. He does not spare himself, and I imagine that few can read these books, and they are not easy to read, since they are in parts dull and often repetitive, without asking themselves whether, if they were unwise enough to expose themselves with so much frankness, they would make a much better showing.

When Stendhal died, only two Paris papers troubled to report the fact, and only three persons, of whom Mérimée was one, attended his funeral. It looked as though he would be entirely forgotten; and, indeed, he might well have been but for the efforts of two devoted friends who succeeded in persuading an important firm of publishers to issue an edition of his principal works. The public, however, notwithstanding two articles which the powerful critic, Sainte-Beuve, devoted to them, remained indifferent. That is not surprising, since Sainte-Beuve's first article was concerned with Stendhal's early works, which his contemporaries neglected and which posterity has decided to ignore, and in the second article he reserved his praise for Stendhal's books of travel, *Promenades dans Rome* and *Mémoires d'un Touriste*, and found nothing to his liking in the novels. He claimed that the characters were puppets, ingeniously constructed, but whose every movement revealed the mechanism within; and the incidents he condemned as frankly incredible. Balzac, while Stendhal was still alive, had written a laudatory article on *La Chartreuse de Parme*; Sainte-Beuve wrote: "It is evident that I am far from sharing the enthusiasm of M. de Balzac for *La Chartreuse de Parme*. The simple fact is that he has written of Beyle, as a novelist, as he would have liked people to write of himself"; and then, a little later, rather maliciously, he tells how after Stendhal's death among his papers was found one which showed that he had given or lent Balzac three thousand francs (and with Balzac a loan always was a gift), and thus paid for the eulogy. Upon this Sainte-Beuve quoted: "*Ce mélange de gloire et de gain m'importune.*" Perhaps he needn't have been so censorious: his two articles on Stendhal were paid for by the publishers of the edition, and the two articles he wrote on Stendhal's cousin, Pierre Daru, whose only distinction as a writer was that he had translated Horace and written a history of Venice in nine volumes, were commissioned as an act of piety by the family.

Stendhal never doubted that his works would survive, but he was prepared to wait till 1880, or even to 1900, to receive the appreciation that was his due. Many an author has consoled himself for the neglect of his contemporaries by a confidence that posterity will recognize his merits. It seldom does. Posterity is busy and careless and, when it concerns itself with the literary productions of the past, makes its choice among those that were successful in their own day. It is only by a remote chance that a dead author is rescued from the obscurity in which he languished during his lifetime. In the case of Stendhal, a professor, otherwise unknown, in his lectures at the École Normale enthusiastically praised his books, and there happened to be among his students some clever young men who later made a name for themselves. They read them, and finding in them something that suited the climate of opinion at the time prevalent among the young, became fanatical admirers. The ablest of these young men was Hippòlyte Taine, and many years later, by which time he was become a well-known and influential man of letters, he wrote a long essay in which he called attention especially to Stendhal's psychological insight. In passing, I should remark that when literary critics speak of a novelist's psychology, they do not use the term in quite the sense that psychologists use it. So far as I can make out, what they mean is that the novelist lays a greater emphasis on the motives, thoughts and emotions of his characters than on their actions; but in practice this results in the novelist chiefly displaying the more sinister parts of man's nature, his envy, his malignity, his selfishness, his pettiness—in fact, his baser rather than his better nature; and this has an air of truth, for, unless we are perfect fools, we are well aware how much there

335

is in us all that is hateful. "But for the grace of God there goes John Bradford." Since Taine's essay, an immense amount has been written about Stendhal, and it is generally agreed that he is one of the three great novelists that France produced in the nineteenth century.

His case is a very singular one. Most of the great novelists have been voluminous creators, and none more so than Balzac and Dickens. One can be pretty sure that, if they had lived to old age, they would have gone on concocting story after story. One would think that, of all the gifts a novelist needs, invention on a large scale is the most essential. This gift Stendhal almost completely lacked. Yet he is, perhaps, the most original of novelists. Just as, when in his youth he wanted to become a famous dramatist, he could never think of an idea on which to construct a play; so, when it came to writing novels, it looks as though he was unable to evolve a plot out of his own head. His first novel, as I have said, was *Armance*. The Duchesse de Duras had written two novels which by their somewhat daring subjects had had a *succès de scandale*, and a writer of some note in his day, by name Henri de Latouche, wrote one, which he issued anonymously, hoping it would be ascribed to the Duchess, and of which the hero was impotent. I have not read it, and can speak of it only from hearsay. From this I gather that Stendhal for *Armance* took not only the theme, but also the plot, of Latouche's book. With what looks like brazen effrontery, he even gave his hero the same name as Latouche had given his, and it was only later that he changed it from Olivier to Octave. He embroidered upon the idea with what I suppose would be called psychological realism; but the novel remains a poor one: the incidents are wildly improbable, and for my part I find it impossible to believe that a man suffering from the peculiar disability which gives the book its theme could fall passionately in love with a young girl. In *Le Rouge et le Noir*, as I shall show later, Stendhal followed closely the story of a young man who was the subject of a celebrated trial. The only part of *La Chartreuse de Parme* which Sainte-Beuve saw fit to praise is the description of the Battle of Waterloo, and Stendhal's description was suggested by the memoirs of an English soldier who had been at the Battle of Vittoria. For the rest of that particular book he depended on old Italian annals and memoirs. Now, a novelist obviously gets his plots from somewhere, sometimes from incidents in real life that he has experienced, witnessed or been told of, but as a rule, I should say, from an elaboration of characters who have for some reason excited his imagination. I know of no novelist of the first rank, other than Stendhal, who has so directly found his inspiration in what he has read. I do not remark on this in disparagement, but merely as a curious fact. Stendhal was not greatly inventive; but, how it came about none can tell, nature had endowed this vulgar buffoon with a wonderful gift of accurate observation, and with a piercing insight into the intricacies, vagaries and bizarreries of the human heart. He had a very poor opinion of his fellow-creatures, but was intensely interested in them. In his *Mémoires d'un Touriste* there is a revealing passage in which he relates how, on a journey through France, he took a post-chaise in order to admire the scenery at his leisure, but after a while, finding himself desperately bored, abandoned it for the crowded stage-coach where he could talk to his fellow-travellers and, at *table d'hôte*, listen to their stories.

Though Stendhal's travel books are lively and can still be read with pleasure, if only for what they tell you of their author's singular character, his fame rests on two novels and on a few passages in *De l'Amour*. One of these was not original: early in 1817 he was at Bologna, and at a party a certain Madame Gherardi, "the prettiest woman that Brescia, the land of fine eyes, ever produced", said to him:

"There are four different kinds of love:
(1) Physical love, that of beasts, savages and degraded Europeans.
(2) Passionate love, that of Héloise for Abelard, of Julie d'Étange for Saint-Preux.
(3) L'Amour Goût, which during the eighteenth century amused the French, and which Marivaux, Crébillon, Duclos, Madame d'Epinay have described with such grace. (I have left *l'amour goût* in French, because I do

not know how to translate it. I think it means the kind of love you feel for a person to whom you have taken a fancy, and, if the word were in the Oxford Dictionary, I should prefer to call it "lech" rather than love.)

(4) Love from Vanity, that which made your Duchesse de Chaulnes say when she was about to marry M. de Gial: 'For a commoner, a duchess is always thirty.' "

Then Stendhal adds: "the act of folly which makes one see every perfection in the object of one's love, is called *crystallization* in Madame Gherardi's circle." It would have been unlike him not to seize upon the fruitful idea that was thus presented to him; but it was not till months later that, on what he called "a day of genius", the analogy occurred to him which has since become famous. Here it is: "At the salt mines of Salzburg you throw into the depths of a disused shaft a leafless branch; two or three months afterwards you take it out covered with brilliant crystallizations: the smallest twigs, no bigger than a titmouse's foot, are adorned with an infinity of scintillating diamonds. One can no longer recognize the original branch.

"What I call crystallization is the operation of the mind that draws from everything around it the discovery that the beloved object has new perfections."

Everyone who has fallen in, and fallen out of, love must recognize the aptness of the illustration.

5

Of the two great novels, *La Chartreuse de Parme* is the more agreeable to read. I do not think Sainte-Beuve was right when he called the characters lifeless puppets. It is true that Fabrice, the hero, and Clelia Conti, the heroine, are shadowy, and for the most part play a somewhat passive role in the story; but Count Mosca and the Duchess Sanseverino are intensely alive. The gay, licentious, unscrupulous duchess is a masterpiece of characterization. But *Le Rouge et le Noir* is by far the more striking, the more original, and the more significant perform-ance. It is because of it that Zola called Stendhal the father of the naturalistic school, and that Bourget and André Gide have claimed him (not quite accurately) as the originator of the psychological novel.

Unlike most authors, Stendhal accepted criticism, however damning, with good humour; but what is even more remarkable, when he sent manuscripts of his books to friends whose opinions he wanted, he adopted without hesitation the revisions, often ample, which they recommended. Mérimée states that though he constantly re-wrote, he never corrected. I am not sure that this is a fact. In a manuscript of his that I have seen he put a little cross over a number of words that he was not satisfied with, and did this surely with the intention of altering them when he came to revise. He hated the flowery manner of writing made fashionable by Chateaubriand, and which a hundred lesser authors had sedulously aped. Stendhal's aim was to set down whatever he had to say as plainly and exactly as he could, without frills, rhetorical flourishes or picturesque verbiage. He said (probably not quite truly) that before starting to write he read a page of the *Code Napoléon* in order to chasten his language. He eschewed description of scenery and the abundant metaphors which were popular in his day. The cold, lucid, self-controlled style he adopted admirably increases the horror of the story he has to tell in *Le Rouge et le Noir*, and adds to its enthralling interest.

It is to *Le Rouge et le Noir* that Taine in his famous essay gave most of his attention; but being an historian and a philosopher, he was chiefly interested in Stendhal's psychological acuteness, his shrewd analysis of motives, and the freshness and originality of his opinions. He pointed out with justice that Stendhal was concerned not with action for its own sake, but only in so far as it was occasioned by the emotions of his personages, the singularities of their character and the vicissitudes of their passions. This made him avoid describing dramatic incidents in a dramatic manner. As an illustration of this, Taine quoted Stendhal's description of his hero's execution, and very truly remarked that most authors would have looked upon this as an event on which they could expatiate. This is how Stendhal treated it:

"The bad air of the cell was becoming intolerable to Julien; happily, on the day on which they told him he was to die, a lovely sun enlivened nature, and Julien was in a courageous mood. To walk in the open air was to him a delicious sensation, as to walk on land might be to a sailor who has been long at sea. Well, everything is going well, he told himself, I don't lack courage. Never had that head been so poetic as when it was about to fall. The sweet moments he had passed in the woods of Vergy crowded upon his memory with the utmost force. Everything took place simply, decently, and on his side without affectation."

But Taine was apparently not interested in the novel as a work of art. His aim in writing was to awaken interest in a neglected author, and it was a panegyric he wrote rather than a critical study. The reader who is induced by Taine's essay to acquaint himself with *Le Rouge et le Noir* may well be a trifle disappointed. For as a work of art it is sadly imperfect.

Stendhal was more interested in himself than in anyone else, and he was always the hero of his novels, Octave in *Armance*, Fabrice in *La Chartreuse de Parme*, and Lucien Leuwen in the unfinished novel of that name. Julien Sorel, the hero of *Le Rouge et le Noir*, is the kind of man Stendhal would have liked to be. He made him attractive to women and successful in winning their love, as he himself would have given everything to be, and too seldom was. He made him achieve his ends with them by just those methods that he had concocted for his own use, and that had consistently failed. He made him as brilliant a talker as he was himself; he was wise enough, however, never to give an example of his brilliance, but only affirmed it, since he knew that when a novelist has told his reader that a character is witty, and then gives examples of his wit, they are apt not to come up to the reader's expectation. He gave him his own astonishing memory, his own courage, his own timidity, his own ambition, sensitiveness, calculating brain, his own suspiciousness and vanity and quickness to take offence, his own unscrupulousness and his own ingratitude. The pleasantest trait he gives him, again one that he found in himself, is Julien's faculty of being moved to tears when he meets with disinterestedness and loving-kindness: it suggests that if the circumstances of his life had been different, he would not have been so vile.

As I have said, Stendhal had no gift for making up a story out of his own head, and he took the plot of *Le Rouge et le Noir* from newspaper reports of a trial that at the time had excited great interest. A young seminarist called Antoine Berthet was tutor in the house of a M. Michoud, then in that of a M. de Cordon; he tried to seduce, or did seduce, the wife of the first and the daughter of the second. He was discharged. He attempted then to resume his studies for the priesthood, but owing to his bad reputation no seminary would receive him. He took it into his head that the Michouds were responsible for this, and in revenge shot Madame Michoud while she was in church, and then himself. The wound was not fatal and he was tried; he sought to save himself at the expense of the unfortunate woman, but was condemned to death.

This ugly, sordid story appealed to Stendhal. He regarded Berthet's crime as the reaction of a strong, rebellious nature against the social order, and as the expression of the natural man, untrammelled by the conventions of an artificial society. He held his fellow-Frenchmen in scorn because they had lost the energy which they had had in the Middle Ages, and were become law-abiding, respectable, prosaic, commonplace and incapable of passion. It might, perhaps, have occurred to him that after the horrors of the Terror, after the catastrophic wars of Napoleon, it was natural that they should welcome peace and quiet. Stendhal prized energy above all other qualities of man, and if he adored Italy, and sooner lived there than in his native land, it was because he persuaded himself that it was the "country of love and hate". There men loved with frenzy and for love's sake died. There men and women surrendered to their passions, careless of the disaster that might ensue. There men, in a sudden attack of blind rage, killed, and killing, dared to be themselves. This is pure romanticism, and it is plain that what Stendhal called energy is what most people call violence. And condemn.

"The people alone," he wrote, "nowadays have some

remnants of energy. There is none of it in the upper classes";
so, when he came to write *Le Rouge et le Noir*, he made Julien a
working-class boy; but he furnished him with a better brain,
more strength of will, and greater courage than were possessed
by his wretched model. The character he drew with consummate skill is of perennial interest; he is devoured with envy
and hatred of those born in a more privileged class, and well
represents a type that occurs in every generation, and will presumably continue to do so until there is a classless society. Then
human nature will doubtless have changed, and the less intelligent, the less competent, the less enterprising will no longer
resent it if the more enterprising, the more competent and the
more intelligent enjoy advantages that are denied them. Here,
when we catch our first glimpse of Julien, is how Stendhal
describes him: "He was a small young man of eighteen or
nineteen, weakly to look at, with irregular, delicate features
and an aquiline nose. His large black eyes, which in moments
of tranquillity suggested reflection and fire, were lit up at that
instant with an expression of the fiercest hate. His dark chestnut
hair, growing very low, gave him a small forehead and in
moments of anger a look of wickedness. . . . His slender, well-
set figure suggested lightness rather than vigour." Not an
attractive portrait, but a good one, because it does not pre-
dispose the reader in Julien's favour. The principal character
in a novel, as I have said, naturally enlists the reader's sympathy,
and Stendhal, having chosen a villain for his hero, had to take
care from the start that his readers should not sympathize with
him overmuch. On the other hand, he had to interest them in
him. He could not afford to make him too repulsive, so he
modified his first description by dwelling repeatedly on his fine
eyes, his graceful figure and his delicate hands. On occasion,
he describes him as positively beautiful. But he does not forget
from time to time to call your attention to the malaise he
arouses in persons who come in contact with him, and to the
suspicion with which he is regarded by all save those who have
most cause to be on their guard against him.

Madame de Rênal, the mother of the children Julien is
engaged to teach, is an admirably drawn character of a kind

most difficult to depict. She is a good woman. Most novelists at one time have tried to create one, but have only succeeded in producing a goose. I suppose the reason is that there is only one way of being good, whereas there are dozens of being bad. This obviously gives the novelist greater scope. Madame de Rênal is charming, virtuous, sincere; and the narrative of her growing love for Julien, with its fears and hesitations, and the flaming passion which it becomes, is told in a masterly fashion. She is one of the most touching creatures of fiction. Julien, feeling that it is a duty he owes himself, decides that if one evening he does not hold her hand he will take his own life; just as Stendhal, wearing his best trousers, vowed that if, on reaching a certain point, he did not declare his love to the Countess Daru, he would blow his brains out. Julien eventually seduces Madame de Rênal, not because he is in love with her, but partly to revenge himself on the class she belongs to, and partly to satisfy his own pride; but he *does* fall in love with her and, for a while, his baser instincts are dormant. For the first time in his life he is happy, and you begin to feel sympathy for him. But the imprudence of Madame de Rênal gives rise to gossip, and it is arranged that Julien should enter a seminary to study for the priesthood. I don't see how the parts that deal with Julien's life with the Rênals and at the seminary could be better; there is no need to exercise a willing suspension of disbelief, the truth of what Stendhal tells you is manifest; it is when the scene is changed to Paris that I, for my part, find myself incredulous. When Julien has finished his course at the seminary, the principal secures him a post as secretary to the Marquis de la Môle, and he finds himself admitted to the most aristocratic circle in the capital. The picture Stendhal draws of it does not carry conviction. He had never moved in good society; he was familiar chiefly with the bourgeoisie, which the Revolution and the Empire had brought into prominence; and he did not know how well-bred people behave. He had never encountered pride of birth. Stendhal was at heart a realist, but no one, however hard he tries, can fail to be influenced by the psychic atmosphere of his time. Romanticism was rampant. Stendhal, notwithstanding his appreciation of the good sense

343

and urbane culture of the eighteenth century, was deeply affected by it. As I have indicated, he was fascinated by the ruthless men of the Italian Renaissance who were troubled neither by scruple nor remorse, and hesitated at no crime to satisfy their ambition, gratify their lust, or avenge their honour. He prized their energy, their disregard of consequences, their scorn of convention and their freedom of soul. It is because of this romantic predilection that the last half of *Le Rouge et le Noir* is unsatisfactory. You are asked to accept improbabilities that you cannot swallow, and to interest yourself in episodes that are pointless.

M. de la Môle had a daughter. Her name was Mathilde. She was beautiful, but haughty and wilful; she was intensely conscious of her high descent, and proud of those ancestors of hers who, risking their lives for a great prize, had been executed, one under Charles IX and another under Louis XIII. By a natural coincidence, she attached the same high value to 'energy' as Stendhal did, and she despised the commonplace young nobles who sought her hand. Now, Emile Faguet in an interesting essay has pointed out that Stendhal in his enumeration of the kinds of love left out *l'amour de tête*. That is the love that starts in the imagination, grows and thrives in the imagination and is apt to perish when it is consummated in sexual congress. That is the love that little by little stole upon Mlle de la Môle for her father's secretary, and its stages have been described by Stendhal with the utmost subtlety. She was both attracted and repelled by Julien. She fell in love with him because he was unlike the young aristocrats who surrounded her, because he despised them as much as she did, because of his humble origins, because of his pride which was equal with her own, because she sensed his ambition, his ruthlessness, his lack of scruple, his depravity; and because she was afraid of him.

Eventually Mathilde sends Julien a note, and bids him take a ladder and come up to her room when everyone is asleep. Since we learn later that he could just as well have walked quietly up the stairs, she asked him to do this presumably to test his courage. Clémentine de Curial had used a ladder to come down to the cellar in which she had hidden Stendhal, and this had evidently fired his romantic imagination; for he made Julien, on his way to Paris, stop off at Verrières, the town in which Madame de Rênal lived, get hold of a ladder, and in the middle of the night climb up to her bedroom. It may be that Stendhal felt it awkward to let his hero use this means of access to a lady's chamber twice in one novel, for on receiving Mathilde's note he makes Julien, referring to the ladder, say with irony: "It is an instrument I am fated to use." But no irony suffices to conceal the fact that here Stendhal's inventiveness failed him. What happens after the seduction is again admirably described. Those two self-centred, irritable, moody creatures scarcely know if they love with passion, or hate with frenzy. Each tries to dominate the other; each seeks to anger, wound and humiliate the other. At length Julien, by means of a banal trick, brings the proud girl to his feet. Presently she finds herself pregnant, and tells her father that she intends to marry her lover. M. de la Môle is obliged to consent. But now, when Julien, by dissimulation, diplomacy and self-restraint, is in sight of achieving all his ambition craved, he commits a foolish error. From then on the book goes to pieces.

We are told that Julien is clever and immensely cunning; and yet, to recommend himself to his future father-in-law, he asks him to write to Madame de Rênal for a certificate of character. He knew that she sincerely repented the sin of adultery that she had committed, and might bitterly blame him, as women all over the world are accustomed to do, for her own weakness; he knew, also, that she loved him passionately, and it should have occurred to him that she might not welcome the prospect of his marrying another woman. On the direction of her confessor, she wrote a letter to the Marquis in which she told him that it was Julien's practice to insinuate himself into a family in order to destroy its peace, and that his great and sole object was by a show of disinterestedness to contrive to secure control of the master of the house, and over his fortune. She had no reason whatever to make either of these charges. She said he was a hypocrite and a vile intriguer: Stendhal does not seem to have noticed that though we readers, to whom every movement of Julien's mind has been exposed, know that indeed he was, Madame de Rênal did not; she knew only that he had performed his duties as tutor to her children in an exemplary manner, and had won their affection; and that he loved her so much that on the last occasion on which she had seen him he had risked his career, and even his life, to pass a few hours with her. She was a conscientious woman, and it is hard to believe that, whatever pressure her confessor brought to bear, she would have consented to write things which she had no reason to think were true. Anyhow, when M. de la Môle receives the letter, he is horrified and refuses absolutely to let the marriage proceed. Why did not Julien say that the letter was a tissue of lies and merely the hysterical outburst of a madly jealous woman? He might have admitted that he had been Madame de Rênal's lover; but she was thirty and he was nineteen: was it not more probable that it was she who had seduced him? It was not a fact, as we know, but it was uncommonly plausible. M. de la Môle was a man of the world. The man of the world has an inclination to think the worst of his fellow-creatures, a mild cynicism which leads him to believe that where there is smoke there is fire; and, at the same time, an easy tolerance of human frailty. It would surely have seemed to M. de la Môle amusing, rather than shocking, that his secretary should have had an affair with the wife of a provincial gentleman of no social consequence.

But in any case Julien held all the cards. M. de la Môle had got him a commission in a crack regiment, and given him an estate which produced a sufficient income. Mathilde refused to have an abortion and, madly in love, had expressed her determination to live with Julien, married or not. Julien had only to state the plain facts of the situation, and the Marquis would have been obliged to give in. We have been shown, from the beginning of the novel, that the strength of Julien consisted precisely in his self-control. His passions, envy, hatred, pride, never dominated him; and his lust, the strongest passion of all, was, as with Stendhal himself, not so much a matter of urgent desire as of vanity. At the crisis of the book, Julien does the fatal thing in a novel: he acts out of character. Just when he most needs his self-control, he behaves like a fool. On reading Madame de Rênal's letter, he takes pistols, drives down to Verrières, and shoots her, not killing, but wounding her.

This unintelligible behaviour of Julien's has greatly puzzled the critics, and they have sought explanations for it. One is that it was the fashion of the day to end a novel with a melodramatic incident, preferably with a tragic death; but if such was the fashion, that would surely have been sufficient reason for Stendhal, with his determination to run counter to accepted usage, to eschew it. Others have suggested that an explanation may be found in his fantastic cult of the crime of violence as the supreme manifestation of energy. I find this no more likely. It is true, of course, that Stendhal looked upon Berthet's monstrous action as a *beau crime*, but can he have failed to see that he had made Julien a very different creature from the miserable blackmailer? Verrières was two hundred and fifty miles from Paris, and even with a change of horses at every stage, even if Julien drove day and night, the journey would take nearly two days, long enough for his rage to lessen and give way to the counsels of common sense. Then, the character that Stendhal has so penetratingly drawn would have turned back and, having faced M. de la Môle with the brutal fact of Mathilde's pregnancy, forced him to consent to the marriage.

What then made Stendhal make the strange mistake which everyone agrees is a flaw in his great novel? It is evident that he could not allow Julien to succeed and, achieving his ambition, with Mathilde and M. de la Môle behind him, win place, power and fortune. That would have been a different book, and Balzac wrote it later in the various novels that tell of the rise of Rastignac. Julien had to die. It may be that Balzac, with his wonderful fecundity, might have found a means to end *Le Rouge et le Noir* in a way that the reader would accept not only as plausible, but as inevitable. I don't think Stendhal could have ended it in any way other than he did. I believe that the facts which had been given him exercised an hypnotic power over him from which he was unable to break loose; he had followed the story of Antoine Berthet very closely and he felt himself under a compulsion to pursue it, against all credibility, to its wretched end. But God, fate, chance, whichever you like to call the mystery that governs men's lives, is a poor story-teller; and it is the business, and the right, of the novelist to correct the improbabilities of brute fact. It was not in Stendhal's capacity to do this. It is a great pity. But, as I have urged, no novel is perfect, owing partly to the natural inadequacy of the medium, and partly to the deficiencies of the human being who writes it. Notwithstanding its grave defects, *Le Rouge et le Noir* is a very great book, and to read it is a unique experience.

CHAPTER FIVE

Balzac and *Le Père Goriot*

I

OF all the great novelists that have enriched with their works the spiritual treasures of the world, Balzac is to my mind the greatest. He is the only one to whom I would without hesitation ascribe genius. Genius is a word that is very loosely used nowadays. It is ascribed to persons to whom a more sober judgment would be satisfied to allow talent. Genius and talent are very different things. Many people have talent; it is not rare: genius is. Talent is adroit and dexterous; it can be cultivated: genius is innate, and too often strangely allied to grave defects. But what is genius? The Oxford Dictionary tells us that it is a "native intellectual power of an exalted type, such as is attributed to those who are esteemed greater in any department of art, speculation or practice; (an) instinctive and extraordinary capacity for imaginative creation, original thought, invention, or discovery". Well, instinctive and extraordinary capacity for imaginative creation is precisely what Balzac had. He was not a realist, as Stendhal in part was, and as Flaubert was in *Madame Bovary*, but a romantic; and he saw life not as it really was, but coloured, often garishly, by the predispositions he shared with his contemporaries.

There are writers who have achieved fame on the strength of one or two books; sometimes because, from the mass they have written, only a fragment has proved of enduring value—such is l'Abbé Prévost's *Manon Lescaut*; sometimes because their inspiration, growing out of a special experience, or owing to a peculiarity of temper, only served for a production of little bulk. They say their say once for all and, if they write again, repeat themselves or write what is negligible. Balzac's fertility was prodigious. Of course he was uneven. In such a volume of work as he produced, it was impossible for him always to be at his best. Literary critics are apt to look askance at fertility. I think they are wrong. Matthew Arnold, indeed, looked upon it as a characteristic of genius. He said of Wordsworth that what struck him with admiration, what established in his own opinion the poet's superiority, was the great and ample body of powerful work which remained to him, even after all his inferior work had been cleared away. He goes on to say: "If it were a comparison of single pieces, or of three or four pieces, by each poet, I do not say that Wordsworth would stand decisively above Gray, or Burns, or Coleridge or Keats. . . . It is in his ampler body of powerful work that I find his superiority." Balzac never wrote a novel with the epic grandeur of *War and Peace*, one with the sombre, thrilling power of *The Brothers Karamazov*, nor one with the charm and distinction of *Pride and Prejudice*: his greatness lies not in a single work, but in the formidable mass of his production.

Balzac's field was the whole life of his time, and his range was as extensive as the frontiers of his country. His knowledge of men, however come by, was rare, though in some directions less exact than in others; and he described the middle class of society, doctors, lawyers, clerks and journalists, shopkeepers, village priests, more convincingly than either the world of fashion, the world of the city workers, or of the tillers of the soil. Like all novelists, he wrote of the wicked more successfully than of the good. His invention was stupendous; his power of creation extraordinary. He was like a force of nature, a tumultuous river overflowing its banks and sweeping everything before it, or a hurricane blustering its wild way across quiet country places and through the streets of populous cities.

As a painter of society, his distinctive gift was not only to envisage men in their relations to one another—all novelists, except the writers of adventure-stories pure and simple, do that —but also, and especially, in their relations to the world they live in. Most novelists take a group of persons, sometimes no more than two or three, and treat them as though they lived under a glass case. This often produces an effect of intensity, but at the same time, unfortunately, one of artificiality. People not only live their own lives, they live also in the lives of others:

350

in their own, they play leading parts; in those of others, parts that are sometimes important, but often trivial. You go to the barber's to get your hair cut; it means nothing to you, but because of some casual remark of yours it may be a turning-point in the barber's life. By realizing all that this implies, Balzac was able to give a vivid and exciting impression of the multifariousness of life, its confusions and cross-purposes, and of the remoteness of the causes that result in significant effects. I believe he was the first novelist to dwell on the paramount importance of economics in everybody's life. He would not have thought it enough to say that money is the root of all evil; he thought the desire for money, the appetite for money, was the mainspring of human action.

One must ever bear in mind that Balzac was a romantic. Romanticism, as we know, was a reaction from classicism, but to-day it is more convenient to contrast it with realism. The realist is a determinist, and he aims in his narratives at a logical verisimilitude. His observation is naturalistic. The romantic finds the life of every day humdrum and platitudinous, and he seeks to escape from the real world to a world of the imagination. He pursues strangeness and adventure; he wishes to surprise, and if he can only do so at the expense of probability he does not care. The characters he invents are intense and extreme. Their appetites are unfettered. They despise self-control, which they look upon as the dull virtue of the bourgeois. They approve with their whole being that saying of Pascal's: *Le cœur a ses raisons que la raison ne connaît point.* Their admiration goes to him who is prepared to sacrifice everything and hesitates at nothing to achieve wealth and power. This attitude towards life exactly suited Balzac's exuberant temper; it is hardly too much to say that if romanticism had not existed, he would have invented it. His observation was minute and precise, but he used it as a basis for the fabrications of his fantastic imagination. The idea that every man has a ruling passion suited his instinct. It is one that has always attracted the writers of fiction, for it enables them to give a dramatic force to the creatures of their invention; these stand out vividly, and the reader, from whom nothing is demanded but to know that they are misers or lechers, harpies or saints, understands them without effort. We of to-day, largely through the works of the novelists who have sought to interest us in the psychology of their characters, no longer believe that men are all of a piece. We know that they are made up of contradictory and seemingly irreconcilable elements; it is just these discordances in them that intrigue us and, because we know them in ourselves, excite our sympathy. Balzac's greatest characters are formed on the model of those older writers who drew every man in his humour. Their ruling passion has absorbed them to the exclusion of all else. They are propensities personified; but they are presented with such wonderful power, solidity and distinctness that, even though you may not quite believe in them, you can never forget them.

2

If you had met Balzac in his early thirties, when he was already successful, this is the man you would have seen: a short, stumpy fellow, rather stout, with powerful shoulders and a massive chest, so that he would not have struck you as small, with a neck like a bull's, its whiteness contrasting with the redness of his face; and thick, smiling lips, noticeably red. His teeth were bad and discoloured. His nose was square, with wide nostrils, and when David d'Angers did a bust of him, he said: "Take care of my nose! My nose is a world!" His brow was noble; his hair dense and black, swept back on his skull like a lion's mane. His brown eyes, flecked with gold, had a life, a light, a magnetism, that were quite thrilling; they obscured the fact that his features were irregular and vulgar. His expression was jovial, frank, kindly and good-natured. Lamartine said of him: "His goodness was not a goodness of indifference or insouciance, it was an affectionate, charming, intelligent goodness, which inspired gratitude and defied you not to love him." His vitality was abounding, so that you felt it exhilarating merely to be in his company. If you had given his hands a glance, you would have been struck by their beauty. They were small, white and fleshy, and the nails were rosy. He was very proud of them; and, indeed, they would have become a bishop. Had you run across him in the day-time you would have found him in a shabby old coat, his trousers muddy, his shoes uncleaned, and in' a shocking old hat. But in the evening, at a party, he was grand in a blue coat with gold buttons, black trousers, a white waistcoat, black silk openwork socks, patent leather shoes, fine linen and yellow gloves. His clothes never fitted him, and Lamartine adds that he looked like a school-boy who has grown so much in the year that he's bursting out of them.

Balzac's contemporaries are agreed that at this time he was ingenuous, childish, kindly and genial. George Sand wrote that he was sincere to the point of modesty, boastful to the point of braggadocio, confident, expansive, very good and quite crazy, drunk on water, intemperate in work and sober in other passions, equally matter-of-fact and romantic, credulous and sceptical, puzzling and contrary. He was not a good talker. He was not quick in the uptake, and he had no gift of repartee; his conversation was neither allusive nor ironical; but as a monologuist his verve was irresistible. He roared with laughter at what he was going to say, and everybody laughed with him. They laughed to listen to him, and they laughed to look at him; André Billy says that the phrase, "he burst out laughing", might have been invented for him.

The best life of Balzac has been written by André Billy, and it is from his admirable book that I have gained the information which I now propose to impart to the reader. The novelist's real name was Balssa, and his ancestors were farm-labourers and weavers; but his father, who started life as clerk to an attorney, having after the Revolution come up in the world changed his name to Balzac. At the age of fifty-one he married the daughter of a draper who had made a fortune by govern-ment contracts, and Honoré, the eldest of his four children, was born in 1799 at Tours, where his father was administrator of the hospital. He had presumably got the job because Madame Balzac's father, the ex-draper, had somehow become director-general of the Paris hospitals. Honoré appears to have been idle and troublesome at school. At the end of 1814 his father was put in charge of the catering to a division of the army in Paris and moved there with his family. It was decided that Honoré should become an attorney and, after passing the necessary examinations, he entered the office of a certain Maître Guyonnet. How he got on there is pretty well indicated by a note sent him one morning by the head clerk: "Monsieur Balzac is requested not to come to the office to-day, as there is a lot of work." In 1819 his father was retired on a pension and decided to live in the country. He settled down at Ville-parisis, a village on the road to Meaux. Honoré stayed in Paris, since it had been decided that a friend of the family, a lawyer, should hand over his business to him when, after a few years of practice, he was competent to deal with it.

But Honoré rebelled. He wanted to be a writer. He insisted on being a writer. There were violent family scenes; but at last, notwithstanding the continuous opposition of his mother, a severe and practical woman whom he never liked, his father yielded so far as to give him a chance. It was arranged that he should have two years to see what he could do. He installed himself in an attic at sixty francs a year, and furnished it with a table, two chairs, a bed, a wardrobe and an empty bottle to serve as a candlestick. He was twenty. Free.

The first thing he did was to write a tragedy; and when his sister was about to be married and he went home, he took his play with him. He read it to the assembled family and two of their friends. All agreed that it was worthless. It was then sent to a professor, whose verdict was that the author should do whatever else he liked, but not write. Balzac, angry and discouraged, went back to Paris. He decided that, since he could not be a tragic poet, he would be a novelist, and he wrote two or three novels inspired by those of Walter Scott, Anne Radcliffe and Maturin. But his parents had come to the conclusion that the experiment had failed, and they ordered him to come back to Villeparisis by the first stage-coach. Presently a friend, a hack writer whose acquaintance Balzac had made in the Latin Quarter, came to see him and suggested that they should write a novel in collaboration. So began a long series of potboilers which he wrote sometimes alone, sometimes in collaboration, under various pseudonyms. No one knows how many books he turned out between 1821 and 1825. Some authorities claim as many as fifty. I don't know that anyone has read them in quantity except George Saintsbury, and he acknowledges that it required an effort. They were for the most part historical, for then Walter Scott was at the height of his fame and they were designed to cash in on his great vogue. They were very bad, but they had their use in teaching Balzac the value of swift action to hold the reader's attention, and the value of dealing with the subjects that people regard as of primary importance—love, wealth, honour and life. It may be that they taught him, too, what his own proclivities must also have suggested to him, that to be read the author must concern himself with passion. Passion may be base, trivial or unnatural, but, if violent enough, is not without some trace of grandeur.

While thus engaged, Balzac lived at home. There he made the acquaintance of a neighbour, a Madame de Berny, the daughter of a German musician who had been in the service of Marie Antoinette and of one of her maids. She was forty-five. Her husband was sick and querulous; she had had, however, six children by him, besides one by a lover. She became Balzac's friend, then his mistress, and remained devoted to him till her death fourteen years later. It was a curious relation. He loved her as a lover, but he transferred to her, besides, the love he had never felt for his mother. She was not only a mistress, but a confidant, whose advice, encouragement and disinterested affection were always his for the asking. The affair gave rise to scandal in the village, and Madame Balzac, as was natural, highly disapproved of her son's entanglement with a woman old enough to be his mother. His books, moreover, brought in little money, and she was concerned about his future. An acquaintance suggested that he should go into business, and the idea seems to have appealed to him. Madame de Berny put up forty-five thousand francs, and with a couple of partners he became a publisher, a printer and a type-founder. He was a poor business man and wildly extravagant. He charged up to the firm his personal expenditure with jewellers, tailors, bootmakers, and even laundresses. At the end of three years the firm went into liquidation, and his mother had to provide fifty thousand francs in order to pay his creditors.

Since money played so large a part in Balzac's existence, it is worth while to consider what these sums really amounted to. Fifty thousand francs was two thousand pounds, but two thousand pounds then was worth far, far more than it is worth now. It is difficult to say how much. Perhaps the best way is to state what at that time could be done on a certain number of francs. The Rastignacs were gentry. The family, consisting of six persons, lived in the provinces, thriftily, but according to their station with decency, on three thousand francs a year. When they sent their eldest son, Eugène, to Paris to study law, he took a room in the pension of Madame Vauquer and paid forty-five francs a month for board and lodging. Several young men had rooms out, but came in for their meals, since the house had a reputation for good food, and for this they paid thirty francs a month. Board and lodging to-day in an establishment of the same class as Madame Vauquer's would cost at least thirty-five thousand francs a month. The fifty thousand francs that Balzac's mother paid to save him from bankruptcy would be equivalent now to a very considerable sum.

The experience, though disastrous, provided him with a good deal of special information and a knowledge of business which were useful to him in the novels he afterwards wrote.

After the crash, Balzac went to stay with friends in Brittany, and there found the material for a novel, *Les Chouans*, which was his first serious work, and the first which he signed with his own name. He was thirty. From then on, he wrote with frenzied industry till his death twenty-one years later. The number of his works is astounding. Every year produced one or two long novels, and a dozen novelettes and short stories. Besides this, he wrote a number of plays, some of which were never accepted, and, of those that were, all, with one exception, lamentably failed. At least once, for a short period, he conducted a newspaper, most of which he wrote himself. When at work, he led a chaste and regular life. He went to bed soon after his evening meal, and was wakened by his servant at one. He got up, put on his white robe, immaculate, for he claimed that to write one should be clad in garments without spot or stain; and then by candle-light, fortifying himself with cup after cup of black coffee, wrote with a quill from a raven's wing. He stopped writing at seven, took a bath (in principle) and lay down. Between eight and nine his publisher came to bring him proofs, or get a piece of manuscript from him; then he set to work again till noon, when he ate boiled eggs, drank water and had more coffee; he worked till six, when he had his light dinner, which he washed down with a little Vouvray. Sometimes a friend or two would drop in, but after a little conversation, he went to bed. Though when alone he was thus abstemious, in company he ate voraciously. One of Balzac's publishers declares that at one meal he saw him devour a hundred oysters, twelve cutlets, a duck, a brace of partridges, a sole, a number of sweets and a dozen pears. It is not surprising that in time he became very fat and his belly enormous. Gavarni says that he ate like a hog. His table manners were certainly inelegant: that he used a knife to eat with, in preference to a fork, does not offend me—I have no doubt that Louis XIV did, too; but I recoil at Balzac's habit of blowing his nose in his napkin.

He was a great note-taker. Wherever he went he had his notebook with him, and when he happened upon something that might be useful to him, hit upon an idea of his own or was taken with someone else's, he jotted it down. When possible, he visited the scene of his stories, and sometimes drove long distances to see a street or a house that he wished to describe. He chose the names of his characters with care, for he had a notion that the name should correspond with the personality and appearance of the individual who bore it. It is generally conceded that he wrote badly. George Saintsbury thought this was owing to the fact that for ten years he had written, post-haste, a mass of novels just to make a bare living. That does not convince me. Balzac was a vulgar man (but was not his vulgarity an integral part of his genius?) and his prose was vulgar. It was prolix, portentous and too often incorrect.

357

Emile Faguet, a critic, in his time, of importance, has given in his book on Balzac a whole chapter to the faults of taste, style, syntax and language of which the author was guilty; and, indeed, some of them are so gross that it needs no profound knowledge of French to perceive them. Balzac had no feeling for the elegance of his native tongue. It can never have occurred to him that prose may have a comeliness and a grace as delightful in its different way as verse. But for all that, when his exuberant volubility did not run away with him, he could give succinct and pithy expression to the apophthegms and maxims that are scattered about his novels. Neither in their matter nor in their manner would they have dishonoured La Rochefoucauld.

Balzac was not a writer who knew what he wanted to say from the start. He began with a rough draft, which he re-wrote and corrected so drastically that the manuscript which he finally sent to the printers was almost impossible to decipher. The proof was returned to him, and this he treated as if it were but an outline of the projected work. He not only added words, he added sentences, not only sentences but paragraphs, and not only paragraphs but chapters. When his proofs were once more set up, with all the alterations and corrections he had made, and a fair set delivered to him, he went to work on them again and made more changes. Only after this would he consent to publication, and then only on condition that in a future edition he should be allowed to make further revisions. The expense of all this was great, and resulted in constant quarrels with his publishers.

The story of Balzac's relations with editors is long, dull and sordid, and I will deal with it very shortly. He was unscrupulous. He would get an advance on a book and guarantee to deliver it at a certain date; and then, tempted by an offer of quick money, would stop working on it to give another editor or publisher a novel or a story he had written with haste. Actions were brought against him for breach of contract, and the costs and damages he had to pay greatly increased his already heavy debts. For no sooner did success come to him, bringing him contracts for books he was engaged to write (and sometimes never did), than he moved into a spacious apartment, which he furnished at great cost, and bought a cabriolet and a pair of horses. He engaged a groom, a cook and a manservant, bought clothes for himself and a livery for his groom, and quantities of plate that he decorated with a coat of arms which did not belong to him. It was that of an ancient family, by name Balzac d'Entragues, and he assumed it when he added the *de*, the *particule*, to his own name to make believe that he was of noble birth. To pay for all this splendour, he borrowed from his sister, his friends, his publishers, and signed bills that he kept on renewing. His debts increased, but he continued to buy—jewellery, porcelain, cabinets, pieces of buhl, pictures, statues; he had his books bound gorgeously in morocco, and one of his many canes was studded with turquoises. For one dinner he gave, he had his dining-room refurnished and the decoration entirely changed. At intervals, when his creditors were more than usually pressing, many of these possessions were pawned; now and then the brokers came in, seized his furniture, and sold it by public auction. Nothing could cure him. To the end of his life, he went on buying with senseless extravagance. He was a shameless borrower, but so great was the admiration his genius excited that he seldom exhausted the generosity of his friends. Women are not as a rule willing lenders, but Balzac apparently found them easy. He was completely lacking in delicacy, and there is no sign that he had qualms about taking money from them.

It will be remembered that his mother had cut into her fortune to save him from bankruptcy; the dowries of her two daughters had further reduced her means, and at last the only property she had left was a house she owned in Paris. The time came when she found herself so desperately in need that she wrote a letter to her son, which André Billy quoted in the first edition of his *Vie de Balzac*, and which I shall translate: "The last letter I had from you was in November 1834. In it you agreed to give me, from April 1st, 1835, two hundred francs every quarter to help me with my rent and my maid. You understood that I could not live as fitted my poverty; you had made your name too conspicuous and your luxury too obvious for the difference in our situations not to be shocking. Such a promise as you made me was for you, I think, an acknowledged debt. It is now April 1837, which means that you owe me for two years. Of these 1600 francs, you gave me last December 500 francs, as though they were a charity churlishly bestowed. Honoré, for two years my life has been a constant nightmare. You weren't able to help me, I don't doubt it, but the result is that the sums I've borrowed on my house have diminished its value and now I can raise no more, and everything I have of value is in pawn; and that I've at last come to the moment when I have to say to you: 'Bread, my son.' For several weeks I've been eating what was given me by my good son-in-law, but, Honoré, it can't go on like that: it seems that you have the means to make long and costly journeys of all sorts, costly in money and in reputation—for yours will be cruelly compromised when you come back because of the contracts you have failed to keep—when I think of all this my heart breaks! My son, as you've been able to afford . . . mistresses, mounted canes, rings, silver, furniture, your mother may also without indiscretion ask you to carry out your promise. She has waited to do so till the last moment, but it has come . . ."

To this letter he replied: "I think you'd better come to Paris and have an hour's talk with me."

His biographer says that since genius has its rights, the conduct of Balzac should not be judged by ordinary standards. That is a matter of opinion. I think it better to admit that he was selfish, unscrupulous and dishonest. The best excuse one can make for his financial shiftiness is that with his buoyant, optimistic temper he was always firmly convinced that he was going to make vast sums out of his writings (for the time he made a great deal) and fabulous amounts out of the specula-tions which one after another tempted his ardent imagination. But, whenever he actually engaged in one, the result was to leave him still more heavily in debt. He could never have been the writer he was if he had been sober, practical and thrifty. He was a show-off; he adored luxury, and he could not help spending money. He worked like a dog to fulfil his obligations, but, unfortunately, before ever he paid off his more pressing debts he had contracted new ones. There is one curious fact worth mentioning. It was only under the pressure of debt that he could bring himself to write. Then he would work till he was pale and worn out, and in these circumstances he wrote some of his best novels; but when by some miracle he was not in harrowing straits, when the brokers left him in peace, when editors and publishers were not bringing actions, his invention seemed to fail him and he could not bring himself to put pen to paper. He claimed to the end of his life that it was his mother who had ruined him; that was a shocking thing to say; for, it was he who had ruined her.

3

Balzac's literary success brought him, as success does, many new friends; and his immense vitality, his radiant good humour, his charm, made him a welcome guest in all but the most exclusive *salons*. One great lady to be attracted by his celebrity was the Marquise de Castries, the daughter of the Duc de Maillé and niece of the Duc de Fitz-James, a direct descendant of James the Second. She wrote to him under an assumed name, he answered, and she wrote again disclosing her identity. He called upon her; he pleased, and presently he went to see her every day. She was pale, blonde, flower-like. He fell in love with her; but though she allowed him to kiss her aristocratic hands, she resisted his further advances. He scented himself, he put on new yellow gloves every day: it availed him nothing. He grew impatient and irritable, and began to suspect that she was playing with him. The fact is plain that she wanted an admirer and not a lover. It was doubtless flattering to have a clever young man, already famous, at her feet, but she had no intention of becoming his mistress. The crisis came at Geneva, where, with her uncle, Fitz-James, as a chaperon, she and Balzac were staying on their way to Italy. No one knows exactly what happened. Balzac and the Marquise went for an excursion, and he returned in tears. It may be supposed that he made summary demands on her, which she rejected in a manner that deeply mortified him. Pained and angry, feeling himself abominably used, he went back to Paris. But he was not a novelist for nothing; every experience, even the most humiliating, was grist to his mill; and Madame de Castries was to serve in future as a model for the heartless flirt of high rank.

While still laying fruitless siege to her, Balzac had received a fan-letter from Odessa signed *L'Étrangère*. A second, similarly signed, arrived after the break. He put an advertisement in the only French paper allowed to enter Russia: "M. de B has received the communication sent to him; he has only this day been able by this paper to acknowledge it and regrets that he does not know where to send his reply." The writer was Eveline Hanska, a Polish lady of noble birth and great wealth. She was thirty-two, and married, but her husband was in the fifties. She had had five children by him, but only one, a girl, was living. She saw Balzac's advertisement, and so arranged that she might receive his letters if he wrote to her in care of a bookseller at Odessa. A correspondence cnsued.

Thus began what Balzac was wont to call the great passion of his life.

The letters soon grew intimate. In the high-flown manner of the time, Balzac so laid bare his heart as to arouse the lady's pity and sympathy. She was romantic, and bored with the monotony of life in the great château in the Ukraine in the middle of fifty thousand acres of dull country. She admired the author, she was interested in the man. When they had been exchanging letters for a couple of years, Madame Hanska, with her elderly husband, who was in poor health, her daughter, a governess and a retinue of servants, went to Neufchâtel in Switzerland; and there, on her invitation, Balzac went too. There is a pleasant, but too fanciful, account of how they met. Balzac was walking in the public gardens when he saw a lady seated on a bench reading a book. She dropped her handkerchief, and on politely picking it up he noticed that the book was one of his. He spoke. It was the woman he had come to see. She was then a handsome creature, of somewhat opulent charms; her eyes were fine, though with ever so slight a cast, her hair was beautiful and her mouth ravishing. She may have been a trifle taken aback at the first sight of this short, fat, red-faced man, like a butcher to look at, who had written her such lyrical and passionate letters; but if she was, the brilliance of his gold-flecked eyes, his exuberant vitality, his animation, the rare goodness of his heart, made her forget the shock, and in the five days he spent at Neufchâtel he became her lover. He was obliged to return to Paris, and they parted with the arrangement that they should meet again early in the winter at Geneva. He arrived for Christmas and passed six weeks there, during which, in the intervals of making love to Madame Hanska, he wrote *La Duchesse de Langeais*, in which he revenged himself on Madame de Castries for the affront she had made him suffer. He left Geneva with Madame Hanska's promise to marry him when her spouse, whose health had not improved, left her a widow. Soon after getting back to Paris, however, Balzac met the Countess Guidoboni-Visconti and was immediately fascinated by her. She was an Englishwoman, an ash-blonde, and, notwithstanding her nationality, voluptuous; and notoriously unfaithful to her easy-going Italian husband. It was not long before she became Balzac's mistress. But the romantics of those days conducted their love affairs in a blaze of publicity, and soon Eveline Hanska, then living in Vienna, heard what had happened. She wrote Balzac a letter full of bitter reproaches, and announced that she was about to return to the Ukraine. It was an appalling blow. He had been counting on marrying her on the death of her ailing lord, an event which he persuaded himself could not be long delayed, and being put in possession of her vast fortune. He borrowed two thousand francs and hurried off to Vienna to make his peace. He travelled as the Marquis de Balzac, with his bogus coat of arms on the luggage, and a valet; this added to the expense of the journey since, as a man of title, it was beneath his dignity to haggle with hotel-keepers and he had to give tips suitable to the rank he had assumed. He arrived penniless. Fortunately, Eveline was generous; but she did not forbear to heap more reproaches on him, and he had to lie his head off to allay her suspicions. Three weeks later she left for the Ukraine, and they did not meet again for eight years.

Balzac went back to Paris and resumed his relations with the Countess Guidoboni. For her sake, he indulged in extravagance greater than ever. He was arrested for debt, and she paid the sum necessary to save him from going to prison. Thenceforward, from time to time she came to his rescue when his financial situation was desperate. In 1836 to his real grief Madame de Berny, his first mistress, died; and he said of her that she was the only woman he had ever loved: others have said that she was the only woman who had ever loved him. In the same year the blonde Countess informed him that she was with child by him. When it was born, her husband, a tolerant man, remarked: "Well, I knew that Madame wanted a dark child. So she's got what she wanted." Of his other affairs, I will mention only one, with a widow called Hélène de Valette, because it began, as had those with Madame de Castries and Eveline Hanska, with a fan-letter. It is odd that three of his five chief love affairs should have so started. It may be that that is why they were unsatisfactory. When a woman is attracted to a man by his fame, she is too much concerned with the credit she may get through the connection with him to be capable of that blessed something of disinterestedness that genuine love evokes. She is a thwarted exhibitionist who snatches at a chance to gratify her instinct. The affair with Hélène de Valette lasted four or five years. Oddly enough, Balzac broke off his relations with her because he discovered that she was not so highly connected as she had led him to believe. He had borrowed a large sum from her, and after his death she tried, seemingly in vain, to get it back from his widow.

Meanwhile, he continued to correspond with Eveline Hanska. His early letters left no doubt about the nature of their relations, and two of them, which Eveline had left carelessly in a book, were read by her husband. Balzac, apprised of this embarrassing occurrence, wrote to M. Hanski and told him that they were merely a joke; Eveline had taunted him with the fact that he could not write a love letter, and he had written those two to show how well he could. The explanation was thin, but M. Hanski apparently accepted it. After that, Balzac's letters were sufficiently discreet, and it was only indirectly, expecting her to read between the lines, that he was able to assure Eveline that he loved her as passionately as ever and longed for the day when they could be united for the rest of their lives. The suggestion is plausible that during an absence of eight years, in which time, besides passing flutters, he had had two serious affairs, one with the Countess Guidoboni, the other with Hélène de Valette, his love for Eveline Hanska was somewhat less ardent than he pretended. Balzac was a novelist, and it is natural enough that, when he sat down to write a letter to her, he should have thrown himself into his character of the love-lorn swain as easily as when, wanting to give an example of Lucien de Rubempré's literary gift, he threw himself into the character of a brilliant young journalist and wrote an admirable article. I have little doubt that when he wrote a love letter to Eveline he felt exactly what he eloquently said. She had promised to marry him on her husband's death, and his future security depended on her keeping her word; no one can blame him if in his letters he forced the note a little. For eight interminable years Monsieur Hanski had enjoyed moderate health. He died suddenly. The moment Balzac had been so long awaiting arrived, and at last his dream was to come true. At last he was going to be rich. At last he was to be free of his petty bourgeois debts.

But the letter in which Eveline told him of her husband's death was followed by another, in which she told him that she would not marry him. She could not forgive him his infidelities, his extravagance, his debts. He was reduced to despair. She had told him in Vienna that she did not expect him to be physically faithful so long as she had his heart. Well, that she had always had. He was outraged by her injustice. He came to the conclusion that he could only win her back by seeing her, and so, after a good deal of correspondence, notwithstanding her marked reluctance, he made the journey to St. Petersburg, where she then was to settle her husband's affairs. His calculations proved correct; both were fat and middle-aged; he was forty-three and she was forty-two; but it looked as though, such was his charm, such his vitality and the power of his genius, when with him she could refuse him nothing. They became lovers again, and again she promised to marry him. It was seven years before she kept her word. Why she hesitated so long has puzzled the biographers, but surely the reasons are not far to seek. She was a great lady, proud of her noble lineage, as proud as Prince Andrew in *War and Peace* was of his, and it is likely enough that she saw a great difference between being the mistress of a celebrated author and the wife of a vulgar upstart. Her family did all they could to persuade her not to contract such an unsuitable alliance. She had a marriageable daughter, whom it was her duty to settle in accordance with her rank and circumstances: Balzac was a notorious spendthrift; she may well have feared that he would play ducks and drakes with her fortune. He was always wanting money from her. He did not dip into her purse, he plunged both hands into it. She was rich, and herself extravagant, but it is very different to fling your money about for your own pleasure and to have someone else fling it about for his.

The strange thing is not that Eveline Hanska waited so long to marry Balzac, but that she married him at all. They saw one another from time to time, and as a result of one of these meetings she became pregnant. Balzac was enchanted. He thought he had won her at last and begged her to marry him at once; but she, unwilling to have her hand forced, wrote to tell him that after her confinement she intended to go back to the Ukraine to economize and would marry him later. The child was born dead. This was in 1845 or 1846. She married Balzac in 1850. He had spent the winter in the Ukraine, and the ceremony took place there. Why did she at last consent? She didn't want to marry him. She never had. She was a devout woman and at one time had seriously thought of entering a convent: perhaps her confessor urged her to regularize her unconventional situation. During the winter Balzac's prolonged and arduous labour, his abuse of strong coffee, had at length shattered his vigorous constitution, and his health failed. Heart and lungs were affected. It was evident that he had not long to live. Perhaps Eveline was moved to pity for a dying man who, notwithstanding his infidelities, had loved her so long. Her brother Adam Rzewuski wrote to beg her not to marry Balzac, and her reply is quoted by Pierre Descaves in *Les Cent Jours de M. de Balzac*: "No, no, no . . . I owe something to the man who has suffered so much by me and for me, whose inspiration and whose joy I have been. He is ill; his days are numbered! . . . He has been betrayed so often; I shall remain faithful to him, in spite of everything and notwithstanding everything, faithful to the ideal that he has made of me, and if, as the doctors say, he must soon die, let it be at least with his hand in mine, and with the image of me in his heart, and may his last glance be fixed on me, on the woman he has loved so much, and who has loved him so sincerely and so truly." The letter is moving, and I don't see why we should doubt its sincerity.

She was no longer a rich woman. She had dispossessed herself of her vast possessions in favour of her daughter and retained only an annuity. If Balzac was disappointed, he did not show it. The couple went to Paris, where, on Eveline's money, he had bought and expensively furnished a large house.

It is lamentable to have to relate that after all this eager waiting, when at last Balzac's hopes were realized, the marriage was not a success. They had lived together for months at a time in the Ukraine, and one would have thought that they must have come to know one another so well, with all their difficulties of character, that they would have fallen easily enough into the intimacy of married life. It is possible that mannerisms and tricks which Eveline had regarded with indulgence in a lover irritated her in a husband. For years Balzac had been in the position of a suppliant: it may be that when safely married he became dictatorial and high-handed. Eveline was haughty, exacting and quick-tempered. She had made great sacrifices to marry him, and she resented the fact that he did not seem properly grateful. She had always said that she would not marry him till all his debts were paid, and he had assured her that this was done; but, on arriving in Paris, she found that the house was mortgaged and that he still owed large sums. She had been accustomed to be mistress of a large house, with a score of house-serfs at her beck and call;

she was unused to French servants, and she resented the interference of Balzac's family in the management of her household.
She did not like them. She found them second-rate and
pretentious. The quarrels between husband and wife were so
bitter and so open that all their friends became aware of them.

Balzac had arrived in Paris ill. He grew worse. He took
to his bed. One complication followed another, and on the
17th of August, 1850, he died.

Eveline Hanska, like Kate Dickens and the Countess
Tolstoy, has had a bad press with posterity. She survived Balzac
for thirty-two years. At some sacrifice she paid his debts, and
gave his mother till her death the three thousand francs a year
which Balzac had promised her but never paid. She arranged
for a re-issue of his complete works. In connection with this, a
young man, Champfleury by name, came to see her within a
few months after her husband's death; and when, being very
much of a lady's man, he made advances to her there and then,
she did not resist. The affair lasted three months. He was
succeeded by a painter called Jean Gigoux; and the connection,
which one may presume from its length grew platonic, lasted
till her own death at the age of eighty-two. Posterity would
have preferred her to remain chaste and inconsolable for the
rest of her long life.

4

George Sand rightly said that each of Balzac's books was in
fact a page of one great book, which would be imperfect if he
had omitted that page. In 1833 he conceived the idea of
combining the whole of his production into one whole under
the name of *La Comédie Humaine*. When it occurred to him, he
ran to see his sister: "Salute me," he cried, "because I'm quite
plainly (*tout simplement*) on the way to become a genius." He
described as follows what he had in mind: "The social world
of France would be the historian, I should be merely the
secretary. In setting forth an inventory of vices and virtues, in
assembling the principal facts of the passions, in painting
characters, in choosing the principal incidents of the social

world, in composing types by combining the traits of several homogeneous characters, perhaps I could manage to write the history forgotten by so many historians, the history of manners and customs." It was an ambitious scheme. He did not live to carry it to completion. It is evident that some of the pages in the vast work he left, though perhaps necessary, are less interesting than others. In a production of such bulk, that was inevitable. But in almost all Balzac's novels there are two or three characters which, because they are obsessed by a simple, primitive passion, stand out with extraordinary force. It was in the depiction of just such characters that his strength lay; when he had to deal with a character of any complexity, he was less happy. In almost all his novels there are scenes of great power, and in several an absorbing story.

If I were asked by someone who had never read Balzac to recommend the novel which best represented him, which gave the reader pretty well all the author had to give, I should without hesitation advise him to read *Le Père Goriot*. The story it tells is continuously interesting. In some of his novels, Balzac interrupts his narrative to discourse on all sorts of irrelevant matters, or to give you long accounts of people in whom you cannot take the faintest interest; but from these defects *Le Père Goriot* is free. He lets his characters explain themselves by their words and actions as objectively as it was in his nature to do. The novel is extremely well constructed; and the two threads, the old man's self-sacrificing love for his ungrateful daughters, and the ambitious Rastignac's first steps in the crowded, corrupt Paris of his day, are ingeniously interwoven. It illustrates the principles which in *La Comédie Humaine* Balzac was concerned to bring to light: "Man is neither good nor bad, he is born with instincts and aptitudes; the world (*la société*), far from corrupting him, as Rousseau pretended, perfects him, makes him better; but self-interest then enormously develops his evil propensities."

So far as I know, it was in *Le Père Goriot* that Balzac first conceived the notion of bringing the same characters into novel after novel. The difficulty of this is that you must create characters who interest you so much that you want to know what happens to them. Balzac here triumphantly succeeds and, speaking for myself, I read with added enjoyment the novels in which I learn what has become of certain persons, Rastignac for instance, whose future I am eager to know about. Balzac himself was profoundly interested in them. He had at one time as his secretary a man of letters called Jules Sandeau, who is chiefly known in literary history as one of George Sand's many lovers: he had gone home because his sister was dying; she died, and he buried her; and on his return Balzac, having offered his condolences and asked after Sandeau's family, said, so the story goes: "Come, that's enough of that, let's get back to serious things. Let's talk of Eugénie Grandet." The device which Balzac adopted (and which, incidentally, Sainte-Beuve in a moment of petulance roundly condemned) is useful because it is an economy of invention; but I cannot believe that Balzac, with his marvellous fertility, resorted to it on that account. I think he felt that it added reality to his narrative, for in the ordinary course of events we have repeated contacts with a fair proportion of the same people; but more than that, I think his main object was to knit his whole work together in a comprehensive unity. His aim, as he said himself, was not to depict a group, a set, a class or even a society, but a period and a civilization. He suffered from the delusion, not uncommon to his countrymen, that France, whatever disasters had befallen it, was the centre of the universe; but perhaps it was just on that account that he had the self-assurance to create a world, multicoloured, various and profuse, and the power to give it the convincing throb of life.

Balzac started his novels slowly. A common method with him was to begin with a detailed description of the scene of action. He took so much pleasure in these descriptions that he often tells you more than you need to know. He never learned the art of saying only what has to be said, and not saying what needn't be said. Then he tells you what his characters look like, what their dispositions are, their origins, habits, ideas and defects; and only after this sets out to tell his story. His characters are seen through his own exuberant temperament and their reality is not quite that of real life; they are painted in primary colours, vivid and sometimes garish, and they are more exciting than ordinary people; but they live and breathe; and you believe in them, I think, because Balzac himself intensely believed in them, so intensely indeed that when he was dying he cried: "Send for Bianchon. Bianchon will save me." This was the clever, honest doctor who appears in many of the novels. He is one of the very few disinterested characters to be met with in *La Comédie Humaine*.

I believe Balzac to have been the first novelist to use a boarding-house as the setting for a story. It has been used many times since, for it is a convenient way of enabling the author to present together a variety of characters in sundry predicaments, but I don't know that it has ever been used with such happy effect as in *Le Père Goriot*. We meet in this novel perhaps the most thrilling character that Balzac ever created—Vautrin. The type has been reproduced a thousand times, but never with such striking and picturesque force, nor with such convincing realism. Vautrin has a good brain, will-power and immense vitality. These were traits that appealed to Balzac, and, ruthless criminal though he was, he fascinated his author. It is worth the reader's while to notice how skilfully, without giving away a secret he wanted to keep till the end of the book, he has managed to suggest that there is something sinister about the man. He is jovial, generous and good-natured; he has great physical strength, he is clever and self-possessed; you cannot but admire him, and sympathize with him, and yet he is strangely frightening. He obsesses you, as he did Rastignac, the ambitious, well-born young man who comes to Paris to make his way in the world; but you feel in the convict's company the same uneasiness as Rastignac felt. Vautrin is a great creation.

His relations with Eugène de Rastignac are admirably presented. Vautrin sees into the young man's heart and proceeds subtly to sap his moral sense: true, Eugène revolts when he learns to his horror that Vautrin has had a man killed to enable him to marry an heiress; but the seeds are sown.

Le Père Goriot ends with the old man's death. Rastignac goes to his funeral and afterwards, remaining alone in the cemetery, surveys Paris lying below him along the two banks of the Seine. His eyes dwell on that part of the city in which reside the denizens of the great world he wishes to enter. "*À nous deux maintenant*," he cries. It may interest the reader who has not felt inclined to read all the novels in which Rastignac plays a part, more or less conspicuous, to know what came of Vautrin's influence. Madame de Nucingen, old Goriot's daughter and the wife of the rich banker, the Baron de Nucingen, having fallen in love with him, took and expensively furnished for him an apartment, and provided him with money to live like a gentleman. Since her husband kept her short of cash, Balzac has not made clear how she managed to do this: perhaps he thought that when a woman in love needs money to support a lover she will somehow manage to get it. The Baron seems to have taken a tolerant view of the situation, and in 1826 made use of Rastignac in a financial transaction in which a number of the young man's friends were ruined, but from which he, as his share of the swag, received from Nucingen four hundred thousand francs. On part of this he dowered his two sisters, so that they could make good marriages, and was left with twenty thousand francs a year: "The price of keeping a stable", he told his friend Bianchon. Being thus no longer dependent on Madame de Nucingen, and realizing that a liaison that lasts too long has all the drawbacks of marriage, without its advantages, he made up his mind to throw her over and become the lover of the Marquise d'Espard, not because he was in love with her, but because she was rich, a great lady and influential. "Perhaps some day I'll marry her," he added. "She'll put me in a position in which at length I shall be able to pay my debts." This was in 1828. It is uncertain whether Madame d'Espard succumbed to his blandishments, but if she did, the affair did not last long, and he continued to be the lover of Madame de Nucingen. In 1831 he thought of marrying an Alsatian girl, but drew back on discovering that her fortune was not so great as he had been led to believe. In 1832, through the influence of Henry de Marsay, a former lover of Madame de Nucingen, who, Louis Philippe being then King of France, was a Minister, Rastignac was made Under-Secretary of State. He was able, while holding this office, largely to increase his fortune. His relations with Madame de Nucingen apparently continued till 1835, when, perhaps by mutual agreement, they were broken off; and three years later he married her daughter Augusta. Since she was the only child of a very rich man, Rastignac did well for himself. In 1839 he was created a Count and again entered the Ministry. In 1845 he was made a peer of France and had an income of three hundred thousand francs a year (£12,000), which for the time was great wealth.

Balzac had a marked predilection for Rastignac. He endowed him with noble birth, good looks, charm, wit; and made him immensely attractive to women. Is it fanciful to suggest that he saw in Rastignac the man he would have given all but his fame to be? Balzac worshipped success. Perhaps Rastignac was a rascal, but he succeeded. True, his fortune was founded on the ruin of others, but they were fools to let themselves be taken in by him, and Balzac had little sympathy with fools. Lucien de Rubempré, another of Balzac's adventurers, failed because he was weak; but Rastignac, because he had courage, determination and strength, succeeded. From the day when, at Père-Lachaise, he had flung his challenge in the face of Paris, he had let nothing stand in his way. He had resolved to conquer Paris; he conquered it. Balzac could not bring himself, I fancy, to regard Rastignac's moral delinquencies with censure. And after all, he was a good sort: though ruthless and unscrupulous where his interests were concerned, he was to the end ever willing to do a service to the old friends of his poverty-stricken youth. From the beginning, his aim had been to live in splendour, to have a fine house with a host of servants, carriages and horses, a string of mistresses and a rich wife. He had achieved his aim: I don't suppose it ever occurred to Balzac that it was a vulgar one.

CHAPTER SIX

Charles Dickens and *David Copperfield*

I

CHARLES DICKENS, though far from tall, was graceful and of a pleasing appearance. A portrait of him, painted by Maclise when he was twenty-seven, is in the National Portrait Gallery. He is seated in a handsome chair at a writing-table, with a small, elegant hand resting lightly on a manuscript. He is grandly dressed, and wears a vast satin neck-cloth. His brown hair is curled and falls well below the ears down each side of his face. His eyes are fine; and the thoughtful expression he wears is such as an admiring public might expect of a very successful young author. What the portrait does not show is the animation, the shining light, the activity of heart and mind, which those who came in contact with him saw in his countenance. He was always something of a dandy, and in his youth favoured velvet coats, gay waistcoats, coloured neck-cloths and white hats; but he never quite achieved the effect he sought: people were surprised and even shocked by his dress, which they described as both slipshod and flashy.

His grandfather, William Dickens, began life as a footman, married a housemaid and eventually became steward at Crewe Hall, the seat of John Crewe, Member of Parliament for Chester. William Dickens had two sons, William and John; but the only one that concerns us is John, first because he was the father of England's greatest novelist, and secondly because he served as a model for his son's greatest creation, Mr. Micawber. William Dickens died, and his widow stayed on at Crewe Hall as housekeeper. After thirty-five years she was pensioned off, and, perhaps to be near her two sons, went to live in London. The Crewes educated her fatherless boys, and provided them with a means of livelihood. They got John a post in the Navy Pay Office. There he made friends with a fellow-clerk and

374

presently married his sister, Elizabeth Barrow. From the beginning of his married life he appears to have been in financial trouble, and he was always ready to borrow money from anyone who was foolish enough to lend it. But he was kind-hearted and generous, no fool, industrious, though perhaps but fitfully; and he evidently had a taste for good wine, since the second time he was arrested for debt, it was at the suit of a wine-merchant. He is described in later life as an old buck who dressed well and was for ever fingering the large bunch of seals attached to his watch.

Charles, the first son, but second child, of John and Elizabeth Dickens, was born in 1812 at Portsea. Two years later his father was transferred to London, and three years after that to Chatham. There the little boy was put to school, and there he began to read. His father had collected a few books, *Tom Jones*, *The Vicar of Wakefield*, *Gil Blas*, *Don Quixote*, *Roderick Random*, *Peregrine Pickle*; Charles read and re-read them. His own novels show how great and persistent an influence they had on him.

In 1822 John Dickens, who by this time had five children, was moved back to London. Charles was left at Chatham to continue his schooling, and did not rejoin his family for some months. He found them settled in Camden Town on the outskirts of the city, in a house which he was later to describe as the home of the Micawbers. John Dickens, though earning a little more than three hundred pounds a year, which to-day would be equivalent to at least four times as much, was apparently in more than usually desperate straits, and it would seem that there was not enough money to send little Charles to school again. To the boy's disgust, he was put to minding the children, cleaning the boots, brushing the clothes and helping the maid Mrs. Dickens had brought with her from Chatham with the housework. In the intervals he roamed about Camden Town, "a desolate place surrounded by fields and ditches", and the neighbouring Somers Town and Kentish Town, and sometimes he was taken farther afield and got a glimpse of Soho and Limehouse.

Things grew so bad that Mrs. Dickens decided to open a

school for the children of parents living in India; she borrowed money, presumably from her mother-in-law, and had hand-bills printed for distribution, which her own children were sent to push into the letter-boxes in the neighbourhood. Naturally enough, no pupils were brought. Debts meanwhile grew more and more pressing. Charles was sent to pawn whatever articles they had on which cash could be raised; the books, the precious books which meant so much to him, were sold. Then James Lamert, vaguely related by marriage to Mrs. Dickens, offered Charles a job at six shillings a week in a blacking factory of which he was part-owner. His parents thankfully accepted the offer, but it cut the boy to the quick that they should be so manifestly relieved to get him off their hands. He was twelve years old. Shortly afterwards, John Dickens was arrested for debt and taken to the Marshalsea; and there his wife, after pawning the little that was left to pawn, joined him with her children. The prison was filthy, insanitary and crowded, for not only was it occupied by the prisoners, but by the families they might, if they chose, bring with them; though whether they were allowed to do this to alleviate the hardships of prison life or because the unfortunate creatures had nowhere else to go, I do not know. If a debtor had money, loss of liberty was the worst of the inconveniences he had to endure, and this loss in some cases might be mitigated: particular prisoners were permitted, on observing certain conditions, to reside outside the prison walls. In the past, the warden was in the habit of practising outrageous extortion on the prisoners and often treated them with barbarous cruelty; but by the time John Dickens was consigned to jail the worst abuses had been done away with, and he was able to make himself sufficiently com-fortable. The faithful little maid lived out and came in daily to help with the children and prepare meals. He still had his salary of six pounds a week, but made no attempt to pay his debt; and it may be supposed that, content to be out of reach of his other creditors, he did not especially care to be released. He soon recovered his usual spirits. The other debtors "made him chairman of the committee by which they regulated the internal economy of the prison", and presently he was on cordial terms with everyone from the turnkeys to the meanest inmate. The biographers have been puzzled by the fact that John Dickens continued meanwhile to receive his wages. The only explanation appears to be that, since government clerks were appointed by influence, such an accident as being imprisoned for debt was not considered so grave a matter as to call for the drastic step of cutting off a salary.

At the beginning of his father's imprisonment, Charles lodged in Camden Town; but since this was a long way from the blacking factory, which was at Hungerford Stairs, Charing Cross, John Dickens found him a room in Lant Street, Southwark, which was near the Marshalsea. He was then able to breakfast and sup with his family. The work he was put to do was not hard; it consisted in washing the bottles, labelling them and tying them up. In April, 1824, Mrs. William Dickens, the Crewes' old housekeeper, died and left her savings to her two sons. John Dickens's debt was paid (by his brother), and he regained his freedom. He settled his family once more in Camden Town, and went back to work at the Navy Pay Office. Charles continued to wash bottles at the factory for a while, but then John Dickens quarrelled with James Lamert, "quarrelled by letter", wrote Charles later, "for I took the letter from my father to him which caused the explosion." James Lamert told Charles that his father had insulted him, and that he must go. "With a relief so strange that it was like oppression, I went home." His mother tried to smooth things down, so that Charles should retain his job and the weekly wage, seven shillings by then, which she still sorely needed; and for this he never forgave her. "I never afterwards forgot, I never shall forget, I never can forget that my mother was warm for my being sent back," he added. John Dickens, however, would not hear of it, and sent his son to a school, very grandly called the Wellington House Academy, in the Hampstead Road. He stayed there two and a half years.

It is difficult to make out how long the boy spent at the blacking factory: he was there early in February and was back with his family by June, so that at the outside he could not have been at the factory for more than four months. It appears, however, to have made a deep impression upon him, and he came to look upon the experience as so humiliating that he could not bear to speak of it. When John Forster, his intimate friend and first biographer, by chance hit upon some inkling of it, Dickens told him that he had touched upon a matter so painful that "even at the present hour", and this was twenty-five years later, "he could never lose the remembrance of it while he remembered anything."

We are so used to hearing eminent politicians and captains of industry boast of having in their early youth washed dishes and sold newspapers that it is hard for us to understand why Charles Dickens should have worked himself up into looking upon it as a great injury that his parents had done him when they sent him to the blacking factory, and a secret so shameful that it must be concealed. He was a merry, mischievous, alert boy, and already knew a good deal of the seamy side of life. From an early age he had seen to what a pass his father's improvidence reduced the family. They were poor people, and they lived as poor people. At Camden Town he was put to sweep and scrub; he was sent to pawn a coat or a trinket to buy food for dinner; and, like any other boy, he must have played in the streets with boys of the same sort as himself. He went to work at an age when at the time it was usual for boys of his class to go to work, and at a fair wage. His six shillings a week, presently raised to seven, was worth at least twenty-five to thirty shillings to-day. For a short time he had to feed himself on that, but later, when he lodged near enough to the Marshalsea to have breakfast and supper with his family, he only had to pay for his dinner. The boys he worked with were friendly, and it is hard to see why he should have found it such a degradation to consort with them. He had from time to time been taken to see his grandmother in Oxford Street, and he could hardly have helped knowing that she had spent her life in 'service'. It may be that John Dickens was a bit of a snob and made pretensions that had no basis, but a lad of twelve surely has little sense of social distinctions. One must suppose, further, that if Charles was sophisticated enough to think himself a cut above the other boys at the factory, he would be smart enough to understand how necessary his earnings were to his family. One would have expected it to be a source of pride to him that he was become a wage-earner.

As a result, one may presume, of Forster's discovery, Dickens wrote, and gave Forster, the fragment of autobiography from which the details of this episode in his life have been made known to us. As his imagination went to work on his recollections, he was filled, I suspect, with pity for the little boy he had been; he gave him the pain, the disgust, the mortification which he thought he, famous, affluent, beloved, would have felt if he had been in the little boy's place. And seeing it all so vividly, his generous heart bled, his eyes were dim with tears, as he wrote of the poor lad's loneliness and his misery at being betrayed by those in whom he had put his trust. I do not think he consciously exaggerated; he couldn't help exaggerating: his talent, his genius if you like, was based on exaggeration. It was by dwelling upon, and emphasizing, the comic elements in Mr. Micawber's character that he excited his readers' laughter; and it was by intensifying the pathos of Little Nell's slow decline that he reduced them to tears. He would not have been the novelist he was if he had failed to make his account of the four months he spent at the blacking factory as moving as he alone knew how to make it; and, as everyone knows, he used it again to harrowing effect in *David Copperfield*. For my part, I do not believe that the experience caused him anything like the suffering that in after years, when he was famous and respectable, a social as well as a public figure, he persuaded himself that it had; and I believe even less that, as biographers and critics have thought, it had a decisive effect on his life and work.

While still at the Marshalsea, John Dickens, fearing that as an insolvent debtor he would lose his job in the Navy Pay Office, solicited the head of his department to recommend him for a superannuation grant on the ground of his ill-health; and eventually, in consideration of his twenty-years' service and six children, he was granted "on compassionate grounds" a pension of one hundred and forty pounds a year. This was little enough for such a man as John Dickens to support a family and he had to find some means of adding to his income. He had somehow acquired a knowledge of shorthand; and with the help of his brother-in-law, who had connections with the press, he got employment as a parliamentary reporter. Charles remained at school till, at fifteen, he went to work as an errand-boy in a lawyer's office. He does not seem to have considered this beneath his dignity. He had joined what we now call the white-collar class. A few weeks later his father managed to get him engaged as a clerk in another lawyer's office at ten shillings a week, which in course of time rose to fifteen shillings. He found the life dull and, with the hope of bettering himself, studied shorthand—to such purpose that after eighteen months he was sufficiently competent to set up as a reporter in the Consistory Court of Doctors' Commons. By the time he was twenty he was qualified to report the debates in the House of Commons, and soon gained the reputation of being "the fastest and most accurate man in the Gallery".

Meanwhile, he had fallen in love with Maria Beadnell, the pretty daughter of a bank clerk. They met first when Charles was seventeen. Maria was a flirtatious young person, and she seems to have given him a good deal of encouragement. There may even have been a secret engagement between them. She was flattered and amused to have a lover, but Charles was penniless, and she can never have intended to marry him. When after two years the affair came to an end, and in true romantic fashion they returned one another's presents and letters, Charles thought his heart would break. They did not meet again till many years later. Maria Beadnell, long a married woman, dined with the celebrated Mr. Dickens and his wife: she was fat, commonplace and stupid. She served then as the model for Flora Finching in *Little Dorrit*. She had already served as the model for Dora in *David Copperfield*.

In order to be near the paper for which he was working, Dickens had taken lodgings in one of the dingy streets off the Strand, but, finding them unsatisfactory, he presently rented unfurnished rooms in Furnival's Inn. But before he could furnish these, his father was again arrested for debt, and he had to provide money for his keep at the sponging-house. "As it had to be assumed that John Dickens would not rejoin his family for some time," Charles took cheap lodgings for his family and camped out with his brother Frederick, whom he took to ljve with him in the "three-pair back" at Furnival's Inn. "Just because he was open-hearted as well as open-handed," wrote the late Una Pope-Hennessy in her very readable biography of Charles Dickens, "and seemed able to deal with difficulties of the kind easily, it became the custom in his family, and later on in his wife's family, to expect him to find money and appointments for as spineless a set of people as ever breadwinner was saddled with."

2

When he had been working for a year or so in the Gallery of the House of Commons, Dickens began to write a series of sketches of London life; the first were published in *The Monthly Magazine*, and later ones in *The Morning Chronicle*; he was paid nothing for them, but they attracted the attention of a publisher named Macrone, and on the author's twenty-fourth birthday they were issued in two volumes, with illustrations by Cruickshank, under the title *Sketches by Boz*. Macrone paid him one hundred and fifty pounds for the first edition. The book was well reviewed, and within a short time brought him an offer of further work. There was a vogue at the time for anecdotic novels of a humorous character, which were issued in monthly parts at a shilling, with comic illustrations. They were the remote ancestors of the funnies of our own time, and they had the same prodigious popularity. One day a partner in the firm of Chapman and Hall called upon Dickens to ask him to write a narrative about a club of amateur sportsmen to serve as a vehicle for the illustrations of a well-known artist. There were to be twenty numbers, and he offered fourteen pounds a month for what we should now call the serial rights, with further payments when later they were published as a book. Dickens protested that he knew nothing about sport and did not think he could write to order, but "the emolument was too tempting to resist". I need hardly say that the result was *The*

Posthumous Papers of the Pickwick Club. The first five numbers had no great success, but with the introduction of Sam Weller the circulation leaped up. By the time the work appeared in book form, Charles Dickens was famous. Though the critics made their reservations, his reputation was made. It is well to record that *The Quarterly Review*, speaking of him, said that "it requires no gift of prophecy to foretell his fate—he has risen like a rocket and he will come down like a stick". But indeed, throughout his career, while the public devoured his books the critics carped.

A couple of days before the appearance of the first number of *The Pickwick Papers*, in 1836, Dickens married Kate, the eldest daughter of George Hogarth, a colleague of Dickens on *The Morning Chronicle*. George Hogarth was the father of six sons and eight daughters. The daughters were small, plump, fresh-coloured and blue-eyed. Kate was the only one of marriageable age. That seems to have been the reason why Dickens married her rather than one of the others. After a short honeymoon, they settled down in Furnival's Inn and invited Kate's pretty sister, Mary Hogarth, a girl of sixteen, to live with them. Dickens accepted a contract to write another novel, *Oliver Twist*, and started it while he was still at work on *The Pickwick Papers*. This also was to appear in monthly numbers, and he devoted a fortnight to one and a fortnight to the other. Most novelists are so absorbed in the characters which are at the moment engaging their attention that, by no effort of will, they thrust back into their unconscious what other literary ideas they have had in mind; and that Dickens should have been able to switch, apparently with ease, from one story to another is an amazing feat.

He took a fancy to Mary Hogarth, and when Kate found herself with child and could not go about with him, Mary became his constant companion. Kate's baby was born, and as she might be expected to have several more, a move was made from Furnival's Inn to a house in Doughty Street. Mary grew every day more lovely and more delightful. One May evening, Dickens took Kate and Mary to a play; they enjoyed themselves and came home in high spirits. Mary was taken ill. A doctor was sent for. In a few hours she was dead. Dickens took the ring from her finger and put it on his own. He wore it till his death. He was prostrated with grief. Not long after, he wrote in his diary: "If she were with us now, the same winning, happy, amiable companion, sympathizing with all my thoughts and feelings more than anyone I know ever did or will, I think I should have nothing to wish for but a continuance of such happiness. But she is gone, and pray God I may one day, through his mercy, rejoin her." These are significant words, and they tell us a great deal. He arranged to be buried by Mary's side. I think that there can be no doubt that he had fallen deeply in love with her. We shall never know whether he was aware of it.

At the time of Mary's death, Kate was once more pregnant, and the shock brought on a miscarriage. When she was well enough, Charles took her for a short trip abroad so that they might both recover their spirits. By the summer he, at all events, had sufficiently done so to have a boisterous flirtation with a certain Eleanor P.

3

With *Oliver Twist, Nicholas Nickleby* and *The Old Curiosity Shop*, Dickens was soundly launched on his triumphant career. He was a hard worker, and for several years started to write a new book long before he had finished with the old one. He wrote to please and kept his eye on the public reaction to the monthly numbers in which many of his novels appeared, and it is interesting to learn that he had no intention of sending Martin Chuzzlewit to America till the declining sales showed that his numbers were not so attractive as usual. He was not the sort of author who looks upon popularity as something to be ashamed of. His success was enormous. But the life of a literary man who has achieved it is not as a rule eventful. It follows a uniform pattern. His profession obliges him to devote a certain number of hours a day to his work, and he discovers a routine to suit him. He is brought into contact with the celebrated people of the day, literary, artistic and polite. He is taken up by great ladies. He goes to parties and gives parties. He travels. He makes public appearances. This, broadly, was the pattern of Dickens's life. The success he enjoyed, indeed, was such as has been the fortune of few authors to experience. His energy seemed inexhaustible. Not only did he produce long novels in quick succession, he founded and edited magazines and, for a short period, even edited a daily paper; he wrote a quantity of occasional pieces; he delivered lectures, he spoke at banquets, and later gave readings of his works. He rode, he thought nothing of walking twenty miles a day, he danced and played the fool with gusto, he did conjuring tricks to amuse his children, he acted in amateur theatricals. He had always been fascinated by the theatre, and once had seriously thought of going on the stage; at that time he took lessons in elocution from an actor, learned parts by heart and practised before a mirror how to enter a room, sit down on a chair and make a bow. One must suppose that these accomplishments were useful to him when he was introduced into the world of fashion. The censorious, notwithstanding, thought him faintly vulgar and his mode of dress showy. Accent in England has always "placed" a man, and it is likely enough that Dickens, who had lived almost all his life in London, and in very modest circumstances, had something of a cockney accent. But he charmed by his good looks, the brightness of his eyes, his exuberance, vivacity and joyous laugh. He may have been dazzled by the adulation of which he was the object, but his head was not turned. He retained an attractive modesty. He was a genial, delightful, affectionate creature. He was one of those persons who, when they come into a room, bring with them delight.

Oddly enough, though he had an immense power of observation and, in course of time, came to be on familiar terms with persons in the higher ranks of society, he never succeeded in his novels in making such characters as he created in those walks of life quite credible. One of the commonest charges against him, during his lifetime, was that he couldn't draw a gentleman. His lawyers and lawyer's clerks, whom he had known when he worked in an office, have a distinctiveness of feature which is lacking in his doctors and parsons; he was at his best when dealing with the ragtag and bobtail among whom his boyhood was spent. It looks as though a novelist can only know intimately enough, to use them with profit as models for creatures of his own invention, the persons with whom he has been connected at an early age. A child's year, a boy's year, is much, much longer than the year of a grown-up man, and he is thus given what seems like all the time in the world to make himself aware of the idiosyncrasies of the people who form his environment. "One reason why many English writers have totally failed in describing the manners of upper life," wrote Henry Fielding, "may possibly be, that in reality they knew nothing of it. . . . Now it happens that this higher order of mortals is not to be seen, like all the rest of the human species, for nothing, in the streets, shops, and coffee houses: nor are they shown, like the upper ranks of animals, for so much a-piece. In short, this is a sight to which no persons are admitted without one or other of these qualifications, viz., either title or fortune, or, what is equivalent to both, the honourable profession of gamester. And, very unluckily for the world, persons so qualified very seldom care to take upon themselves the bad trade of writing; which is generally entered upon by the lower and poorer sort, as it is a trade which many think requires no kind of store to set up with."

As soon as circumstances permitted, the Dickenses moved into a new house in a more fashionable quarter, and ordered from firms of repute complete suites for the reception rooms and bedrooms. Thick pile carpets were laid on the floors and festooned curtains adorned the windows. They engaged a good cook, three maids and a manservant. They set up a carriage. They gave dinner parties, to which noble and distinguished people came. The profusion somewhat shocked Jane Carlyle, and Lord Jeffrey wrote to his friend, Lord Cockburn, that he had dined in the new house and had "a rather too sumptuous dinner for a man with a family and only beginning to be rich". It was part of the generosity of Dickens's spirit that he liked to surround himself with people, and after the meanness of his origins it is only natural that it should have pleased him to be lavish. But it cost money. His father and his father's family, his wife's family, were a constant drain on him. It was partly to meet his heavy expenses that he founded the first of his magazines, *Master Humphrey's Clock*, and to give it a good send-off published *The Old Curiosity Shop* in it.

In 1842, leaving the four children in the care of Georgina Hogarth, Kate's sister, but taking Kate with him, he went to America. He was lionized as no author has ever been before or since. But the trip was not a complete success. A hundred years ago the people of the United States, though ready enough to disparage things European, were exceedingly sensitive of any criticism of themselves. A hundred years ago the press of the United States was ruthless in its invasion of the privacy of any hapless person who was "news". A hundred years ago in the United States the publicity-minded looked upon the distinguished foreigner as a God-given opportunity to get into the limelight, and called him conceited and supercilious when he showed a disinclination to be treated like a monkey in a zoo. A hundred years ago the United States was a land where speech was free, so long as it did not offend the susceptibilities or affect the interests of other people, and where everyone was entitled to his own opinions, so long as they agreed with those of everyone else. Of all this Charles Dickens was ignorant, and he made bad blunders. The absence of an International Copyright not only deprived English authors of any profit in the United States from the sale of their books, but also damaged American authors, since the booksellers very naturally preferred to publish books by English authors, which they could get for nothing, rather than books by American authors, for which they had to pay. But it was tactless of Dickens to introduce the subject in the speeches he made at the banquets given for him on his arrival. The reaction was violent, and the newspapers described him as "no gentleman, but a mercenary scoundrel". Though he was mobbed by admirers, and at Philadelphia shook hands for two hours with the crowd who wanted to meet him, his rings and diamond pins, his gaudy waistcoats, excited a good deal of criticism, and there were some who found his behaviour far from well-bred. But he was natural and unpretending, and few in the end could resist his youth, comely looks and gaiety. He made some good friends, with whom he remained on affectionate terms till his death.

The Dickenses returned to England after four eventful, but exhausting, months. The children had grown attached to their Aunt Georgina, and the weary travellers asked her to make her home with them. She was sixteen, the age of Mary when she went to live at Furnival's Inn with the newly-married couple, and so like her that from a distance she might have been taken for her. The resemblance was so strong "that when she and Kate and I are sitting together," wrote Dickens, "I seem to think that what has happened is a melancholy dream from which I am just awakening." Georgy was pretty, attractive and unassuming. She had a gift of mimicry by means of which she could make Dickens roar with laughter. In course of time he came to depend more and more on her. They took long walks together, and he discussed his literary plans with her. He found her a useful and reliable amanuensis. The style of living Dickens had adopted was expensive, and soon he found himself uncomfortably in debt. He decided to let his house and take his family, including Georgy of course, to Italy, where living was cheap and he could retrench. He spent a year there, chiefly at Genoa, and though he did a good deal of sight-seeing up and down the country, he was too insular, and his culture too tenuous, for the experience to have any spiritual effect on him. He remained the typical British tourist. But having discovered how pleasant (and economical) it was to live abroad, Dickens began to spend long periods on the Continent. Georgy, as one of the family, went with them. On one occasion, when they were going to settle in Paris for a considerable time, she went there alone with Charles to find an apartment, while Kate waited in England till they had made everything ready for her.

Kate was of a placid and melancholy disposition. She was not adaptable, and liked neither the journeys Charles took her on, the parties she went to with him, nor the parties at which she acted as hostess. She was clumsy, colourless and rather stupid, it would appear; and it is likely enough that the great and important persons who were eager to enjoy the celebrated author's company found it a nuisance to have to put up with his dull wife. Some of them, to her annoyance, persistently treated her as a cipher. It is not easy to be the wife of a distinguished man. She is unlikely to make a good job of it, unless she has tact and a lively sense of humour. In default of these, she must love her husband, and sufficiently admire him to find it natural that people should be more interested in him than in her. She must be clever enough to find solace in the fact that he loves her and, whatever his intellectual infidelities may be, in the end returns to her for comfort and reassurance. Kate does not appear ever to have been in love with Dickens. There is a letter he wrote to her during their engagement in which he reproaches her for her coldness. It may be that she married him because at that time marriage was the only occupation open to a woman, or it may be that, as the eldest of eight daughters, some pressure was put upon her by her parents to embrace an offer that provided for her future. She was a kindly, gentle little thing, but incapable of meeting the claims which her husband's eminence made on her. In fifteen years she gave birth to ten children, and had four miscarriages. During her pregnancies, Georgy accompanied Dickens on the jaunts he was fond of taking, went to parties with him, and increasingly presided at his table in Kate's place. One would have expected Kate to resent the situation: we do not know that she did.

4

The years passed. In 1857 Charles Dickens was forty-five. Of his nine surviving children, the elder ones were grown up, the youngest was five. His reputation was world-wide and he was the most popular author in England. He was influential. He lived, as greatly appealed to his theatrical instincts, in the public eye. Some years before, he had made the acquaintance of Wilkie Collins, and the acquaintance quickly ripened into a close friendship. Collins was twelve years younger than Dickens. Mr. Edgar Johnson thus writes of him: "He loved rich food, champagne and music halls; he was often involved in intricate tangles with several women at once; he was amusing, cynical, good-humoured, unrestrained to the point of vulgarity." For Dickens, Wilkie Collins stood, again quoting Mr. Johnson, "for fun and freedom". They travelled about England together and went to Paris to have a lark. It is likely enough that Dickens took the opportunity, as many a man in his place would do, to have a little flutter with any young person of easy virtue who was at hand. Kate had not given him all he expected, and for a long time he had been increasingly dissatisfied with her. "She is amiable and complying," he wrote, "but nothing on earth would make her understand me." From early in their marriage she had been jealous of him. I suspect he found the scenes she made him easier to bear when he knew that she had no reason to be jealous than later when she surely had. He persuaded himself then that she had never suited him. He had developed, but she had remained what she was at the beginning. Dickens was convinced that he had nothing to reproach himself with. He was assured that he had been a good father, and had done everything possible for his children. The fact is that, though none too pleased at having to provide for so many, for which he seems to have thought that Kate alone was to blame, he liked them well enough when they were small; but as they grew up he somewhat lost interest in them, and at a suitable age packed the boys off to remote parts of the world. It is true that they were scarcely a promising lot.

But it is likely that, but for an unforeseen accident, nothing very much would have changed the relations between Dickens and his wife. Like many another uncongenial couple, they might have drifted apart and yet to the world retained a semblance of unity. Dickens fell in love. He had, as I have said, a passion for the stage, and on more than one occasion had given amateur performances of one play or another for charitable purposes. At the time with which I am now dealing, he was asked to give some performances in Manchester of a play, *The Frozen Deep*, which Wilkie Collins had written with his help, and which had been performed at Devonshire House with great success before the Queen, the Prince Consort and the King of the Belgians. But when he agreed to repeat the play at Manchester, since he did not think his daughters, who had taken the girls' parts before, would be heard in a big theatre, he decided that their parts should be acted by professionals. A young woman called Ellen Ternan was engaged for one of them. She was eighteen. She was small and fair, and her eyes were blue. The rehearsals took place in Dickens's house, and he directed the play. He was flattered by Ellen's adoring attitude and by her pathetic desire to please him. Before the rehearsals were over, he was in love with her. He gave her a bracelet, which by mistake was delivered to his wife, and she naturally made him a scene. Charles seems to have adopted the attitude of injured innocence which a husband in such an awkward juncture finds it most convenient to adopt. The play was produced, and he played the leading part, that of a self-sacrificing Arctic explorer, with such pathos that there was not a dry eye in the house. He had grown a beard to play it.

The relations between Dickens and his wife grew more and more tense. He, who had always been so genial, so good-humoured, so easy to get on with, now was moody, restless and out of temper with everyone—but Georgy. He was very unhappy. At last he came to the conclusion that he could live with Kate no longer; but his position with the public was such that he was fearful of the scandal that an open break might cause. His anxiety is comprehensible. By his immensely profitable Christmas Books he had done more than anyone to make Christmas the symbolic festival to celebrate the domestic virtues and the beauty of a united and happy family life. For years he had assured his readers in moving terms that there was no place like home. The situation was delicate. Various suggestions were made. One was that Kate should have her own suite of rooms apart from his, act as hostess at his parties and accompany him to public functions. Another was that she should stay in London while he was at Gad's Hill (a house in Kent Dickens had recently bought), and stay at Gad's Hill when he was in London. A third was that she should settle abroad. All these proposals she rejected, and finally a complete separation was decided on. Kate was installed in a little house on the edge of Camden Town with an income of six hundred a year. A little later, Dickens's eldest son, Charles, went to live with her for a period.

The arrangement is surprising. One cannot but wonder why, placid as she was and stupid as she may have been, Kate allowed herself to be driven from her own house, and why she consented to leave her children behind. She knew of Charles's infatuation with Ellen Ternan, and one would have supposed that, with this trump-card in her hand, she could have made what terms she chose. In one of his letters Dickens refers to a "weakness" of Kate's, and in another letter, unfortunately published at the time, he alludes to a mental disorder "which caused his wife to think that she would be better away". It is pretty well certain now that these were discreet references to the fact that Kate drank. It would not be strange if her jealousy, her sense of inadequacy, the mortification of feeling that she was not wanted, had driven her to the bottle. If she was become a confirmed alcoholic, it would explain why Georgy should have managed the house and looked after the children, why they should have remained at home when their mother left it, why Georgy could write that "Poor Kate's incapacity for looking after children was no secret to anyone." It may be that her eldest son went to live with her to see that she did not tipple overmuch.

Dickens was far too celebrated for his private affairs not to give rise to gossip. Scandalous rumours were spread abroad. He heard that the Hogarths, Kate's and Georgy's mother and sister, were saying that Ellen Ternan was his mistress. He was furious and forced them, by threatening to turn Kate out of her house without a penny, to sign a declaration that they did not believe there was anything reprehensible in his relations with the little actress. The Hogarths took a fortnight before they could bring themselves to be thus blackmailed. They must have known that, if he carried out his threat, Kate could go to law with a cast-iron case; if they dared not let things go to such lengths, it can surely only have been because there were faults on Kate's side which they were unwilling to have divulged. There was also a good deal of talk about Georgy. She is, indeed, the enigmatic figure in the whole affair. I wonder that no one has been tempted to make her the central figure of a play. Earlier in this chapter I remarked on the significance of what Dickens wrote in his diary after Mary's death. This made it clear, it seemed to me, not only that he had been in love with her, but was already dissatisfied with Kate. And when Georgy came to live with them, he was charmed with her because of her astonishing resemblance to Mary. Did he then fall in love with her too? Did she love him? No one can tell. Georgy was jealous enough of Kate to cut out all sentences in praise of her when, after Charles's death, she edited a selection of his letters; but the attitude of Church and State towards marriage with a deceased wife's sister had given any connection of the sort an incestuous aspect, and it may never have entered her head that there could be more between herself and the man in whose house she had lived for fifteen years than the fond affection a sister might legitimately feel for a brother by blood. Perhaps it was enough for her to be in the confidence of so famous a man, and to have established a complete ascendancy over him. The strangest part of it all is that when Charles fell passionately in love with Ellen Ternan, Georgy made a friend of her and welcomed her at Gad's Hill. Whatever she felt, she kept to herself.

The connection between Charles Dickens and Ellen Ternan was dealt with, by those in a position to know, so discreetly that the details are uncertain. It seems that she resisted his advances for some time, but in the end yielded to his insistence. It is believed that under the name of Charles Tringham he took a house for her at Peckham, and there she lived till his death. According to his daughter Katie, he had a son by her; since nothing more was heard of him it is presumed that he died in infancy. But Ellen's surrender, it is said, did not bring Dickens the radiant bliss he expected; he was more than twenty-five years older than she was, and he could not but have known that she was not in love with him. Few pains are harder to bear than those of an unrequited passion. He left her a thousand pounds in his will, and she married a parson. She told a clerical friend, a certain Canon Benham, that she "loathed the very thought of the intimacy" Dickens had forced upon her. Like many another member of the gentle sex, she seems to have been ready enough to accept the perquisites of her position, but saw no reason why she should be asked to give anything in return.

At about the time of the break with his wife, Dickens began to give readings of his work, and for this purpose travelled over the British Isles and again went to the United States. His histrionic gift served him well, and his success was spectacular. But the effort he exerted, and the constant journeys, wore him out, and people began to notice that, though still in his forties, he looked an old man. These readings were not his only activity: during the twelve years between the separation and his death he wrote three long novels and conducted an immensely popular magazine called *All the Year Round*. It is not surprising that his health failed. He began to suffer from tiresome ailments, and it was evident that the lectures were wearing him out. He was advised to give them up, but he wouldn't; he loved the publicity, the excitement that attended his appearances, the face-to-face applause, the thrill of power that he felt as he swayed an audience to his will. And is it not just possible that he felt it might make Ellen fonder of him when she saw the adulation of the crowds that thronged his lectures? He decided to make a final tour, but was taken so ill in the middle of it that he had to abandon it. He went back to Gad's Hill and sat down to write *The Mystery of Edwin Drood*. But to make up to his managers for the readings he had had to cut short, he arranged to give twelve more in London. This was in January 1870. "The audiences at St. James's Hall were immense and sometimes they rose and cheered in a body as he entered and when he left." Back at Gad's Hill, he resumed work on his novel. One day in June, while he was dining alone with Georgy, he was taken ill. She sent for the doctor, and for his two daughters who were in London, and next day the younger one, Katie, was despatched by her resourceful and competent aunt to break the news to his wife that he was dying. Katie returned to Gad's Hill with Ellen Ternan. He died the day after, June 9, 1870, and was buried in Westminster Abbey.

393

5

In a famous essay Matthew Arnold insists that poetry to be truly excellent must have a high seriousness, and because he finds it lacking in Chaucer, refuses him, though praising him handsomely, a place among the greatest poets. Arnold was too austere not to look upon humour without a faint misgiving, and I don't suppose he could ever have been brought to admit that there might be as high a seriousness in Rabelais' laughter as in Milton's desire to justify the works of God to man. But I see his point, and it does not apply only to poetry. It may be that it is because this high seriousness is lacking in Dickens's novels that, for all their great merits, they leave us faintly dissatisfied. When we read them now with the great French and Russian novels in mind, and not only theirs, but George Eliot's, we are taken aback by their naïveté. In comparison with them, Dickens's are scarcely adult. But, of course, we must remember that we do not read the novels he wrote. We have changed, and they have changed with us. It is impossible for us to recapture the emotions with which his contemporaries read them, as they came hot from the press. In this connection, I will quote a passage from Una Pope-Hennessy's book: "Mrs. Henry Siddons, a neighbour and friend of Lord Jeffrey, peeped into his library and saw Jeffrey with his head on the table. He raised it with his eyes suffused with tears. She begged to be excused, saying, 'I had no idea that you had any bad news or cause of grief or I would not have come. Is anyone dead?' 'Yes, indeed,' replied Lord Jeffrey. 'I'm a great goose to have given away so, but I could not help it. You'll be sorry to hear that little Nelly, Boz's little Nelly, is dead.' " Jeffrey was a Scottish judge, a founder of *The Edinburgh Review* and a severe, caustic critic.

For my part, I find myself still immensely amused by Dickens's humour, but his pathos leaves me cold. I am inclined to say that he had strong emotions, but no heart. I hasten to qualify that. He had a generous heart, a passionate sympathy with the poor and oppressed, and, as we know, he took a persistent and effective interest in social reform. But it was an actor's heart, by which I mean that he could feel intensely an emotion that he wished to depict in the same way as an actor playing a tragic part can feel the emotion he represents. "What's he to Hecuba or Hecuba to him?" With respect to this, I am reminded of something an actress, at one time in Sarah Bernhardt's Company, told me many years ago. The great artist was playing Phèdre and, in the midst of one of her most moving speeches, when to all appearance she was distraught with anguish, she became aware that some persons standing in one of the wings were loudly talking; she moved towards them and, turning away from the audience as though in her misery to hide her face, hissed out what was the French equivalent to "Stop that bloody row, you lousy bastards"; and then, turning back with a magnificent gesture of woe, went on with her tirade to its impressive end. The audience had noticed nothing. It is hard to believe that she could have given expression so noble and tragic to the words she had to utter unless she had truly felt them; but her emotion was a professional emotion, skin-deep, an affair of nerves rather than of heart which had no effect on her self-possession. I have no doubt that Dickens was sincere, but it was an actor's sincerity; and that, perhaps, is why now, no matter how he piled up the agony, we feel that his pathos was not quite genuine and so are no longer moved by it.

But we have no right to ask of an author more than he can give, and if Dickens lacked that high seriousness which Matthew Arnold demanded of the greatest poets, he had much else. He was a very great novelist. He had enormous gifts. He thought *David Copperfield* the best of all his books. An author is not always a good judge of his own work, but in this case Dickens's judgment seems to me correct. *David Copperfield*, as I suppose everyone knows, is in great part autobiographical; but Dickens was writing a novel, not an autobiography, and though he drew much of his material from his own life, he made only such use of it as suited his purpose. For the rest, he fell back on his vivid imagination. He was never much of a reader, literary conversation bored him, and such acquaintance with literature as he made later in life seems to have had little effect in lessening the very strong impressions he had received from the works he first read as a boy at Chatham. Of these it was, I think, the novels of Smollett that in the long run chiefly influenced him. The figures Smollett presents to the reader are not so much larger than life as more highly coloured. They are "humours" rather than characters.

So to see people well suited the idiosyncrasy of Dickens's temper. Mr. Micawber was drawn from his father. John Dickens was grandiloquent in speech and shifty in money matters, but he was no fool and far from incompetent; he was industrious, kindly and affectionate. We know what Dickens made of him. If Falstaff is the greatest comic character in literature, Mr. Micawber is the greatest but one. Dickens has been blamed, to my mind unjustly, for making him end up as a respectable magistrate in Australia, and some critics have thought that he should have remained reckless and improvident to the end. Australia was a sparsely settled country. Mr. Micawber was a man of fine presence, of some education and of flamboyant address; I do not see why, in that environment and with those advantages, he should not have attained official position. But it was not only in his creation of comic characters that Dickens was masterly. Steerforth's smooth servant is admirably drawn; he has a mysterious, sinister quality which sends cold shivers down one's back. Uriah Heep smacks of what used to be called transpontine melodrama; but for all that he is a powerful, horrifying figure, and he is most skilfully presented. Indeed, *David Copperfield* is filled with characters of the most astonishing variety, vividness and originality. There never were such people as the Micawbers, Peggotty and Barkis, Traddles, Betsy Trotwood and Mr. Dick, Uriah Heep and his mother: they are the fantastic inventions of Dickens's exultant imagination; but they have so much vigour, they are so consistent, they are presented with so much verisimilitude and with so much conviction, that while you read you cannot but believe in them. They may not be real; they are very much alive.

Dickens's general method of creating character was to exaggerate the traits, peculiarities, foibles, of his models and to put into the mouth of each one some phrase, or string of phrases, which stamped his quintessence on the reader's mind. He never showed the development of characters and, on the whole, what his creatures were at the beginning they remain at the end. (There are in Dickens's work one or two exceptions, but the change of nature he has indicated is highly unconvincing; it is occasioned to bring about a happy ending.) The danger of drawing character in this way is that the limits of plausibility may be exceeded, and the result is caricature. Caricature is all very well when the author presents you with a character at whom you can laugh, as you can at Mr. Micawber, but it will not serve when he expects you to sympathize. Dickens was never particularly successful with his female characters unless, like Mrs. Micawber, with her "I will never desert Mr. Micawber", and Betsy Trotwood, they were caricatured. Dora, drawn after Dickens's first love, Maria Beadnell, is too silly and too childish; Agnes, drawn after Mary and Georgy Hogarth, is too good and too sensible: they are both fearfully tiresome. Little Em'ly seems to me a failure. Dickens evidently meant us to feel pity for her: she only got what she asked for. Her ambition was to be a "lady", and in the hope, presumably, that she would be able to get Steerforth to marry her, she ran away with him. She seems to have made him a most unsatisfactory mistress, sullen, tearful and sorry for herself; and it is no wonder that he grew tired of her. The most baffling female character in *David Copperfield* is Rosa Dartle. I suspect that Dickens meant to make greater use of her in his story than he did, and if he did not do so, it was because he feared to offend his public. I can only suppose that Steerforth had been her lover and she hated him because he had abandoned her, but, notwithstanding, loved him still with a jealous, hungry, vindictive love. Dickens here invented a character that Balzac would have made much of. Of the leading actors in *David Copperfield*, Steerforth is the only one that is drawn "straight", using the word as actors do when they speak of a "straight part". Dickens has given the reader an admirable impression of Steerforth's charm, grace and elegance, his friendliness, his kindliness, his amiable gift of being able to get on with all kinds of people, his gaiety, his courage, his selfishness, his unscrupulousness, his recklessness, his callousness. He has drawn here a portrait of the sort of man that most of us have known, who gives delight wherever he goes and leaves disaster behind him. Dickens brought him to a bad end. Fielding, I think, would have been more lenient; for, as Mrs. Honour, speaking of Tom Jones, put it: "And when wenches are so coming, young men are not so much to be blamed neither; for to be sure they do no more than what is natural." To-day, the novelist is under the necessity of making the events he relates not only likely, but so far as possible inevitable. Dickens was under no such constraint. That Steerforth, coming from Portugal by sea after an absence from England of some years, should be wrecked and drowned in sight of Yarmouth just when David Copperfield had gone there on a brief visit to his old friends, is a coincidence that really puts too great a strain on the reader's credulity. If Steerforth had to die in order to satisfy the Victorian demand that vice should be punished, Dickens might surely have thought of a more plausible way of bringing this about.

6

It was a misfortune for English literature that Keats died too soon and Wordsworth too late; it was a misfortune almost as serious that, just at the time when the greatest novelists our country has produced were in full possession of their gifts, the methods of publication then prevalent encouraged, to the detriment of their production, the tendency to diffuseness and prolixity and digression to which by their nature English novelists have for the most part been inclined. The Victorian novelists were working men who lived by their pen. They had to accept contracts to provide a definite amount of copy for eighteen, twenty or twenty-four numbers, and they had so to arrange their narrative as to end each number in such a way as to induce the reader to buy the following one. They doubtless had in mind the main lines of the story they set out to tell, but we know that they were satisfied if they had two or three numbers written before publication started. They wrote the rest as they were needed, trusting that their invention would provide them with enough material to fill the requisite number of pages; and we know, from their own admissions, that on occasion their invention failed them and they had to make the best job they could when they had nothing to write about. Sometimes it happened that their story was finished when there were perhaps two or three numbers still to be written, and then they had to use any device they could think of to delay the conclusion. Naturally their novels were shapeless and long-winded; they were forced to digression and prolixity.

Dickens wrote *David Copperfield* in the first person. This straightforward method served him well, since his plots were often complicated, and the reader's interest was sometimes diverted to characters and incidents that have no bearing on the story's course. In *David Copperfield* there is only one major digression of this kind, and that is the account of Dr. Strong's relations with his wife, his mother and his wife's cousin; it does not concern David and is in itself tedious. I surmise that he used this episode to cover on two occasions a lapse of time which otherwise he didn't know what to do with: the first was the years that David spent at school at Canterbury, and the second was the period between David's disappointment with Dora and her death.

Dickens did not escape the danger that confronts the author of a semi-biographical novel in which himself is the principal character. David Copperfield at the age of ten was put to work by his stern stepfather, as Charles Dickens was by *his* father, and suffered from the "degradation" of having to mix with boys of his own age whom he did not consider his social equals, in the same way as Dickens, in the fragment of autobiography which he gave to Forster, persuaded himself that he had suffered. Dickens did all he could to excite the reader's sympathy for his hero, and indeed on the celebrated journey to Dover, when David ran away in order to seek the protection of his aunt Betsy Trotwood, a delightful, amusing character, he loads his dice without scruple. Innumerable readers have found the narration of this escapade wonderfully pathetic. I am made of sterner stuff. I am surprised that the little boy should have been such a ninny as to let everyone he came across rob and cheat him. After all, he had been in the factory for some months and had wandered about London early and late; one would have thought that the other boys at the factory, even though they were not up to his social standard, would have taught him a thing or two; he had lived with the Micawbers and pawned their bits and pieces for them, and had visited them at the Marshalsea: if he had really been the bright boy he is described to be, even at that tender age he would surely have acquired some knowledge of the world and enough sharpness to fend for himself. But it is not only in his childhood that David Copperfield shows himself sadly incompetent. He is incapable of coping with a difficulty. His weakness with Dora, his lack of common sense in dealing with the ordinary problems of domestic life, are almost more than one can bear; and he is so obtuse that he does not guess that Agnes is in love with him. I cannot persuade myself that in the end he became the successful novelist we are told he did. If he wrote novels, I suspect that they were more like those of Mrs. Henry Wood than those of Charles Dickens. It is strange that his creator should have given him none of his own drive, vitality and exuberance. David was slim and good-looking; and he had charm, or he would not have attracted the affection of almost everyone he encountered; he was honest, kindly and conscientious; but he was surely a bit of a fool. He remains the least interesting person in the book. Nowhere does he show himself in so poor a light, so feckless, so incapable of dealing with an awkward situation, as in the monstrous scene between Little Em'ly and Rosa Dartle in the attic in Soho which David witnesses but, for the very flimsiest reason, makes no attempt to stop. This scene affords a good example of how the method of writing a novel in the first person may result in the narrator being forced into a position so shockingly false, so unworthy of a hero of fiction, that the reader is justly indignant with him. If described in the third person, from the standpoint of omniscience, the scene would still have been melodramatic and repellent, but, even though with difficulty, credible. But of course the pleasure one gets from reading *David Copperfield* does not arise from any persuasion one may have that life is, or ever was, anything like what Dickens describes. That is not to depreciate him. Fiction, like the kingdom of heaven, has many mansions, and the author may invite you to visit whichever he chooses. One has just as much right to exist as another, but you must suit yourselves to the surroundings into which you are led. You must put on different spectacles to read *The Golden Bowl* and to read *Bubu de Montparnasse*. *David Copperfield* is a fantastication, sometimes gay, sometimes pathetic; on life, composed out of recollections and wish-fulfilments by a man of lively imagination and warm feelings. You must read it in the same spirit as you read *As You Like It*. It provides an entertainment almost as delightful.

CHAPTER SEVEN

Flaubert and *Madame Bovary*

I

IF, as I believe, the sort of books an author writes depends on the sort of man he is, and so it is well to know what is relevant in his personal history, this, as will presently appear, in the case of Flaubert is essential. He was a very unusual man. No writer that we know of devoted himself with such a fierce and indomitable industry to the art of literature. It was not with him, as it is with most authors, an activity of paramount importance but one that allows for other activities which rest the mind, refresh the body or enrich experience. He did not think that to live was the object of life; for him the object of life was to write: no monk in his cell more resolutely sacrificed the pleasures of the world to the love of God than Flaubert sacrificed the fullness and variety of life to his ambition to create a work of art. He was at once a romantic and a realist. Now, at the bottom of romanticism, as I said in speaking of Balzac, is a hatred of reality and a passionate desire to escape from it. Like the rest of the romantics, Flaubert sought refuge in the extraordinary and the fantastic, in the Orient and in antiquity; and yet, for all his hatred of reality, for all his loathing for the meanness, the platitude, the imbecility of the bourgeois, he was fascinated by it; for there was something in his nature that horribly attracted him to what he most detested. Human stupidity had a revolting charm for him, and he took a morbid delight in exhibiting it in all its odiousness. It got on his nerves with the force of any obsession; it was like a sore on the body that is pain to touch and that yet you can't help touching. The realist in him pored over human nature as though it were a pile of garbage, not to find something he could value, but to show to all and sundry how base, for all their outward seeming, were human beings.

402

2

Gustave Flaubert was born at Rouen in 1821. His father, a doctor, was head of the hospital and lived there with his wife and children. It was a happy, highly respected and affluent family. Flaubert was brought up like any other French boy of his class; he went to school, made friends with other boys, worked little but read much. He was emotional and imaginative, and, like many another child and boy, was troubled by that sense of inner loneliness which the sensitive carry with them all their lives. "I went to school when I was only ten," he wrote, "and I very soon contracted a profound aversion to the human race." This is not just a quip; he meant it. He was a pessimist from his youth up. It is true that then romanticism was in full flower and pessimism the fashion: one of the boys at Flaubert's school blew his brains out, another hanged himself with his necktie; but one cannot quite see why Flaubert, with a comfortable home, affectionate and indulgent parents, a doting sister and friends to whom he was devoted, should have really found life intolerable and his fellow-creatures hateful. He was well-grown and to all appearance healthy.

When he was fifteen, he fell in love. His family went in summer to Trouville, then a modest village by the sea with one hotel; and there, that year, they found staying Maurice Schlesinger, a music publisher and something of an adventurer, with his wife and child. It is worth while to transcribe the portrait Flaubert drew of her later: "She was tall, a brunette with magnificent black hair that fell in tresses to her shoulders; her nose was Greek, her eyes burning, her eyebrows high and admirably arched, her skin was glowing and as if it were misty with gold; she was slender and exquisite, one saw the blue veins meandering on her brown and purple throat. Add to that a fine down that darkened her upper lip and gave her face a masculine and energetic expression such as to throw blonde beauties into the shade. She spoke slowly, her voice was modulated, musical and soft." I hesitate to translate *pourpré* with purple, which does not sound alluring, but that *is* the translation, and I can only suppose that Flaubert used the word as a synonym for bright-hued.

Elisa Schlesinger, then twenty-six, was nursing her baby. Flaubert was timid, and would never have summoned up the courage even to speak to her if her husband had not been a jovial, hearty fellow with whom it was easy to make friends. Maurice Schlesinger took the boy riding with him and, on one occasion, the three of them went for a sail. Flaubert and Elisa sat side by side, their shoulders touching and her dress against his hand; she spoke in a low, sweet voice, but he was in such a turmoil that he could not remember a word she said. The summer came to an end, the Schlesingers left, the Flauberts went back to Rouen and Gustave to school. He had entered upon the one genuine passion of his life. Two years later, he returned to Trouville and was told that Elisa had been and gone. He was seventeen. It seemed to him then that before he had been too stirred really to love her; he loved her differently now, with a man's desire, and her absence only exacerbated his passion. When he got home, he took up again a book he had started and abandoned, *Les Mémoires d'un Fou*, and told the story of the summer when he fell in love with Elisa Schlesinger.

At nineteen, to reward him for having matriculated, his father sent him with a certain Dr. Cloquet on a trip to the Pyrenees and Corsica. He was then full-grown and broad-shouldered. His contemporaries have described him as a giant, and so he called himself, though he was not quite six feet tall, which nowadays is no great height; but the French at that time were a good deal shorter than they are now, and he evidently towered over his fellows. He was thin and graceful; his black lashes veiled enormous, sea-green eyes, and his long fair hair fell to his shoulders. Forty years later, a woman who knew him as a youth said that then he was as beautiful as a Greek God. On the way back from Corsica, the travellers stopped at Marseilles, and one morning, coming in from a bathe, Flaubert noticed a young woman sitting in the courtyard of the hotel. He addressed her, and they got into conversation. She was called Eulalie Foucaud and was waiting till the ship sailed to take her back to her husband, an official, in French Guiana.

Flaubert and Eulalie Foucaud passed that night together, a night, according to his own account, of that flaming passion which is as beautiful as the setting of the sun on the snow. He left Marseilles and never saw her again. The experience made a deep impression upon him.

Shortly after this, he went to Paris to study law, not because he wanted to be a lawyer, but because he had to adopt some profession; he was bored there, bored by his law-books, bored by the life of the university; and he despised his fellow-students for their mediocrity, their poses and their bourgeois tastes. While in Paris, he wrote a novelette called *Novembre* in which he described his adventure with Eulalie Foucaud. But he gave her the high arched eyebrows, the upper lip with its bluish down and the lovely neck of Elisa Schlesinger. He had got in touch with the Schlesingers again by calling on the publisher at his office, and was asked by him to dine with him and his wife. Elisa was as beautiful as ever. When last Flaubert had seen her, he was a hobbledehoy; now he was a man, eager, passionate and handsome. He was soon on intimate terms with the couple, dined with them regularly and went on little trips with them. But he was no less timid than before, and for long he hadn't the courage to declare his love. When at last he did, Elisa was not angry, as he had feared she might be, but made it plain that she was not prepared to be anything more to him than a good friend. Her story was curious. When first Flaubert met her, in 1836, he thought, as did everyone else, that she was the wife of Maurice Schlesinger; she was not; she was married to a certain Emile Judéa who through dishonesty had got into serious trouble, whereupon Schlesinger had come forward with the offer to provide money sufficient to save him from prosecution on the condition that he left France and gave up his wife. This he did, and Schlesinger and Elisa Judéa lived together, there being at the time no divorce in France, till Judéa's death in 1840 enabled them to marry. It is said that, notwithstanding his absence and death, it was this abject creature that Elisa continued to love; and it may be that this, and a sense of loyalty to the man who had given her a home and was the father of her child, combined to make her hesitate to accede to Flaubert's desires. But he was ardent, Schlesinger was flagrantly unfaithful, and perhaps she was touched by Flaubert's boyish devotion; at length he persuaded her to come one day to his apartment; he awaited her with feverish anxiety: she never came. Such is the story that Flaubert's biographers have accepted on the strength of what he wrote in *L'Education Sentimentale*, and since it is plausible, it may well be a faithful account of the facts. What is certain is that Elisa never became his mistress.

Then, in 1844, an event occurred that was to change Flaubert's life and, as I hope to show later, affect his literary production. One dark night he was driving back to Rouen with his brother from a property of their mother's which they had been visiting. His brother, nine years older than he, had adopted his father's profession. Suddenly, without warning, Flaubert "felt himself carried away in a torrent of flames and fell like a stone to the floor of the trap". When he recovered consciousness, he was covered with blood; his brother had carried him into a neighbouring house and bled him. He was taken to Rouen, where his father bled him again; he was dosed with valerian and indigo, and he was forbidden to smoke, drink wine or eat meat. He continued for some time to have fits of great violence. For days after, his shattered nerves were in a state of frantic tension. A great deal of mystery has surrounded this illness, and the doctors have discussed it from various points of view. Some have frankly said it was epilepsy, and that is what his friends thought it was; his niece in her recollections has passed the matter over in silence; M. Réne Dumesnil, himself a doctor and the author of an important work on Flaubert, claims that it was not epilepsy, but what he calls hystero-epilepsy. But whatever it was, the treatment was very much the same: Flaubert for some years was given enormous doses of quinine sulphate, and later, and more or less for the rest of his life, potassium bromide.

It is possible that the attack did not come as a complete surprise to Flaubert's family. He is reputed to have told Maupassant that he had first had auditory and visual hallucinations when he was twelve. When at the age of nineteen he was sent on a journey, it was with a doctor and, since change of scene was part of the treatment his father afterwards prescribed, it does not seem unlikely that he had already had something in the nature of a fit. The Flauberts, though rich, were provincial, humdrum and thrifty: it is hard to believe that they would have thought of letting their son go on a trip, with a medical man, merely because he had passed the examination which every educated French boy has to undergo. Even as a lad, Flaubert had never felt himself quite like the people with whom he came in contact, and it seems probable that the sombre pessimism of his early youth had its cause in the mysterious disease which, even then, must have been affecting his nervous system. Anyhow, he was faced now with the fact that he was afflicted with a terrifying malady, the attacks of which were unpredictable, and it was necessary to change his mode of life. He decided, willingly enough, it may be supposed, to abandon the law, and made up his mind never to marry.

In 1845 his father died, and two or three months later Caroline, his only sister, whom he adored, after giving birth to a daughter died also. As children they had been inseparable, and till her marriage she was his dearest companion.

Some time before his death, Dr. Flaubert had bought a property, called Croisset, on the banks of the Seine, with a fine stone house two hundred years old, a terrace in front of it and a little pavilion looking over the river. Here the widow settled with her son, Gustave, and the baby daughter of Caroline; her elder son, Achille, was married and succeeded his father at the Rouen hospital. Croisset was to be Flaubert's home for the rest of his life. He had been writing off and on from a very early age, and now, unable through his illness to live a normal life, he made up his mind to devote himself wholly to literature. He had a large work-room on the ground floor, with windows on the river and the garden. He adopted methodical habits. He got up about ten, read his letters and the papers, lunched lightly at eleven and, till one, lounged about the terrace or sat in the pavilion reading. At one, he set to work and worked till dinner at seven, then he took another stroll in the garden and went back to work till far into the night.

He saw nobody but the few friends whom, now and then, he invited to stay with him so that he might discuss his work with them. They were three: Alfred Le Poittevin, older than Flaubert, but a friend of the family; Maxime du Camp, whom he had met when reading law in Paris; and Louis Bouilhet, who earned his meagre living by giving lessons in Latin and French at Rouen. They were all interested in literature, and Bouilhet was a poet. Flaubert had an affectionate disposition and was devoted to his friends, but he was possessive and exacting. When Le Poittevin, who had had a considerable influence over him, married a Mademoiselle de Maupassant he was outraged. "It meant to me," he said later, "what the news of a great scandal caused by a bishop would have meant to a believer." Of Maxime du Camp and Louis Bouilhet I shall have something to say presently.

When Caroline died, Flaubert took a cast of her face and hands, and some months later went to Paris to commission Pradier, then a well-known sculptor, to make a bust of her. At Pradier's studio he met a poetess called Louise Colet. She was one of those writers, far from rare in the world of letters, who suppose that push and pull are an adequate substitute for talent; and, with beauty to help, she had acquired something of a position in literary circles. She had a *salon* frequented by celebrities, and was known as 'the Muse.' Her husband, Hippolite Colet, was a professor of music; her lover, by whom she had a child, was Victor Cousin, philosopher and statesman. She wore her fair hair in ringlets that framed her face, and her voice was passionate and tender. She acknowledged to thirty, but was in fact some years older. Flaubert was twenty-five. Within forty-eight hours, after a slight contretemps owing to his nervousness and excitement, he became her lover, not of course displacing the philosopher, whose attachment, though according to her by then platonic, was official; and three days later, leaving Louise in tears, he returned to Croisset. The same night Flaubert wrote to her the first of as strange a series of love letters as ever lover wrote to his mistress. Many years later, he told Edmond de Goncourt that he had loved Louise Colet "furiously"; but he was always prone to exaggeration and the correspondence hardly bears out the statement. I think we may surmise that he was proud to have a mistress who was in the public eye; but he lived a rich life of the imagination and, like many another day-dreamer, found that he loved his mistress more when he was away from her than when he was with her. Somewhat unnecessarily, he told her so. She urged him to come and live in Paris; he told her that he could not leave his mother, broken by the death of her husband and her daughter; then she begged him at least to come more often to Paris; he told her that he could only get away if he had a reasonable excuse, whereupon she answered angrily: "Does that mean that you're watched over like a girl?" That is, in point of fact, pretty well what it did mean. His epileptiform fits left him for days weak and depressed, and it was natural that his mother should be anxious. She would not let him swim in the river, which was his delight, nor go in a boat on the Seine, without someone to look after him. He could not ring the bell for a servant to bring him something he wanted without his mother rushing upstairs to see if he was well. He told Louise that his mother would raise no objection if he proposed leaving her for a few days, but he could not bear the distress it would cause her. Louise can hardly have failed to see that, if he loved her as passionately as she loved him, that would not have prevented him from joining her. Even at this time of day, it is easy to think of plausible reasons he could have given that made it essential for him to go to Paris. He was a very young man, and if he consented to see Louise so seldom, it is likely enough that, constantly under the influence of powerful sedatives as he was, his sexual desires were not pressing.

"Your love isn't love," Louise wrote, "in any case it doesn't mean much in your life." To this he replied: "You want to know if I love you. Well, yes, as much as I can love; that's to say, for me love isn't the first thing in life, but the second." Flaubert prided himself on his frankness; it was indeed brutal. His tactlessness was amazing. On one occasion, he asked Louise to find out from a friend of hers who had lived at Cayenne what had happened to Eulalie Foucaud, the object of his adventure at Marseilles, and even asked her to have a letter delivered to her; he was frankly astonished when she accepted the commission with irritation. He even told her of his encounters with prostitutes, for whom he had, according to his own story, an inclination which he frequently gratified. But there is nothing men lie about so much as about their sex life, and it is probable that he was boasting of powers which he did not possess. He certainly treated Louise cavalierly. Once, yielding to her importunity, he suggested a meeting at a hotel at Mantes, where, if she started early from Paris and he from Rouen, they could spend an afternoon together, and he could still get home by nightfall. He was astounded when the proposal excited her indignation. In the two years the affair lasted they met six times, and it was apparently she who broke it off.

Meanwhile, Flaubert had been busy writing *La Tentation de St. Antoine*, a book that he had long had in mind; and it had been settled that as soon as he was through with it, he and Maxime du Camp should go on a jaunt to the Near East. Madame Flaubert's consent had been obtained because her son, Achille, and Dr. Cloquet, the medical man who had years before accompanied Flaubert to Corsica, agreed that a sojourn in warm countries would benefit his health. When then the book was finished, Flaubert summoned du Camp and Bouilhet to Croisset so that he might read it to them. He read for four days, four hours in the afternoon and four hours at night. It was decided that no opinion should be given till the whole work had been heard. At midnight on the fourth day, Flaubert, having read to the end, banged his fist on the table and said: "Well?" One of them answered: "We think you ought to throw it on the fire and not speak of it again." It was a shattering blow. They argued for hours, and finally Flaubert accepted their verdict. Then Bouilhet suggested that Flaubert, taking Balzac as his model, should write a realistic novel. By this time it was eight in the morning, and they went to bed. Later in the day, they met again to continue the discussion and, according to Maxime du Camp in his *Souvenirs Littéraires*, it was then that Bouilhet proposed the story that eventually became

Madame Bovary; but since, on the journey on which Flaubert and du Camp soon after set out, Flaubert in his letters home mentioned various subjects for novels that he was considering, but not *Madame Bovary*, it is pretty certain that du Camp was mistaken. The two friends visited Egypt, Palestine, Syria and Greece. They returned to France in 1851. Flaubert was still undecided about what he should try his hand at, and it is probably then that Bouilhet told him the story of Eugène Delamare. Delamare had been an *interne*, house surgeon or house physician, at the hospital at Rouen, and he had a practice in a small town near-by. On the death of his first wife, a widow much older than himself, he married the pretty young daughter of a neighbouring farmer. She was pretentious and extravagant. She soon grew bored with her dull husband and took a series of lovers. She spent on clothes money she could not afford and ran hopelessly into debt. Finally she took poison, and eventually Delamare killed himself. As everyone knows, Flaubert followed this mean little story very closely.

Soon after his return to France, he again met Louise Colet. During his absence things had gone badly with her. Her husband had died, Victor Cousin had ceased to assist her financially, and she could get no one to accept a play she had written. She wrote to Flaubert that she was passing through Rouen on her way back from England; they met, and their correspondence was renewed. After a while he went to Paris and again became her lover. One wonders why. She was by now in her forties, a blonde, and blondes don't wear well, and at that time women with any pretentions to respectability did not make up. Perhaps he was touched by her feeling for him; she was the only woman who had ever been in love with him, and perhaps, sexually uncertain as he seems to have been, he felt at his ease with her on the rare occasions on which they had sexual intercourse. Her letters were destroyed, but his remain. From them you can gather that Louise had learnt nothing: she was as domineering, as exacting and as tiresome as she had been from the first. Her letters seem to have become increasingly acrimonious. She continued to press Flaubert to come to Paris, or to let her come to Croisset; and he continued to find excuses not to do the one nor to let her do the other. His letters are chiefly concerned with literary subjects, and they end with very perfunctory expressions of affection; their chief interest lies in the remarks he makes on the difficult progress of *Madame Bovary*, which he was by then absorbed in. Every now and then Louise sent him a poem she had written. His criticism was harsh. It was inevitable that the affair should come to an end. Louise brought it about by her own rashness. It appears that, for the sake of their daughter, Victor Cousin had offered to marry her, and she seems to have let Flaubert know that it was on his account that she had refused. She had in point of fact made up her mind to marry Flaubert, and very imprudently told friends that she was going to. When it came to his ears, he was aghast; and after a series of violent scenes, which not only frightened but humiliated him, he told her that he would never see her again. Undeterred, however, she arrived at Croisset one day to make yet another scene; he threw her out so brutally that even his mother was outraged. Notwithstanding the stubborn determination of her sex to believe only what they want to believe, 'the Muse' was at last obliged to face the fact that Flaubert was finished with her for good and all. She revenged herself by writing a novel, said to be very poor, in which she drew a vicious portrait of him.

3

Now I must hark back. When the two friends returned from the East, Maxime du Camp settled in Paris and bought an interest in the *Revue de Paris*. He came to Croisset to urge Flaubert and Bouilhet to write for him. After Flaubert's death, du Camp published two stout volumes of reminiscences which he called *Souvenirs Littéraires*. All who have written about Flaubert have made free use of them, and it seems ungrateful that they should have treated their author with contumely. In this book du Camp wrote: "Authors are divided into two classes: those for whom literature is a means, those for whom literature is an end. I belonged, I have always belonged, to the former category; I have never asked from literature more than

412

the right to love it and to cultivate it as best I could." The class of literary men to which Maxime du Camp was satisfied to belong has always been a large one. These are the men who have literary inclinations, a love of literature, and often talent, taste, culture and facility; but no gift of creation. In their youth they are apt to write accomplished verse or an indifferent novel, but after a while they settle down to what they find comes more easily to them. They review books, or become editors of literary magazines; write prefaces to the selected works of dead authors, biographies of eminent persons, essays on literary subjects; and in the end, like du Camp, their reminiscences. They perform a useful function in the world of letters, and since they often write with elegance, their productions are generally pleasant to read. There is no reason to regard them with the scorn with which Flaubert came to regard du Camp.

People have said, I think unjustly, that du Camp was jealous of Flaubert. In his reminiscences he wrote: "Never has the thought come to me of so exalting myself as to compare myself with Flaubert, and never have I allowed myself to dispute his superiority." No man could say fairer than that. As lads in the Latin Quarter, when Flaubert was reading law, they had been intimate; they had eaten in the same inexpensive restaurants, and interminably talked of literary subjects in the same cafés. Later, on their travels in the Near East they had been sea-sick together in the Mediterranean, got drunk together in Cairo and whored together when they had the opportunity. Flaubert was not easy to get on with, for he was impatient of contradiction, irritable and overbearing. For all that, du Camp felt a sincere affection for him and thought highly of him as a writer; but he knew the man too well to be unaware of his weaknesses; it is not in human nature that he should have looked upon the boon-companion of his youth with the veneration with which he was regarded by his fanatical admirers. For this the poor wretch has been unmercifully abused.

Du Camp thought that his old friend made a mistake in burying himself at Croisset; and on one of his numerous visits urged him to settle down in Paris, where he could meet people, and by mixing in the intellectual life of the capital, by exchanging ideas with his fellow writers, widen his mind. On the face of it, there was much to say for the notion. The novelist must live among his raw material. He cannot wait for experience to come to him; he must go in search of it. Flaubert had lived a very narrow life. He knew little of the world. The only women with whom he had been more than casually acquainted were his mother, Elisa Schlesinger and 'the Muse.' But he was impetuous and imperious. He resented interference. Du Camp, however, would not let well alone, and in a letter he wrote from Paris went so far as to tell Flaubert that if he continued to lead that constricted life he would soon suffer from softening of the brain. The remark infuriated Flaubert and he never forgot it. It was of course an unfortunate one to make, since he was always afraid that these epileptiform attacks of his would result in something of the sort. In fact, in one of his letters to Louise he said that in four years he might become an idiot. Flaubert replied to du Camp with an angry letter, in which he told him that the life he led was exactly what suited him, and that he had only contempt for the wretched hacks who composed the literary life of Paris. An estrangement ensued, and though later the old friends renewed relations, they were never cordial. Du Camp was an active, energetic man, and he quite frankly wanted to make his way in the literary world of his day; but that he should wish to do this seemed to Flaubert disgusting: "he is lost to us," he wrote, and for the next three or four years never mentioned his name without contempt. He found his productions despicable, his style abominable and his borrowings from other authors scandalous. Flaubert was glad, all the same, that du Camp should print in his magazine the poem in three thousand lines that Bouilhet had written on a Roman subject, and when *Madame Bovary* was finished, he accepted du Camp's offer to serialize it in the *Revue de Paris*.

Louis Bouilhet remained his only intimate friend. Flaubert, mistakenly it is held now, thought him a great poet and trusted his judgment as he trusted that of no one else. He owed a great deal to him. Except for Bouilhet, *Madame Bovary* would very likely never have been written, and certainly would not have been the book it is. It was he who after interminable arguments persuaded Flaubert to write a synopsis, which Mr. Francis Steegmuller in his excellent work, *Flaubert and Madame Bovary*, has printed. Bouilhet found it very promising and at last, in 1851, Flaubert, being then thirty, set to work. With the exception of *La Tentation de St. Antoine*, the more important of his early works had been strictly personal; they were, in fact, novelizations of his amorous experience: his aim now was to be strictly objective. He determined to tell the truth without bias or prejudice, narrating the facts and exposing the characters of the persons he had to deal with without comment of his own, neither condemning nor praising: if he sympathized with one, not to show it; if the stupidity of another exasperated him, the malice of a third outraged him, not to allow word of his to reveal it. This, on the whole, is what he succeeded in doing, and that is perhaps why many readers have found a certain coldness in the novel. There is nothing heart-warming in this calculated, obstinate detachment. Though it may be a weakness in us, my impression is that, as readers, we find comfort in knowing that the author shares the emotions he has made us feel.

But the attempt at complete impersonality fails with Flaubert, as it fails with every novelist, because complete impersonality is impossible to achieve. It is very well that the writer should let his characters explain themselves and, as far as may be, let their actions be the outcome of their natures, and he may easily make a nuisance of himself when he draws your attention to his heroine's charm or his villain's malevolence, when he moralizes or irrelevantly digresses, when, in short, he is a personage in the story he is telling; but this is only a matter of method, one that some very good novelists have used and, if it happens to have gone out of fashion at the moment, that is not to say it is a bad one. But the author who avoids it keeps his personality only out of the surface of his novel; he reveals it willy-nilly by his choice of subject, his choice of characters and the point of view from which he describes them. Flaubert eyed the world with gloomy indignation. He was violently intolerant.

He had no patience with stupidity. The bourgeois, the commonplace, the ordinary filled him with exasperation. He had no pity. He had no charity. Most of his adult life he was a sick man, oppressed by the humiliation which his distemper caused him to feel. His nerves were in a constant state of perturbation. He was, as I have said, at once a romantic and a realist; and he flung himself into the sordid story of Emma Bovary with the fury of a man revenging himself by wallowing in the gutter because life has not met the demands of his passion for the ideal. We are introduced to many persons in the course of the novel's five hundred pages, and but for Dr. Larivière, a minor character, they have hardly a redeeming feature. They are base, mean, stupid, trivial and vulgar. A great many people are, but not all; and it is inconceivable that in a town, however small, there should not be found one person at least, if not two or three, who is sensible, kindly and helpful. Flaubert failed to keep his personality out of his novel.

His deliberate intention was to choose a set of characters who were thoroughly commonplace, and devise incidents that would inevitably arise from their nature and their circumstances; but he was well aware of the possibility that no one would be interested in persons so dull, and that the incidents he had to relate would prove tedious. How he proposed to deal with this I will come to later. Before doing so, I want to consider how far he succeeded in his attempt. The characters are drawn with consummate skill. We are persuaded of their truth. We no sooner meet them than we accept them as living creatures, standing on their own feet, in the world we know. We take them for granted, as we take our plumber, our grocer, our doctor. It never occurs to us that they are figures in a novel. Homais, to mention one, is a creature as humorous as Mr. Micawber, and he has become as familiar to the French as Mr. Micawber is to us; and we believe in him as we can never quite believe in Mr. Micawber, for, unlike Mr. Micawber, he is always consistently himself. But Emma Bovary is not by any means the ordinary farmer's daughter. That there is in her something of every woman and of every man is true. We are all given to extravagant and absurd reveries, in which we see ourselves rich, handsome, successful, the heroes or heroines of romantic adventures; but most of us are too sensible, too timorous or too unadventurous to let our day-dreams seriously affect our behaviour. Emma Bovary was exceptional in that she tried to live her fantasies; she was exceptional in her beauty. As is well known, when the novel was published author and printer were prosecuted on the charge that it was immoral. I have read the speeches of the public prosecutor and of the defending counsel. The prosecutor recited a number of passages which he claimed were pornographic: they make one smile now, they are so restrained in comparison with the descriptions of sexual intercourse to which modern novelists have accustomed us; but one cannot believe that even then (in 1875) the prosecutor was shocked by them. The defending counsel pleaded that the passages were necessary, and that the moral of the novel was good because Emma Bovary suffered for her misconduct. The judges accepted this view, and the defendants were acquitted. It is evident, however, that if Emma came to a bad end, it was not, as the morality of the time demanded, because she had committed adultery, but because she ran up bills that she hadn't the money to pay, and if she had had the notoriously thrifty instincts of the Norman peasant, there was no reason why she should not have gone from lover to lover without coming to harm.

On publication, Flaubert's great novel was enthusiastically received by readers and immediately became a best-seller, but the critics were, when not hostile, indifferent. Strange as it may seem, they were more inclined to attach importance to a novel called *Fanny* by a certain Ernest Feydeau, which was issued about the same time; and it was only the deep impression that *Madame Bovary* made on the public, and the influence it had on subsequent writers of fiction, that obliged them in the end to take it seriously.

Madame Bovary is a hard-luck story rather than a tragedy. I should say that the difference between the two is that in a hard-luck story the events that occur are brought about by chance, whereas in a tragedy they are the result of the characters of the persons engaged. It was bad luck that, with her good looks and charm, Emma should have married such a dull fool as Charles Bovary. It was bad luck that when she was pregnant and wanted a son to make up for the disillusionment of her marriage, she should have a daughter. It was bad luck that Rodolphe Boulanger, Emma's first lover, was a selfish, brutal fellow who let her down. It was bad luck that her second was mean, weak and timorous. It was bad luck that when she was desperate, the village priest, to whom she went for help and guidance, should be a callous and fatuous dolt. It was bad luck that when Emma found herself hopelessly in debt and, threatened with proceedings, so far humiliated herself as to ask Rodolphe for money, he couldn't give it her, though we are told he would have been ready to do so, because he didn't happen to have any by him. It was bad luck that it never occurred to him that his credit was good and his lawyer would immediately have given him the required sum. The story Flaubert had to tell necessarily ended in Emma's death, but it must be confessed that the means by which he brought it about strains the reader's credulity to the breaking-point.

Some have found it a fault that, though Emma is the central character, the novel begins with an account of Bovary's early youth and his first marriage, and ends with his disintegration and death. I surmise that Flaubert's idea was to enclose the story of Emma Bovary within that of her husband, as you enclose a painting in a frame. He may have felt that thus he rounded off his narrative and gave it the unity of a work of art. If this was his intention, it would have been more evident if the end were not hurried and arbitrary. Throughout the book, Charles Bovary has been shown to be weak and easily led. Flaubert tells us that after Emma's death he changed utterly. That is very summary. Broken as he was, it is hard to credit that he should have become quarrelsome, self-willed and obstinate. Though a stupid man, he was conscientious, and it seems strange that he should have neglected his patients. He badly needed their money. He had Emma's debts to pay and his daughter to provide for. The radical change in Bovary's character requires a good deal more explanation than Flaubert has given it. Finally he dies. He was a robust man in the prime of life, and the only reason one can give for his death is that Flaubert, after fifty-five months of exhausting labour, wanted to be done with the book. Since we are expressly told that Bovary's memories of Emma with time grew dim, and so presumably less poignant, one cannot but ask oneself why Flaubert did not let Bovary's mother arrange a third marriage for him, as she had arranged the first. It would have added one more note of futility to the story of Emma Bovary, and accorded well with Flaubert's ferocious sense of irony.

A work of fiction is an arrangement of incidents devised to display a number of characters in action and to interest the reader. It is not a copy of life as it is lived. Just as in a novel conversations cannot be reproduced exactly as they take place in real life, but have to be summarized so that only the essential points are given, and then with clearness and concision, so facts have to suffer some deformation in order to accord with the author's plan and to hold the reader's attention. Irrelevant incidents must be omitted; repetitions must be avoided—and, heaven knows, life is full of repetitions; isolated occurrences and events that in real life would be separated by a passage of time may often have to be brought into proximity. No novel is entirely free of improbabilities, and to the more usual ones readers have become so accustomed that they accept them as a matter of course. The novelist cannot give a literal transcript of life, he draws a picture for you which, if he is a realist, he tries to make life-like; and if you believe him he has succeeded.

On the whole, *Madame Bovary* gives an impression of intense reality, and this arises, I think, not only because Flaubert's characters are eminently lifelike, but because he has described detail with extreme accuracy. The first four years of Emma's married life were passed in a village called Tostes; she was hideously bored there, but for the balance of the book this period had to be described at the same pace and with the same detail as the rest. Now, it is difficult to describe a boring time without boring the reader; yet you read the long passage with interest. Flaubert has narrated a series of very trivial incidents, and you are not bored because you are reading something fresh all the time; but since each little incident, whether it is something Emma does, feels or sees, is so commonplace, so trivial, you do get a vivid sensation of her boredom. There is a set description of Yonville, the little town in which the Bovarys settled after leaving Tostes, but it is the only one; for the rest, the descriptions of country and town, beautifully done all of them, are interwoven with the narrative and enforce its interest. Flaubert introduces his characters in action, and we learn of their appearance, their mode of living, their setting, in a continuous process; as, in fact, we come to know people in real life.

4

I remarked a few pages back that Flaubert was aware that in setting out to write a book about commonplace people he ran the risk of writing a dull one. He desired to produce a work of art, and he felt that he could only surmount the difficulties presented by the sordid nature of his subject and the vulgarity of his characters by means of beauty of style. Now, I do not know whether such a creature exists as the natural born stylist; certainly Flaubert was not; his early works, unpublished in his lifetime, are said to be verbose, turgid and rhetorical. It is generally stated that his letters show little sign that he had a feeling for the elegance and distinction of his native tongue. I don't think that is true. They were, for the most part, written late at night, after a hard day's work, and sent to their recipients uncorrected. Words are misspelt and the grammar is often faulty; they are slangy and sometimes vulgar; but there are in them brief descriptions of scenery so real, so rhythmical, that they would not have seemed out of place in *Madame Bovary*; and there are passages, when he was moved to fury, that are so incisive, so direct, that you feel no revision would have served to improve them. You hear the sound of his voice in the short, crisp sentences. But that was not the way in which Flaubert wanted to write a book. He was prejudiced against the conversational style, and was blind to its advantages. He took for his models La Bruyère and Montesquieu. His aim was to write

420

a prose that was logical, precise, swift and various, rhythmical, sonorous, musical as poetry, and yet preserving the qualities of prose. He was of opinion that there were not two ways of saying a thing, but only one, and that the wording must fit the thought as the glove fits the hand. "When I find an assonance or a repetition in one of my phrases," he said, "I know that I am ensnared in something false." (As examples of assonance, the Oxford Dictionary gives man and hat, nation and traitor, penitent and reticent.) Flaubert claimed that an assonance must be avoided, even if it took a week to manage it. He would not allow himself to use the same word twice on a page. That does not seem sensible: if it is the right word in each place, it is the right word to use, and a synonym or a periphrase can never be as apt. He was careful not to allow the sense of rhythm which was natural to him, as it is to every writer, to obsess him (as George Moore in his later works was obsessed) and took pains to vary it. He exercised all his ingenuity to combine words and sounds to give an impression of speed or languor, lassitude or intensity; in short, of whatever state he desired to express.

When writing, Flaubert would sketch out roughly what he wished to say, and then work on what he had written, elaborating, cutting, re-writing, till he got the effect he wanted. That done, he would go out on his terrace and shout out the words he had written, convinced that if they did not sound well, there must be something wrong with them. In that case, he would take them back and work over them again till he was satisfied. Théophile Gautier thought that Flaubert attached too great a value to the cadence and harmony with which he sought to enrich his prose; they were, according to him, only evident when Flaubert in his booming voice read them aloud; but a phrase, he added, is made to read to oneself, not to be bellowed. Gautier was inclined to mock at Flaubert's fastidiousness: "You know," he said, "the poor chap suffers from a remorse that poisons his life. You don't know what the remorse is; it's to have put two genitives together in *Madame Bovary*, one on the top of the other: *une couronne de fleurs d'oranger*. It tortures him, but however hard he tried, he found it impossible to avoid." It is fortunate for us that by means of our English genitive we can escape this difficulty. We can say: "Where is the bag of the doctor's wife"; but in French you would have to say: "Where is the bag of the wife of the doctor." It must be confessed that it is not pretty.

Louis Bouilhet would come to Croisset of a Sunday; Flaubert read to him what he had written during the week, and Bouilhet criticized. Flaubert stormed and argued, but Bouilhet held his ground, and in the end Flaubert accepted the emendations, the elimination of superfluous incidents and irrelevant metaphors, the correction of false notes, which his friend insisted on. No wonder the novel proceeded at a snail's pace. In one of his letters Flaubert wrote: "The whole of Monday and Tuesday was taken up with the writing of two lines." This does not mean that he wrote only two lines in two days, he may well have written a dozen pages; it means that with all his labour he only succeeded in writing two lines to his satisfaction. Flaubert found the strain of composition exhausting. Alphonse Daudet believed that this was attributable to the bromide that his malady obliged him to make constant use of. If there is anything in this, it may account for the effort it evidently was to him to set down on paper in coherent order the huddle of ideas in his mind. We know how laborious a task he found it to write the well-known scene in *Madame Bovary* of the agricultural show. Emma and Rodolphe are seated at a window of the local inn. A representative of the *préfet* has come to deliver a speech. What Flaubert wanted to do he told in a letter to Louise Colet: "I have to situate together in the same conversation five or six people (who talk), several others (of whom one hears), the spot where this occurs, the feel of the place, while giving physical descriptions of people and things, and to show in the midst of all a man and a woman who begin (by their common sympathies of taste) to feel a little attracted to one another." That does not seem a very difficult thing to do, and Flaubert has in fact done it extremely well, but, though it was only twenty-seven pages long, it took him two solid months. Balzac would have written it in his own way no less well in the inside of a week. The great novelists, Balzac, Dickens and Tolstoy, had what we are accustomed to call inspiration. It is only in a scene here and there that you feel that Flaubert had it; for the rest he seems to have depended on sheer hard work, the advice and suggestions of Bouilhet, and his own acuteness of observation. This is not to depreciate *Madame Bovary*; but it is strange that so great a work should have been produced, not as we feel *Le Père Goriot* or *David Copperfield* was produced in the free flow of an exuberant fancy, but by almost pure ratiocination.

It is not unreasonable to ask oneself how near Flaubert came, by taking the immense pains I have described, to achieve the perfect style at which he aimed. Style is a matter of which a foreigner, even though he knows a language pretty well, can be but an uncertain judge: the finer points, the music, the subtlety, the aptness, the rhythm, can hardly fail to escape him. He must accept the opinions of the native born. For a generation after Flaubert's death his style was highly regarded in France; now it is less admired. The French writers of to-day find in it a lack of spontaneity. He had, as I have before mentioned, a horror of "this new maxim that one must write as one speaks". And of course one must no more write as one speaks than one must speak as one writes; but written language has life and vitality only if it is firmly grounded on current speech. Flaubert was a provincial, and in his prose was apt to use provincialisms which offend the purists; I don't suppose that a foreigner, unless they were pointed out to him, would be aware of them; nor would he notice the grammatical mistakes of which Flaubert, like nearly every writer who ever wrote, was sometimes guilty. Few Englishmen, though able to read French with ease and pleasure, could point out what is grammatically wrong with the following phrase: "*Ni moi! reprit vivement M. Homais, quoiqu'il lui faudra suivre les autres au risque de passer pour un Jésuite*"; and fewer still could tell how to put it right.

The French language tends to rhetoric, as the English to imagery (thereby marking a profound difference between the two peoples), and the basis of Flaubert's style is rhetorical. He made abundant, even excessive, use of the triad. This is the sentence of three members which are arranged, as a rule, either in an ascending or descending scale of importance. It is both an easy and a satisfying way of achieving balance, and orators have taken full advantage of it. Here is an example from Burke: "Their wishes ought to have great weight with him; their opinion, high respect; their business, unremitted attention." The danger of this sort of sentence, and one from which Flaubert did not escape, is that when used too often it is monotonous. Flaubert in one of his letters wrote: "I'm devoured with similes as one is with lice, and I spend all my time crushing them, my phrases swarm with them." Critics have observed that in his letters the similes are spontaneous, whereas in *Madame Bovary* they are too studied, too neatly balanced, to be natural. Here is a good example: Charles Bovary's mother has come to pay Emma and her husband a visit. "*Elle observait le bonheur de son fils, avec un silence triste, comme quelqu'un de ruiné qui regarde, à travers les carreaux, des gens attablés dans son ancienne maison.*" This is admirably put, but the simile is in itself so striking that it distracts your attention from the mood it is supposed to illustrate; the object of a simile, however, is to add force and importance to a statement, not to weaken it.

The best French writers of to-day, so far as I have been able to discover, deliberately avoid rhetoric. They attempt to say what they have to say simply and naturally. They eschew the effective triad. They avoid similes, as though they were indeed the vermin to which Flaubert likened them. That, I believe, is why they are apt to hold his style in small esteem, at least the style of *Madame Bovary*, for when he came to write *Bouvard et Pécuchet* he abandoned every form of ornament and decoration; and that is why they prefer the easy, flowing, animated and natural manner of his letters to the laboured manner of his greater novels. This is, of course, merely a matter of fashion, and justifies us in forming no judgment on the merits of Flaubert's style. A style may be stark, like Swift's, flowery, like Jeremy Taylor's, or grandiloquent, like Burke's: each is good, and whether you prefer one to another depends merely on your individual taste.

5

After the publication of *Madame Bovary* Flaubert wrote *Salammbô*, which is generally considered a failure, then another version of *L'Education Sentimentale*, in which he again described his love for Elisa Schlesinger. Many men of letters in France look upon it as his masterpiece. It is confused and hard to read. Frédéric Moreau, the hero, is partly a portrait of Flaubert, as he saw himself, and partly a portrait of Maxime du Camp, as he saw *him*; but the two men were too different to make a plausible amalgam, and the character remains unconvincing. He is singularly uninteresting. The book, however, begins admirably, and towards the end there is a parting scene between Madame Arnoux (Elisa Schlesinger) and Frédéric (Flaubert) of rare beauty. Then, for the third time, he wrote *La Tentation de St. Antoine*. Though Flaubert said he had enough ideas for books to last him to the end of his life, they remained vague projects. It is curious that with the exception of *Madame Bovary*, the story of which was given him ready-made, the only novels he wrote were founded on ideas he had had early in life. He aged prematurely. At thirty he was already bald and pot-bellied. It may well be, as Maxime du Camp said, that his nerve storms and the depressing sedatives he took to counteract them impaired his power of imaginative creation.

Time passed, and Caroline, his niece, married. Flaubert and his mother were left alone. His mother died. For some years he had had an apartment in Paris, but there he lived almost as solitarily as at Croisset. He had few friends, except the literary men who met once or twice a month to dine together at Magny's. He was a provincial, and Edmond de Goncourt said that the more he lived in Paris the more provincial he became. When dining at a restaurant, he insisted on a private room, because he could not bear noise or to have people near him; and he could not eat at his ease without taking off his coat and his boots. After the defeat of France in 1870, Caroline's husband found himself in financial difficulties, and finally, to save him from bankruptcy, Flaubert handed over his entire fortune. He was left with little except his old home. The worry of this brought on again the fits from which for some years he had been free, and when he dined out, Guy de Maupassant went to fetch him to see him safely home. Goncourt describes him at this time as irritable, sarcastic, irascible and quick to take offence at anything or nothing; but, he added in another note in his journal, "so long as you give him the principal part and let yourself catch cold because he keeps on opening the windows, he's an agreeable companion. He has a ponderous gaiety and the laughter of a child, which is contagious, and in the contact of everyday life a hearty affectionateness which is not without charm." There Goncourt did him no less than justice. Du Camp said of him: "This impetuous, imperious giant, exploding at the least contradiction, was the most respectful, the gentlest, the most attentive son that a mother could dream of." And you have only to read his charming letters to his niece to see of what tenderness he was capable.

Flaubert's last years were lonely. He spent most of the year at Croisset. He smoked too much. He ate too much and drank too much. He took no exercise. His means were straitened. Friends eventually got him the offer of a sinecure which would bring him in three thousand francs a year, and though it deeply humiliated him, he was obliged to accept it. He did not live long enough to profit by it.

The last work he published was a volume of three stories, one of which, *Un Coeur Simple*, is of a rare excellence. He engaged upon a novel called *Bouvard et Pécuchet*, in which he determined to have still another fling at the stupidity of the human race, and with his usual thoroughness he read fifteen hundred books to provide himself with the material he thought necessary. It was to be in two volumes, and he almost reached the end of the first. On the morning of May 8, 1880, the maid went into the library at eleven to bring him his lunch. She found him lying on the divan, muttering incomprehensible words. She ran for the doctor and brought him back with her. He could do nothing. In less than an hour Gustave Flaubert was dead.

The only woman he sincerely, devotedly and disinterestedly loved in his life was Elisa Schlesinger. One evening at dinner *chez Magny*, when Théophile Gautier, Taine and Edmond de Goncourt were present, Flaubert made a curious statement: he said that he had never really possessed a woman, that he was virgin, that all the women he had had were never anything but "mattresses" for another woman, the woman of his dreams. Maurice Schlesinger's speculations had ended in disaster, and he took his wife and children to live in Baden. In 1871 he died. Flaubert, after loving Elisa for thirty-five years, wrote his first love letter to her. Instead of beginning as he had been used to do, "*Chère Madame*," he began: "My old love, my only loved one." She came to Croisset. Both were greatly changed since they had last seen one another. Flaubert was gross and fat, his face red and blotchy; he wore an immense moustache and to cover his baldness a black cap. Elisa had grown thin, her skin had lost its delicate hues and her hair was white. The lovely description in *L'Education Sentimentale* of the last meeting of Madame Arnoux and Frédéric Moreau probably faithfully describes the meeting of Flaubert and Elisa after so many years. They met once or twice after that, and then, so far as anyone knows, never again.

A year after Flaubert's death, Maxime du Camp spent the summer at Baden, and one day, when he was out shooting, found himself near the lunatic asylum of Illenau. The gates were opened to allow the female inmates, under the care of keepers, to take their daily walk. They came out two by two. Among them was one who bowed to him. It was Elisa Schlesinger, the woman whom Flaubert so long and so vainly loved.

CHAPTER EIGHT

Herman Melville and *Moby Dick*

I

HITHERTO I have been dealing with novels which, with all their differences, descend in a fairly direct line from the novels of a remote past. "The novel," I learn from *The Encyclopaedia Britannica*, "has been made a vehicle for satire, for instruction, for political or religious exhortation, for technical information; but these are side issues. The plain and direct purpose of the novel is to amuse by a succession of scenes painted from nature, and by a thread of emotional narrative." This puts the matter in a nutshell. The novel, I learn further, came into favour in Alexandrian times, when life was sufficiently easy for people to take pleasure in accounts, realistic or fanciful, of the adventures and emotions of imaginary characters; but the first work of fiction that has come down to us which can strictly be called a novel is one that was written by a Greek called Longus and entitled *Daphnis and Chloe*. From this, through unnumbered generations, with many ups and downs, with many diversions, are derived the novels I have been briefly considering, whose direct purpose is, as the *Encyclopaedia* puts it, to amuse by a succession of scenes painted from nature, and by a thread of emotional narrative.

But now I come to a small group of novels which are so different in their effect on the reader, which seem to be written with an intention so extraneous, that they must be put in a class by themselves. Such novels are *Moby Dick*, *Wuthering Heights* and *The Brothers Karamazov*; and such are the novels of James Joyce and Kafka. Novelists are, of course, mutations from the common stock of bishops and bar-tenders, policemen and politicians, and so forth; and mutations occur repeatedly. But biologists tell us that most are harmful, and many lethal. Now, since the sort of book an author writes depends on the sort of man he is, and this depends partly on the association in the chromosome of genes from different parents and partly on the environment, it is surely significant that novelists are inclined to sterility; there are only two in history, Tolstoy and Dickens, who were greatly fertile. The mutation is evidently lethal. But perhaps that is just as well, since, whereas oysters when they proliferate produce oysters, novelists generally produce nitwits. The particular mutation I am now concerned with has left, so far as I know, no literary descendants.

I am going to take first the author of that strange and powerful book, *Moby Dick*. I have read Raymond Weaver's *Herman Melville, Mariner and Mystic*, Lewis Mumford's *Herman Melville*, Charles Roberts Anderson's *Melville in the South Seas*, William Ellery Sedgwick's *Herman Melville: The Tragedy of Mind*, and Newton Arvin's *Melville*. I have read them with interest, profited by most of them, and learnt from them a number of facts useful to my modest purpose; but I cannot persuade myself that I know more about Melville, the man, than I knew before.

According to Raymond Weaver, an "uncircumspect critic at the time of Melville's centenary in 1919" wrote: "Owing to some odd psychological experience, that has never been definitely explained, his style of writing, his view of life underwent a complete change." I don't quite know why this unnamed critic should be described as uncircumspect. He hit upon the problem which must puzzle everyone who is interested in Melville. It is on this account that one scrutinizes every known detail of his life and reads his letters and books, books some of which can only be read by a determined effort of will, to discover some hint that may help to elucidate the mystery.

But first let us take the facts, so far as they are made known to us by the biographers. On the face of it, but only on the face of it, they are simple enough.

Herman Melville was born in 1819. His father, Allan Melville, and his mother, Maria Gansevoort, were gentlefolk. Allan was a cultivated, travelled man, and Maria an elegant, well-bred and pious woman. For the first five years of their marriage they lived at Albany, and after that settled in New York, where Allan's business—he was an importer of French dry goods—for a time prospered, and where Herman was born. He was the third of their eight children. But by 1830 Allan Melville had fallen on evil days and moved back to Albany, where two years later he died bankrupt and, it is said, insane. He left his family penniless. Herman went to the Albany Classical Institute for boys and, on leaving school at the age of fifteen, was employed as a clerk in the New York State Bank; in 1835 he worked in his brother Gansevoort's fur store, and the following year on his uncle's farm at Pittsfield. For a term he was a teacher at the common school in the Sykes district. At seventeen he went to sea. Much has been written to account for this, but I cannot see why any further reason need be sought than the one he gives himself: "Sad disappointments in several plans which I had sketched out for my future life; the necessity of doing something for myself, united to a naturally roving disposition, had now conspired within me, to send me to sea as a sailor." He had tried his hand without success at various occupations, and from what we know of his mother we may surmise that she did not hesitate to express her displeasure. He went to sea, as many a boy before and after has done, because he was unhappy at home. Melville was a very strange man, but it is unnecessary to look for strangeness in a perfectly natural proceeding.

He arrived in New York wet through, in patched trousers and a hunting jacket, without a penny in his pocket, but with a fowling-piece his brother Gansevoort had given him to sell; he walked across town to the house of a friend of his brother's, where he spent the night, and next day with this friend went down to the waterfront. After some search, they came across a ship that was sailing for Liverpool, and Melville was signed on as a "boy" at three dollars a month. Twelve years later he wrote in *Redburn* an account of the voyage there and back, and of his stay in Liverpool. He looked upon it as hack-work; but it is vivid and interesting, and it is written in English that is simple, straightforward, easy and unaffected. It is one of the most readable of his works.

Nothing much is known about how he spent the next three years. According to the accepted accounts, he "taught school" in various places: at one, Greenbush, N.Y., he received six dollars a quarter and board; and he wrote a number of articles for provincial papers. One or two of them have been discovered. They are without interest, but give signs that he had done a lot of desultory reading; and they have a mannerism of which to the end of his life he could never rid himself, namely that of bringing in without rhyme or reason allusions to mythological gods, to historical and romantic characters, and to all kinds of authors. As Raymond Weaver neatly puts it: "He called up Burton, Shakespeare, Byron, Milton, Coleridge and Chesterfield, as well as Prometheus and Cinderella, Mahomet and Cleopatra, Madonna and Houris, Medici and Mussulman, to strew carelessly across his pages."

But he had an adventurous spirit, and it may be supposed that in the end he could no longer endure the tameness of life to which it seemed circumstances had condemned him. Though he had disliked life before the mast, he made up his mind to go to sea again; and in 1841 he sailed from New Bedford in the whaler *Acushnet*, bound for the Pacific. With one exception, the men in the forecastle were coarse, brutal and uneducated; the exception was a boy of seventeen called Richard Tobias Greene. This is how Melville describes him: "Toby was endowed with a remarkably prepossessing exterior. Arrayed in his blue frock and duck trousers, he was as smart a looking sailor as ever stepped upon a deck; he was singularly small and slightly made, with great flexibility of limb. His naturally dark complexion had been deepened by exposure to the tropical sun, and a mass of jetty locks clustered about his temples, and threw a darker shade into his large black eyes."

After fifteen months of cruising, the *Acushnet* put in at Nuku-Hiva, an island of the Marquesas. The two lads, disgusted with the hardship of life aboard the whaler and the brutality of the captain, decided to desert. They stowed away as much tobacco, ship's biscuit and calico (to give the natives) as they could get into the front of their frocks, and made off for the interior of the island. After several days, during which they had sundry mishaps, they reached the valley inhabited by the Typees, and were by them hospitably received. Shortly after their arrival, Toby was sent away on the pretext of getting

431

medical help, for Melville on the way had hurt his leg so badly that he could only walk with pain, but in fact to arrange their escape. The Typees were reputed to be cannibals, and prudence suggested that it would be unwise to reckon too long on the continuance of their good will. Toby never returned, and it was discovered much later that, on reaching the coast, he had been kidnapped on to a whaler. Melville, by his own account, spent four months in the valley. He was well treated. He made friends with a girl called Fayaway, swam and boated with her, and except for his fear of being eaten was happy enough. Then it chanced that the captain of a whaler, coming to anchor at Nuka-Hiva, heard that there was a sailor in the hands of the Typees. Many of his own crew having deserted, he sent a boatload of taboo natives to secure the man's release. Melville, again by his own account, persuaded the natives to let him go down to the beach and, after a skirmish in which he killed a man with a boat-hook, effected his escape.

Life in the ship he now boarded, the *Julia*, was even worse than in the *Acushnet*, and after some weeks of fruitless cruising on the look-out for whales, the skipper hove his craft to off the island of Tahiti. The crew mutinied and presently, after trial at Papeete, were consigned to the local jail. The *Julia*, having signed on a new crew, sailed, and the prisoners were in a short time released. With another member of the old crew, a medical man who had come down in the world and whom he calls Doctor Long Ghost, Melville sailed to the neighbouring island of Moorea, and there the pair hired themselves out to two planters to hoe potatoes. Melville had not liked farming when he worked for his uncle in Massachusetts, and he liked it less still under the tropical sun of Polynesia. With Doctor Long Ghost he wandered off, living on the natives, and eventually, leaving the doctor behind, persuaded the captain of a whaler which he calls the *Leviathan* to sign him on. In this ship he reached Honolulu. What he did there is uncertain. It is supposed that he found employment as a clerk. Then he shipped as an ordinary seaman in an American frigate, the *United States*, and after a year, upon the ship's arrival home, was discharged from the service.

We have now reached the year of 1844. Melville was twenty-five. No portrait of him in youth exists, but, from those taken in middle age, we can picture him in his twenties as a tall, well-set-up man, strong and active, with rather small eyes, but with a straight nose, a fresh colour and a fine head of waving hair.

He came home to find his mother and sisters settled at Lansingburg, a suburb of Albany. His elder brother, Gansevoort, had given up his fur shop and was become a lawyer and a politician; his second brother, Allan, a lawyer too, had settled in New York; and his youngest, Tom, soon to go to sea like Herman, was still in his teens. Herman found himself the centre of interest as "the man who had lived among cannibals", and he told the story of his adventures to eager listeners; they urged him to write a book, and this forthwith he set out to do.

He had tried his hand at writing before, though with little success; but he had to earn money, and to write seemed to him, as to many another misguided author, before and since, an easy way to do so. When *Typee*, the book in which he described his sojourn on the island of Nuka-Hiva, was finished, Gansevoort Melville, who had gone to London as secretary to the American Minister, submitted it to John Murray, who accepted it, and some time later Wiley and Putnam published it in America. It was well received and Melville, encouraged, wrote the continuation of his adventures in the South Pacific in a book which he called *Omoo*.

It appeared in 1847, and in this year he married Elizabeth, the only daughter of Chief Justice Shaw, whose family had long been known to the Melvilles. The young couple moved to New York, where they lived in Allan Melville's house at 103 Fourth Avenue, together with Herman's and Allan's sisters, Augusta, Fanny and Helen. We are not told why the three young women left their mother and Lansingburg. Herman settled down to write. In 1849, two years after his marriage and a few months after the birth of his first child, a boy named Malcolm, he crossed the Atlantic again, this time as a passenger, to see publishers and arrange for the publication of *White Jacket*, the book in which he describes his experiences in the frigate

United States. From London he went to Paris, Brussels and up the Rhine. His wife wrote as follows in her arid memoir: "Summer of 1849 we remained in New York. He wrote *Redburn* and *White Jacket.* Same fall went to England and published the above. Took little satisfaction in it from mere home-sickness, and hurried home, leaving attractive invitations to distinguished people—one from the Duke of Rutland to pass a week at Belvoir Castle—see his journal. We went to Pittsfield and boarded in the summer of 1850. Moved to Arrowhead in fall—October 1850."

Arrowhead was the name Melville gave to a farm at Pittsfield which he bought on money advanced by the Chief Justice, and here he settled with his wife, child and sisters. Mrs. Melville, in her matter-of-fact way, says in her journal: "Wrote *White Whale* or *Moby Dick* under unfavourable circumstances—would sit at his desk all day not writing anything till four or five o'clock—then ride to the village after dark—would be up early and out walking before breakfast—sometimes splitting wood for exercise. We all felt anxious about the strain on his health in the Spring of 1853."

When Melville established himself at Arrowhead, he found Hawthorne living in the neighbourhood. He took something that very much resembles a schoolgirl crush for the older writer, a crush which may have somewhat disconcerted that reserved, self-centred and undemonstrative man. The letters he wrote to him were impassioned: "I shall leave the world, I feel, with more satisfaction for having come to know you," he said in one of them. "Knowing you persuades me more than the Bible of our immortality." Of an evening he would ride over to the Red House at Lenox to talk—a little, it appears, to Hawthorne's weariness—of "Providence and futurity and of everything else that lies beyond human ken." While the two authors discoursed, Mrs. Hawthorne sewed at her stand, and in a letter to her mother she thus described Melville: "I am not quite sure that I do not think him a very great man . . . A man with a true, warm heart, and a soul and an intellect—with life to his finger-tips; earnest, sincere and reverent; very tender and modest . . . He has very keen perceptive power; but what astonishes me is, that his eyes are not large and deep. He seems to see everything very accurately; and how he can do so with his small eyes, I cannot tell. They are not keen eyes, either, but quite undistinguished in any way. His nose is straight and rather handsome, his mouth expressive of sensibility and emotion. He is tall, and erect, with an air free, brave and manly. When conversing, he is full of gesture and force, and loses himself in his subject. There is no grace, nor polish. Once in a while, his animation gives place to a singularly quiet expression, out of these eyes to which I have objected; an indrawn, dim look, but which at the same time makes you feel that he is at that moment taking deepest note of what is before him. It is a strange, lazy glance, but with a power in it quite unique. It does not seem to penetrate through you, but to take you into itself."

The Hawthornes left Lenox; and the friendship, eager and deep-felt on Melville's side and on Hawthorne's sedate, and perhaps embarrassed, came to an end. Melville dedicated *Moby Dick* to him. The letter he wrote after reading the book no longer exists, but from Melville's reply it looks as though he guessed that Hawthorne did not like it. Nor did the public, nor did the critics; and *Pierre*, with which he followed it, fared even worse. It was received with contemptuous abuse. He made very little money from his writings, and he had to provide not only for his wife, his two sons and two daughters, but also, presumably, for his three sisters. Melville, to judge from his letters, found farming his own land as little to his taste as he had found cutting his uncle's hay at Pittsfield or digging potatoes in Moorea. The fact is that he had never cared for manual labour: "See my hand—four blisters on this palm, made by hoes and hammers within the last few days. It is a rainy morning, so I am indoors, and all work suspended. I feel cheerfully disposed . . ." A farmer with hands as soft as that is unlikely to have farmed with profit.

His father-in-law, the Chief Justice, seems periodically to have come to the financial assistance of the family; and as he was a sensible man, besides being a very kind one, it may be supposed that it was he who suggested to Melville that he should look for some other way of earning his living. Various strings were pulled to obtain a consulship for him, but without success, and he was obliged to go on writing. He ailed, and the Chief Justice once more came to the rescue; in 1856 he went abroad again, this time to Constantinople, Palestine, Greece and Italy, and on his return managed to earn a little money by lecturing. In 1860 he made his last journey. Tom, his youngest brother, commanded a clipper in the China trade, the *Meteor*, and in this Melville sailed, round the Horn, to San Francisco; one would have expected him to have still enough of the spirit of adventure to seize the opportunity to go to the Far East, but for some unknown reason, either because he was bored with his brother or his brother had grown impatient of him, he left the ship at San Francisco and went home. For some years the Melvilles had lived in great poverty, but in 1861 the Chief Justice died and left his daughter a handsome legacy; they decided to leave Arrowhead and bought a house in New York from Allan, Herman's prosperous brother, and in part payment turned Arrowhead over to him. In this house, 104 East Twenty Sixth Street, Melville lived for the rest of his life.

At this time, according to Raymond Weaver, it was a good year if he earned a hundred dollars in royalties on his books; in 1866 he managed to secure an appointment as Inspector of Customs; for this he was paid four dollars a day. In the following year Malcolm, his eldest son, shot himself in his room, but whether by design or accident is not clear; his second son, Stanwix, ran away from home and of him nothing more is heard. Melville held his modest post in the Customs for twenty years; and then his wife inherited money from her brother, Samuel, and he resigned. In 1878 he published, at the expense of his Uncle Gansevoort, a poem of twenty thousand lines called *Clarel*. Shortly before his death he wrote, or re-wrote, a novelette called *Billy Budd*. He died, forgotten, in 1891. He was seventy-two.

2

Such, in brief, is the story of Melville's life as it is told by his biographers, but it is evident that there is much that they have not told. They pass over Malcolm's death, and the flight of Stanwix from home, as though they were matters of no consequence. Surely the untoward death of their elder son distressed his parents; surely the disappearance of their second perturbed them; letters must have passed between Mrs. Melville and her brothers when the boy, eighteen years of age, shot himself; one can only suppose that they have been suppressed; it is true that by 1867 Melville's fame had dwindled, but one would expect that such an event would have reminded the press of his existence, and that some mention would have been made of it in the newspapers. It was news, and American papers have never hesitated to make the most of it. Was there no enquiry into the circumstances of the boy's death? If he committed suicide, what made him do so? And why did Stanwix run away? What were the conditions of his life at home that drove him to such a step, and how does it happen that nothing more is heard of him? Mrs. Melville, so far as we know, was a good and affectionate mother: it is strange that, again so far as we know, she seems to have taken no steps to get in touch with him. From the fact that only she and her two daughters attended Melville's funeral, the only members, we are told, of his immediate family still alive, we must suppose that Stanwix was dead. The records show that in his old age Melville was fond of his grandchildren, but his feeling for his own children is ambiguous. Lewis Mumford, whose biography of Melville is sensible, and to all appearance trustworthy, gives a grim picture of his relations with them. He seems to have been a harsh, impatient parent. "One of his daughters could not recur to the image of her father without a certain painful revulsion ... When he purchased a work of art, a print or a statue for ten dollars, when there was scarcely bread to go round who can wonder at their black memories?" Revulsion is a strong word: one would have thought impatience or irritation better suited to express what his daughters may have felt when their father showed himself thus thoughtless. There must have been something more to cause their bitterness. Melville, it appears, had a jocularity which was little to their taste, and if you read between the lines, you can hardly escape the suspicion that he sometimes came home the worse for liquor. I hasten to add that this is mere surmise. Professor Stoll, in an article published in *The Journal of the History of Ideas*, suggests that Melville was "an emphatic teetotaller". I cannot believe it. He was a convivial creature and surely it is very probable that as a sailor before the mast he drank with the rest. We know that on his first journey to Europe as a passenger he sat up until all hours, drinking whisky punches and talking metaphysics with a young scholar named Adler, and later at Arrowhead, when friends came up from the city to visit him, "one hears a good deal about champagne, gin and cigars" on the excursions taken to neighbouring places of interest. Part of Melville's duty was to inspect incoming ships, and unless American skippers have changed very much from that day to this, it is pretty well certain that he would not have been long on board before being taken below to have a drink. It would be very natural if in his disappointment with life he sought solace in liquor. I should add that, unlike many of his fellows in the Customs, he performed his duties with the greatest integrity.

Melville was a very singular fellow, and there is little definite evidence for any view you may take of his character; but from his first two books you can get a pretty good idea of what he was like as a young man. For my part, I find *Omoo* more readable than *Typee*. It is a straightforward narrative of his experience on the island of Moorea, and on the whole may be accepted as true: *Typee*, on the other hand, seems to be a hotch-potch of fact and fancy. According to Charles Roberts Anderson, Melville spent only a month on the island of Nuku-Hiva and not four, as he pretended, and his adventures on his way to the valley of the Typees were not so startling as he makes out, nor the dangers he ran from their supposed predilection for human flesh so great; and the story of his escape, as he gives it, is highly improbable: "the whole scene of the rescue itself is romantic and unconvincing, apparently written in haste and more with a view to making himself a hero than with a proper regard to logic and dramatic finesse." Melville should not be found fault with for this; we are told that he repeatedly gave an account of his adventures to willing listeners, and everyone knows how hard it is to resist the temptation to make a story a little better, and a little more exciting, each time you tell it. It would have been embarrassing for him when he came to write it to state the sober and not peculiarly thrilling facts when in numberless talks he had freely embroidered upon them. *Typee*, in fact, appears to be a compilation of matter which Melville found in contemporary travel books, combined with a highly coloured version of his own experiences. The industrious Mr. Anderson has shown that on occasion he not only repeated the errors these travel books contained, but in various instances used the very words of their authors. I think this accounts for a certain heaviness the reader may find in it. But both *Typee* and *Omoo* are well enough written in the idiom of the period. Melville was already inclined to use the literary word rather than the plain one: so, for example, he prefers to call a building an *edifice*; one hut is not near another, nor even in its neighbourhood, but in the *vicinity*; he is more apt to be *fatigued* than, like most people, tired; and he prefers to *evince*, rather than to show, feeling.

But the portrait of the author of both these books emerges clearly, and you need make no imaginative effort to see that he was a hardy, brave and determined youth, high-spirited and fond of fun, work-shy but not lazy; gay, amiable, friendly and carefree. He was charmed with the prettiness of the Polynesian girls, as any young fellow of his age would be, and it would be strange if he did not accept the favours they were certainly willing to grant him. If there was anything unusual in him, it was that he took a keen delight in beauty, something to which youth is apt to be indifferent; and there is some intensity in his admiring descriptions of the sea and the sky and the green mountains. Perhaps the only indication there is that there was more in him than in any other sailor-man of three-and-twenty is that he was of "a pondering turn", and conscious of it. "I am of a meditative humour", he wrote much later, "and at sea used often to mount aloft at night, and, seating myself in one of the upper yards, tuck my jacket about me and give loose to reflection."

How is one to account for the transformation of this apparently

439

normal young man into the savage pessimist who wrote *Pierre*? What turned the undistinguished writer of *Typee* into the darkly imaginative, powerful, inspired and eloquent author of *Moby Dick*? Some have thought, an attack of insanity. This has been hotly denied by his admirers, as though it were something disgraceful: it is, of course, no more disgraceful than to have an attack of jaundice. I have not in this essay to deal with *Pierre*. It is a preposterous book. There are in it pregnant sayings: Melville wrote in pain and bitterness, and his passion from time to time gave rise to passages that are powerful and eloquent; but the incidents are improbable, the motives unconvincing and the conversations stilted. *Pierre* gives one the impression that it was written in a condition of advanced neurasthenia. But that is not insanity. If there is any evidence that Melville was ever out of his mind, it has not, so far as I know, been produced. It has been suggested, also, that Melville was so profoundly affected as to become a different man by the intensive reading he undertook when he moved from Lansingburg to New York; the notion that he was crazed by Sir Thomas Browne, as Don Quixote was crazed by romances of chivalry, is really too naïve to carry conviction. In some unknown way the commonplace writer became a writer of something very like genius. In these days of sex-consciousness, it is natural to look for a sexual cause to explain so strange a circumstance.

Typee and *Omoo* were written before Melville married Elizabeth Shaw. During the first year of their union he wrote *Mardi*. It begins as a straightforward continuation of his adventures before the mast, but then it becomes wildly fanciful. It is long-winded and, to my mind, tedious. I cannot put its theme better than has been done by Raymond Weaver: "*Mardi* is a quest after some total and undivided possession of that holy and mysterious joy that touched Melville during the period of his courtship: a joy he had felt in the crucifixion of his love for his mother; a joy that had dazzled him in his love for Elizabeth Shaw . . . And *Mardi* is a pilgrimage for a lost glamour . . . It is a quest after Yillah, a maiden from Oroolia, the Island of Delight. A voyage is made through the civilized world for her; and though they (the persons of the novel) find occasion for much discourse on international politics, and an array of other topics, Yillah is not found."

If one wants to indulge in conjecture, one may take this strange story as the first sign of his disappointment with the married state. One has to guess what Elizabeth Shaw, Mrs. Melville, was like from the few letters of hers that remain. She was not a good letter-writer, and it may be that there was more in her than they reveal; but they show, at least, that she was in love with her husband and that she was a sensible, kindly, practical, though narrow and conventional, woman. She bore poverty without complaint. She was doubtless puzzled by her husband's development, and perhaps regretful that he seemed bent on throwing away the reputation and popularity *Typee* and *Omoo* had won him, but she continued to believe in him and to admire him to the end. She was not a woman of intellect, but she was a good, tolerant and affectionate wife.

Did Melville love her? No letters that he may have written during his courtship remain, and it is no more than a sentimental assumption that he was then touched by a "holy and mysterious joy". He married her. But men do not only marry for love. It may be that he had had enough of a wandering life, and wanted to settle down: one of the strange things about this strange man is that though, as he says himself, of "a naturally roving disposition," after his first journey as a boy to Liverpool and his three years in the South Seas, his thirst for adventure was quenched. Such journeys as he took later were mere tourist trips. It may be that Melville married because his family and friends thought it was high time he did, or it may be that he married in order to combat inclinations that dismayed him. Who can tell? Lewis Mumford says that "he was never quite happy in Elizabeth's company, nor was he quite happy away from it", and suggests that he felt not merely affection for her, but "on these long absences, passion would gather within him", only to be followed by quick satiety. He would not have been the first man to find that he loved his wife more when he was parted from her than when he was with her, and that the expectation of sexual intercourse was more exciting than the realization. I think it probable that Melville was impatient with the marriage tie; it may be that his wife gave him less than he had hoped, but he continued to have marital relations long enough for her to bear him four children. He remained, so far as anyone knows, faithful to her.

No one who has occupied himself with Melville has failed to notice his delight in male beauty. In a lecture he gave on sculpture after his return from Palestine and Italy, he singled out for special comment the Greco-Roman statue known as the Apollo Belvedere. Its chief merit is that it represents a very handsome young man. I have already described the impression made on Melville by Toby, the boy in whose company he deserted the *Acushnet*, and in *Typee* he dwells on the physical perfection of the youths with whom he consorted. They are much more vividly presented than the girls with whom he flirted. But before that, at the age of seventeen, he sailed in a ship bound for Liverpool. There he made friends with a boy called Harry Bolton. This is how he described him in *Redburn*: "He was one of those small, but perfectly formed beings with curling hair, and silken muscles, who seem to have been born in cocoons. His complexion was a mantling brunette, feminine as a girl's; his feet were small, his hands very white; and his eyes were large, black and womanly; and, poetry aside, his voice was as the sound of a harp." Doubt has been thrown on the hurried jaunt the two boys made to London, and even on the existence of such a person as Harry Bolton; but if Melville invented him to add an interesting episode to his narrative, it is queer that such a manly fellow as he should have invented a character who was so obviously homosexual.

In the frigate *United States*, Melville's great friend was an English sailor, Jack Chase, "tall and well-knit, with a clear open eye, a fine brow, and an abounding nut-brown beard." "There was such an astounding air of good sense and good feeling about the man," he wrote in *White Jacket*, "that he who could not love him, would thereby pronounce himself a knave," and further: "Wherever you may be now rolling over the blue billows, dear Jack, take my best love with you, and God bless you, wherever you go." A touch of tenderness rare in Melville.

So deep an impression did this sailor make on him that he dedicated to him the novelette, *Billy Budd*, which he completed only three months before his death, fifty years later. The story hangs on the hero's amazing beauty. It is this that causes everyone in the ship to love him, and it is this that indirectly brings about his tragic end.

It seems fairly evident that Melville was a repressed homosexual, a type which, if we may believe what we read, was more common in the United States of his time than it is to-day. The sexual proclivities of an author are no business of his readers, except in so far as they influence his work, as is the case with André Gide and Marcel Proust; when they do, and the facts are put before you, much that was obscure or even incredible may be made plain. If I have dwelt on this idiosyncrasy of Melville's, it is because it may account for his dissatisfaction with married life; and it may be that a sexual frustration occasioned the change in him which has puzzled all those who have interested themselves in him. The probabilities are great that his moral sense prevailed; but who can tell what instincts, perhaps even unrecognized and, even if recognized, angrily repressed and never, except perhaps in imagination, indulged in—who can tell, I say, what instincts may dwell in a man's being which, though never yielded to, may yet have an overwhelming effect on his disposition?

3

Melville's reading, though desultory, had always been wide. It seems that he was chiefly attracted by the poets and prose writers of the seventeenth century, and one must presume that he found in them something that peculiarly accorded with his own confused propensities. Whether their influence was harmful to him or beneficial is a matter of personal opinion. His early education was slight and, as often happens in such cases, he did not quite assimilate the culture he acquired in later years. Culture is not something you put on like a ready-made suit of clothes, but a nourishment you absorb to build up your personality, just as food builds up the body of a growing boy; it is not an ornament to decorate a phrase, still less to show off your knowledge, but a means, painfully acquired, to enrich the soul.

Melville was making a dangerous experiment when, in order to write *Moby Dick*, he devised for himself a style founded on that of the seventeenth-century writers. At its best, it is impressive and has a poetic power; but after all it remains a pastiche. That is not to belittle it. A pastiche may have great beauty. The Venus of Milo, a work of the first century B.C., is a pastiche; and so is the even later Spinario in Rome. Both were formerly supposed to be works of mid-fifth-century sculptors. Duccio, the great Siennese painter, based his style on early twelfth-century Byzantine painting, and not on the Byzantine painting current in his own day, two centuries later. When, however, a writer attempts pastiche, he is faced with the difficulty that consistency is practically unattainable. Just as Dr. Johnson's old schoolfellow, Mr. Edwards, found it impossible to philosophize because cheerfulness would break in, so in a pastiche the contemporary idiom natural to the author breaks in to jar with the idiom he has affected. "To produce a mighty book," wrote Melville, "you must choose a mighty theme," and it is pretty clear that he thought it must be dealt with in the grand style. Robert Louis Stevenson claimed that Melville had no ear; I don't know what he meant by that. Melville had a true sense of rhythm, and the balance of his sentences, however long, is in general excellent. He liked the high-sounding phrase, and the stately vocabulary he employed in fact enabled him frequently to get effects of great beauty. Sometimes this inclination led him to tautology, as when he speaks of the "umbrageous shade", which only means the shady shade; but you can scarcely deny that the sound is rich. Sometimes one is pulled up by such a tautology as "hasty precipitancy" only to discover with some awe that Milton wrote: "Thither they hasted with glad precipitance." Sometimes Melville uses common words in an unexpected way, and often obtains by this means a pleasant novelty of effect; and even when it seems to you that he has used them in a sense they cannot bear, it is rash to blame him with "hasty precipitancy", for he may well have authority to go on. When he speaks of "redundant hair", it may occur to you that hair may be redundant on a maiden's lip, but hardly on a young man's head; but if you look it out in the dictionary you will find that the second sense of redundant is copious, and Milton wrote of "redundant locks".

The difficulty of the kind of writing Melville set himself to use in *Moby Dick* is that the rhetorical level must be maintained throughout. The matter must fit the manner. The writer cannot afford to be sentimental or humorous. Melville was too often both, and then you read him with embarrassment.

His taste was unsure and sometimes, attempting the poetic, he only succeeded in being absurd: "But few thoughts of Pan stirred Ahab's brain, as standing like an iron statue at his accustomed place beside the mizzen rigging, with one nostril he unthinkingly sniffed the sugary musk from the Banshee isles (in whose sweet woods mild lovers must be walking), and with the other consciously inhaled the salt breath of the new-found sea. . . ." To smell one odour with one nostril and, at the same time, another with the other is more than a remarkable feat; it is an impossible one. I have little sympathy with Melville's partiality for archaic words and words only in poetic usage: *o'er* for over; *nigh* for near; *ere* for before; *anon* and *eftsoons*; they give a fusty, meretricious air to prose that at its best is solid and virile. He had an extensive vocabulary, and sometimes it ran away with him. He found it hard to set down a noun without tacking on to it an adjective and often two or three. He was peculiarly fond of the adjective *mystic*, and used it as though it meant strange, mysterious, awe-inspiring, frightening, in fact whatever at the moment he wanted it to mean. Professor Stoll in the article to which I have already referred, and which is as eminently, and even as devastatingly, sensible as everything he writes, has justly stigmatized this as pseudo-poetic. In this article Professor Stoll has remarked on a characteristic that must disturb all readers of Melville, and that is his predilection for adverbs formed out of participles. It may be that it is on this account that Stevenson claimed that Melville had no ear, for one has to admit that these constructions seldom have euphony to recommend them. The most ill-sounding that I

445

have noticed is *whistlingly*, but Professor Stoll has quoted others, *burstingly*, *suckingly*, and he might have quoted a hundred more that run it pretty close. Newton Arvin in his painstaking, but to my mind wrong-headed, book in the American Men of Letters Series has given examples of Melville's coining of words: *footmanism*, *omnitooled*, *uncatastrophied*, *domineerings*; and appears to think that they add a peculiar excellence to his style. They add certainly to its idiosyncrasy, but surely not to its beauty. If Melville had had an education more catholic, and a taste less uncertain, he could have achieved the effects he was presumably aiming at without the distortions of language he affected.

Melville's dialogue has little resemblance to ordinary speech. It is highly stylized. Since the principal persons on the *Pequod* are Quakers, it is natural enough that Melville should have used the second person singular, but I think, moreover, that he found it suited the deliberate purpose he had in view. He may well have felt that it gave an hieratic turn to the conversations he reported and a poetic flavour to the words used. He had no great skill in differentiating the speech of different characters: they all talk very much like one another, Ahab like his mates, the mates like the carpenter and the blacksmith, in a highly figurative manner, with an abundant use of metaphor and simile. Queequeg, thinking he is about to die, is lying in the coffin he has made for himself, and Pip, a little coloured boy who has lost his wits, "drew nigh to him where he lay, and with soft sobbings, took him by the hand; in the other, holding his tambourine"; and this is how he addressed the Kanaka: "Poor rover! will ye never have done with all this weary roving? Where go ye now? But if the currents carry ye to those sweet Antilles where the beaches are only beat with water-lilies, will ye do one little errand for me? Seek out one Pip, who's now been missing long, for he must be very sad for look! he's left his tambourine behind;—I found it. Rig-a-dig, dig, dig! Now, Queequeg, die; and I'll beat ye your dying march." Starbuck, the first mate, is "gazing down the scuttle" on this scene, and he murmurs as follows: "I have heard that in violent fevers, men, all ignorance, have talked in ancient tongues; and that when the mystery is probed, it turns out always that in their wholly forgotten childhood those ancient tongues have been really spoken in their hearing by some lofty scholars. So, to my fond faith, poor Pip, in this strange sweetness of his lunacy, brings heavenly vouchers of all our heavenly homes. Where learned he that, but there?"

Of course, in fiction dialogue is necessarily stylised. To reproduce it accurately would be intolerable. It is a question of degree. It should surely have such verisimilitude as not to shock the reader. Ahab, speaking to Stubb, the second mate, about the white whale, cries: "I'll ten times girdle the unmeasured globe; yea and dive straight through it, but I'll slay him yet!" You dismiss the high-sounding bombast with a laugh.

But for all that, notwithstanding the reservations one may make, Melville wrote English uncommonly well. Sometimes, as I have pointed out, the manner he had acquired led him to rhetorical extravagance, but at its best it has a copious magnificence, a sonority, a grandeur, an eloquence that no modern writer, so far as I know, has achieved. It does, indeed, at times recall the majestic phrase of Sir Thomas Browne and the stately period of Milton. I should like to call the reader's attention to the ingenuity with which Melville wove into the elaborate pattern of his prose the ordinary nautical terms used by sailormen in the course of their daily work. The effect is to bring a note of realism, a savour of the fresh salt of the sea, to the sombre symphony which is the strange and powerful novel of *Moby Dick*. Every author has the right to be judged by his best. How good Melville's best is the reader can judge for himself by reading the chapter entitled 'The Great Armada.' When he has action to describe, he does it magnificently, with force, and then his formal manner of writing grandly enhances the thrilling effect.

4

No one who has read anything I have written will expect me to speak of *Moby Dick*, Melville's only title to rank with the great writers of fiction, as an allegory. Readers must go elsewhere for that. I can only deal with it from my own standpoint of a not inexperienced novelist. The purpose of fiction is to give æsthetic pleasure. It has no practical ends. The business of the novelist is not to advance philosophical theories; that is the business of the philosopher, who can do it better. But since some very intelligent persons have taken *Moby Dick* for an allegory, it is proper that I should deal with the matter. They have regarded as ironical Melville's own remark: "He feared," he wrote, "that his work might be looked upon as a monstrous fable, or still worse and more detestable, a hideous and intolerable allegory." Is it rash to assume that when a practised writer says a thing, he is more likely to mean what he says than what his commentators think he means? It is true that in a letter to Mrs. Hawthorne he stated that he had, while writing, "some vague idea that the whole book was susceptible of an allegorical construction"; but that is slender evidence that he had the intention of writing an allegory. May it not be possible that if, in fact, it is susceptible to such an interpretation, it is something that came about by accident and, as his words to Mrs. Hawthorne seem to indicate, not a little to his dismay? I don't know how critics write novels, but I have some notion how novelists write them. They do not take a general proposition, such as Honesty is the Best Policy or All is not Gold that Glitters, and say: "Let's write an allegory about that." A group of characters, generally suggested by persons they have known, excites their imagination, and sometimes simultaneously, sometimes after an interval, an incident or a string of incidents, experienced, heard of or invented, appears to them out of the blue to enable them to make suitable use of it in the development of the theme that has arisen in their minds by a sort of collaboration between the characters and the incidents. Melville was not fanciful, or at least, when he attempted to be so, as in *Mardi*, he came a cropper. To imagine, and his imagination was powerful, he needed a solid basis of fact. Indeed, certain critics have on this account accused him of lacking invention—I think, without reason. It is true that he invented more convincingly when he had a substratum of experience, his own or that of others, to sustain him; but then so do most novelists; and when he had this, his imagination worked freely and with power. When, as in *Pierre*, he had not, he wrote absurdly. It is true that Melville was of a "pondering" turn and, as he grew older, he became absorbed in metaphysics, which Raymond Weaver, strangely enough, states is "but misery dissolved in thought". That is a narrow view: there is no subject to which a man can more fitly give his attention, for it deals with the greatest problems that confront his soul. Melville's approach to them was not intellectual, but emotional; he thought as he did because he felt as he did; but this does not prevent many of his reflections from being memorable. I should have thought that deliberately to write an allegory required an intellectual detachment of which Melville was incapable.

Professor Stoll has shown how ridiculous and contradictory are the symbolic interpretations of *Moby Dick* that have been hurled at the heads of an inoffensive public. He has done it so conclusively that there is no need for me to enlarge upon the topic. In defence of these critics, however, I would say this: the novelist does not copy life, he arranges it to suit his purpose. He disposes of the data given him according to the peculiarity of his own temperament. He draws a coherent pattern, but the pattern he draws varies according to the attitude, interests and idiosyncrasy of the reader. According to your proclivities, you may take a snow-clad Alpine peak, as it rises to the empyrean in radiant majesty, as a symbol of man's aspiration to union with the Infinite; or since, if you like to believe that, a mountain range may be thrown up by some violent convulsion in the earth's depths, you may take it as a symbol of the dark and sinister passions of man that lour to destroy him; or, if you want to be in the fashion, you may take it as a phallic symbol. Newton Arvin regards Ahab's ivory leg as "an equivocal symbol both of his own impotence and of the independent male principle directed cripplingly against him", and the white whale as "the archetypal Parent; the father, yes, but the mother also, so far as she becomes a substitute for the father". For Ellery Sedgwick, who claims that it is its symbolism that makes

449

the book great, Ahab is "Man—Man sentient, speculative, purposive, religious, standing his full stature against the immense mystery of creation. His antagonist, Moby Dick, is that immense mystery. He is not the author of it, but is identical with that galling impartiality in the laws and lawlessness of the universe which Isaiah devoutly fathered on the Creator". Lewis Mumford takes Moby Dick as a symbol of evil, and Ahab's conflict with him as the conflict of good and evil in which good is finally vanquished. There is a certain plausibility in this, and it accords well with Melville's moody pessimism.

But allegories are awkward animals to handle; you can take them by the head or by the tail, and it seems to me that an interpretation quite contrary is equally plausible. Why should it be assumed that Moby Dick is a symbol of evil? It is true that Melville causes Ishmael, the narrator, to adopt Ahab's crazy passion to revenge himself on the dumb beast that had maimed him; but that is a literary artifice which he had to make use of, first, because there was Starbuck already there to represent common sense, and second, because he needed someone to share, and to an extent sympathize with, Ahab's tenacious purpose, and so induce the reader to accept it as not quite unreasonable. Now, the "empty malice" of which Professor Mumford speaks consists in Moby Dick defending himself when he is attacked.

> *"Cet animal est très méchant,*
> *Quand on l'attaque, il se défend."*

Why should the White Whale not represent goodness rather than evil? Splendid in beauty, vast in size, great in strength, he swims the seas in freedom. Ahab, with his insane pride, is pitiless, harsh, cruel and vindictive; *he* is evil; and when the final encounter comes and Ahab with his crew of "mongrel renegades, castaways and cannibals" is destroyed, and the White Whale, imperturbable, justice having been done, goes his mysterious way, evil has been vanquished and good at last triumphed. This seems to me as plausible an interpretation as any other; for let us not forget that *Typee* is a glorification of the noble savage, uncorrupted by the vices of civilization, and that Melville looked upon the natural man as good.

Fortunately *Moby Dick* may be read, and read with intense interest, without a thought of what allegorical or symbolic significance it may or may not have. I cannot repeat too often that a novel is not to be read for instruction or edification, but for intelligent enjoyment, and if you find you cannot get this from it you had far better not read it at all. But it must be admitted that Melville seems to have done his best to hinder his readers' enjoyment. He was writing a strange, original and thrilling story, but a perfectly straightforward one. The romantic beginning is admirable. Your interest is aroused and held. The characters, as they are introduced one by one, are clearly presented, alive and plausible. The tension rises and, with the acceleration of the action, your excitement increases. The climax is intensely dramatic. It is hard to understand why Melville should have deliberately sacrificed the grip he had got on his readers by pausing here and there to write chapters dealing with the natural history of the whale, its size, skeleton, amours and so forth. It is as senseless, on the face of it, as it would be for a man telling a story over the dinner table to stop now and then to tell you the etymological meaning of some word he had used. Montgomery Belgion, in a judicious introduction to an edition of *Moby Dick*, has supposed that since it is a tale of pursuit, and the end of a pursuit must be perpetually delayed, Melville wrote these chapters merely to do so. I cannot believe that. Had he had any such purpose, during the three years he spent in the Pacific he must surely have witnessed incidents, or been told tales, that he could have woven into his narrative more fitly to effect it. I myself think that Melville wrote these chapters for the simple reason that, like many another self-educated man, he attached an exaggerated importance to the knowledge he had so painfully acquired and could not resist the temptation to parade it, just as in his earlier writings he "called up Burton, Shakespeare, Byron, Milton, Coleridge and Chesterfield, as well as Prometheus and Cinderella, Mahomet and Cleopatra, Madonna and

451

Houris, Medici and Mussulman, to strew carelessly across his pages".

For my part, I can read most of these chapters with interest, but it cannot be denied that they are digressions which sadly impair the tension. Melville lacked what the French call *l'esprit de suite*, and it would be stupid to assert that the novel is well-constructed. But if he composed it in the way he did, it is because that is how he wanted it. You must take it or leave it. He knew very well that *Moby Dick* would not please. He was of an obstinate temper, and it may be that the neglect of the public, the savage onslaught of the critics, and the lack of understanding in those nearest to him only confirmed him in his determination to write exactly as he chose. You must put up with his vagaries, his faulty taste, his ponderous playfulness, his errors of construction, for the sake of his excellencies, the frequent splendour of his language, his vivid and thrilling descriptions of action, his delicate sense of beauty and the tragic power of his "mystic" ponderings which, perhaps because he was somewhat muddle-headed, with no striking gift for ratiocination, for just that reason are emotionally impressive. But, of course, it is the sinister and gigantic figure of Captain Ahab that pervades the book and gives it its unique force. You must go to the Greek dramatists for anything like that sense of doom with which everything you are told about him fills you, and to Shakespeare to find beings of such terrible power. It is because Herman Melville created him that, notwithstanding any reservation one may make, *Moby Dick* is a great book.

I have said, and said again, that in order to get a real insight into a great novel you must know what there is to be known about the man who wrote it. I have an idea that in the case of Melville something like the contrary obtains. When one reads, and re-reads, *Moby Dick*, it seems to me that one gets a more convincing, a more definite, impression of the man than from anything one may learn of his life and circumstances; an impression of a man endowed by nature with a great gift blighted by an evil genius, so that, like the agave, no sooner had it put forth its splendid blooming than it withered; a moody, unhappy man tormented by instincts he shrank from with horror; a man conscious that the virtue had gone out of him, and embittered by failure and poverty; a man of heart craving for friendship, only to find that friendship too was vanity. Such, as I see him, was Herman Melville, a man whom one can only regard with deep compassion.

CHAPTER NINE

Emily Brontë and *Wuthering Heights*

I

HUGH PRUNTY, a young peasant-farmer in County Down, in 1776 married Elinor McClory; and on St. Patrick's Day in the following year the eldest of his ten children was born and given the name of Ireland's patron saint. It looks as though he could neither read nor write, for he seems to have been uncertain how his name was spelt. In the baptismal register it is given as Brunty and Bruntee. The small-holding he farmed was insufficient to provide for his large family, and he worked in a lime-kiln and, when things were slack, as a labourer on the estate of one of the neighbouring gentry. It may be supposed that Patrick, his eldest son, did odd jobs about his father's bit of land till he was old enough to earn a wage. Then he became a hand-loom weaver. But he was a clever lad, and ambitious; and, somehow or other, by the time he was sixteen he had got enough education to become a teacher at a village school near his birth-place. Two years later he got a similar job at the parish school at Drumballyroney, and held it for eight years. There are two accounts of what happened then: one states that Methodist ministers, impressed by his ability and expecting him to train himself for the ministry, subscribed a few pounds which, added to the little he had saved, enabled him to go to Cambridge; another states that he left the parish school to become a tutor in a clergyman's family, and it was with his help that he entered St. John's College. He was then twenty-five, old to enter a university, a tall, very strong young man, handsome and vain of his good looks. He subsisted on a scholarship, two exhibitions and what he was able to earn by coaching. He took his B.A. at the age of twenty-nine, and was ordained in the Church of England. If the Methodist ministers

454

really helped him to go to Cambridge, they must have felt that they had made a bad investment.

It was while he was at Cambridge that Patrick Branty, as his surname is spelt in the list of admissions, changed it to Bronte, but it was not till later that he adopted the diæresis, and signed himself Patrick Brontë. He was appointed to a curacy at Withersfield in Essex and there fell in love with a Miss Mary Burder. She was eighteen and, though not rich, well off. They became engaged. For some reason that has remained obscure, Mr. Brontë jilted her, and it has been supposed that, having a good opinion of his advantages, he thought that by waiting he could do better for himself. Mary Burder was bitterly hurt. It may be that the handsome curate's behaviour caused a good deal of acid comment in the parish, for he left Withersfield and took a curacy at Wellington in Shropshire and, after a few months, another at Hartshead in Yorkshire. There he met a plain little woman of thirty called Maria Branwell. She had fifty pounds a year of her own and belonged to a respectable middle-class family; Patrick Brontë was thirty-five and perhaps thought that by then, notwithstanding his good looks and agreeable brogue, this was about as well as he could expect to do for himself. He proposed, was accepted and in 1812 the couple were married. While still at Hartshead Mrs. Brontë had two children, and they were named Maria and Elizabeth. Then Mr. Brontë was appointed to still another curacy, this time near Bradford, and here Mrs. Brontë had four more children. They were named Charlotte, Patrick Branwell, Emily and Anne. A year before his marriage Mr. Brontë had published at his own expense a volume of verse entitled *Cottage Poems*, and a year after that another, *The Rural Minstrel*. While living near Bradford he wrote a novel, called *The Cottage in the Wood*. People who have read these productions say that they are devoid of merit. In 1820 Mr. Brontë was appointed to the "perpetual curacy" of Haworth, a Yorkshire village, and there he remained, his ambitions, one may suppose, satisfied, till his death. He never went back to Ireland to see the parents, brothers and sisters he had left there, but as long as she lived he sent his mother twenty pounds a year.

In 1821, after nine years of marriage, Maria Brontë died of cancer. The widower persuaded his sister-in-law, Elizabeth Branwell, to leave Penzance, where she lived, to come and look after his six children; but he wanted to marry again, and after a decent interval he wrote to Mrs. Burder, mother of the girl he had treated so ill fourteen years before, to enquire whether she was still single. After some weeks he received a reply and forthwith wrote to Mary herself. The letter is smug, self-complacent, unctuous and, considering the facts, in execrable taste. He had the impudence to say that his ancient love was rekindled and that he had a longing desire to see her. It was in effect a proposal of marriage. Her reply was stinging, but, undeterred, he wrote again. With amazing tactlessness he told her: "You may think and write as you please, but I *have not the least doubt* that if you had been mine you would have been happier than you *now* are, or *can* be as one in *single life*." (The italics are his.) Having failed with Mary Burder, he turned his thoughts in another direction. It does not seem to have occurred to him that a widower of forty-five, with six young children, was no great catch. He made an offer to Miss Elizabeth Frith, whom he had known when he was a curate near Bradford, but she also refused him; upon which he seems to have given it up as a bad job. It was, at all events, something to be thankful for that Elizabeth Branwell was there to look after the house and take care of the children.

Haworth Parsonage was a small brownstone house on the brow of the steep hill down which the village straggled. There was a tiny strip of garden in front of it and behind, and, on either side, the graveyard. Biographers of the Brontës have thought this depressing, and to a doctor it might have been, but a clergyman may well have thought it an edifying and even consoling sight; anyhow, this particular clergyman's family must have grown so accustomed to it that in all probability they noticed it as little as the fisherman at Capri notices the view of Vesuvius or of Ischia in the setting sun. There was a parlour, a study for Mr. Brontë, a kitchen and a storeroom on the ground floor, and four bedrooms and a lobby on the floor above. There were no carpets, except in the parlour and the study, and no curtains to the windows because Mr. Brontë had the greatest dread of fire. The floors and the stairs were of stone, cold and damp in winter, and Miss Branwell, for fear of catching cold, always went about the house in pattens. A narrow pathway led from the house to the moor. With the idea, perhaps barely conscious, of making the story of the Brontës more poignant, it has been customary for authors to write as though it were always bleak, bitter cold and dreary at Haworth. But, of course, even in winter there were days of blue sky and brilliant sunshine, when the frosty air was invigorating, and meadows, moor and woods were painted in the tender colours of pastel. On such a day I went to Haworth. The countryside was bathed in a haze of silver-grey so that the distance, its outlines dim, was mysterious. The leafless trees had the elegance of trees in a wintry scene in a Japanese print, and the hawthorn hedges by the roadside glistened white with hoar frost. Emily's poems and *Wuthering Heights* tell you how thrilling the spring was on the moor, and how rich in beauty and how sensuous in summer.

Mr. Brontë walked long and far on the moor. In his old age he boasted that he had been able to walk forty miles a day. He was a man who shunned company—somewhat of a change, for as a curate he had been a social creature, fond of parties and flirtations; and, with the exception of the neighbouring parsons who sometimes came down the hills to drink a dish of tea, he saw no one but the churchwardens and his parishioners. If these sent for him he went to see them, and if they asked a service he was glad to do it, but he and his family "kept themselves very close". He, the son of a poverty-stricken Irish peasant, would not let his children associate with the village children, and they were driven to sit in the cold little lobby on the first floor, which was their study, reading or whispering low in order not to disturb their father, who, when annoyed or displeased, maintained a sullen silence. He gave them their lessons in the morning, and Miss Branwell taught them sewing and housework.

Even before his wife's death, Mr. Brontë had taken to having his meals in his study by himself, and this habit he retained for the rest of his life. The reason given for this is that he suffered from indigestion. Emily wrote in a diary: "We are going to have for dinner boiled beef, turnips, potatoes and apple pudding." And in 1846 Charlotte wrote from Manchester: "Papa requires nothing you know but plain beef and mutton, tea and bread and butter." This does not seem a very good régime for someone who suffers from chronic dyspepsia. I am inclined to think that if Mr. Brontë took his meals by himself, it was because he did not much care for the company of his children and was irritable when they interrupted him. At eight o'clock at night he read family prayers, and at nine locked and barred the front door. As he passed the room in which his children were sitting, he told them not to sit up late and, halfway up the stairs, stopped to wind the clock.

Mrs. Gaskell knew Mr. Brontë for several years, and the conclusion she came to was that he was selfish, irascible and domineering; and Mary Taylor, one of Charlotte's intimate friends, wrote to another of her friends, Ellen Nussey: "I can never think without gloomy anger of Charlotte's sacrifices to the selfish old man." Of late, attempts have been made to whitewash him. But no whitewashing can get over the letters he wrote to Mary Burder. They are published in full in Clement Shorter's *The Brontës and their Circle*. Nor can whitewashing get over his behaviour when his curate, Mr. Nicholls, proposed to Charlotte. I will come to that later. Mrs. Gaskell writes as follows: "Mrs. Brontë's nurse told me that one day when the children had been on the moors, and rain had come on, she thought they would be wet, and accordingly she rummaged out some coloured boots which had been given them by a friend. These little pairs she ranged round the kitchen fire to warm; but when the children came back, the boots were nowhere to be found; only a very strong odour of burnt leather was perceived. Mr. Brontë had come in and seen them; they were too gay and luxurious for his children; so he had put them into the fire. He spared nothing that offended his antique simplicity. Long before this, someone had given Mrs. Brontë a silk gown; either the make, the colour, or the material was not according to his notions of consistent propriety, and Mrs. Brontë in consequence had never worn it. But, for all that, she kept it treasured up in her drawers, which were generally locked. One day, however, while in the kitchen, she remembered that she had left the key in her drawer, and hearing Mr. Brontë upstairs, she augured some ill of her dress, and, running up in haste, she found it cut into shreds." The story is circumstantial, but it is hard to see why the nurse should have invented it. "Once he got the hearthrug, and stuffing it up the grate, deliberately set it on fire, and remained in the room in spite of the stench, until it had smouldered and shrivelled away into uselessness. Another time he took some chairs, and sawed away at the backs till they were reduced to the condition of stools." It is only fair to add that Mr. Brontë declared that these stories were untrue. But no one has doubted that he had a violent temper, nor that he was stern and peremptory. I have asked myself whether these unamiable traits of Mr. Brontë's may not be ascribed to his disappointment with life. Like many another man of humble origins who has had a galling struggle to raise himself above the class in which he was born and to get an education, he may well have had an exaggerated opinion of his abilities. We know that he was vain of his good looks. His literary efforts had met with no success. It would not be strange if it embittered him to realize that the only reward he had got for his long tussle with adversity was a perpetual curacy in the wilds of Yorkshire.

The hardships and loneliness of life at the parsonage have been made too much of. The talented sisters seem to have been quite satisfied with it; and indeed, if they ever stopped to consider their father's origin, they may well have thought themselves far from unlucky. They were neither better nor worse off than hundreds of parsons' daughters all over England whose lives were as isolated and whose means as limited. The Brontës had neighbours, clergymen within walking distance, gentry, mill-owners and manufacturers in a small way, with whom they might have consorted; and if they lived secluded lives it was by choice. They were not rich, but neither were they poor. Mr. Brontë's benefice provided him with a house and two hundred pounds a year, his wife had fifty pounds a year which, on her death, he presumably inherited, and Elizabeth Branwell, when she came to live at Haworth, brought her fifty pounds a year with her. The household thus had three hundred pounds a year to dispose of, which at that time was worth at least twelve hundred pounds now. Many a clergyman to-day, even with income-tax as it is, would look upon such a sum as riches. Many a clergyman's wife to-day would be thankful to have one maid: the Brontës generally had two, and whenever there was pressure of work, girls were brought in from the village to help.

In 1824 Mr. Brontë took his four elder daughters to a school at Cowan Bridge. It had been recently established to give an education to the daughters of poor clergymen. The place was unhealthy, the food bad and the administration incompetent. The two elder girls died, and Charlotte and Emily, whose health was affected, were, though strangely enough only after another term, removed. Such schooling as they got, from then on, seems to have been given them by their aunt. Mr. Brontë thought more of his son than of the three girls and, indeed, Branwell was looked upon as the clever one of the family. Mr. Brontë would not send him to school, but undertook his education himself. The boy had a precocious talent, and his manners were engaging. His friend, F. H. Grundy, thus describes him: "He was insignificantly small—one of his life's trials. He had a mass of red hair, which he wore brushed high off his forehead—to help his height, I fancy—a great, bumpy, intellectual forehead, nearly half the size of the whole facial contour; small ferrety eyes, deep sunk and still further hidden by the never removed spectacles, prominent nose, but weak lower features. He had a downcast look, which never varied, save for a rapid momentary glance at long intervals. Small and thin of person, he was the reverse of attractive at first sight." He had parts, and his sisters admired him and expected him to do great things. He was a brilliant, eager talker, and from some Irish ancestor, for his father was a morose, silent man, he had inherited a gift for social intercourse and an agreeable loquacity. When a traveller, putting up for the night at the Black Bull, seemed lonely, the landlord would ask him: "Do you want someone to help you with your bottle, sir? if so, I'll send up for Patrick." Branwell was always glad to be of service. I should add that when, years later, Charlotte Brontë then being famous, the landlord was asked about this, he denied that he had ever done anything of the kind: "Branwell," he said, "never needed to be sent for." You are still shown at Haworth the room at the Black Bull, with its windsor chairs, in which Branwell tippled with his friends.

When Charlotte was just under sixteen, she went to school once more, this time at Roe Head, and was happy there; but after a year she came home again to teach her two younger sisters. Though the family, as I have pointed out, were not so poor as has been made out, the girls had nothing to look forward to. Mr. Brontë's stipend would naturally cease at his death, and Miss Branwell was leaving the little money she had to her amusing nephew; they decided, therefore, that the only way they could earn a living was by training themselves to be governesses or school-mistresses. At that time there was no other calling open to women who looked upon themselves as ladies. Branwell, by now, was eighteen and a decision had to be made on what trade or profession he was to adopt. He had some facility for drawing, as his sisters had too, and he was eager to become a painter. It was settled that he should go to London and study at the Royal Academy. He went, but nothing came of the project, and after a while, which he spent in sightseeing and presumably having as good a time as he could, he returned to Haworth. He tried writing, but with no success; then he persuaded his father to set him up in a studio in Bradford where he might earn a living by painting portraits of the local people; but this failed too, and Mr. Brontë called him home. Then he became tutor to a Mr. Postlethwaite at Barrow-in-Furness. He seems to have done well enough there, but, for reasons unknown, after six months Mr. Brontë brought him back to Haworth. Presently, a job was found for him as clerk-in-charge at the station of Sowerby Bridge on the Leeds and Manchester Railway, and later at Luddenden Foot. He was bored and lonely, he drank too much, and eventually was discharged for gross neglect of his duties. Meanwhile, in 1835,

Charlotte had returned to Roe Head as a teacher, and taken Emily with her as a pupil. But Emily became so desperately homesick that she fell ill, and had to be sent home. Anne, who was of a calmer, more submissive temper, took her place. Charlotte held her job for three years, at the end of which, her health failing, she too went home.

She was twenty-two. Branwell was not only a source of worry, but a source of expense; and Charlotte, as soon as she was well enough, felt herself obliged to take a situation as a nursery governess. It was not work she liked. Neither she nor her sisters liked children, any more than their father did. "I find it so hard to repel the rude familiarity of children," she wrote to Ellen Nussey. She hated to be in a dependent position, and was continually on the look-out for affronts. She was not an easy person to get on with and, so far as one can judge from her letters, seems to have expected to be asked to do as a favour what her employers quite naturally thought they could demand as a right. She left after three months and returned to the parsonage, but some two years later took another situation with a Mr. and Mrs. White at Rawdon, near Bradford. Charlotte did not think them refined. "Well can I believe that Mrs. W. has been an exciseman's daughter, and I am convinced also that Mr. W's extraction is very low." She was, however, fairly happy in this place, but, as she wrote to the same intimate friend: "No one but myself can tell how hard a governess's life is to me—for no one but myself is aware how utterly averse my whole mind and nature are for the employment." She had long been toying with the idea of keeping a school of her own, with her two sisters, and now she took it up again; the Whites, who seem to have been very kind, decent people, encouraged her, but suggested that before she could hope to be successful she must acquire certain qualifications. Though she could read French, she could not speak it, and knew no German, so she decided that she must go abroad to learn languages. Miss Branwell was persuaded to advance money for the cost of this; and then Charlotte and Emily, with Mr. Brontë to look after them on the journey, set out for Brussels. The two girls, Charlotte being then twenty-six, Emily twenty-two, became pupils at the Pensionnat Héger. After ten months they were recalled to England by the illness of Miss Branwell. She died, and having disinherited Branwell, owing to his bad behaviour, left the little she had to her nieces. It was enough for them to carry out the plan they had so long discussed of having a school of their own; but since their father was old and his sight failing, they made up their minds to set it up at the parsonage. Charlotte did not think she was sufficiently equipped, and so accepted Monsieur Héger's offer to go back to Brussels and teach English at his school. She spent a year there and on her return to Haworth the three sisters issued prospectuses, and Charlotte wrote to her friends asking them to recommend the school they intended to start. How they expected to house pupils in the parsonage, which had only four bedrooms, all of which they occupied themselves, has never been explained, and as no pupils came it certainly never will be.

2

They had been writing off and on since they were children, and in 1846 the three of them published a volume of verse at their own expense under the names of Currer, Ellis and Acton Bell. It cost them fifty pounds, and two copies were sold. Each of them then wrote a novel. Charlotte's (Currer Bell) was called *The Professor*, Emily's (Ellis Bell) *Wuthering Heights* and Anne's (Acton Bell) *Agnes Grey*. They were refused by publisher after publisher; but when Smith, Elder & Co., to whom Charlotte's *The Professor* had finally been sent, returned it, they wrote to say that they would be glad to consider a longer novel by her. She was finishing one, and within a month was able to send it to the publishers. They accepted it. It was called *Jane Eyre*. Emily's novel, and Anne's, had also at last been accepted by a publisher, Newby by name, "on terms somewhat impoverishing to the two authors", and they had corrected the proofs before Charlotte sent *Jane Eyre* to Smith, Elder & Co. Though the reviews of *Jane Eyre* were not particularly good, readers liked it and it became a best-seller. Mr. Newby, upon this, tried to persuade the public that *Wuthering Heights* and

Agnes Grey, which he then published together in three volumes, were by the author of *Jane Eyre*. They made, however, no impression, and indeed were regarded by a number of critics as early and immature work by Currer Bell. Mr. Brontë had consented, after some persuasion, to read *Jane Eyre*. When he came in to tea, after finishing it, he said: "Girls, do you know Charlotte has been writing a book, and it is much better than likely?"

At the time of Miss Branwell's death, Anne was in a situation at Thorpe Green as governess to the children of a certain Mrs. Robinson. Her nature was sweet and gentle, and she was apparently better able to get on with people than the exacting and prickly Charlotte. She was not unhappy in her situation. She went back to Haworth for her aunt's funeral, and on her return to Thorpe Green took with her Branwell, then idling at home, as tutor to Mrs. Robinson's son. Mr. Edmund Robinson, a wealthy clergyman, was an elderly invalid with a youngish wife, and Branwell, though she was seventeen years older than he, fell in love with her. What their relations were is uncertain. Anyhow, whatever they were, they were discovered. Branwell was sent packing, and Mr. Robinson ordered him "never to see again the mother of his children, never set foot in her house, never write or speak to her." Branwell "stormed, raved, swore he could not live without her; cried out against her for staying with her husband. Then prayed the sick man might die soon; they would yet be happy." Branwell had always drunk too much; now in his distress he took to eating opium. It seems, however, that he was able to communicate with Mrs. Robinson, and, some months after his dismissal, they appear to have met at Harrogate. "It is said that she proposed flight together, ready to forfeit all her grandeur. It was Branwell who advised patience and a little longer waiting." Since this can only have been told by Branwell himself, and is in any case very unlikely to be true, we may accept it as an invention of a young man who was both silly and conceited. Suddenly he received a letter to announce the death of Mr. Robinson; "he fair danced down the churchyard as if he was out of his mind; he was so fond of that woman," someone told Mary Robinson, Emily's biographer.

"The next morning he rose, dressed himself with care and prepared for a journey; but before he had even set out from Haworth, two men came riding to the village post-haste. They sent for Branwell and when he arrived, in a great state of excitement, one of the riders dismounted and went with him into the Black Bull." He brought a message from the widow begging him not to come near her again, for if she even saw him once she would lose her fortune and the custody of her children. This is what he told, but since the letter was never produced and it has been discovered that Mr. Robinson's will contained no such clause, there is no knowing whether he told the truth. The only thing sure is that Mrs. Robinson let him know that she wanted to have nothing more to do with him, and it may be that she made up this excuse to render the blow less mortifying. The Brontë family were convinced that she had been Branwell's mistress, and ascribed his consequent behaviour to her evil influence. It is possible that she was, but it is just as possible that, like many a man before and after him, he boasted of a conquest he had never made. But if she had been for a brief period infatuated with him, there is no reason to suppose that it had ever entered her head to marry him. He proceeded to drink himself to death. When he knew the end was near, one who attended him in his last illness told Mrs. Gaskell that, wanting to stand up to die, he insisted upon getting up. He had only been in bed a day. Charlotte was so upset that she had to be led away, but her father, Anne and Emily looked on while he rose to his feet and after a struggle that lasted twenty minutes died, as he wished, standing.

Emily never went out of doors after the Sunday following his death. She had a cold and a cough. It grew worse, and Charlotte wrote to Ellen Nussey: "I fear she has pain in the chest, and I sometimes catch a shortness in her breathing, when she has moved at all quickly. She looks very, very thin and pale. Her reserved nature causes me great uneasiness of mind. It is useless to question her; you get no answer. It is still more useless to recommend remedies; they are never adopted." A week or two later, Charlotte wrote to another friend: "I would fain hope that Emily is a little better this evening, but it is difficult to ascertain this. She is a real stoic in illness; she neither seeks nor will accept sympathy. To put any questions, to offer any aid, is to annoy; she will not yield a step before pain or sickness till forced; not one of her ordinary avocations will she voluntarily renounce. You must look on and see her do what she is unfit to do, and not dare say a word . . ." One morning Emily got up as usual, dressed herself and began to sew; she was short of breath and her eyes were glazed, but she went on working. She grew steadily worse. She had always refused to see a doctor, but at last, at midday, asked that one should be sent for. It was too late. At two she died.

Charlotte was at work on another novel, *Shirley*, but she put it aside to nurse Anne, who was attacked by what was then known as galloping consumption, the disease from which Branwell and Emily had died, and did not finish it till after the gentle creature's death only five months after Emily's. She went to London in 1849 and 1850, and was made much of; she was introduced to Thackeray and had her portrait painted by George Richmond. A Mr. James Taylor, a member of the firm of Smith, Elder, whom she described as a stern and abrupt little man, asked her to marry him, but she refused. Before that, two young clergymen had proposed to her, only to be rejected, and two or three curates, her father's or those of neighbouring parsons, had shown her marked attention; but Emily discouraged suitors (her sisters called her the Major, because of the effective way she dealt with them), and her father disapproved, so that nothing had come of it. It was, however, a curate of her father's whom she at last married. This was the Rev. Arthur Nicholls. He went to Haworth in 1844. Writing to Ellen Nussey in that year, she said of him: "I cannot for my life see those interesting germs of goodness you discovered; his narrowness of mind always strikes me chiefly." And, a couple of years later, she included him in her sweeping contempt of curates in general. "They regard me as an old maid, and I regard them, one and all, as highly uninteresting, narrow and unattractive specimens of the coarser sex." Mr. Nicholls, an Irishman, went to Ireland on his holiday, and Charlotte wrote to her usual correspondent: "Mr.

Nicholls is not yet returned. I am sorry to say that many of the parishioners express a desire that he should not trouble himself to recross the Channel."

In 1852 Charlotte wrote a long letter to Ellen Nussey. She enclosed a note from Mr. Nicholls which, she said, "has left on my mind a feeling of deep concern . . ." "What papa has seen or guessed I will not inquire, though I may conjecture. He has irritably noticed all Mr. Nicholls's low spirits, all his threats of expatriation, all his symptoms of impaired health— noticed them with little sympathy and much indirect sarcasm. On Monday evening Mr. Nicholls was here to tea. I vaguely felt without clearly seeing, as without seeing I have felt for some time, the meaning of his constant looks, and strange feverish restraint. After tea I withdrew to the dining-room as usual. As usual Mr. Nicholls sat with papa till between eight and nine o'clock; I then heard him open the parlour door as if going. I expected the clash of the front door. He stopped in the passage; he tapped; like lightning it flashed on me what was coming. He entered; he stood before me. What his words were you can guess; his manner you can hardly realize, nor can I forget it. Shaking from head to foot, looking deadly pale, speaking low, vehemently, yet with difficulty, he made me for the first time feel what it costs a man to declare affection where he doubts response.

"The spectacle of one ordinarily so statue-like thus trembling, stirred, and overcome, gave me a kind of strange shock. He spoke of sufferings he had borne for months, of sufferings he could endure no longer, and craved leave for some hope. I could only entreat him to leave me then and promise a reply on the morrow. I asked him if he had spoken to papa. He said he dared not. I think I half led, half put him out of the room. When he was gone I immediately went to papa, and told him what had taken place. Agitation and anger disproportionate to the occasion ensued; if I had *loved* Mr. Nicholls, and had heard such epithets applied to him as were used, it would have transported me past my patience; as it was, my blood boiled with a sense of injustice. But papa worked himself into a state not to be trifled with; the veins on his temples started up like whipcord, and his eyes became suddenly bloodshot. I made haste to promise that Mr. Nicholls should on the morrow have a distinct refusal."

In another letter, dated three days later, Charlotte writes: "You ask how papa demeans himself to Mr. Nicholls. I only wish you were here to see papa in his present mood: you would know something of him. He just treats him with a hardness not to be bent, and a contempt not to be propitiated. The two have had no interview as yet; all has been done by letter. Papa wrote, I must say, a most cruel note to Mr. Nicholls on Wednesday." She went on to say that her father thought "a little too much about his want of money; he says the match would be a degradation, that I should be throwing myself away, that he expects me, if I marry at all, to do very differently." Mr. Brontë, in fact, behaved as badly as he had behaved years before to Mary Burder. Relations between Mr. Brontë and Mr. Nicholls grew so strained that the latter resigned his curacy. But his successors at Haworth did not give Mr. Brontë satisfaction, and Charlotte, at last exasperated by his complaints, told him that he had only himself to blame. He had only to let her marry Mr. Nicholls and all would be well. Papa continued "very, very hostile, bitterly unjust," but she saw and corresponded with Mr. Nicholls. They became engaged and in 1854 were married. She was then thirty-eight. She died in childbirth nine months later.

So the Rev. Patrick Brontë, having buried his wife, her sister and his six children, was left to eat his dinner alone in the solitude he liked, walk on the moors as far as his waning strength permitted, read the papers, preach his sermons and wind up the clock on his way to bed. There is a photograph of him in his old age. A man in a black suit with an immense white choker round his neck, with white hair cut short, a fine brow and a large straight nose, a tight mouth and ill-tempered eyes behind his spectacles. He died at Haworth at the age of eighty-four.

3

It is not without intention that in writing of Emily Brontë and *Wuthering Heights*, I have said so much more about her father, her brother and her sister Charlotte than about her; for in the books written about the family it is of them that we hear most. Emily and Anne hardly come into the picture. Anne was a gentle, pretty little thing, but insignificant; and her talent was small. Emily was very different. She is a strange, mysterious and shadowy figure. She is never seen directly, but reflected, as it were, in a moorland pool. You have to guess what sort of woman she was from her one novel, her poems, from an allusion here and there and from scattered anecdotes. She was aloof, an intense, uncomfortable creature; and when you hear of her given over to unrestrained gaiety, as on walks over the moor she sometimes was, it makes you uneasy. Charlotte had friends, Anne had friends, Emily had none. Her character was full of contradictions. She was harsh, dogmatic, self-willed, sullen, angry and intolerant; and she was pious, dutiful, hard-working, uncomplaining, tender to those she loved and patient.

Mary Robinson describes her at fifteen as "a tall, long-armed girl, full grown, elastic as to tread; with a slight figure that looked queenly in her best dresses, but loose and boyish when she slouched over the moors, whistling the dogs, and taking long strides over the rough earth. A tall, thin, loose-jointed girl—not ugly, but with irregular features and a pallid thick complexion. Her dark hair was naturally beautiful, and in later days looked well, loosely fastened with a tall comb at the back of her head; but in 1833 she wore it in an unbecoming tight curl and frizz. She had beautiful eyes of a hazel colour." Like her father, her brother and her sisters, she wore spectacles. She had an aquiline nose and a large, expressive, prominent mouth. She dressed regardless of fashion, with leg-of-mutton sleeves long after they had ceased to be worn; in straight long skirts clinging to her lanky figure.

She went to Brussels with Charlotte. She hated it. Friends, wishing to be nice to the two girls, asked them to spend Sundays and holidays at their house, but they were so shy that to go was agony for them, and after a while their hosts came to the conclusion that it was kinder not to invite them. Emily had no patience with social small-talk, which of course is for the most part trivial; it is merely an expression of general amiability, and people take part in it because they have good manners. Emily was too shy to take part in it and was irritated by those who did. There was in her shyness both diffidence and arrogance. If she was so retiring, it is strange that she should have made herself so conspicuous in her dress. The very shy not uncommonly have in them a streak of exhibitionism, and it may occur to one that she wore those absurd leg-of-mutton sleeves to flaunt her contempt for the commonplace people in whose company she was tongue-tied.

At school, during the hours of recreation, the two sisters always walked together, Emily leaning heavily on her sister, and generally in silence. When they were spoken to, Charlotte answered. Emily rarely spoke to anyone. They were both of them several years older than the rest of the girls, and they disliked their noisiness, their high spirits and the sillinesses natural to their age. Monsieur Héger found Emily intelligent, but so stubborn that she would listen to no reason when it interfered with her wishes or beliefs. He found her egotistical, exacting and, with Charlotte, tyrannical. But he recognized that there was something unusual in her. She should have been a man, he said: "Her strong, imperious will would never have been daunted by opposition or difficulty; never have given way but with life."

When Emily went back to Haworth after Miss Branwell's death, it was for good. She never left it again. It looks as though only there was she able to live the reveries which were the solace and the torment of her life.

She got up in the morning before anyone else and did the roughest part of the day's work before Tabby, the maid, who was old and frail, came down. She did the household ironing and most of the cooking. She made the bread, and the bread was good. While kneading the dough, she would glance at the book propped up before her. "Those who worked with her in the kitchen, young girls called in to help in stress of business, remember how she would keep a scrap of paper, a pencil at her side, and how when the moment came that she could pause in her cooking or her ironing, she would jot down some impatient

470

thought and then resume her work. With these girls she was always friendly and hearty—pleasant, sometimes quite jovial like a boy! So genial and kind, a little masculine, 'say my informants', but of strangers she was exceedingly timid, and if the butcher's boy or the baker's man came to the kitchen door she would be off like a bird into the hall or the parlour till she heard their hobnails clumping down the path." The people of the village said that she "was more like a boy than a girl", and that her figure looked "loose and boyish when she slouched over the moors, whistling to her dogs and taking long strides". She disliked men and, with one exception, was not even ordinarily polite to her father's curates; this was the Rev. William Weightman. He is described as young and fair, eloquent and witty; and there was about him "a certain girlishness of looks, manner and taste". He was known in the family as Miss Celia Amelia. Emily got on famously with him. It is not difficult to know why. May Sinclair, in her book called *The Three Brontës*, constantly uses the word virile when she speaks of her. Romer Wilson, speaking of Emily, asks: "Did the lonely father see himself in her and feel that she was the only other male spirit in his house? . . . She early knew the boy in herself, and later knew the man." Shirley, in Charlotte's novel, is understood to have been modelled on Emily; it is curious that Shirley's old governess should reprove her for constantly speaking of herself as though she were a male; it is not a usual thing for a girl to do, and one can only suppose that it was a habit of Emily's. Much in her character and behaviour that disconcerted her contemporaries can to-day be easily explained. Homosexuality was not at that period openly discussed as it is now, often to an embarrassing extent, but it existed, both in men and women, as it has always done, and it may well be that neither Emily herself, her family nor her family's friends, for, as I have said, she had none of her own, recognized what made her so strange.

Mrs. Gaskell did not like her. Someone told her that Emily "never showed regard to any human creature; all her love was reserved for animals". She liked them wild and intractable. She was given a bulldog called Keeper, and concerning him

Mrs. Gaskell tells a curious story: "Keeper was faithful to the depths of his nature so long as he was with friends; but he who struck him with stick or whip, roused the relentless nature of the brute, who flew at his throat forthwith, and held him there till one or the other was at the point of death. Now Keeper's household fault was this. He loved to steal upstairs, and stretch his square, tawny limbs on the comfortable beds, covered over with delicate white counterpanes. But the cleanliness of the parsonage arrangements was perfect; and this habit of Keeper's was so objectionable, that Emily, in reply to Tabby's remonstrances, declared that, if he was found again transgressing, she herself, in defiance of warning and his well-known ferocity of nature, would beat him so severely that he would never offend again. In the gathering dusk of an autumn evening Tabby came, half-triumphantly, half-tremblingly, but in great wrath, to tell Emily that Keeper was lying on the best bed, in drowsy voluptuousness. Charlotte saw Emily's whitening face and set mouth, but dared not speak to interfere, no one dared when Emily's eyes glowed in that manner out of the paleness of her face, and when her lips were compressed into stone. She went upstairs, and Tabby and Charlotte stood in the gloomy passage below, full of the dark shadows of the coming night. Downstairs came Emily, dragging after her the unwilling Keeper, his hind legs set in a heavy attitude of resistance, held by the 'skuft of his neck', but growling low and savagely all the time. The watchers would fain have spoken, but durst not, for fear of taking off Emily's attention, and causing her to avert her head for a moment from the enraged brute. She let him go, planted in a dark corner at the bottom of the stairs; no time was there to fetch stick or rod, for fear of the strangling clutch at her throat—her bare clenched fist struck against his red fierce eyes, before he had time to make his spring, and in the language of the turf, she 'punished' him till his eyes were swelled up, and the half-blind stupefied beast was led to his accustomed lair, to have his swollen head fomented and cared for by the very Emily herself."

Charlotte wrote of her: "Disinterested and energetic she certainly is; but if she be not quite so tractable and open to

472

conviction as I could wish, I must remember perfection is not the lot of humanity." Emily's temper was uncertain and her sisters appear to have been not a little afraid of her. From Charlotte's letters one gathers that she was puzzled and often irritated by Emily, and it is plain that she didn't know what to make of *Wuthering Heights*; she had no notion that her sister had produced a book of astonishing originality, and one compared with which her own were commonplace. She felt constrained to apologize for it. When it was proposed to republish it, she undertook to edit it. "I am likewise compelling myself to read it over, for the first time of opening the book since my sister's death," she wrote. "Its power fills me with renewed admiration; but yet I am oppressed: the reader is scarcely permitted a taste of unalloyed pleasure, every beam of sunshine is poured down through black bars of threatening cloud; every page is surcharged with a sort of moral electricity; and the writer was unconscious of it." And again: "If the auditor of her work, when read in manuscript, shuddered under the guiding influence of natures so relentless and so implacable—of spirits so lost and fallen; if it was complained that the mere hearing of certain vivid and fearful scenes banished sleep by night, and disturbed mental peace by day, Ellis Bell would wonder what was meant, and suspect the complainant of affectation. Had she but lived, her mind would of itself have grown like a strong tree—loftier, straighter, wider-spreading—and its matured fruits would have attained a mellower ripeness and sunnier bloom; but on that mind time and experience alone could work; to the influence of other intellects it was not amenable." One is inclined to think that Charlotte never knew her sister.

4

Wuthering Heights is an extraordinary book. For the most part, novels betray their period, not only in the manner of writing common to the time at which they were written, but also by their concurrence with the climate of opinion of their day, the moral outlook of their authors, the prejudices they accept or reject. Young David Copperfield might very well

473

have written (though with less talent) the same sort of novel as *Jane Eyre*, and Arthur Pendennis might have written a novel something like *Villette*, though the influence of Laura would doubtless have led him to eschew the naked sexuality which gives Charlotte Brontë's book its poignancy. But *Wuthering Heights* is an exception. It is related in no way to the fiction of the time. It is a very bad novel. It is a very good one. It is ugly. It has beauty. It is a terrible, an agonizing, a powerful and a passionate book. Some have thought it impossible that a clergyman's daughter who led a retired humdrum life, and knew few people and nothing of the world, could have written it. This seems to me absurd. *Wuthering Heights* is wildly romantic. Now, romanticism eschews the patient observation of realism; it revels in the unbridled flight of the imagination and indulges, sometimes with gusto, sometimes with gloom, in horror, mystery, passion and violence. Given Emily Brontë's character, and fierce, repressed emotions, which what we know of her suggests, *Wuthering Heights* is just the sort of book one would have expected her to write. But, on the face of it, it is much more the sort of book that her scapegrace brother Branwell might have written, and a number of people have been able to persuade themselves that he had in whole or in part done so. One of them, Francis Grundy, wrote: "Patrick Brontë declared to me, and what his sister said bore out the assertion, that he wrote a great part of *Wuthering Heights* himself. . . . The weird fancies of diseased genius with which he used to entertain me on our long walks at Luddenden Foot, reappear in the pages of the novel, and I am inclined to believe that the very plot was his invention rather than his sister's." On one occasion two of Branwell's friends, Dearden and Leyland by name, arranged to meet him at an inn on the road to Keighley to read their poetical effusions to one another; and this is what Dearden some twenty years later wrote to the Halifax *Guardian*: "I read the first act of the Demon Queen; but when Branwell dived into his hat—the usual receptacle of his fugitive scraps—where he supposed he had deposited his manuscript poem, he found he had by mistake placed there a number of stray leaves of a novel on which he had been trying

474

his 'prentice hand'. Chagrined at the disappointment he had caused, he was about to return the papers to his hat, when both friends earnestly pressed him to read them, as they felt a curiosity to see how he could wield the pen of a novelist. After some hesitation, he complied with the request, and riveted our attention for about an hour, dropping each sheet, when read, into his hat. The story broke off abruptly in the middle of a sentence, and he gave us the sequel, *viva voce*, together with the real names of the prototypes of his characters, but, as some of these persons are still living, I refrain from pointing them out to the public. He said he had not yet fixed upon a title for the production, and was afraid he would never be able to meet with a publisher who would have the hardihood to usher it into the world. The scene of the fragment which Branwell read, and the characters introduced in it—so far as they developed—were the same as those in *Wuthering Heights*, which Charlotte confidently asserts was the production of her sister Emily."

Now this is either a pack of lies, or it is true. Charlotte despised and, within the bounds of Christian charity, hated her brother; but, as we know, Christian charity has always been able to make allowances for a lot of good honest hatred, and Charlotte's unsupported word cannot be accepted. She may have persuaded herself, as people often do, to believe what she wanted to believe. The story is circumstantial, and it is odd that anyone should, for no particular reason, have invented it. What is the explanation? There is none. It has been suggested that Branwell wrote the first four chapters, and then, drunk and doped as he was, gave it up, whereupon Emily took it over. The argument that these chapters are written in a more stilted manner than the subsequent ones does not, to my mind, hold water; and if there is in them a somewhat greater pomposity in the writing, I should ascribe it to a not unsuccessful attempt on Emily's part to show that Lockwood was a silly, conceited ape. I have no doubt at all that Emily, and Emily alone, wrote *Wuthering Heights*.

It must be admitted that it is badly written. The Brontë sisters did not write well. Like the governesses they were, they affected the turgid and pedantic style for which the word

475

littératise has been coined. The main part of the story is told by Mrs. Dean, a Yorkshire maid of all work like the Brontës' Tabby; a conversational style would have been suitable; Emily makes her express herself as no human being could. Here is a typical utterance: "I tried to smooth away all disquietude on the subject, by affirming, with frequent iteration, that that betrayal of trust, if it merited so harsh an appellation, should be the last." Emily Brontë seems to have been aware that she was putting into Mrs. Dean's mouth words that it was unlikely she would have known, and, to explain it, makes her say that in the course of her service she has had the opportunity to read books, but, even at that, the pretentiousness of her discourse is appalling. She does not read a letter, she peruses an epistle; she doesn't send a letter, but a missive. She does not leave a room, she quits a chamber. She calls her day's work her diurnal occupation. She commences rather than begins. People don't shout or yell, they vociferate; nor do they listen, they hearken. There is pathos in this parson's daughter striving so hard to write in a lady-like way, only to succeed in being genteel. Yet one would not wish *Wuthering Heights* to have been written with grace: it would be none the better for being better written. Just as in one of those early Flemish pictures of the burial of Christ the anguished grimaces of the emaciated creatures concerned, their stiff, ungainly gestures, seem to add a greater horror, a matter-of-fact brutality, to the scene, which makes it more poignant, more tragic, than when the same event is pictured in beauty by Titian; so there is in this uncouth stylization of the language something which strangely heightens the violent passion of the story.

Wuthering Heights is clumsily constructed. That is not surprising, for Emily Brontë had never written a novel before, and she had a complicated story to tell, dealing with two generations. This is a difficult thing to do because the author has to give some sort of unity to two sets of characters and two sets of events; and he must be careful not to allow the interest of one to overshadow the interest of the other. This Emily did not succeed in doing. After the death of Catherine Earnshaw there is, until you come to the last finely imaginative pages, some loss of power. The younger Catherine is an unsatisfactory character, and Emily Brontë seems not to have known what to make of her; obviously she could not give her the passionate independence of the older Catherine, nor the foolish weakness of her father. She is a spoilt, silly, wilful and ill-mannered creature; and you cannot greatly pity her sufferings. The steps are not made clear which led to her falling in love with young Hareton. He is a shadowy figure, and you know no more of him than that he was sullen and handsome. The author of such a story as I am now considering has also to compress the passage of years into a period of time that can be accepted by the reader with a comprehensive glance, as one seizes in a single view the whole of a vast fresco. I do not suppose that Emily Brontë deliberately thought out how to get a unity of impression into a straggling story, but I think she must have asked herself how to make it coherent; and it may have occurred to her that she could best do this by making one character narrate the long succession of events to another. It is a convenient way of telling a story, and she did not invent it. Its disadvantage is that it is impossible to maintain anything like a conversational manner when the narrator has to *tell* a number of things, descriptions of scenery for instance, which no sane person would think of doing. And of course if you have a narrator (Mrs. Dean) you must have a listener (Lockwood). It is possible that an experienced novelist might have found a better way of telling the story of *Wuthering Heights*, but I cannot believe that if Emily Brontë used it, it was because she was working on a foundation of someone else's invention.

But more than that, I think the method she adopted might have been expected of her, when you consider her extreme, her morbid, shyness and her reticence. What were the alternatives? One was to write the novel from the standpoint of omniscience, as, for instance, *Middlemarch* and *Madame Bovary* were written. I think it would have shocked her harsh, uncompromising virtue to tell the outrageous story as a creation of her own; and if she had, moreover, she could hardly have avoided giving some account of Heathcliff during the few years he spent away from Wuthering Heights—years in which he managed to acquire an education and make quite a lot of money. She couldn't do this, because she simply didn't know how he had done it. The fact the reader is asked to accept is hard to believe, and she was content to state it and leave it at that. Another alternative was to have the story narrated to her, Emily Brontë, by Mrs. Dean, say, and tell it then in the first person; but I suspect that that, too, would have brought her into a contact with the reader too close for her quivering sensitivity. By having the story in its beginning told by Lockwood, and unfolded to Lockwood by Mrs. Dean, she hid herself behind, as it were, a double mask. Mr. Brontë told Mrs. Gaskell a story which in this connection has significance. When his children were young, he, desiring to find out something of their natures, which their timidity concealed from him, made each in turn put on an old mask, under cover of which they could answer more freely the questions he put to them. When he asked Charlotte what was the best book in the world, she answered, "The Bible"; but when he asked Emily what he had best do with her troublesome brother Branwell, she said: "Reason with him; and when he won't listen to reason, whip him."

And why did Emily need to hide herself when she wrote this powerful, passionate and terrible book? I think because she disclosed in it her innermost instincts. She looked deep into the well of loneliness in her heart, and saw there unavowable secrets of which, notwithstanding, her impulse as a writer drove her to unburden herself. It is said that her imagination was kindled by the weird stories her father used to tell of the Ireland of his youth, and by the tales of Hoffmann which she learned to read when she went to school in Belgium, and which she continued to read, we are told, back at the parsonage, seated on a hearthrug by the fire with her arm around Keeper's neck. I am willing to believe that she found in the stories of mystery, violence and horror of the German romantic writers something that appealed to her own fierce nature; but I think she found Heathcliff and Catherine Earnshaw in the hidden depths of her own soul. I think she was herself Heathcliff, I think she was herself Catherine Earnshaw. Is it strange that she should have put herself into the two chief characters of her book? Not at all. We are none of us all of a piece; more than one person dwells within us, often in uncanny companionship with his fellows; and the peculiarity of the writer of fiction is that he has the power to objectify the diverse persons of which he is compounded in individual characters: his misfortune is that he cannot bring to life characters, however necessary to his story they may be, in which there is no part of himself. That is why the younger Catherine in *Wuthering Heights* is unsatisfactory.

I think Emily put the whole of herself into Heathcliff. She gave him her violent rage, her sexuality, vehement but frustrated, her passion of unsatisfied love, her jealousy, her hatred and contempt of human beings, her cruelty, her sadism. The reader will remember the incident when, with so little reason, she beat with her naked fist the face of the dog she loved as perhaps she loved no human being. There is another curious circumstance related by Ellen Nussey. "She enjoyed leading Charlotte where she would not dare to go of her own free will. Charlotte had a mortal dread of unknown animals, and it was Emily's pleasure to lead her into close vicinity, and then tell her of how and what she had done, laughing at her horror with great amusement." I think Emily loved Catherine Earnshaw with Heathcliff's masculine, animal love; I think she laughed, as she had laughed at Charlotte's fears, when, as Heathcliff, she kicked and trampled on Earnshaw and dashed his head against the stone flags; and I think when, as Heathcliff, she hit the younger Catherine in the face and heaped humiliations upon her, she laughed. I think it gave her a thrill of release when she bullied, reviled and browbeat the persons of her invention, because in real life she suffered such bitter mortification in the company of her fellow-creatures; and I think, as Catherine, doubling the roles, as it were, though she fought Heathcliff, though she despised him, though she knew him for the beast he was, she loved him with her body and soul, she exulted in her power over him, and since there is in the sadist something of the masochist too, she was fascinated by his violence, his brutality and his untamed nature. She felt they were kin, as indeed they were, if I am right in supposing they were both Emily Brontë. "Nelly, I *am* Heathcliff," Catherine cried. "He's always in my mind: not as a pleasure, any more than I am always a pleasure to myself, but as my own being."

Wuthering Heights is a love story, perhaps the strangest that was ever written, and not the least strange part of it is that the lovers remain chaste. Catherine was passionately in love with Heathcliff, as passionately in love with him as Heathcliff was with her. For Edgar Linton, Catherine felt only a kindly, and often exasperated, tolerance. One wonders why those two people who were consumed with love did not, whatever the poverty that might have faced them, run away together. One wonders why they didn't become real lovers. It may be that Emily's upbringing caused her to look upon adultery as an unforgivable sin, or it may be that the idea of sexual intercourse between the sexes filled her with disgust. I believe both the sisters were highly sexed. Charlotte was plain, with a sallow skin and a large nose on one side of her face. She had proposals of marriage when she was obscure and penniless, and at that period a man expected his wife to bring a portion with her. But beauty is not the only thing that makes a woman attractive; indeed, great beauty is often somewhat chilling: you admire, but are not moved. If young men fell in love with Charlotte, a captious and critical young woman, it can surely have only been because they found her sexually attractive, which means that they felt obscurely that she was highly sexed. She was not in love with Mr. Nicholls when she married him; she thought him narrow, dogmatic, sullen and far from intelligent. It is clear from her letters that after she married him she felt very differently towards him; for her they are positively skittish. She fell in love with him, and his defects ceased to matter. The most probable explanation is that those sexual desires of hers were at last satisfied. There is no reason to suppose that Emily was less highly sexed than Charlotte.

5.

The genesis of a novel is a very curious affair. In a novelist's first novel, and Emily, so far as we know, wrote but one, it is not unlikely that there will be something of wish-fulfilment and something of imagined autobiography. It is conceivable that *Wuthering Heights* is the product of pure fantasy. Who can tell what erotic reveries Emily had during the long watches of her sleepless nights, or when she lay all the summer day among the flowering heather? Everybody must have noticed how strong the family likeness is between Charlotte's Rochester and Emily's Heathcliff. Heathcliff might be a by-blow, the bastard a younger son in the Rochester family might have had by an Irish biddy met in Liverpool. Both men are swarthy, violent, hard-featured, fierce, passionate and mysterious. They differ only as differed the natures of the two sisters who constructed them to satisfy their urgent, thwarted desires for sexual satisfaction. But Rochester is the dream of the woman of normal instincts who hankers to give herself to the domineering, ruthless male; Emily gave Heathcliff her own masculinity, her violence and her savage temper. But the primary model on which the sisters created these two uncouth, difficult men was, I surmise, their father, the Rev. Patrick Brontë.

But though, as I have said, it is conceivable that Emily constructed *Wuthering Heights* entirely out of her own fantasies, I do not believe it. I should have thought that it was only very rarely that the fruitful idea which will give rise to a fiction comes to an author, like a falling star, out of the blue; for the most part, it comes to him from an experience, generally emotional, of his own, or, if it is told him by another, emotionally appealing; and then his imagination in travail, character and incidents little by little grow out of it, until at length the finished work comes into being. Few people, however, know how small a hint, how trivial to all appearances an occurrence, may be that will serve to set the spark that will kindle the author's invention. When you look at the cyclamen with its heart-shaped leaves surrounding a profusion of flowers, their careless petals wearing a wilful look as though they grew at haphazard, it seems incredible that this luscious beauty, this rich colour, should have come from a seed hardly larger than a pin's head. So it may be with the productive seed that will give rise to an immortal book.

It seems to me that one only has to read Emily Brontë's

poems to guess what the emotional experience was that led her to seek release from cruel pain by writing *Wuthering Heights*. She wrote a good deal of verse. It is uneven; some of it is commonplace, some of it moving, some of it lovely. She seems to have been most at home with the metres of the hymns which she sang of a Sunday in the parish church at Haworth, but the commonplace metres she used do not veil the intense emotion beneath. Many of the poems belong to the Gondal Chronicles, that long history of an imaginary island with which she and Anne amused themselves when they were children, and which Emily continued to write when she was a grown woman. It may be that she found this a convenient way to deliver her tortured heart of emotions which, with her natural secretiveness, she could not have borne to set out in any other way. Other poems seem to be the direct expression of feeling. In 1845, three years before her death, she wrote a poem called *The Prisoner*. So far as is known, she had never read the works of any of the mystics, yet in these verses she so describes the mystical experience that it is impossible to believe that they do not tell of what she knew from personal acquaintance. She uses almost the very words that the mystics use when they describe the anguish felt on the return from union with the Infinite:

"Oh dreadful is the check—intense the agony—
When the ear begins to hear, the eye begins to see;
When the pulse begins to throb, the brain to think again;
The soul to feel the flesh, and the flesh to feel the chain."

These lines surely reflect a felt, a deeply felt, experience. Why should one suppose that Emily Brontë's love poems were no more than a literary exercise? I should have thought they pointed very clearly to her having fallen in love, to her love having been repulsed, and then to her having been bitterly hurt. She wrote these particular poems when she was teaching at a girls' school at Law Hill, near Halifax. She was nineteen. There was little chance of her meeting men there (and we know how she fled from men), and so, from what we surmise of her disposition, it is likely enough that she fell in love with one or other of the mistresses, or with one of the girls. It was the only love of her life. It may well be that the unhappiness it caused her sufficed to implant the seed in the fruitful soil of her tortured sensibility which enabled her to create the strange book we know. I can think of no other novel in which the pain, the ecstasy, the ruthlessness of love have been so powerfully set forth. *Wuthering Heights* has great faults, but they do not matter; they matter as little as the fallen tree-trunks, the strewn rocks, the snow-drifts which impede, but do not stem, the alpine torrent in its tumultuous course down the mountain-side. You cannot liken *Wuthering Heights* to any other book. You can liken it only to one of those great pictures of El Greco in which in a sombre, arid landscape, under clouds heavy with thunder, long, emaciated figures in contorted attitudes, spellbound by an unearthly emotion, hold their breath. A streak of lightning, flitting across the leaden sky, gives a mysterious terror to the scene.

CHAPTER TEN

Dostoevsky and *The Brothers Karamazov*

I

FYODOR DOSTOEVSKY was born in 1821. His father, a surgeon
at the Hospital of St. Mary in Moscow, was a member of the
nobility, a fact to which Dostoevsky seems to have attached
importance, since he was distressed when on his condemnation
his rank, such as it was, was taken away from him; and on his
release from prison he pressed influential friends to have it
restored. But nobility in Russia was different from what it was
in other European countries; it could be acquired, for instance,
by reaching a certain modest rank in the government service,
and appears to have had little more significance than to set you
apart from the peasant and the tradesman, and allow you to
look upon yourself as a gentleman. In point of fact, Dostoevsky's
family belonged to the white-collar class of poor professional
men. His father was a stern man. He deprived himself not
only of luxury, but even of comfort, in order to give his seven
children a good education; and from their earliest years taught
them that they must accustom themselves to hardship and misfortune to prepare themselves for the duties and obligations of
life. They lived crowded together in the two or three rooms at
the hospital which were the doctor's quarters. They were never
allowed to go out alone, they were given no pocket money,
they had no friends. The doctor had some private practice
besides his hospital salary and, in course of time, acquired a
small property some hundred miles from Moscow, and there,
from then on, mother and children spent the summer. It was
their first taste of freedom.

When Dostoevsky was sixteen, his mother died, and the
doctor took his two elder sons, Michael and Fyodor, to St.
Petersburg to put them to school at the Military Engineering
Academy. Michael, the elder, was rejected on account of his

poor physique, and Fyodor was thus parted from the only person he cared for. He was lonely and unhappy. His father either would not, or could not, send him money, and he was unable to buy such necessities as books and boots, or even to pay the regular charges of the institution. The doctor, having settled his elder sons, and parked three other children with an aunt in Moscow, gave up his practice and retired with his two youngest daughters to his property in the country. He took to drink. He had been severe with his children, he was brutal with his serfs, and one day they murdered him.

Fyodor was then eighteen. He worked well, though without enthusiasm, and, having completed his term at the Academy, was appointed to the Engineering Department of the Ministry of War. What with his share of his father's estate and his salary, he had then five thousand roubles a year. That, at the time, in English money would have been a little more than three hundred pounds. He rented an apartment, conceived an expensive passion for billiards, flung money away right and left, and when a year later he resigned his commission, because he found service in the Engineering Department "as dull as potatoes", he was deeply in debt. He remained in debt till the last years of his life. He was a hopeless spendthrift, and though his thriftlessness drove him to despair, he never acquired the strength of mind to resist his caprices. It has been suggested by one of his biographers that his want of self-confidence was to an extent responsible for his habit of squandering money, since it gave him a passing sense of power and so gratified his exorbitant vanity. It will be seen later to what mortifying straits this unhappy failing reduced him.

While still at the Academy, Dostoevsky had begun a novel and now, having decided to earn his living as a writer, he finished it. It was called *Poor Folk*. He knew no one in the literary world; but an acquaintance, Grigorovich by name, was familiar with a man, Nekrasov, who was proposing to start a review, and offered to show him the story. One day Dostoevsky came back to his lodging late. He had spent the evening reading his novel to a friend and discussing it with him. At four in the morning he walked home. He did not go to sleep, but opened the window and sat by it. He was startled by a ring. Grigorovich and Nekrasov rushed into the room in transports and almost in tears, and embraced him again and again. They had begun to read the book, taking it in turns to read aloud, and when they had finished, late though it was, decided to seek Dostoevsky out. "Never mind if he is asleep," they said to one another, "let us wake him. This thing transcends sleep." Nekrasov took the manuscript next day to Belinsky, the most important critic of the time, and he was as enthusiastic as had been the other two. The novel was published, and Dostoevsky found himself famous.

He did not take success well. A certain Madame Panaev-Golovachev has described the impression he made when he was brought to see her: "At first glance one could perceive that the newcomer was a young man of an extremely nervous and impressionable temperament. Short and thin, he had fair hair, an unhealthy complexion, small grey eyes which wandered uneasily from object to object, and pale lips which maintained a restless twitching. Almost everyone present was known to him, yet he seemed bashful and took no part in the general conversation, even though successive members of the party, to banish his reserve and to make him feel that he was a member of our circle, tried to draw him out. After that evening, however, he came frequently to see us, and his restraint began to wear off: he even took to . . . engaging in disputes in which sheer contradictoriness seemed to impel him to give everyone the lie. The truth was that his youthfulness combined with his nervous temperament to deprive him of all self-control, and to lead him to over-parade his presumption and conceit as a writer. That is to say, dazed with his sudden and brilliant entry into the literary arena, and overwhelmed with the praises of the great ones in the world of letters, he, like most impressionable spirits, could not conceal his triumph over young writers whose entry had been of a more modest order . . . through his captiousness and his tone of overweening pride he showed that he considered himself to be immeasurably superior to his companions . . . Particularly did Dostoevsky suspect all and sundry of attempting to pooh-pooh his talent; and since he discerned in every guileless word a desire to belittle his work, and to affront him personally, it was in a mood of scathing resentment which yearned to pick a quarrel, to vent upon his fancied detractors the whole measure of spleen that was choking his breast, that he used to visit our house."

On the strength of his success, Dostoevsky signed contracts to write a novel and a number of stories. With the advances he received, he proceeded to lead so dissipated a life that his friends, for his own good, took him to task. He quarrelled with them, even with Belinsky, who had done so much for him, because he was not convinced of "the purity of his admiration"; for he had persuaded himself that he was a genius, and the greatest of Russian writers. His debts increased, and he was obliged to work with haste. He had long suffered from an obscure nervous disorder, and now, falling ill, feared he was going mad, or falling into a consumption. The stories written in these circumstances were failures, and the novel proved unreadable. The people who had so extravagantly praised him now violently attacked him, and the opinion was general that he was written out.

2

Early one morning, on the 29th of April, 1849, Dostoevsky was arrested and taken to the fortress of Peter-Paul. He had joined a group of young men, imbued with the socialistic notions then current in Western Europe, who were bent on certain measures of reform, especially on the emancipation of the serfs and the abolition of censorship, and who met once a week to discuss their ideas. They set up a printing-press for the purpose of circulating, in secret, articles written by members of the group. The police had for some time had them under surveillance, and all were arrested on the same day. After some months in prison, they were tried, and fifteen of them, among them Dostoevsky, were condemned to death. One winter morning, they were taken to the place of execution, but as the soldiers prepared to carry out the sentence, a messenger arrived to say that the penalty was commuted to penal servitude in Siberia. Dostoevsky was sentenced to four years' imprisonment at Omsk, after which he was to serve as a common soldier. When he was taken back to the fortress of Peter-Paul, he wrote the following letter to his brother Michael.

"To-day the 22nd of December, we were all taken to Semenovsky Square. There the death sentence was read to us, we were given the Cross to kiss, the dagger was broken over our heads, and our funeral toilet (white shirts) was made. Then three of us were put standing before the palisades for the execution of the death sentence. I was sixth in the row; we were called up by groups of three, and so I was in the second group, and had not more than a moment to live. I thought of you, my brother, and of yours; in that last moment you alone were in my mind; then first I learnt how much I love you, my beloved brother! I had time to embrace Plestchiev and Durov, who stood near me, and to take my leave of them. Finally, retreat was sounded, those who were bound to the palisades were brought back, and it was read to us that His Imperial Majesty granted us our lives. Then the final sentences were recited. . . ."

In *The House of the Dead* Dostoevsky has described the horrors of his life in prison. One point is worthy of remark. He notes that, within two hours of arriving, a newcomer would find himself at home with the other convicts and live on familiar terms with them. "But with a gentleman, a nobleman, things were different. No matter how unassuming and good-tempered and intelligent he might be, he would to the end remain a person unanimously hated and despised, and never understood and, still more, never trusted. No one would ever come to look upon him as a friend or a comrade, and though, as the years went on, he might at least attain the point of ceasing to serve as a butt for insult, he would still be powerless to live his own life, or to get rid of the torturing thought that he was lonely and a stranger."

Now, Dostoevsky was not such a great gentleman as all that; his origins were as modest as his life and, but for a brief period of glory, he had been poverty-stricken. Durov, his friend and fellow-prisoner, was loved by all. It looks very much as though

Dostoevsky's loneliness, and the suffering it caused him, were in part at least occasioned by his own defects of character, his conceit, his egoism, his suspiciousness and his irritability. But his loneliness, amid two hundred companions, drove him back on himself: "Through this spiritual isolation," he writes, "I gained an opportunity of reviewing my past life, of dissecting it down to the pettiest detail, of probing my heretofore existence, and of judging myself strictly and inexorably." The New Testament was the only book he was allowed to possess, and he read it incessantly. Its influence on him was great. From then on, he practised humility and the necessity of suppressing the human desires of normal men. "Before all things humble yourself," he wrote, "consider what your past life has been, consider what you may be able to effect in the future, consider how great a mass of meanness and pettiness and turpitude lies lurking at the bottom of your soul." Prison, for the time at least, cowed his overweening, imperious spirit. He left it a revolutionary no longer, but a firm upholder of the authority of the Crown and the established order. He left it also an epileptic.

When his term of imprisonment came to an end, he was sent to complete his sentence as a private in a small garrison town in Siberia. It was a hard life, but he accepted its pains as part of the punishment he merited for his crime, for he had come to the conclusion that his activities for reform were sinful; and he wrote to his brother: "I do not complain; this is my cross and I have deserved it." In 1856, through the intercession of an old schoolfellow, he was raised from the ranks, and his life became more tolerable. He made friends and he fell in love. The object of his affections was a certain Maria Dmitrievna Isaeva, wife of a political deportee who was dying of drink and consumption, and mother of a young son; she is described as a rather pretty blonde of middle height, very thin, passionate and *exaltée*. Little seems to be known of her, except that she was of a nature as suspicious, as jealous and as self-tormenting as Dostoevsky himself. He became her lover. But after some time Isaev, her husband, was moved from the village in which Dostoevsky was stationed to another frontier post some four hundred miles away, and there died. Dostoevsky wrote and proposed marriage. The widow hesitated, partly because they were both destitute and partly because she had lost her heart to a "high-minded and sympathetic" young teacher, called Vergunov, and had become his mistress. Dostoevsky, deeply in love, was frantic with jealousy, but with his passion for lacerating himself, and perhaps with his novelist's proneness to see himself as a character of fiction, he did a characteristic thing. Declaring Vergunov to be dearer to him than a brother, he besought one of his friends to send him money so as to make it possible for Maria Isaeva to marry her lover.

He was able, however, to play the part of a man with a breaking heart, ready to sacrifice himself to the happiness of his well-beloved, without serious consequences, for the widow had an eye to the main chance. Vergunov, though "high-minded and sympathetic", was penniless, whereas Dostoevsky was now an officer, his pardon could not long be delayed, and there was no reason why he should not again write successful books. The couple were married in 1857. They had no money, and Dostoevsky had borrowed till he could borrow no more. He turned again to literature; but as an ex-convict he had to get permission to publish, and this was not easy. Nor was married life. In fact it was very unsatisfactory, which Dostoevsky ascribed to his wife's suspicious, painfully fanciful nature. It escaped his notice that he was himself as impatient, quarrelsome, neurotic and unsure of himself as he had been in the first flush of success. He began various pieces of fiction, put them aside, began others, and in the end produced little, and that little of no importance.

In 1859, as the result of his appeals and by the influence of friends, he received permission to return to Petersburg. Professor Ernest Simmons, of the University of Columbia, in his interesting and instructive book on Dostoevsky, justly remarks that the means he employed to regain his freedom of action were abject. "He wrote patriotic poems, one celebrating the birthday of the Dowager Empress Alexandra, another on the coronation of Alexander II, and a threnody on the death of Nicholas I. Begging letters were addressed to people in power and to the new Tsar himself. In them he protests that he adores the young monarch, whom he describes as a sun shining on the just and the unjust alike, and he declares that he is ready to give up his life for him. The crime for which he was convicted he readily confesses to, but insists that he has repented and is suffering for opinions that he had abandoned."

He settled down with his wife and stepson in the capital. It was ten years since he had left it as a convict. With his brother Michael, he started a literary journal. It was called *Time*, and for it he wrote *The House of the Dead* and *The Insulted and Injured*. It was a success, and his circumstances were easy. In 1862, leaving the magazine in charge of Michael, he visited Western Europe. He was not pleased with it. He found Paris "a most boring town" and its people money-grubbing and small-minded. He was shocked by the misery of the London poor and the hypocritical respectability of the well-to-do. He went to Italy, but he was not interested in art, and he spent a week in Florence without going to the Uffizi and passed the time reading the four volumes of Victor Hugo's *Les Misérables*. He returned to Russia without seeing Rome or Venice. His wife, whom he had ceased to love, had contracted tuberculosis and was now a chronic invalid.

Some months before going abroad, Dostoevsky, who was then forty, had made the acquaintance of a young woman who brought a short story for publication in his literary journal. Her name was Polina Suslova. She was twenty, a virgin and handsome, but, to show that her views were advanced, she bobbed her hair and wore dark glasses. Dostoevsky was greatly taken with her, and after his return to Petersburg seduced her. Then, owing to an unfortunate article by one of his contributors, the magazine was suppressed and he decided to go abroad again. The reason he gave was to get treatment for his epilepsy, which for some time had been growing worse, but this was only an excuse; he wanted to go to Wiesbaden to gamble, for he had invented a system to break the bank, and he had made a date with Polina Suslova in Paris. He parked his sick wife at Vladimir, a town some distance from Moscow, borrowed money from the Fund for Needy Authors, and set out.

At Wiesbaden he lost much of his money, and tore himself

from the tables only because his passion for Polina Suslova was stronger than his passion for roulette. They had arranged to go to Rome together; but, while waiting for him, the emancipated young lady had had a short affair with a Spanish medical student; she was upset when he walked out on her, a proceeding women are not apt to take with equanimity, and refused to resume her relations with Dostoevsky. He accepted the situation and proposed that they should go to Italy "as brother and sister", and to this, being presumably at a loose end, she consented. The arrangement, complicated by the fact that they were so short of money they had on occasion to pawn their knick-knacks, was not a success, and after some weeks of "lacerations" they parted. Dostoevsky went back to Russia. He found his wife dying. Six months later she was dead. He wrote as follows to a friend:

"My wife, the being who adored me, and whom I loved beyond measure, expired at Moscow, whither she had removed a year before her death of consumption. I followed her thither and never once throughout that winter left her bedside. . . . My friend, she loved me beyond measure, and I returned her affection to a degree transcending all expression; yet our joint life was not a happy one. Some day, when I meet you, I will tell you the whole story. But for the present let me confine myself to saying that, apart from the fact that we lived unhappily together, we should never have lost our mutual love for one another, but have become more attached in proportion to our misery. This may seem strange to you; yet it is but the truth. She was the best, the noblest, woman I have ever known. . . ."

Dostoevsky somewhat exaggerated his devotion. During that winter he went twice to Petersburg in connection with a new magazine he had started with his brother. It was no longer liberal in tendency, as *Time* had been, and failed. Michael died after a short illness, leaving heavy debts, and Dostoevsky found himself obliged to support his widow and children, his mistress and her child. He borrowed ten thousand roubles from a rich aunt, but by 1865 had to declare himself bankrupt. He owed sixteen thousand roubles on note of hand, and five thousand on the security of his word alone. His creditors were troublesome and, to escape from them, he again borrowed money from the Fund for Needy Authors and got an advance on a novel which he contracted to deliver by a certain date. Thus provided, he went to Wiesbaden to try his luck once more at the tables and to meet Polina. He made her an offer of marriage. She refused it. It is evident that, if she had ever loved him, she loved him no longer. One may surmise that she had yielded to him because he was a well-known author and, as editor of a magazine, might be of use to her. But the magazine was dead. His appearance had always been insignificant, and now he was forty-five, bald and epileptic. Nothing, I suppose, exasperates a woman more than the sexual desire for her of a man who is physically repellent to her, and when, to put it bluntly, he will not take no for an answer, she may very well come to hate him. Thus it was, I imagine, with Polina. Dostoevsky attributed her change of heart to a reason more flattering to himself. I shall come to it, and the effect it had on him, in due course. They had gambled their money away, and Dostoevsky wrote to Turgenev, with whom he had quarrelled and whom he detested and despised, for a loan. Turgenev sent him fifty thalers, and on this Polina was able to get to Paris. For a month longer Dostoevsky remained in Wiesbaden. He was ill and wretched. He had to sit quietly in his room so as not to get up an appetite which he had no money to satisfy. His straits were such that he wrote Polina for money. She was, it appears, already occupied with another affair and does not seem to have replied. He began another book, under the lash, he says, of necessity and against time. This was *Crime and Punishment*. At last, in answer to a begging letter he had written to an old friend of his Siberian days, he received enough money to leave Wiesbaden and, with his friend's further help, managed to go back to Petersburg.

While still at work on *Crime and Punishment*, he remembered that he had contracted to deliver a book by a certain date. By the iniquitous agreement he had signed, if he did not do so the publisher had the right to issue everything he wrote for the following nine years without paying him a penny. The date was at hand. Dostoevsky was at his wits' end. Then some bright person suggested that he should employ a stenographer; this he did, and in twenty-six days finished a novel called *The Gambler*. The stenographer, Anna Grigorievna by name, was twenty, but homely; she was, however, efficient, practical, patient, devoted and admiring; and early in the year 1867 he married her. His stepson, his brother's widow and her children, foreseeing that he would not thenceforward support them as he had done before, were bitterly antagonistic to the poor girl and, indeed, behaved so badly, and made her so miserable, that she persuaded Dostoevsky to leave Russia once more. He was again heavily in debt.

This time he spent four years abroad. At first, Anna Grigorievna found life difficult with the celebrated author. His epilepsy grew worse. He was irritable, thoughtless and vain. He continued to correspond with Polina Suslova, which did not conduce to Anna's peace of mind, but, being a young woman of uncommon sense, she kept her dissatisfaction to herself. They went to Baden-Baden and there Dostoevsky again began to gamble. As usual he lost all he had and, as usual, wrote to everyone likely to help for money and more money, and whenever it arrived slunk off to the tables to lose it. They pawned whatever they had of value, they moved into cheaper and cheaper lodgings, and sometimes they had barely enough to eat. Anna Grigorievna was pregnant. Here is an extract from one of his letters. He had just won four thousand francs:

"Anna Grigorievna begged me to be content with the four thousand francs, and to leave at once. But there was a chance, so easy and possible to remedy everything. And the examples? Besides one's own personal winnings, one sees every day others winning 20,000 and 30,000 francs (one does not see those who lose). Are there saints in the world? Money is more necessary to me than to them. I staked more than I lost. I began to lose my last resources, enraging myself to fever point. I lost. I pawned my clothes, Anna Grigorievna has pawned everything that she has, her last trinkets. (What an angel!) How she consoled me, how she wearied in that accursed Baden in our two little rooms above the forge where we had to take refuge! At last, no more, everything was lost. (Oh, those Germans are vile. They are all, without exception, usurers, scoundrels and rascals. The proprietor, knowing that we had nowhere to go till we received money, raised his prices.) At last we had to escape and leave Baden."

The child was born at Geneva. Dostoevsky continued to gamble. He was bitterly repentant when he lost the money that would have provided his wife and child with the necessities they so badly needed; but hurried back to the gambling house whenever he had a few francs in his pocket. After three months, to his intense grief, the baby died. Anna Grigorievna was again pregnant. The couple were in such want that Dostoevsky had to borrow sums of five and ten francs from casual acquaintances to buy food for himself and his wife. *Crime and Punishment* had been a success and he set to work on another book. He called it *The Idiot*. His publisher agreed to send him two hundred roubles a month; but his unhappy weakness continued to leave him in straits, and he was obliged to ask for further and further advances. *The Idiot* failed to please, and he started on yet another novel, *The Eternal Husband*, and then on a long one named, in English, *The Possessed*. Meanwhile, according to circumstances, which I take to mean when they had exhausted their credit, Dostoevsky, his wife and child moved from place to place. But they were homesick. He had never overcome his dislike of Europe. He was untouched by the culture and distinction of Paris, the *gemütlichkeit*, the music of Germany, the splendour of the Alps, the smiling yet enigmatic beauty of the lakes of Switzerland, the gracious loveliness of Tuscany, and that treasury of art which is Florence. He found Western civilization bourgeois, decadent and corrupt, and convinced himself of its approaching dissolution. "I am becoming dull and narrow here," he wrote from Milan, "and am losing touch with Russia. I lack the Russian air and the Russian people." He felt he could never finish *The Possessed* unless he went back to Russia. Anna was pining to go home. But they had no money, and Dostoevsky's publisher had already advanced as much as the serial rights were worth. In desperation Dostoevsky appealed to him again. The first two numbers had already appeared in a magazine and, faced with the fear of getting no further instalments, he sent money for the fares. The Dostoevskys returned to Petersburg.

This was in 1871. Dostoevsky was fifty and had ten more years to live.

The Possessed was received with favour, and its attack on the young radicals of the day brought its author friends in reactionary circles. They thought he could be made use of in the Government's struggle against reform and offered him the well-paid editorship of a paper called *The Citizen*, which was officially supported. He held it for a year, and then resigned over a disagreement with the publisher. Anna had persuaded her husband to let her publish *The Possessed* herself; the experiment was successful, and thenceforward she brought out editions of his works so profitably that for the rest of his life he was released from want. His remaining years can be passed over briefly. Under the title of *The Journal of an Author*, he wrote a number of occasional essays. They were very popular, and he came to look upon himself as a teacher and a prophet. This is a role which few authors have been disinclined to play. He had become an ardent Slavophil and he saw in the Russian masses, with their brotherly love, which he regarded as the peculiar genius of the Russian people, with their thirst for universal service for the sake of mankind, the only possibility of healing the ills, not only of Russia, but of the world. The course of events suggests that he was unduly optimistic. He wrote a novel called *A Raw Youth* and finally *The Brothers Karamazov*. His fame increased, and when he died, rather suddenly, in 1881, he was esteemed by many the greatest writer of his time. His funeral is said to have been the occasion for "one of the most remarkable demonstrations of public feeling ever witnessed in the Russian capital."

3

I have tried to relate the main facts of Dostoevsky's life without comment. The impression one receives is of a singularly

496

unamiable character. Vanity is an occupational disease of artists, whether writers, painters, musicians or actors, but Dostoevsky's was outrageous. It seems never to have occurred to him that anyone could have enough of hearing him talk about himself and his works. With this was combined, necessarily maybe, that lack of self-confidence which is now called the inferiority complex. It was, perhaps, on this account that he was so openly contemptuous of his fellow-writers. A man of any strength of character would hardly have been reduced by the experience of prison to submission so cringing; he accepted his sentence as the due punishment for his sin in resisting authority, but this did not prevent him from doing all he could to get it remitted. It does not seem logical. I have told to what depths of self-abasement he descended in his appeals to persons of power and influence. He was utterly lacking in self-control. Neither prudence nor common decency served to restrain him when he was in the grip of passion. So, when his first wife was ill and had not long to live, he abandoned her to follow Polina Suslova to Paris, and only rejoined her when that flighty young woman threw him over. But his weakness is nowhere more manifest than in his mania for gambling. It brought him time after time to destitution.

The reader will remember that, to fulfil a contract, Dostoevsky wrote a short novel called *The Gambler*. It is not a good one. Its chief interest is that in it he vividly described the feelings he knew so well which seize the unfortunate victim; and after you have read it, you understand how it came about that, notwithstanding the humiliations it caused him, the misery to him and those he loved, the dishonourable proceedings it occasioned (when he got money from the Fund for Needy Authors it was to enable him to write, not to gamble), the constant need to apply to others, already wearied with providing him with money, notwithstanding everything, he could not resist temptation. He was an exhibitionist, as to a greater or less extent are all those who, whatever art they practise, have the creative instinct; and he has described the way in which a run of luck may gratify this discreditable tendency. The onlookers crowd round and stare at the fortunate gambler, as though he were a superior being. They wonder and admire. He is the centre of attraction. Balm to the unhappy man cursed with a morbid diffidence! When he wins, it gives him an intoxicating sense of power; he feels himself the master of his fate, for his cleverness, his intuition, are so infallible that he can control chance.

"I have only for once to show will-power and in an hour I can transform my destiny," he makes his gambler exclaim. "The great thing is will-power. Only remember what happened to me seven months ago at Roulettenburg just before my final failure. Oh! it was a remarkable instance of determination. I had lost everything then, everything. I was going out of the Casino, I looked, there was still one golden gulden in my waist-coat pocket: 'Then I shall have something for dinner,' I thought. But after I had gone a hundred paces I changed my mind and went back. I staked that gulden . . . and there really is something peculiar in the feeling when, alone in a strange land, far from home and from friends, not knowing whether you will have anything to eat that day—you stake your last gulden, your very last. I won, and twenty minutes later I went out of the Casino, having a hundred and seventy gulden in my pocket. That's a fact. That's what the last gulden can sometimes do. And what if I had lost heart then? What if I had not dared to risk it?"

Dostoevsky's official life was written by a certain Strakhov, an old friend of his; and, in connection with this work, he wrote a letter to Tolstoy which Aylmer Maude has printed in his biography of that author and which, with some omissions, I now give in his translation:

"All the time I was writing I had to fight against a feeling of disgust and tried to suppress my bad feelings . . . I cannot regard Dostoevsky as a good or happy man. He was bad, debauched, full of envy. All his life long he was a prey to passions that would have rendered him ridiculous and miserable had he been less intelligent or less wicked. I was vividly aware of these feelings while writing his biography. In Switzerland, in my presence, he treated his servant so badly that the man revolted and said to him: 'But I too am a man!' I remember how I was struck by those words which reflected the ideas current in free Switzerland about the rights of man and were addressed to one who was always preaching sentiments of humanity to the rest of mankind. Such scenes were of constant occurrence; he could not control his temper . . . the worst of it was that he prided himself on the fact that he never repented of his dirty actions. Dirty actions attracted him and he gloried in the fact. Viskovatov (a professor) told me how Dostoevsky had boasted of having outraged a little girl at the bath-house, who had been brought to him by her governess . . . With all this he was given to a sort of mawkish sentimentality and high-flown humanitarian dreams, and it is these dreams, his literary message and the tendency of his writings, which endear him to us. In a word, all these novels endeavour to exculpate their author, they show that the most hidebound villainies can exist side by side with the noblest sentiments . . ."

It is true that his sentimentality was mawkish and his humanitarianism bootless. He had small acquaintance with the "people", to whom, as opposed to the intelligentsia, he looked for the regeneration of Russia, and he had little sympathy with their hard and bitter lot. He violently attacked the radicals who sought to alleviate it. The remedy he offered to the frightful misery of the poor was "to idealise their sufferings and make out of it a way of life. Instead of practical reforms, he offered them religious and mystical consolation".

The story of the violation of the little girl has grievously disturbed Dostoevsky's admirers and they have discredited it. Anna asserted that he had never spoken of it to her. Strakhov's account is obviously based on hearsay; but to confirm it is a report that, overcome by remorse, Dostoevsky told it to an old friend who advised him by way of penance to confess it to the man whom he hated most in the world. This was Turgenev. He had warmly praised Dostoevsky when he entered upon the literary scene, and had helped him with money, but Dostoevsky hated him because he was a "Westerner", and aristocratic, rich and successful. He made his confession to Turgenev, who heard it in silence. Dostoevsky paused. Perhaps, as André Gide has suggested, he expected Turgenev to act as one of his own (Dostoevsky's) characters would have acted, to take him in his arms and kiss him with the tears running down his cheeks, upon which they would be reconciled. But nothing happened.

"Mr. Turgenev, I must tell you," said Dostoevsky, "I must tell you. I despise myself profoundly." He waited for Turgenev to speak. The silence continued. Then Dostoevsky, losing his temper, cried: "But I despise you still more. That was all I had to say to you." He flung out of the room, slamming the door behind him. He had been robbed of one of those scenes which no one could write better than himself.

It is curious that he twice used the shocking episode in his books. Svidrigailov in *Crime and Punishment* confesses to the same ugly action, and so does Stavrogin in a chapter in *The Possessed* which Dostoevsky's publisher refused to print. It is perhaps significant that in this very book Dostoevsky wrote a malicious caricature of Turgenev. It is dull and stupid. It serves only to make a shapeless work more shapeless, and looks as if it were merely introduced to give Dostoevsky a chance to vent his malice. He is not the only author who has bit the hand that fed him. Before he married Anna Grigorievna, Dostoevsky, with an amazing lack of tact, told the ugly story to a girl he was courting; but as a fiction. And that, I think, is what it was. He had, as have the characters of his novels, a passion for self-abasement, and it seems to me not improbable that he narrated the discreditable incident to others as a personal experience. For all that, I do not believe that he actually committed the revolting crime of which he accused himself. I hazard the suggestion that it was a persistent day-dream which at once fascinated and horrified him. His characters so often have day-dreams that it is likely enough he had them too. In fact we all do. The novelist, by the nature of his gift, probably has day-dreams more precise and circumstantial than most people. Sometimes they are of such a nature that he can use them in his fiction, and then he forgets them. That is what seems to me likely to have happened with Dostoevsky. Having twice used the shameful story in his novels, he was no longer interested in it. That, perhaps, is why he never told it to Anna Grigorievna.

Dostoevsky was vain, envious, quarrelsome, suspicious, cringing, selfish, boastful, unreliable, inconsiderate, narrow and intolerant. In short he had an odious character. But that is not the whole story. If it had been, it is unimaginable that he could have created Alyosha Karamazov, perhaps the most engaging creature in all fiction. It is unimaginable that he could have created the saintly Father Zosima. Dostoevsky was the least censorious of men. While in prison, he had learned that men may commit fearful crimes, murder, rape or banditry, and yet have qualities of courage, generosity and loving-kindness towards their fellows. He was charitable. He never refused money to a beggar or a friend. When himself destitute, he managed to scrape something together to give to his sister-in-law and his brother's mistress, to his worthless stepson and to the drunken good-for-nothing, his younger brother Andrew. They sponged on him as he sponged on others and, far from resenting it, he seems only to have been distressed that he could not do more for them than he did. He loved, admired and respected Anna Grigorievna; he looked upon her as in every way superior to himself; and it is touching to learn that during their four years of absence from Russia he was tormented by the fear that, alone with him, she would grow bored. He could hardly bring himself to believe that he had at last found someone who, notwithstanding his defects, of which he was only too well aware, loved him devotedly.

I can think of no one in whom the dichotomy between the man and the writer has been greater than it was in Dostoevsky. It probably exists in all creative artists, but it is more conspicuous in authors than in others because their medium is words, and the contradiction between their behaviour and their communication is more shocking. It may be that the creative gift, a normal faculty of childhood and early youth, if it persists after adolescence is a disease which can only flourish at the expense of normal human attributes and, just as the melon is sweeter when grown in manure, thrives best in a soil compounded of vicious traits. It was not the good in Dostoevsky, it was the bad that was the source of the startling originality which made him one of the supreme novelists of the world.

.4

Balzac and Dickens created an immense number of characters. They were fascinated by the diversity of human beings, and their imagination was kindled by the differences they saw in them and the peculiarities that individualized them. No matter if men were good or bad, stupid or clever, they were themselves, and so, material to be put to good use. I suspect that Dostoevsky was interested in no one but himself, and in others only as they intimately affected him. He was in a way like those people who care for beautiful objects only if they own them. He was content to make do with a very small number of characters, and they are repeated in novel after novel. Alyosha in *The Brothers Karamazov* is the same man, less the epilepsy, as Prince Myshkin in *The Idiot*; Stavrogin in *The Possessed* is merely an elaboration of Svidrigailov in *Crime and Punishment*. The hero of that book, Raskolnikov, is a less forcible version of Ivan in *The Brothers Karamazov*. All are emanations of Dostoevsky's tortured, warped, morbid sensibility. There is even less variety in his female characters. Polina Alexandrovna in *The Gambler*, Lizabeta in *The Possessed*, Nastasia in *The Idiot*, Katrina and Grushenka in *The Brothers Karamazov* are the same woman; they are modelled directly on Polina Suslova. The suffering she caused him, the indignities she heaped upon him, were the fillip he needed to satisfy his masochism. He knew that she hated him; he felt sure that she loved him; and so the women who are modelled on her want to dominate and torture the man they love, and at the same time submit to him and suffer at his hands. They are hysterical, spiteful and malevolent because Polina was. Some years after the break, Dostoevsky met her in Petersburg and made her still another proposal of marriage. She refused it. He could not bring himself to believe that she simply did not like him, and so conceived the idea, to salve, one may suppose, his wounded vanity, that a woman attaches so great an importance to her virginity that she can only hate a man who has taken it without being married to her.

"You cannot forgive me," he told Polina, "for the fact that you once gave yourself to me, and you are taking revenge for that."

Dostoevsky was sufficiently convinced of the truth of this to use the notion more than once. In *The Brothers Karamazov*, Grushenka, some time before the story begins, has been seduced by a Pole and, though in the interval she has been kept by a rich merchant, feels she can only redeem herself by marrying her seducer. Again, in *The Idiot* Nastasia cannot forgive Totsky because he seduced her. Here, I think, Dostoevsky's psychology was at fault. The particular value attached to virginity is a fabrication of the male, due partly to superstition, partly to masculine vanity and partly, of course, to a disinclination to father someone else's child. Women, I should say, have ascribed importance to it chiefly because of the value men place on it, and also from fear of the consequences. I think I am right in saying that a man, to satisfy a need as natural as eating his dinner when he is hungry, may have sexual intercourse without any particular feeling for the object of his appetite; whereas with a woman sexual intercourse, without something in the nature, if not of love, at least of sentiment, is merely a tiresome business which she accepts as an obligation, or from the wish to give pleasure. I cannot bring myself to believe that when a virgin "gives herself" to a man to whom she is indifferent or actually averse, it is anything but an unpleasant and painful experience. That it should rankle for years and alter her whole character seems to me incredible.

Dostoevsky was deeply conscious of the duality in himself, and he ascribed it to all his self-willed characters. His meek characters, of which Prince Myshkin and Alyosha are examples, with all their sweetness are strangely ineffectual. But the very word duality suggests a simplification of human nature which does not accord with the facts. Man is an imperfect creature. The mainspring of his being is self-interest, it is folly to deny it; but it is folly to deny that he is capable of a disinterestedness which is sublime. We all know to what heights he may rise in a moment of crisis, and then show a nobility which neither he nor anyone else knew was in him. Spinoza has told us that "everything in so far as it is in itself endeavours to persevere in its own being"; and yet we know that it is not so rare for a man to lay down his life for his friend. Man is a jumble of vices and virtues, goodness and badness, of selfishness and unselfishness, of fears of all kinds and the courage to face them, of tendencies and predispositions which lure him this way and that. He is made up of elements so discordant that it is amazing that they can exist together in the individual, and yet so come to terms with one another as to form a plausible harmony. There is no such complication in the creatures of Dostoevsky's invention. They are constituted of a desire to dominate and a desire to submit themselves, of love devoid of tenderness and hate charged with malice. They are strangely lacking in the normal attributes of human beings. They only have passions. They have neither self-control nor self-respect. Their evil instincts are not mitigated by education, the experience of life or that sense of decency which prevents a man from disgracing himself. That is why, to common sense, their activities seem wildly improbable and the motives of them madly inconsequential.

We in Western Europe consider their unaccountable behaviour with astonishment and accept it, if we do accept it, as the natural behaviour of Russians. But are Russians like that? Were Russians like that in Dostoevsky's day? Turgenev and Tolstoy were his contemporaries. Turgenev's characters very much resemble ordinary people. We have all known young Englishmen like Tolstoy's Nicolas Rostov, gay, careless, extravagant, brave and affectionate, good fellows; and we have known at least a few girls as pretty, charming, ingenuous and good as his sister Natasha; nor would it be hard to find in our own country a man like fat, stupid, generous and good-hearted Peter Bezukhov. Dostoevsky claimed that those strange characters of his were more real than reality. I don't know what he meant by that. An ant is just as real as an archbishop. If he meant that they have moral qualities which raise them above the common run of men, he was mistaken. If there is any value in art, music and literature to correct the perversities of character, to assuage distress and to liberate the soul in part from human bondage, they know nothing of it.

504

They are devoid of culture. They have atrocious manners. They take a malignant pleasure in being rude to one another merely in order to wound and humiliate. In *The Idiot* Varvara spits in her brother's face because he is proposing to marry a woman she does not approve of, and in *The Brothers Karamazov* Dmitri, when Madame Hohlakov refuses him the loan of a large sum of money which there is no reason for her to lend him, in his anger spits on the floor of the room in which she has received him. They are an outrageous lot. But they are extraordinarily interesting. Raskolnikov, Stavrogin, Ivan Karamazov are of the same breed as Emily Brontë's Heathcliff and Melville's Captain Ahab. They palpitate with life.

5

Dostoevsky had been pondering over *The Brothers Karamazov* for a long time, and he took more pains over it than his financial difficulties had allowed him to take with any novel since his first. On the whole it is his best constructed work. As his letters show, he implicitly believed in that mysterious entity which we call inspiration, and counted upon it to enable him to write what he vaguely saw in his mind's eye. Now, inspiration is uncertain. It is more apt to come in isolated passages. To construct a novel, you need *esprit de suite*, that logical sense by means of which you may arrange your material in a coherent order, so that the various parts shall follow one another with verisimilitude and the whole shall be complete, with no loose ends hanging. Dostoevsky had no great capacity for this. That is why he is his best in scenes. He had a truly remarkable gift for creating suspense and dramatizing a situation. I know no scene in fiction more terrifying than that in which Raskolnikov murders the old pawnbroker, and few more striking than that in *The Brothers Karamazov* in which Ivan meets in the form of a devil his troubled conscience. With the prolixity of which he could not correct himself, Dostoevsky indulges in conversations of immense length; but even though the persons concerned express themselves with such abandon that you can hardly believe that human beings can so conduct themselves, they are almost always enthralling. In passing, I may mention a device he often used to excite in the reader a tremulous susceptibility. His characters are agitated out of proportion to the words they utter. They tremble with emotion, they insult one another, they burst into tears, they redden, they go green in the face or fearfully pallid. A significance the reader finds it hard to account for is given to the most ordinary remarks, and presently he is so wrought up by these extravagant gestures, these hysterical outbursts, that his own nerves are set on edge and he is prepared to receive a real shock when something happens which otherwise would have left him little perturbed.

Alyosha was designed to be the central figure of *The Brothers Karamazov*, as is plainly indicated by the first sentence: "Alexey Fyodorovitch Karamazov was the third son of Fyodor Pavlovitch Karamazov, a landowner well-known in the district in his own day, and still remembered among us owing to his gloomy and tragic death, which happened thirteen years ago, and which I shall describe in its proper place." Dostoevsky was too practised a novelist to have without intention begun his book with a definite statement that marks Alyosha out. But in the novel, as we have it, he plays a subordinate role compared with those of his brothers Dmitri and Ivan. He passes in and out of the story, and seems to have little influence on the persons who play their more important parts in it. His own activity is chiefly concerned with a group of schoolboys whose doings, beyond showing Alyosha's charm and loving-kindness, have nothing to do with the development of the theme.

The explanation is that *The Brothers Karamazov*, which runs in Mrs. Garnett's translation to 838 pages, is but a fragment of the novel Dostoevsky proposed to write. He intended in further volumes to continue the development of Alyosha, taking him through a number of vicissitudes, in which it is supposed he was to undergo the great experience of sin and finally, through suffering, achieve salvation. But death prevented Dostoevsky from carrying out his intention, and *The Brothers Karamazov* remains a fragment. It is, nevertheless, one of the greatest novels ever written, and stands at the head of the small, wonderful group of works of fiction which by their intensity and power hold a place apart from other novels, conspicuous as their different merits may be, and of which two thrilling examples are *Wuthering Heights* and *Moby Dick*.

Fyodor Pavlovitch Karamazov, a besotted buffoon, has four sons, Dmitri, Ivan and Alyosha, whom I have already spoken of, and a bastard, Smerdyakov, who lives in his house as cook and valet. The two elder sons hate their disgraceful father; Alyosha, the only lovable character in the book, is incapable of hating anyone. Professor E. J. Simmons thinks Dmitri should be considered the hero of the novel. He is the sort of man whom the tolerant are apt to describe as his own worst enemy, and, as such men often are, he is attractive to women. "Simplicity and deep feeling are the essence of his nature," says Professor Simmons; and further: "There is poetry in his soul which is reflected in his behaviour and colourful language. His whole life is like an epic in which the turbulent action is relieved by occasional lyric flights." It is true that he makes high-flown protestations of his moral aspirations, but as they do not lead to any change for the better in his conduct, I think one is justified in attaching small importance to them. It is true that he is capable on occasion of great generosity, but he is also capable of shocking meanness. He is a drunken, boastful bully, recklessly extravagant, dishonest and dishonourable. Both he and his father are furiously in love with Grushenka, a kept woman who lives in the town, and he is insanely jealous of the old man.

Ivan, to my mind, is a more interesting character. He is highly intelligent, prudent, determined to make his way in the world and ambitious. At the age of twenty-four he has already made something of a name for himself by the brilliant articles he has contributed to the reviews. Dostoevsky describes him as practical, and intellectually superior to the mass of needy and unfortunate students who hang about newspaper offices. He, too, hates his father. The sensual old wretch is murdered by Smerdyakov for the three thousand roubles he had hidden away to give Grushenka if she could be induced to go to bed with him, and Dmitri, who had often threatened to kill his father, is accused of the crime, tried and convicted. It was in accordance with Dostoevsky's plan that he should be, but in order to effect this he was obliged to make the various persons concerned behave in a manner that outrages probability. On the eve of the trial, Smerdyakov goes to Ivan and confesses that it was he who had committed the crime and returns him the money he had stolen. He makes it plain to Ivan that he had murdered the old man on his (Ivan's) instigation, and with his connivance. Ivan goes all to pieces, just as Raskolnikov does after murdering the old pawnbroker. But Raskolnikov was wildly neurotic, half-starved and destitute. Ivan was not. His first impulse is to go at once to the public prosecutor and tell him the facts, but he decides to wait and do so at the trial. Why? So far as I can see, only because Dostoevsky saw that then the confession would come with more thrilling effect. Then comes the very curious scene, to which I have already referred, in which Ivan has an hallucination in which his double, in the form of a shabby gentleman in reduced circumstances, confronts him with his worse self, with its baseness and insincerity. There is a furious knocking at the door. It is Alyosha. He comes in and tells Ivan that Smerdyakov has hanged himself. The situation is critical. Dmitri's fate is in the balance. It is true that Ivan was distraught, but he was not demented. From what we know of his character, we would have expected him at such a moment to have the strength to pull himself together and act with common sense. The natural thing, the obvious thing, was for the two of them to go there and then to the defending counsel, tell him of Smerdyakov's confession and suicide and give him the three thousand roubles he had stolen. With these materials the defending counsel, who, we are told, was an uncommonly able man, would surely have thrown enough doubt in the jury's minds to cause them to hesitate to bring in a verdict of guilty. Alyosha puts cold compresses on Ivan's head and tucks him up in bed. I have mentioned before that, for all his goodness, the gentle creature was strangely ineffectual. He was never more so than on this occasion.

Nor is an explanation given of Smerdyakov's suicide. He has been shown to be the most calculating, callous, clear-headed and self-confident of Karamazov's four sons. He had made his plans beforehand. With great presence of mind, he seized the opportunity that a lucky chance presented to him, and killed the old man. He had a reputation for complete honesty and no one could have suspected him of stealing the money. The evidence pointed to Dmitri. So far as I can see, there was no reason for Smerdyakov to hang himself, except to give Dostoevsky the occasion to end a chapter with a highly dramatic announcement. Dostoevsky was a sensational, not a realistic, writer, and so felt himself justified in using methods which the latter is bound to eschew.

After Dmitri has been found guilty, he makes a statement in which he proclaims his innocence and ends it with the words: "I accept the torture of accusation, and my public shame. I want to suffer, and by suffering I shall purify myself." Dostoevsky had a deep-rooted belief in the spiritual value of suffering, and thought that by the willing acceptance of it one atoned for one's sins, and so reached happiness. From this the surprising inference seems to emerge that, since sin gives rise to suffering and suffering leads to happiness, sin is necessary and profitable. But was Dostoevsky right in thinking that suffering cleanses and refines the character? There is no evidence in *The House of the Dead* that it had any such effect on his fellow convicts, and it certainly had none on him: as I have said, he emerged from prison the same man as he entered it. So far as physical suffering is concerned, my experience is that long and painful illness makes people querulous, egotistic, intolerant, petty and jealous. Far from making them better, it makes them worse. Of course I know that there are some, and I have known one or two myself, who in a long and distressing illness, from which recovery was impossible, have shown courage, unselfishness, patience and resignation; but they had those qualities before. The occasion revealed them. There is spiritual suffering too. No one can have lived long in the world of letters without having known men who had enjoyed success and then, for one reason or another, lost it. It made them sullen, bitter, spiteful and envious. I can think of only one case in which this misfortune, accompanied as it is by humiliations which only those who have witnessed them know, has been borne with courage, dignity and good humour. The man of whom I speak no doubt had those qualities before, but the mask of frivolity he wore prevented one from discerning them. Suffering is part of our human lot, but that does not make it any the less evil.

Though one may deplore Dostoevsky's prolixity, a fault he was well aware of, but could not, or would not, correct; though one may wish he had seen fit to avoid the improbabilities—improbabilities of character, improbabilities of incident—which cannot but disconcert the attentive reader; though one may think some of his ideas erroneous, *The Brothers Karamazov* remains a stupendous book. It has a theme of profound significance. Many critics have said that this was the quest of God; I, for my part, should have said it was the problem of evil. It is in the section called "Pro and Contra", which Dostoevsky rightly considered the culminating point of his novel, that it is dealt with. "Pro and Contra" consists of a long monologue which Ivan delivers to the sweet Alyosha. To the human intelligence the existence of a God who is all-powerful and all-good seems incompatible with the existence of evil. That men should suffer for their sins seems reasonable enough, but that innocent children should suffer revolts the heart as well as the head. Ivan tells Alyosha a horrible story. A little serf boy, a child of eight, threw a stone and by accident lamed his master's favourite dog. His master, owner of great estates, had the child stripped naked and made to run; and as he ran he set his pack of hounds on him and he is torn to pieces before his mother's eyes. Ivan is willing to believe that God exists, but he cannot accept the cruelty of the world God created. He insists that there is no reason for the innocent to suffer for the sins of the guilty; and if they do, and they do, God either is evil or does not exist. Dostoevsky never wrote with greater power than in this piece; but having written it, he was afraid of what he had done. The argument was cogent, but the conclusion repugnant to what with all his heart he wished to believe, namely, that the world, for all its evil, is beautiful because it is the creation of God. He hastened to write a refutation. No one was better aware than he that he had not succeeded. The section is tedious and the refutation unconvincing.

The problem of evil still awaits solution, and Ivan Karamazov's indictment has not yet been answered.

CHAPTER ELEVEN

Tolstoy and *War and Peace*

I

The last three chapters have dealt with novels which, in one way or another, stand apart. They are atypical. Now I come to one which, for all its complication, by its form and content takes its place in the main line of fiction, which, as I said on a previous page, began with the pastoral romance of Daphnis and Chloë. *War and Peace* is surely the greatest of all novels. It could only have been written by a man of high intelligence and of powerful imagination, a man with wide experience of the world and a penetrating insight into human nature. No novel with so grand a sweep, dealing with so momentous a period of history and with so vast an array of characters, was ever written before; nor, I surmise, will ever be written again. Novels as great will perhaps be written, but none quite like it. With the mechanization of life, with the State assuming ever greater power over the lives of men, with the uniformity of education, the extinction of class distinctions and the diminution of individual wealth, with the equal opportunities which will be offered to all (if such is the world of the future), men will still be born unequal. Some will be born with the peculiar gift that makes them become novelists, but the world they will know, with men and manners so conditioned, is more likely to produce a Jane Austen to write *Pride and Prejudice* than a Tolstoy to write *War and Peace*. It has been justly called an epic. I can think of no other work of fiction in prose that can with truth be so described. Strakhov, a friend of Tolstoy's and an able critic, put his opinion in a few energetic sentences: "A complete picture of human life. A complete picture of the Russia of that day. A complete picture of what may be called the history and struggle of people. A complete picture of everything in which people find their happiness and greatness, their grief and humiliation. That is *War and Peace*."

2

Tolstoy was born in a class that has not often produced writers of eminence. He was the son of Count Nicholas Tolstoy and of Princess Marya Volkonska, an heiress; and he was born, the youngest but one of their five children, at his mother's ancestral home, Yasnaya Polyana. His parents died when he was a child. He was educated first by private tutors, then at the University of Kazan, and later at that of Petersburg. He was a poor student, and took a degree at neither. His aristocratic connections enabled him to enter society, and first at Kazan, then at Petersburg and Moscow, he engaged in the fashionable diversions of his set. He was small and in appearance unprepossessing. "I knew very well that I was not good-looking," he wrote. "There were moments when I was over-come with despair: I imagined that there could be no happiness on earth for one with such a broad nose, such thick lips and such small grey eyes as mine; and I asked God to perform a miracle, and make me handsome, and all I then had and everything I might have in the future I would have given for a handsome face." He did not know that his homely face revealed a spiritual strength which was wonderfully attractive. He could not see the look of his eyes which gave charm to his expression. He dressed smartly (hoping like poor Stendhal that modish clothes would make up for his ugliness,) and he was unbecomingly conscious of his rank. A fellow-student at Kazan wrote of him as follows: "I kept clear of the Count, who from our first meeting repelled me by his assumption of coldness, his bristly hair, and the piercing expression of his half closed eyes. I had never met a young man with such a strange, and to me incomprehensible, air of importance and self-satisfaction . . . He hardly replied to my greetings, as if wishing to intimate that we were far from being equals . . ."

In 1851 Tolstoy was twenty-three. He had been spending some months in Moscow. His brother Nikolai, who was an artilleryman, arrived there on leave from the Caucasus, and when it was up and he had to return, Tolstoy decided to accompany him. After some months he was persuaded to enter the army and, as a cadet, engaged in the raids Russian troops made now and then on the rebellious mountain tribes. He seems to have judged his brother officers without indulgence. "At first," he wrote, "many things in this society shocked me, but I have accustomed myself to them without, however, attaching myself to these gentlemen. I have formed a happy mean in which there is neither pride nor familiarity." A supercilious young man! He was very sturdy, and could walk a whole day or spend twelve hours in the saddle without fatigue. A heavy drinker and a reckless, though unlucky, gambler, on one occasion, to pay a gambling debt, he had to sell the house on his estate at Yasnaya Polyana which was part of his inheritance. His sexual desires were violent, and he contracted syphilis. Except for this misadventure, his life in the army was very much like that of numberless young officers in all countries who are of good birth and have money. Dissipation is the natural outlet of their exuberant vitality, and they indulge in it the more readily since they think, perhaps rightly, that it adds to their prestige among their fellows. According to Tolstoy's diaries, after a night of debauchery, a night with cards or women, or in a carousal with gipsies, which if we may judge from novels is, or was, the usual but somewhat naïve Russian way of having a good time, he suffered pangs of remorse; he did not, however, fail to repeat the performance when the opportunity offered.

In 1854 the Crimean War broke out, and at the siege of Sevastopol Tolstoy was in charge of a battery. He was promoted to the rank of lieutenant for "distinguished bravery and courage" at the battle at the Chernaya River. In 1856, when peace was signed, he resigned his commission. During his military service Tolstoy wrote a number of sketches and stories, and a romanticized account of his childhood and early youth; they were published in a magazine and aroused highly favourable notice, so that when he returned to Petersburg he was warmly welcomed. He did not like the people he met there. Nor did they like him. Though convinced of his own sincerity, he could never bring himself to believe in the sincerity of others, and had no hesitation in telling them so. He had no patience with received opinions. He was irritable, brutally contradictory, and arrogantly indifferent to other people's feelings. Turgenev has said that he never met anything more disconcerting than Tolstoy's inquisitorial look, which, accompanied by a few biting words, could goad a man to fury. He took criticism very badly, and when he accidentally read a letter in which there was a slighting reference to himself, he immediately sent a challenge to the writer, and his friends had difficulty in preventing him from fighting a ridiculous duel.

Just then there was a wave of liberalism in Russia. The emancipation of the serfs was the pressing question of the day, and Tolstoy, after spending some months in the capital, returned to Yasnaya Polyana to put before the peasants on his estates a plan to grant them their freedom; but they suspected there was a catch in it and refused. After a time he went abroad and, on his return, started a school for their children. His methods were revolutionary. The pupils had the right not to go to school and, even when in school, not to listen to their teacher. There was complete absence of discipline, and no one was ever punished. Tolstoy taught, spending the whole day with them, and in the evening joined in their games, told them stories and sang songs with them till late into the night.

About this time he had an affair with the wife of one of his serfs, and a son was born. It was something more than a passing fancy, and in his diary he wrote: "I'm in love as never before." In later years the bastard, Timothy by name, served as coachman to one of Tolstoy's younger sons. The biographers have found it quaint that Tolstoy's father also had an illegitimate son who also served as coachman to a member of the family. To me it points to a certain moral obtuseness. I should have thought that Tolstoy, with his troublesome conscience, with his earnest desire to raise the serfs from their degraded state, to educate them and teach them to be clean, decent and self-respecting, would have done at least something for the boy. Turgenev too had an illegitimate child, a daughter, but he took care of her, had governesses to teach her and was deeply concerned with her welfare. Did it cause Tolstoy no embarrassment when he saw the peasant who was his natural son on the box of his legitimate son's carriage?

One of the peculiarities of Tolstoy's temper was that he could embark on a new undertaking with all the enthusiasm in the world, but sooner or later grew bored with it. He somewhat lacked the solid virtue of perseverance. So, after conducting the school for two years, finding the results of his activity disappointing, he closed it. He was tired, dissatisfied with himself, and in poor health. He wrote later that he might have despaired had there not been one side of life which lay still unexplored and which promised happiness. This was marriage.

He decided to make the experiment. After considering a number of eligible young women and discarding them for one reason or another, he married Sonya, a girl of eighteen and the second daughter of a Dr. Bers, who was a fashionable physician in Moscow and an old friend of his family's. Tolstoy was thirty-four. The couple settled down at Yasnaya Polyana. During the first eleven years of their marriage the Countess had eight children, and during the next fifteen five more. Tolstoy liked horses and rode well, and he was passionately fond of shooting. He improved his property and bought new estates east of the Volga, so that in the end he owned some sixteen thousand acres. His life followed a familiar pattern. There were in Russia scores of noblemen who gambled, got drunk and wenched in their youth, who married and had a flock of children, who settled down on their estates, looked after their property, rode and shot; and there were not a few who shared Tolstoy's liberal principles and, distressed at the ignorance of the peasants, sought to ameliorate their lot. The only thing that distinguished him from all of them was that during this time he wrote two of the world's greatest novels, *War and Peace* and *Anna Karenina*.

3

Sonya Tolstoy as a young woman seems to have been attractive. She had a graceful figure, fine eyes, a rather fleshy

515

nose and dark lustrous hair. She had vitality, high spirits and a beautiful speaking voice. Tolstoy had long kept a diary in which he recorded not only his hopes and thoughts, his prayers and self-reproachings, but also the faults, sexual and otherwise, of which he was guilty. On their engagement, in his desire to conceal nothing from his future wife, he gave her his diary to read. She was deeply shocked, but after a sleepless night, passed in tears, returned it and forgave. She forgave; she did not forget. They were both violently emotional and had what is known as a lot of character. This generally means that the person thus endowed has some very unpleasant traits. The Countess was exacting, possessive and jealous; Tolstoy was harsh, dogmatic and intolerant. He insisted on her nursing her children, which she was glad to do; but when, on the birth of one of them, her breasts were so sore that she had to give the child to a wet nurse, he was unreasonably angry with her. They quarrelled now and then, but made it up. They were very much in love with one another and, on the whole, their marriage for many years was a happy one. Tolstoy worked hard, and wrote assiduously. His handwriting was often difficult to read, but the Countess, who copied his manuscripts as each portion was written, grew very skilful in deciphering it, and was even able to guess the meaning of his hasty jottings and incomplete sentences. She is said to have copied *War and Peace* seven times.

In writing this essay I have quoted largely from Aylmer Maude's *Life of Tolstoy*, and I have used his translation of *A Confession*. Maude had the advantage of knowing Tolstoy and his family, and his narrative is very readable. It is unfortunate that he should have thought fit to tell more about himself and his opinions than most people can want to know. I am deeply indebted to Professor E. J. Simmons's full, detailed and convincing biography. He gives many interesting facts which Aylmer Maude, presumably from discretion, omitted. It must long remain the standard biography in English.

Professor Simmons has thus described Tolstoy's day: "All the family assembled at breakfast, and the master's quips and jokes rendered the conversation gay and lively. Finally he would get up with the words, 'It's time to work now,' and he would disappear into his study, usually carrying a glass of strong tea with him. No one dared disturb him. When he emerged in the early afternoon it was to take his exercise, usually a walk or ride. At five he returned for dinner, ate voraciously, and when he had satisfied his hunger he would amuse all present by vivid accounts of any experience he had had on his walk. After dinner he retired to his study to read, and at eight would join the family and any visitors in the living-room for tea. Often there was music, reading aloud or games for the children."

It was a busy, useful and contented life, and there seemed no reason why it should not run in the pleasant groove for many years to come, with Sonya bearing children, looking after them and the house, helping her husband in his work, and with Tolstoy riding and shooting, superintending his estates and writing books. He was approaching his fiftieth year. That is a dangerous period for men. Youth is past and, looking back, they are apt to ask themselves what their life amounts to; looking forward, with old age looming ahead, they are apt to find the prospect chilling. And there was one fear that had haunted Tolstoy all his life—the fear of death. Death comes to all men, and most are sensible enough, except in moments of peril or grave illness, not to think of it. This is how in *A Confession* he describes his state of mind at that time: "Five years ago something very strange began to happen to me. At first I experienced moments of perplexity and arrest of life, as though I did not know how to live or what to do; and I felt lost and became dejected. But this passed and I went on living as before. Then these moments of perplexity recurred oftener and oftener and always in the same form. They were always expressed by the questions: What is it for? What does it lead to? I felt that what I had been standing on had broken down and that I had nothing left under my feet. What I had lived on no longer existed, and I had nothing else to live on. My life came to a standstill. I could breathe, eat, drink and sleep, and I could not help doing these things, but there was no life, for there were no wishes the fulfilment of which I could consider reasonable.

"And all this befell me at a time when all around me I had what is considered complete good fortune. I was not yet fifty;

I had a good wife who loved me and whom I loved; good children, and a large estate which without much effort on my part improved and increased . . . I was praised by people, and without much self-deception could consider that my name was famous . . . I enjoyed a strength of mind and body such as I have seldom met among men of my kind: physically I could keep pace with the peasants at mowing, and mentally I could work for eight to ten hours at a stretch without experiencing any ill results from such exertion.

"My mental condition presented itself to me in this way: My life is a stupid and spiteful joke that someone has played on me."

The drunkenness of youth had left him with a bad hangover. When still a boy, he had ceased to believe in God, but his loss of faith left him unhappy and dissatisfied, for he had no theory that enabled him to solve the riddle of life. He asked himself: "Why do I live and how ought I to live?" He found no answer. Now he came once more to believe in God, but, strangely enough for a man of so emotional a temper, by a process of reasoning. "If I exist," he wrote, "there must be some cause of it, and a cause of causes. And that first cause of all is what men call God." For a while Tolstoy clung to the Russian Orthodox Church, but he was repelled by the fact that the lives of its learned men did not tally with their principles, and he found it impossible to believe all they required him to believe. He was prepared to accept only what was true in a plain and literal sense. He began to draw near to the believers among the poor and simple and unlettered; and the more he looked into their lives, the more convinced he became that, notwithstanding the darkness of their superstition, they had a real faith which was necessary to them and, alone, by giving their life a meaning, made it possible for them to live.

It was years before he arrived at the final determination of his views, and they were years of anguish, meditation and study. It is difficult to summarize these views briefly, and I attempt to do so only with hesitation.

He came to believe that the truth was to be found only in the words of Jesus. He rejected as evident absurdities, and an insult to the human intelligence, the creeds in which the tenets of Christianity are set forth. He rejected the divinity of Christ, the Virgin Birth and the Resurrection. He rejected the sacraments, since they were based on nothing in Christ's teaching and served only to obscure the truth. For a time he did not believe in life after death, but later, when he came to think that the Self was part of the Infinite, it seemed inconceivable to him that it should cease with the death of the body. In the end, shortly before his death, he declared that he did not believe in a God who created the world, but in One who lived in the consciousness of men. Such a god, one would have thought, is no less a figment of the imagination than the centaur or the unicorn. Tolstoy believed that the essence of Christ's teaching lay in the precept "Resist not evil"; the commandment "Swear not at all", he decided, applied not only to common expletives, but to oaths of any kind, those taken in the witness box or by soldiers being sworn in; while the charge "Love your enemies, bless them that curse you", forbade men to fight their country's enemies or to defend themselves when attacked. But to adopt opinions with Tolstoy was to act: if he had come to the conclusion that the substance of Christianity was love, humility, self-denial and the returning of good for evil, it was incumbent upon him, he felt, to renounce the pleasures of life, to humble himself, to suffer and be merciful.

Sonya Tolstoy, a pious member of the Orthodox Church, insisted on her children having religious instruction, and in every way did her duty according to her lights. She was not a woman of great spirituality; indeed, what with having so many children, nursing them herself, seeing that they were properly educated and running a great household, she had little time for it. She neither understood nor sympathized with her husband's altered outlook, but she accepted it tolerantly enough. When, however, his change of heart resulted in a change of behaviour, she was displeased, and did not hesitate to show it. Now that he thought it was his duty to consume as little as possible of the work of others, he heated his own stove, fetched water and attended to his clothes himself. With the idea of earning his bread with his own hands, he got a shoemaker to teach him to make boots. At Yasnaya Polyana he worked with the peasants, ploughing, carting hay and cutting wood; the Countess disapproved, for it seemed to her that from morning till evening he was doing unprofitable work which even among the peasants was done by young people.

"Of course you will say," she wrote to him, "that to live so accords with your convictions and that you enjoy it. That is another matter and I can only say: enjoy yourself! But all the same I am annoyed that such mental strength should be lost at log-splitting, lighting samovars and making boots—which are all excellent as a rest or a change of occupation; but not as a special employment." Here she was talking good sense. It was a stupidity on Tolstoy's part to suppose that manual labour is in any way nobler than mental labour. Nor is it more fatiguing. Every author knows that after writing for a few hours he is physically exhausted. There is nothing particularly commendable in work. One works in order to enjoy leisure. It is only stupid people who work because, when not working, they don't know what to do with themselves. But even if Tolstoy thought that to write novels for idle people to read was wrong, one would have thought he could have found a more intelligent employment than to make boots, which he made badly and which the people to whom he gave them could not wear. He took to dressing like a peasant, and became dirty and untidy. There is a story of how he came into dinner one day after loading manure, and the stench he brought with him was such that the windows had to be opened. He gave up shooting, to which he had been passionately addicted and, so that animals should not be killed for the table, became a vegetarian. For many years he had been a very moderate drinker; but now he became a total abstainer, and in the end, at the cost of a bitter struggle, left off smoking.

By this time the children were growing up, and for the sake of their education, and because Tanya, the eldest daughter, would be coming out, the Countess insisted that the family should go to Moscow in the winter. Tolstoy disliked city life, but yielded to his wife's determination. In Moscow he was appalled by the contrast he saw between the riches of the rich and the poverty of the poor. "I felt awful, and shall not cease to feel," he wrote, "that as long as I have superfluous food and some have none, and I have two coats and someone else has none, I share in a constantly repeated crime." It was in vain for people to tell him, as they continued to do, that there always had been rich and poor, and always would be; he felt it was not right; and after visiting a night lodging-house for the destitute, and seeing its horrors, he was ashamed to go home and sit down to a five-course dinner served by two men-servants in dress-clothes, white ties and white gloves. He tried giving money to the down-and-outs who appealed to him in their need, but came to the conclusion that the money they had wheedled out of him did more harm than good. "Money is an evil," he said. "And therefore he who gives money does evil." From this it was a short step to the conviction that property was immoral and to possess it sinful.

For such a man as Tolstoy the next step was obvious: he decided to rid himself of everything he owned; but here he came into violent conflict with his wife, who had no wish to beggar herself or to leave her children penniless. She threatened to appeal to the courts to have him declared incompetent to manage his affairs, and after heaven only knows how much acrimonious argument he offered to turn his property over to her. This she refused, and in the end he divided it among her and the children. On more than one occasion during the year this dispute lasted he left home to live among the peasants, but before he had gone far was drawn back by the pain he was causing his wife. He continued to live at Yasnaya Polyana and, though mortified by the luxury, luxury on a very modest scale, that surrounded him, none the less profited by it. The friction continued. He disapproved of the conventional education the Countess was giving their children, and he could not forgive her for having prevented him from disposing of his property as he wished.

In this brief sketch of Tolstoy's life I have been constrained to omit much that is of interest, and I must deal even more summarily with the thirty years that followed his conversion. He became a public figure, recognized as the greatest writer in

Russia, and with an immense reputation throughout the world as a novelist, a teacher and a moralist. Colonies were founded by people who wished to lead their lives according to his views. They came to grief when they tried to put his principles into practice, and the story of their misadventures is both instructive and comic. Owing to Tolstoy's suspicious nature, his harsh argumentativeness, his intolerance and his unconcealed conviction that if others disagreed with him it was from unworthy motives, he retained few friends; but, with his increasing fame, a host of students, pilgrims visiting the holy places of Russia, journalists, sightseers, admirers and disciples, rich and poor, nobles and commoners, came to Yasnaya Polyana.

Sonya Tolstoy was, as I have said, jealous and possessive; she had always wanted to monopolize her husband, and she resented the invasion of her house by strangers. Her patience was sorely tried: "While describing and relating to people all his fine feelings, he has lived as always, loving sweet food, a bicycle, riding and lust." And on another occasion she wrote in her diary: "I cannot help complaining because all these things he practises for the happiness of people complicate life so much that it becomes more and more difficult for me to live . . . His sermons on love and the good have resulted in indifference to his family and the intrusion of all kinds of rabble into our circle."

Among the first persons to share Tolstoy's views was a young man called Chertkov. He was wealthy, and had been a captain in the Guards, but, when he came to entertain a belief in the principle of non-resistance, he resigned his commission. He was an honest man, an idealist and an enthusiast, but of a domineering temper, with a singular capacity for enforcing his will on others; and Aylmer Maude states that everybody connected with him became his instrument, quarrelled with him or had to escape. An attachment sprang up between him and Tolstoy which lasted till the latter's death, and he acquired an influence over him which bitterly incensed the Countess.

While to most of Tolstoy's few friends his views seemed extreme, Chertkov constantly urged him to go further and apply them more rigidly. Tolstoy had been so occupied with his spiritual development that he had neglected his estates, with the result that, though they were worth something like sixty thousand pounds, they brought in no more than five hundred a year. It was evidently not enough to keep the household going and educate a swarm of children. Sonya persuaded her husband to give her the publishing rights to everything he had written before 1881, and on borrowed money started a business of her own to publish his books. It prospered so well that she was able to meet her commitments. But it was obviously incompatible with Tolstoy's conviction that property was immoral to retain rights on his literary productions and, when Chertkov gained this ascendancy over him, he induced him to declare that everything he had written since 1881 was in the public domain and could be published by anyone. This was enough to enrage the Countess, but Tolstoy did more than that: he asked her to surrender her rights over the earlier books, including of course the very popular novels, and this she absolutely refused to do. Her livelihood, and that of her family, depended upon them. Disputes, acrimonious and protracted, ensued. Sonya and Chertkov gave him no peace. He was torn between conflicting claims, neither of which he felt it right to repudiate.

4

In 1896 Tolstoy was sixty-eight. He had been married for thirty-four years, most of his children were grown up, his second daughter was going to be married; and his wife, at the age of fifty-two, fell ignominiously in love with a man many years younger than herself, a composer called Tanayev. Tolstoy was shocked, ashamed and indignant. Here is a letter he wrote to her: "Your intimacy with Tanayev disgusts me and I cannot tolerate it calmly. If I go on living with you on these terms, I shall only be shortening and poisoning my life. For a year now I have not been living at all. You know this. I have told it you in exasperation and with prayers. Lately I have tried silence. I have tried everything and nothing is of use. The intimacy goes on and I can see that it may well go on like this to the end. I cannot stand it any longer. It is obvious that you cannot give it up, only one thing remains—to part. I have firmly made up my mind to do this. But I must consider the best way of doing it. I think the very best thing would be for me to go abroad. We shall think out what would be for the best. One thing is certain—we cannot go on like this."

But they did not part; they continued to make life intolerable to one another. The Countess pursued the composer with the fury of an ageing woman in love, and though at first he may have been flattered, he soon grew tired of a passion which he could not reciprocate and which made him ridiculous. She realized at last that he was avoiding her, and finally he put a public affront on her. She was deeply mortified, and shortly afterwards came to the conclusion that Tanayev was "thick-skinned and gross both in body and spirit." The undignified affair came to an end.

The disagreement between husband and wife was by then common knowledge, and it was a source of bitterness to Sonya that his disciples, now his only friends, sided with him and, because she prevented him from acting as they thought he should, regarded her with hostility. His conversion had brought him little happiness; it had lost him friends, created discord in his family, and caused dissension between his wife and himself. His followers reproached him because he continued to lead a life of ease, and, indeed, he felt himself to blame. He wrote in his diary: "So I, who am now entering upon my seventieth year, long with all the strength of my spirit for tranquillity and solitude, and though not perfect accord, still something better than this crying disharmony between my life and my beliefs and conscience."

His health gave way. During the next ten years he had several illnesses, one so serious that he nearly died of it. Gorky, who knew him during this period, describes him as very lean, small and grey, but with eyes keener than ever and a glance more piercing. His face was deeply lined, and he had a long, unkempt white beard. He was an old man. He was eighty. A year passed, and another. He was eighty-two. He was failing rapidly, and it was evident that he had only a few more months to live. They were embittered by sordid quarrels. Chertkov, who apparently did not altogether share Tolstoy's notion that property was immoral, had built himself at considerable cost a large house near Yasnaya Polyana, and though Tolstoy deplored the expenditure of money, the propinquity naturally facilitated intercourse between the two men. He now pressed Tolstoy to carry into effect his desire that on his death all his works should go into the public domain. The Countess was outraged that she should be deprived of control over the novels that Tolstoy had handed over to her twenty-five years before. The enmity that had long existed between Chertkov and herself burst into open warfare. The children, with the exception of Alexandra, Tolstoy's youngest daughter, who was completely under Chertkov's domination, sided with their mother; they had no wish to lead the sort of life their father wanted them to lead and, though he had divided his estates among them, saw no reason why they should be deprived of the large income his writings brought in. So far as I know, none of them had been brought up to earn his own living. But notwithstanding the pressure his family brought upon him, Tolstoy made a will in which he bequeathed all his works to the public and declared that the manuscripts extant at the time of his death should be handed to Chertkov, so that he might make them freely accessible to all who might want to publish them. But this apparently was not legal, and Chertkov urged Tolstoy to have another will drawn up. Witnesses were smuggled into the house so that the Countess should not know what was going on, and Tolstoy copied the document in his own handwriting behind the locked doors of his study. In this will the copyrights were given to his daughter Alexandra, whom Chertkov had suggested as a nominee, for, as he wrote with some understatement: "I feel certain that Tolstoy's wife and children would not like to see someone not a member of the family made the official legatee." As the will deprived them of their chief means of subsistence that is credible. But this will again did not satisfy Chertkov, and he drew up another himself, which Tolstoy copied, sitting on the stump of a tree in the forest near Chertkov's house. This left Chertkov in full control of the manuscripts.

The most important of these were Tolstoy's later diaries. Both husband and wife had long been in the habit of keeping diaries, and it was an understood thing that each should have access to the other's. It was an unfortunate arrangement, since the complaints each made of the other, when read over, gave rise to bitter recriminations. The earlier diaries were in Sonya's hands, but those of the last ten years Tolstoy had delivered to Chertkov. She was determined to get them, partly because they could eventually be published at a profit, but especially because Tolstoy had been very frank in his account of their disagreements and she did not want these passages to be made public. She sent a message to Chertkov demanding their return. He refused. Upon this she threatened to poison or drown herself if they were not given back, and Tolstoy, shattered by the scene she made, took them away from Chertkov; but instead of letting Sonya have them, he put them in the bank. Chertkov wrote him a letter on which Tolstoy in his diary commented as follows: "I have received a letter from Chertkov full of reproaches and accusations. They tear me to pieces. Sometimes the idea occurs to me to go far away from them all."

From an early age, Tolstoy from time to time had had the desire to leave the world, with its turmoil and trouble, and retire to some place where he could devote himself in solitude to self-perfection; and, like many another author, he lent his own longing to the two characters in his novels, Pierre in *War and Peace* and Levin in *Anna Karenina*, for whom he had a peculiar predilection. The circumstances of his life at this time combined to give this desire almost the force of an obsession. His wife, his children, tormented him. He was harassed by the disapproval of his friends, who felt that he should at last carry his principles into complete effect. Many of them were pained because he did not practise what he preached. Every day he received wounding letters, accusing him of hypocrisy. One eager disciple wrote to beg him to abandon his estate, give his property to his relations and the poor, leave himself without a kopek, and go as a mendicant from town to town. Tolstoy wrote in reply: "Your letter has profoundly moved me. What you advise has been my sacred dream, but up to this time I have been unable to do it. There are many reasons . . . but the chief reason is that my doing this must not affect others." As we know, people often thrust into the background of their unconscious the real reason for their conduct, and in this case I think the real reason why Tolstoy did not act as both his conscience and his followers urged him to do was simply that he didn't quite enough want to do it. There is a point in the writer's psychology that I have never seen mentioned, though it must be obvious to anyone who has studied the lives of authors. Every creative writer's work is, to some extent at least, a sublimation of instincts, desires, day-dreams, call them what you like, which for one cause or another he has repressed, and by giving them literary expression he is freed of the compulsion to give them the further release of action. But it is not a complete satisfaction. He is left with a feeling of inadequacy. That is the source of the man of letters' glorification of the man of action, and the unwilling, envious admiration with which he regards him. It is possible that Tolstoy would have found in himself the strength to do what he sincerely thought right, for of his sincerity there can be no doubt, if he had not by writing his books blunted the edge of his determination.

He was a born writer, and it was his instinct to put matters in the most effective and interesting way he could. I suggest that in his didactic works, to make his points more telling, he let his pen run away with him, and put his theories in a more uncompromising fashion than he would have done if he had stopped to think what consequences they entailed. On one occasion he did allow that compromise, inadmissible in theory, was inevitable in practice. But there, surely, he gave his whole position away; for if compromise is inevitable in practice, which means only that the practice is impracticable, then something must be wrong with the theory. But, unfortunately for Tolstoy, the friends, the disciples, who came to Yasnaya Polyana in adoring droves could not reconcile themselves to the notion that their idol should condescend to compromise. There is, indeed, something brutal in the persistence with which they pressed the old man to sacrifice himself to their

527

sense of dramatic propriety. He was the prisoner of his message. His writings and the effect they had on so many, for not a few a disastrous effect, since some were exiled and others went to jail, the devotion, the love he inspired, the reverence in which he was held, had forced him into a position from which there was only one way out. He could not bring himself to take it.

For when, at length, he left home on the disastrous but celebrated journey which ended in his death, it was not because he had at last decided to take the step which his conscience and the representations of his followers urged him to take, but to get away from his wife. The immediate cause of his action was fortuitous. He had gone to bed and, after a while, heard Sonya rummaging among the papers in his study. The secrecy with which he had made his will preyed upon his mind, and it may be that he thought then that she had somehow learned of its existence and was looking for it. When she had gone, he got up, took some manuscripts, packed a few clothes and, having roused the doctor who had for some time been living in the house, told him that he was leaving home. Alexandra was awakened, the coachman hauled out of bed, the horses were harnessed, and he drove, accompanied by the doctor, to the station. It was five in the morning. The train was crowded, and he had to stand on the open platform at the end of the carriage in the cold and rain. He stopped first at Shamardin, where his sister was a nun at the convent, and there Alexandra joined him. She brought news that the Countess, on finding that Tolstoy was gone, had tried to commit suicide. She had done this more than once before, but as she took little pains to keep her intention to herself, the attempts resulted not in tragedy, but in fuss and bother. Alexandra pressed him to move on, in case her mother discovered where he was and followed him. They set out for Rostov-on-Don. He had caught cold, and was far from well; in the train he grew so ill that the doctor decided they must stop at the next station. This was at a place called Astapovo. The station-master, hearing who the sick man was, put his house at his disposal.

Next day Tolstoy telegraphed for Chertkov, and Alexandra

sent for her eldest brother and asked him to bring a doctor from Moscow. But Tolstoy was too great a figure for his movements to remain unknown, and within twenty-four hours a newspaper-man told the Countess where he was. With those of her children who were at home, she hastened to Astapovo, but he was so ill by then that it was thought better not to tell him of her arrival, and she was not allowed to enter the house. The news of his illness created world-wide concern. During the week it lasted, the station at Astapovo was thronged by representatives of the Government, police officers, railway officials, pressmen, photographers and many others. They lived in railway carriages, side-tracked for their accommodation, and the local telegraph office could hardly cope with the work put on it. Tolstoy was dying in a blaze of publicity. More doctors arrived, till at last there were five to attend him. He was often delirious, but in his lucid moments worried about Sonya, whom he still believed to be at home and unaware of his whereabouts. He knew he was going to die. He had feared death; he feared it no longer. "This is the end," he said, "and it doesn't matter." He grew worse. In his delirium he continued to cry out: "To escape! To escape!" At last Sonya was admitted into the room. He was unconscious. She fell to her knees and kissed his hand; he sighed, but gave no sign that he knew she had come. A few minutes after six in the morning, on Sunday, November 7, 1910, he died.

5

Tolstoy began to write *War and Peace* when he was thirty-six. That is a very good age at which to set about writing a masterpiece. By then an author has presumably acquired an adequate knowledge of the technique of his craft, he has gained a wide experience of life, he is still in full possession of his intellectual vigour and his creative power is at its height. The period Tolstoy chose to deal with was that of the Napoleonic wars, and the climax is Napoleon's invasion of Russia, the burning of Moscow and the retreat and destruction of his armies. When he started upon his novel, it was with the notion of writing a tale of family life among the gentry, and the historical incidents were to serve merely as a background. The persons of the story were to undergo a number of experiences which would profoundly affect them spiritually, and in the end, after much suffering, they would enjoy a quiet and happy life. It was only in the course of writing that Tolstoy placed more and more emphasis on the titanic struggle between the opposing powers, and conceived what is somewhat grandly called a philosophy of history. Some time ago, Mr. Isaiah Berlin published a most interesting and instructive little book, called *The Hedgehog and the Fox*, in which he showed that Tolstoy's ideas on the subject I must now briefly deal with were inspired by those of Joseph de Maistre, an eminent diplomatist, in a work entitled *Les Soirées de Saint-Pétersbourg*. That is not to discredit Tolstoy. It is no more the novelist's business to originate ideas than it is to invent the persons who serve as his models. Ideas are there, just as are human beings, their environment of town and country, the incidents of their lives, and in fact everything that concerns them, for him to make use of for his private purpose, which is to create a work of art. Having read Mr. Berlin's book, I felt constrained to read *Les Soirées de Saint-Pétersbourg*. The ideas which Tolstoy set forth with some elaboration in the second part of the epilogue to *War and Peace*, de Maistre expounded in three pages, and the gist of them is contained in a phrase: *"C'est l'opinion qui perd les batailles, et c'est l'opinion qui les gagne."* Tolstoy had seen war in the Caucasus and at Sevastopol, and his own experience enabled him to give vivid descriptions of the various battles in which sundry characters in his novel were engaged. What he had observed concorded very well with the views of de Maistre. But the piece he wrote is long-winded and somewhat involved, and I think one gets a better notion of his opinions from scattered remarks in the course of the narrative and from Prince Andrew's reflections. In passing, I may interject that this is the most suitable way in which a novelist can deliver his ideas.

Tolstoy's idea was that owing to fortuitous circumstances, unknown forces, errors of judgment, unforeseen accidents, there could be no such thing as an exact science of war, and so there could be no such thing as military genius. It was not, as commonly supposed, great men who affected the course of history, but an obscure force that ran through the nations and drove them unconsciously to victory or defeat. The leader of an advance was in the position of a horse harnessed to a coach and started full-tilt downhill—at a certain point the horse ceases to know whether he is dragging the coach or the coach is forcing him on. It was not by his strategy or his big battalions that Napoleon won his battles, for his orders were not obeyed, since either the situation had changed or they were not delivered in time; but because the enemy was seized with a conviction that the battle was lost and so abandoned the field. The result depended on a thousand incalculable chances, any one of which might prove decisive in an instant. "So far as their own free will was concerned, Napoleon and Alexander contributed no more by their actions to the accomplishment of such and such an event than the private soldier who was compelled to fight for them as a recruit or a conscript." "Those who are known as great men are really labels in history, they give their name to events, often without having so much connection with the facts as a label has." For Tolstoy they were no more than figure-heads, who were carried on by a momentum they could neither resist nor control. There is surely some confusion here. I do not see how he reconciles his conviction of the "predestined and irresistible necessity" of occurrences with the "caprices of chance"; for when fate comes in at the door, chance flies out of the window.

It is hard to resist the impression that Tolstoy's philosophy of history was, in part at least, occasioned by his wish to depreciate Napoleon. He seldom appears in person in the course of *War and Peace*, but when he does, he is made to seem petty, gullible, silly and ridiculous. Tolstoy calls him "that infinitesimal tool in history, who at no time, not even in exile, showed any manly dignity". Tolstoy is outraged that even the Russians should look upon him as a great man. He had not even a good seat on a horse. Here, I think, it is well to pause. The French Revolution gave rise to scores of young men who were as ambitious, as clever, as resolute and as unscrupulous as the son of the Corsican lawyer; and one cannot but ask oneself how it happened that this particular young man, of insignificant appearance, with a foreign accent, without money or influence, managed so to make his way in the world that after winning battle after battle he made himself dictator of France, and brought half Europe under his sway. If you see a bridge-player win an international tournament, you may ascribe it to luck or to the excellence of his partner; but if, no matter who his partner is, he goes on winning tournaments through a number of years, it is surely simpler to allow that he has a peculiar aptitude for the game, and outstanding gifts, than to claim that his triumphs are the result of the immense, irresistible pressure of antecedent and contingent events. I should have thought a great general needed that same combination of qualities, knowledge, flair, boldness, the intelligence to calculate chances and the intuition that enables him to judge his adversaries' mentality, as are needed by the great bridge-player. Of course Napoleon was aided by the circumstances of his time, but it is only prejudice that can deny that he had the genius to take advantage of them.

All this, however, does not affect the power and interest of *War and Peace*. The narrative carries you along with the impetuous rush of the Rhône at Geneva as it hurries to meet the placid waters of Lake Leman. There are said to be something like five hundred characters. They stand firmly on their feet. This is a wonderful achievement. The interest is not concentrated, as in most novels, on two or three persons, or even on a single group, but on the members of four families belonging to the aristocracy, the Rostovs, the Bolkonskis, the Kuragins and the Bezukhovs. The novel, as the title indicates, deals with war and peace, and that is the sharply contrasted background against which their fates are presented. One of the difficulties a novelist has to cope with when his theme requires him to deal with events violently diverse, with more groups than one, is to make the transition from one set of events to another, from one group to another, so plausible that the reader accepts it with docility. If the author succeeds in doing this, the reader finds he has been told what he needs to be told about one set of circumstances, one set of persons, and is ready to be told about other circumstances, other persons, whereof for a time he had heard nothing. On the whole, Tolstoy has managed to perform this difficult feat so skilfully that you seem to be following a single thread of narration.

Like writers of fiction in general, he framed his characters on persons he knew, or knew of, but it appears that he did not merely use them as models for his imagination to work upon, but drew faithful portraits of them. The thriftless Count Rostov is a portrait of his grandfather, Nicholas Rostov of his father, and the pathetic, charming, ugly Princess Mary of his mother. It has sometimes been thought that in the two men, Pierre Bezukhov and Prince Andrew Bolkonski, Tolstoy had himself in mind; and if this is so, it is perhaps not fantastical to suggest that, conscious of the contradictions in himself, in thus creating two contrasted individuals on the one model of himself he sought to clarify and understand his own character.

Both these men, Pierre and Prince Andrew, are in love with Natasha, Count Rostov's younger daughter, and in her Tolstoy has created the most delightful girl in fiction. Nothing is so difficult as to portray a young girl who is at once charming and interesting. Generally the young girls of fiction are colourless (Amelia in *Vanity Fair*), priggish (Fanny in *Mansfield Park*), too clever by half (Constantia Durham in *The Egoist*), or little geese (Dora in *David Copperfield*), silly flirts or innocent beyond belief. It is understandable that they should be an awkward subject for the novelist to deal with, for at that tender age the personality is undeveloped. Similarly, a painter can only make a face interesting when the vicissitudes of life, thought, love and suffering have given it character. In the portrait of a girl, the best he can do is to represent the charm and beauty of youth. But Natasha is entirely natural. She is sweet, sensitive and sympathetic, childish, womanly already, idealistic, quick-tempered, warm-hearted, headstrong, capricious and in every way enchanting. Tolstoy created many women, and they are wonderfully real, but never another who wins the affection of the reader as does Natasha. She was drawn from Tanya Bers, the younger sister of his wife, and he was charmed by her as

533

Charles Dickens was charmed by his wife's younger sister, Mary Hogarth. An instructive parallel!

To both the men who loved her, to Prince Andrew and Pierre, Tolstoy attributed his own passionate search for the meaning and purpose of life. Prince Andrew is the more obvious. He is a product of the conditions prevalent then in Russia. A rich man, in possession of vast estates, he owns a great number of serfs, from whom he can exact forced labour and, if they displease him, have them stripped and flogged, or wrest them from wife and children and send them to serve as common soldiers in the army. And if a girl or married woman takes his fancy, he can send for her and use her for his pleasure. Prince Andrew is handsome, with marked features, weary eyes and an air of boredom. He is in fact the *beau ténébreux* of romantic fiction. A gallant figure, proud of his race and rank, high-minded, but haughty, dictatorial, intolerant and unreasonable. He is cold and arrogant with his equals, patronizing but kind with his inferiors. He is intelligent, and ambitious to distinguish himself. With a nice touch, Tolstoy wrote of him: "Prince Andrew always became specially keen when he had to guide a young man and help him to wordly success. Under cover of obtaining help for another, which from pride he would never accept for himself, he kept in touch with the circle which confers success and which attracted him."

Pierre is a more puzzling character. He is a huge, ugly man, so short-sighted that he has to wear spectacles, and very fat. He eats too much and drinks too much. He is a great womaniser. He is clumsy and tactless; but he is so good-natured, so manifestly sincere, so kindly, considerate and unselfish, that it is impossible to know him without loving him. He is wealthy. He allows a horde of hangers-on, however worthless, to dip freely into his purse. He is a gambler and is unmercifully cheated by the members of the aristocratic club in Moscow to which he belongs. He lets himself be jockeyed into an early marriage with a beautiful woman, who marries him for his money and is impudently unfaithful to him. After fighting a grotesque duel with her lover, he leaves her and goes to Petersburg. On the journey he meets by chance a mysterious old man, who turns out to be a Freemason. They converse and Pierre confesses that he does not believe in God. "If He did not exist we could not talk about Him," answers the Freemason, and on these lines goes on to give Pierre an elementary version of what is known as the ontological proof of God's existence. This was devised by Anselm, Archbishop of Canterbury, and runs as follows: We define God as the greatest object of thought, but the greatest object of thought must exist, or else another, as great but having existence, would be greater. From this it follows that God exists. This proof was rejected by Thomas Aquinas and demolished by Kant, but it convinced Pierre, and very shortly after his arrival in Petersburg he was initiated into the Masonic Order. Of course, in a novel events, whether material or spiritual, have to be telescoped, otherwise it would never end: a long-fought battle must be described in a page or two, and everything but what the author thinks essential has to be omitted; it is the same with a change of heart. In this case, it seems to me that Tolstoy has gone too far; so sudden a conversion makes Pierre uncommonly superficial. As a result of it, however, desiring to abandon his dissipated ways, he decides to return to his estates, liberate his serfs and devote himself to their welfare. He is hoodwinked and cheated by his steward, just as he was by his gambling friends, and finds himself thwarted in all his good intentions. His philanthropic schemes for the most part come to nothing for lack of perseverance, and he returns to his old life of idleness. His enthusiasm for the Masonic Order dwindles as he discovers that most of the brethren see nothing in it beyond its forms and ceremonies, while many cling to it "simply for the sake of being intimate with rich people and getting some benefit out of the intimacy." Disgusted and weary, he takes once more to gambling, drink and promiscuous fornication.

Pierre knows his faults and hates them, but he lacks the tenacity of purpose to amend them. He is a modest, humane, good-natured creature, but strangely devoid of common sense. His behaviour at the Battle of Borodino is of a singular ineptitude. Though a civilian, he drives in his carriage to the field of battle, gets in everybody's way, makes a thorough nuisance of himself and finally, to save his life, takes to his heels. When Moscow is evacuated, he stays on, is arrested as an incendiary and condemned to death. The sentence is remitted, and he is imprisoned. He is taken along with other prisoners when the French set out on their disastrous retreat, and is eventually rescued by a band of guerrillas.

It is difficult to know what to make of him. He is good and modest; he has a wonderful sweetness of disposition; he is terribly weak. I am sure he is true to life. I suppose he should be regarded as the hero of *War and Peace*, since in the end he marries the charming and desirable Natasha. I imagine that Tolstoy loved him: he writes of him with tenderness and sympathy; but I wonder if it was necessary to make him quite so silly.

In so long a book as *War and Peace*, and one that took so long to write, it is inevitable that the author's verve should sometimes fail him. Tolstoy ends his novel with an account of the retreat from Moscow and the destruction of Napoleon's army. But this long and, no doubt, necessary narrative has the disadvantage of telling the reader, unless he is abnormally ignorant of history, a great deal of what he knows already. The result is that the quality of surprise, which makes you turn the pages of a book eager to know what is to happen next, is lacking; and, notwithstanding the tragic, dramatic and pathetic incidents which Tolstoy relates, you read with a certain impatience. He used these chapters to tie up various loose ends, and to bring upon the scene again characters of whom we have long lost sight; but I think his main object in writing them was to introduce a fresh character who was to have an important effect on Pierre's spiritual development.

This was one of his fellow-prisoners, Plato Karataev, a serf condemned to serve in the army for stealing wood. He was a type that at this time seems to have much occupied the Russian intelligentsia. Living, as they did, under a severe despotism and knowing the empty, frivolous lives of the aristocracy, the ignorance and narrowness of the merchant class, they had come to believe that the salvation of Russia lay in the down-trodden and ill-used peasantry. Tolstoy in *A Confession* tells us how, despairing of his own class, he turned to the Old Believers for the goodness and faith which gave meaning to life. But, of course, there were good landlords as well as bad ones, honest tradesmen as well as dishonest ones, and bad peasants as well as good ones. It was merely a literary illusion to suppose that in the peasants alone was virtue.

Tolstoy's portrait of the simple soldier is one of the most winning of all the portraits in *War and Peace*. It was natural that Pierre should be drawn to him. Plato Karataev loves all men. He is perfectly unselfish. He endures hardship and danger with cheerfulness. He has a sweet and noble character, and Pierre, as susceptible as ever to every influence, seeing the goodness in him, comes himself to believe in goodness: "the world that had been shattered was once more stirring in his soul with a new beauty and on a new and unshakable foundation." From Plato Karataev, Pierre learns that "happiness for man is only to be found within, and from the satisfaction of simple human needs, that unhappiness arises not from privations but from superabundance, and that there is nothing in life too difficult to face." At last he finds himself possessed of that serenity and peace of mind that he had so long and so vainly sought.

If for some readers there is a certain diminution of interest in Tolstoy's account of the retreat, it is richly made up for in the first part of the Epilogue. It is a brilliant invention.

The older novelists were in the habit of telling the reader what happened to their principal characters after the story they had to tell was finished. He was informed that the hero and heroine lived happily, in prosperous circumstances, and had so and so many children, while the villain, if he had not been polished off before the end, was reduced to poverty and married a nagging wife, and so got what he deserved. But it was done perfunctorily, in a page or two, and the reader was left with the impression that it was a sop the author had somewhat contemptuously thrown him. It remained for Tolstoy to make his epilogue a piece of real importance. Seven years have passed, and we are taken to the house of Nicholas Rostov, who has married a rich wife and has children. Prince Andrew was

537

mortally wounded at the Battle of Borodino. It was his sister that Nicholas married. Pierre's wife conveniently died during the invasion, and he was free to marry Natasha, whom he had long loved. They too have children. They love one another, but oh, how dull they have become, and how commonplace! After the hazards they have run, the pain and anguish they have suffered, they have settled down to a middle-aged complacency. Natasha, who was so sweet, so unpredictable, so delightful, is now a fussy, exacting, shrewish housewife. Nicholas Rostov, once so gallant and high-spirited, has become a self-opinionated country squire; and Pierre, fatter than ever, sweet and good-natured still, is no wiser than he was before. The happy ending is deeply tragic. Tolstoy did not write thus, I think, in bitterness, but because he knew that this is what it would all come to; and he had to tell the truth.

CHAPTER TWELVE

In Conclusion

I

AFTER you have given a party, especially if your guests were of unusual distinction, when you have sped the last one on his way and you return to the sitting-room, it is only natural, human nature being what it is, that you and your wife, if you have one, the friend who lives with you, if you haven't, should discuss them over a final drink before going to bed. A. was in fine form. B. has a tiresome habit of interrupting with an irrelevant remark just as someone is reaching the point of a good story, and so killing it; it was amusing to see A., indefatigably loquacious, take not the smallest notice and go on talking as though B. had never opened his mouth. D. and C. were disappointing. They wouldn't make an effort. It had never occurred to them that, when you go to a party, it is your duty to do what you can to make it go. You defend one of them by saying that he is very shy, and the other by saying that it is a matter of principle with him; he will not speak unless he has something to say worth saying. Your friend justly retorts that if we were all as austere, conversation would perish. You laugh and pass on to E. He was as caustic as usual, and no less truculent: he is disgruntled because he thinks his merits have not been adequately recognized; success would soften him, but perhaps his wit would be less delectable if it lost its sting. You wonder how F.'s latest love affair is going on, and try to remember the exact wording of that brilliant repartee of his which made you laugh. On the whole it was a good party; you finish your drink, turn out the lights and go to your respective bedrooms.

So I, having spent many months in the company of the novelists with whom I have dealt, find myself inclined, before parting from them for good, to sum up in my mind, as though they had been my guests at a party, the various impressions they have made on me. It would have been a mixed gathering, but, taking it all in all, a convivial one. At first the conversation was general. Tolstoy, dressed as a peasant, with his great, untidy beard, his little grey eyes darting from one to another, discoursed with unction of God and with coarseness of sex. He said with complacency that in his youth he had been a great lecher, but in order to show that he was one at heart with the peasantry used a grosser word. Dostoevsky, angrily conscious that no one really appreciated his genius, for long maintained a moody silence; suddenly he broke out into a vituperative harangue which might have caused a quarrel, if the rest of the company had not been so busy talking themselves that they paid no attention. The party broke up into smaller groups. Dostoevsky went and sat by himself in a corner. His ravaged face was contorted by a sardonic sneer as he took note of the fact that Tolstoy's smock was of a fine material that must have cost at least seven roubles a yard. He could not forgive Tolstoy because the editor of a magazine in Moscow had refused to buy a novel of his for serialization, since he had just then paid so much money for *Anna Karenina*. It infuriated him that Tolstoy should talk of God as though He were his own peculiar per-quisite: had he never read *The Brothers Karamazov*? Dostoevsky's eyes wandered with indifference, tinged with sullen dislike, from person to person in the room, till they came to rest on a young woman who was seated by herself. She was not much to look at, but he read on her pale face a contemptuous disapproval of the persons in whose company she found herself, which touched a chord in his own tortured soul. There was in her expression a spirituality which attracted him. He had been told that she was a Miss Emily Brontë. He got up, walked towards her and, taking a chair, sat down beside her. She blushed scarlet. He saw that she was very shy and very nervous. He patted her kindly on the knee, which she withdrew with a start, and to put her at her ease began to tell her his favourite story of how in a bath-house in Moscow a governess had brought him a little girl whom he had raped; but as he spoke very quickly, in broken French, the young lady did not understand a word he said and, before he had half done telling her how agonizing his remorse had been for the sin he had committed, and how terrible his sufferings, she rose abruptly and left him.

When the party dispersed about the spacious room, Miss Austen had chosen a seat somewhat apart. Stendhal, though he had never got over his timidity where women were concerned, felt it was a duty he owed himself to make a pass at her; but her cool amusement disconcerted him, and with a glance at Henry Fielding, who was talking with Herman Melville, he joined the noisy group of Balzac, Charles Dickens and Flaubert. Miss Austen was glad to be left to give her undisturbed attention to her fellow-guests. She saw Miss Brontë leave the ugly little man who had been talking to her, and seat herself in the corner of a sofa. Poor little thing, so badly dressed, with those leg-of-mutton sleeves; her eyes were fine and her hair was pretty, but why did she do it so unbecomingly? She looked distressingly like a governess, and though, of course, a clergyman's daughter, was certainly of very humble origins. Miss Austen thought she looked lost and lonely, and felt it would be a kindness to speak to her. She got up and sat down on the sofa beside her. Emily gave her a startled look, and answered Miss Austen's friendly questions with embarrassed monosyllables. Miss Austen had noticed without surprise that the elder Miss Brontë had not been invited to the party. Perhaps it was just as well, as she had a very low opinion of *Pride and Prejudice*, and thought that its author lacked poetry and sentiment; but, being a well-bred woman, Miss Austen felt it only polite to ask how Miss Charlotte was. Emily again replied with a monosyllable, and Miss Austen came to the conclusion that to talk with people she didn't know was agony to the poor little thing and so she decided that it would be kinder to leave her to herself. She resumed her former seat, and for Cassandra's sake went on with her consideration of the other persons in the room. Of course, there was too much to tell in a letter, and she must wait till they were once more together at Chawton. She smiled when she thought how dear Cassandra would laugh when she described those queer people one by one.

Mr. Dickens was smaller than Miss Austen liked men to be, and much too smartly dressed; but he had a pleasant face and fine eyes, and from his lively air she thought it quite possible that he had a sense of humour. It was a pity he was so vulgar. There were two Russians there, one with an unpronounceable name who looked disagreeable and common; the other, Tolstoy, had the air of a gentleman, but you could never tell with foreigners. Miss Austen could not understand why he wore that strange smock, like an artist's, and those great clumsy boots. They said he was a Count, but she had never thought a foreign title anything but rather ridiculous. And as for the others—Monsieur Beyle, whom they called Stendhal, was fat and ugly, Monsieur Flaubert laughed much too loudly for any-one who had pretensions to elegance, and as to Monsieur de Balzac, his manners were deplorable. The fact was that the only gentleman present was Mr. Fielding, and Miss Austen wondered what he could find to interest him in that American he was talking to. It was a Mr. Melville, a fine figure of a man, tall and upstanding, but he wore a beard, and it made him look like the captain of a merchant vessel. He was telling Mr. Fielding a story, which was evidently amusing, and Mr. Fielding laughed heartily. Mr. Fielding was a little the worse for liquor, but Miss Austen knew that gentlemen often were, and though she regretted it, it did not shock her. Mr. Fielding had a fine presence and, though something of a dissipated look, an air of good breeding. He would have held his own at Godmersham with any of her brother's, Mr. Knight's, friends. After all, he was a cousin of Lady Mary Wortley-Montagu, and through the Earls of Denbigh descended from the Hapsburgs. He caught her look, rose to his feet and, leaving the strange American, came over to Miss Austen, and with a bow asked if he might sit beside her. She smiled her assent and set herself to be suitably gracious. He had a pleasant flow of small-talk, and presently Miss Austen felt emboldened to tell him that she had read *Tom Jones* when she was a girl.

"And I'm sure it did you no harm, Madam," he said.

"None whatever," she answered. "Nor do I believe that it

would ever do so to any young woman of sound principles and good sense."

Then Mr. Fielding, with a smile in which there was something of gallantry, asked Miss Austen how it had happened that, with her charm, wit and grace, she had never married.

"How could I, Mr. Fielding?" she answered gaily. "The only man I could ever have brought myself to marry was Darcy, and he was married to my dear Elizabeth."

Charles Dickens had joined the group of the three eminent novelists, Stendhal, Balzac and Flaubert, but he did not feel quite at ease. Though they were cordial enough, he could not but see that they looked upon him as an amiable barbarian. They were quite plainly of opinion that nothing of literary importance could be produced out of France. That an Englishman should write novels was an amusing performance, like the antics of trained dogs in a circus, but, of course, without any pretension to artistic merit. Stendhal admitted that England had Shakespeare, and was fond of saying every now and then: "To be or not to be"; and once, when Flaubert was more than usually vociferous, he gave Dickens a quizzical look and murmured: "The rest is silence." Dickens, generally the life and soul of a party, tried his best to seem amused at the conversation of those great talkers, but his laughter was forced. He was frankly shocked at the bawdy freedom with which they related their sexual adventures. Sex was not a matter that he cared to hear spoken of. When they asked him if it was not true that English women were frigid, he did not know what to answer, and he listened in pained silence to Balzac's ribald account of his affair with the Countess Guidoboni, a member of the highest English aristocracy. They chaffed him about the English prudishness: "improper" was the commonest word in the English vocabulary; this was improper, that was improper; and Stendhal stated as a fact that in England they put the legs of pianos into trousers so that young girls who were learning to play should not be distracted from their five-finger exercises by lascivious thoughts. Dickens bore their banter with his usual good humour; but he smiled within himself when he thought how little they knew of the larks he and Wilkie Collins had when

543

they went on their jaunts to Paris. On the last one, as they sighted the white cliffs of Dover, Wilkie had turned to him with a solemnity unusual to him: "Charles," he had said, "the respectability of England, thank God, is firmly established on the immorality of France." For a moment, Dickens was speechless, and then, as he realized the profound significance of the remark, his eyes filled with patriotic tears. "God save the Queen," he muttered in a husky voice. Wilkie, always the gentleman, gravely raised his top-hat. A memorable moment!

2

It is evident that these novelists were persons of marked and unusual individuality. They had the creative instinct strongly developed, and they had a passion for writing. If they are anything to go by, one may safely say that it is not much of a writer who hates writing. That is not to say that they found it easy. It is difficult to write well. But still, to write was their passion. It was not only the business of their lives, but a need as urgent as hunger or thirst. There is probably in everyone something of the creative instinct. It is natural for a child to play about with coloured pencils and paint little pictures in water-colour, and then, often enough, when it learns to read and write, to write little verses and little stories. I believe that the creative instinct reaches its height during the twenties and then, sometimes because it was merely a product of adolescence, sometimes because the affairs of life, the necessity of earning a living, leave no time for its exercise, it languishes and dies. But in many persons, in more than most of us know, it continues to burden and enchant them. They become writers because of the compulsion within them. Unfortunately, the creative instinct may be powerful and yet the capacity to create anything of merit may be lacking.

What is it that must be combined with the creative instinct to make it possible for a writer to produce a work of value? Well, I suppose it is personality. It may be a pleasant or an unpleasant one; that doesn't matter. What matters is that, by some idiosyncrasy of nature, the writer is enabled to see in a manner peculiar to himself. It doesn't matter if he sees in a way that common opinion regards as neither just nor true. You may not like the world he sees, the world, for instance, that Stendhal, Dostoevsky or Flaubert saw, and then his world will be distasteful to you; but you can hardly fail to be impressed by the power with which he has presented it; or you may like his world, as you like the world of Fielding and Jane Austen, and then you will take the author to your heart. That depends on your own disposition. It has nothing to do with the merits of the work.

I have been curious to discover, if I could, what precisely were the characteristics of these novelists I have been discussing which made them able to produce books to which the consensus of qualified opinion has agreed to ascribe greatness. Little is known of Fielding, Jane Austen and Emily Brontë, but as regards the others, the material for such an enquiry is overwhelming. Stendhal and Tolstoy wrote volume after volume about themselves; Flaubert's revealing correspondence is enormous; and of the rest, friends and relations have written reminiscences and biographers elaborate lives. Strangely enough, they do not seem to have been highly cultured. Flaubert and Tolstoy were great readers, but chiefly to obtain material for what they wanted to write; the others were no more widely read than the average persons of the class they belonged to. They appear to have taken little interest in any art other than their own. Jane Austen confessed that concerts bored her. Tolstoy was fond of music and played the piano. Stendhal had a predilection for opera, which is the form of musical entertainment which affords pleasure to people who don't like music. He went to the Scala every night when he was in Milan to gossip with his friends, have supper and play cards, and, like them, gave his attention to what was happening on the stage only when a famous singer sang a well-known aria. He had an equal admiration for Mozart, Cimarosa and Rossini. I have not discovered that music meant anything to the rest. Nor did the plastic arts. Such references as you find in their books to painting or sculpture indicate that their taste was distressingly conventional. Tolstoy, as everyone knows, discarded all painting as worthless unless the subject provided a moral lesson. Stendhal deplored the fact that Leonardo had not had the advantage of Guido Reni's guidance and example, and he claimed that Canova was a greater sculptor than Michael Angelo because he had produced thirty masterpieces, whereas Michael Angelo had produced but one.

Of course, it requires intelligence to write a good novel, but of a peculiar, and perhaps not of a very high, order, and these great writers were intelligent; but they were not strikingly intellectual. Their naïveté, when they deal with general ideas, is often startling. They accept the commonplaces of the philosophy current in their day, and when they put them in use in their fiction, the result is seldom happy. The fact is, ideas are not their affair, and their concern with them, when they *are* concerned with them, is emotional. They have little gift for conceptual thought. They are not interested in the proposition, but in the example; for it is the concrete that interests them. But if intellect is not their strong point, they make up for it with gifts that are more useful to them. They feel strongly, even passionately; they have imagination, keen observation and an ability to put themselves in the shoes of the characters of their invention, to rejoice in their joys and suffer with their pains; and, finally, they have a faculty for giving with force and distinctness body and shape to what they have seen, felt and imagined.

These are great gifts, and an author is fortunate to possess them, but they will not suffice unless he has something else besides. Gavarni said of Balzac that in general information on all subjects he was completely *ignare*. One's first impulse is to translate that by "ignorant", but that is a French word too, and *ignare* means more than that. It suggests the crass ignorance of a moron. But when Balzac began to write, Gavarni went on, he had an intuition of things, so that he seemed to know everything about everything. I take intuition to be a judgment one makes on grounds which are, or which one thinks are, legitimate, but which are not present to consciousness. But this, apparently, was not the case with Balzac. There were no grounds for the knowledge he displayed. I think Gavarni used the wrong word; I think a better one would have been inspiration. Inspiration is that something else the author needs in order to write greatly. But what is inspiration? I possess a number of books on psychology, and I have looked through them in vain to find something that would enlighten me. The only piece of writing I have come across that attempts to deal with the subject is an essay by Edmond Jaloux entitled *L'Inspiration Poétique et l'Aridité*. Edmond Jaloux was a Frenchman, and he wrote of his fellow-countrymen. It may be that their response to a spiritual state is more intense than that of the sober Anglo-Saxons. He describes, as follows, the aspect of the French poet when he is under the spell of his inspiration. He is transfigured. His countenance is calm and at the same time radiant; his features are relaxed, his eyes shine with a singular clearness, with a sort of strange desire that reaches out to nothing real. It is an indubitable physical presence. But inspiration, Edmond Jaloux goes on to say, is not permanent. It is followed by aridity, which may last a little while or may last for years. Then the author, feeling himself only half alive, is ill-humoured, afflicted with a bitterness that not only depresses him but makes him aggressive, spiteful, misanthropic and jealous, both of the works of his fellow-writers and of the power to work which he has lost. I find it curious, and even rather alarming, to perceive how like these states are to those of the mystics when, in moments of illumination, they feel themselves at one with the Infinite, and when, in those periods which they call the Dark Night of the Soul, they feel dry, empty and abandoned of God.

Edmond Jaloux wrote as though only poets had inspiration, and it is perhaps true that it is more necessary to them than to the writers of prose. Certainly the difference between the poet's verse when he writes because he is a poet, and the verse he writes when he is inspired, is more obvious; but the writer of prose, the novelist, has his inspiration too. It would be only prejudice that could deny that certain brief passages in *Wuthering Heights*, in *Moby Dick*, in *Anna Karenina*, are as inspired as any poem of Keats or Shelley. The novelist may consciously depend on this mysterious entity. Dostoevsky, in

547

letters to his publisher, frequently outlined some scene he had in mind to write and said it would be masterly if, when he sat down to it, inspiration came. Inspiration pertains to youth. It seldom persists to old age, and then only sporadically. No effort of will can evoke it, but authors have found that it can often be coaxed into activity. Schiller, when he went into his study to work, smelt the rotten apples he kept in a drawer so as to awaken it. Dickens had to have certain objects on his desk, without which he could not write a line. For some reason, it was the presence of those objects that brought his inspiration into play. But it is terribly unreliable. The writer may be seized by an inspiration as genuine as that which seized Keats when he wrote his greatest ode, and yet produce something that is worthless. To this again the mystics offer a parallel: St. Theresa attached no value to the ecstasies, the visions, of her nuns unless they resulted in works. I am well aware that I have not told the reader, as I should have done, just what inspiration is. I wish I could. I do not know. It is a mysterious something that enables the author to write things that he had no idea he knew, so that, looking back, he asks himself: "Where on earth did I get that from?" We know that Charlotte Brontë was puzzled by the fact that her sister Emily could write of things and people that, to her knowledge, she had no acquaintance with. When the author is seized by this welcome power, ideas, images, comparisons, even solid facts, crowd upon him and he feels himself merely an instrument, a stenographer, as it were, taking down what is dictated to him. But I have said enough on this obscure subject. I have spoken of it only to make the point that whatever gifts an author may have, without the influence, or the power, of this mysterious something, none of them will avail.

3

It is an abnormal thing for the creative instinct to possess a person after the age of thirty, and with the exception of Jane Austen, who seems to have had all the virtues that a woman can have, without being a paragon that no one could put up with, in some respects all these writers were abnormal. Dostoevsky was an epileptic; so was Flaubert, and the drugs prescribed to him are generally believed to have affected his production. This brings me to a notion which has been put forward that a physical disability, or an unhappy experience in childhood, is the determining force of the creative instinct. Thus, Byron would never have become a poet if he had not had a club-foot, and Dickens would never have become a novelist if he had not spent a few weeks in a blacking factory. This seems to me non-sensical. Innumerable men have been born with a malformed foot, innumerable children have been put to work they found ignominious, without ever writing ten lines of verse or prose. The creative instinct, common to all, in a privileged number is vigorous and persistent; neither Byron, with his club-foot, Dostoevsky with his epilepsy, nor Dickens with his unfortunate experience at Hungerford Stairs, would have become a writer at all unless he had had the urge from the composition of his nature. It is the same urge as possessed the healthy Henry Fielding, the healthy Jane Austen and the healthy Tolstoy. I have no doubt that a physical or spiritual disability affects the character of an author's work. To some extent it sets him apart from his fellows, makes him self-conscious, prejudices him, so that he sees the world, life and his fellow-creatures from a standpoint, often unduly jejune, which is not the usual one; and more than all, it adds introversion to the extroversion with which the creative instinct is inexorably associated. I do not doubt that Dostoevsky would not have written the sort of books he did if he had not been an epileptic, but neither do I doubt that, in that case, he would still have been the voluminous writer he was.

On the whole, these great writers, with the exception of Emily Brontë and Dostoevsky, must have been very pleasant to meet. They had vitality. They were good company and great talkers, and their charm impressed everyone who came in contact with them. They had a prodigious power of enjoyment, and loved the good things of life. It is a mistake to suppose that the creative artist likes to live in a garret. He does not. There is an exuberance in his nature that leads him to display.

He relishes luxury. Remember Fielding with his prodigality, Stendhal with his fine clothes, his cabriolet and his groom, Balzac with his senseless ostentation, Dickens with his grand dinner parties, his fine house and his carriage and pair. There was nothing of the ascetic about them. They wanted money, not to hoard it, but to squander it, and they were not always scrupulous in the way they got it. Extravagance was natural to their buoyant temper, and if it is a fault, it is one with which most of us can sympathize. But, again with one or two exceptions, they cannot have been easy to live with. They had traits which can hardly fail to disconcert even the most tolerant. They were self-centred. Nothing really mattered to them but their work, and to this they were prepared to sacrifice, without a qualm, everyone connected with them. They were vain, inconsiderate, selfish and pigheaded. They had little self-control, and it never occurred to them not to gratify a whim because it might bring distress to others. They do not seem to have been much inclined to marry, and when they did, either on account of their natural irritability or on account of their inconstancy, they brought their wives scant happiness. I think they married to escape from the hurly-burly of their agitating instincts: to settle down seemed to offer them peace and rest, and they imagined that marriage was an anchorage where they could live safe from the stormy waves of the tempestuous world. But escape, peace and rest, safety, were the last things to suit their temperaments. Marriage is an affair of perpetual compromise, and how could they be expected to compromise when a stubborn egoism was of the essence of their natures? They had love affairs, but they do not appear to have been very satisfactory either to themselves or to the objects of their affections. And that is understandable: real love surrenders, real love is selfless, real love is tender; but tenderness, selflessness and self-surrender were not virtues of which they were capable. With the exception of the eminently normal Fielding, and the lecherous Tolstoy, they do not seem to have been highly sexed. One suspects that when they had love affairs it was more to gratify their vanity, or to prove to themselves their own virility, than because they were carried off their feet by an irresistible attraction. I venture the suggestion that when they had achieved these objects, they returned to their work with a sigh of relief.

These, of course, are generalizations, and generalizations, as we know, are only more or less true. I have chosen a few persons about whom I have learnt something and made statements about them which, in one case or another, might easily be shown to be exaggerated. I have left out of consideration the environment and the climate of opinion (an expression now sadly shop-soiled, but convenient) in which my authors passed their lives, though, evidently, their influence on them was far from negligible. With the exception of *Tom Jones*, the novels with which I have dealt appeared in the nineteenth century. This was a period of revolution, social, industrial and political; men abandoned ways of life and ways of thought which had prevailed with little change for generations. It may be that such a period, when old beliefs are no longer unquestionably accepted, when there is a great ferment in the air and life is a new and exciting adventure, is conducive to the production of exceptional characters and of exceptional works. The fact remains that during the nineteenth century, if you are prepared to hold that it did not end till 1914, greater novels were written than had ever been written before, or have been written since.

I think one may roughly divide novels into the realistic and the sensational. This is very indefinite, since many a realistic novelist on occasion introduces a sensational incident, and contrariwise, the sensational novelist generally tries by realistic detail to make the events he relates more plausible. The sensational novel has a bad name, but you cannot dismiss with a shrug of the shoulders a method which was practised by Balzac, Dickens and Dostoevsky. It is merely a different genre. The enormous popularity of detective stories shows how great an appeal it has to readers. They wish to be excited, shocked and harrowed. The sensational novelist endeavours, by violent and extravagant events, to rivet your attention, to dazzle and amaze. The danger he runs is that you will not believe him. But, as Balzac said, it is essential that you should believe that what he tells you really happened. He can best manage to do this by creating characters so unusual to common experience that their behaviour *is* plausible. The sensational novel demands characters a little more than life-size, such characters as Dostoevsky called more real than reality; creatures of uncontrollable passions, excessive in their emotions, impetuous and unprincipled. Melodrama is their legitimate province and to frown on it, as is usual, is as unreasonable as to disparage a cubist picture because it is not representational.

The realist purports to describe life as it is. He avoids violent incidents because, on the whole, in the lives of the ordinary creatures with whom he deals they do not occur. The occurrences he relates must be not only likely but, so far as may be, inevitable. He does not seek to astound you or make your blood run faster. He appeals to the pleasure of recognition. You know the sort of people in whom he asks you to interest yourself. You are familiar with their ways of life. You enter into their thoughts and feelings because they are very like your own. What happens to them might very well happen to you. But life on the whole is monotonous, and so the realistic novelist is haunted by the fear that he may bore. Then he may be seduced into bringing in a sensational incident. The note is forced, and the reader is disillusioned. Thus, in *Le Rouge et le Noir*, Stendhal's manner is realistic till Julien goes to Paris and is brought into contact with Mathilde de la Môle; then it becomes sensational, and you accompany the author with discomfort along the new path he has unaccountably chosen to follow. The danger of being dull was clear to Flaubert when he set about the composition of *Madame Bovary* ·and he decided that he could only avoid it by beauty of style. Jane Austen escaped it by her unfailing humour. But there are not many novelists who, like Flaubert and Jane Austen, have managed to conserve to the end, without faltering, the realistic mode. It requires consummate tact.

I have quoted somewhere or other a remark of Chekhov's, which, since it is to the point, I venture to quote again. "People don't go to the North Pole and fall off icebergs," he said, "they go to the office, quarrel with their wives and eat

552

cabbage soup." That is unduly to narrow the scope of the realistic novel. People do go to the North Pole, and if they don't fall off icebergs, they undergo adventures as formidable. They go to Africa, Asia and the South Seas. Not the same things happen in those parts as in the squares of Bloomsbury, or the seaside resorts of the South Coast. They may be sensational, but if they are the sort of things that are usual, there is no reason why the realistic novelist should hesitate to describe them. It is true that the ordinary person goes to the office, quarrels with his wife and eats cabbage soup; but it is the realist's business to bring out what is not ordinary in the ordinary person. Then to eat cabbage soup may be of as great moment as falling off an iceberg.

But even the realist does not copy life. He arranges it to suit his purpose. To the best of his ability he avoids improbability, but some improbabilities are so necessary and so general that readers accept them without demur. For instance, if the hero of a novel urgently needs to meet a certain person without delay, he will run across him while walking along the crowded pavement of Piccadilly. "Hulloa," he says, "fancy meeting you! The very person I want to see." The occurrence is as unlikely as for a bridge-player to be dealt thirteen spades, but the reader will take it in his stride. Probability changes with the sophistication of readers: a coincidence which at one time passed unnoticed will cause in the reader of to-day a jolt of unbelief. I do not suppose the contemporary readers of *Mansfield Park* thought it odd that Sir Thomas Bertram should arrive from the West Indies on the very day his family were having private theatricals. A novelist to-day would feel obliged to make his arrival at so awkward a juncture more likely. I make this point merely to indicate that the realistic novel is in fact, though more subtly, less blatantly, no more true to life than the sensational one.

4

The novels I have dealt with in these pages are very different from one another; but one thing they have in common: they tell good stories, and their authors have told them in a very straightforward way. They have narrated events and delved into motives without recourse to any of the tiresome literary tricks, such as the stream of thought, the throw-back, which make so many modern novels tedious. They have told the reader what they wished him to know, and not, as is the present fashion, left him to guess who the characters were, what their calling was and what their circumstances: in fact, they have done all they could to make things easy for him. It does not appear that they sought to impress by their subtlety, or startle by their originality. As men, they are complicated enough; as writers, they are astonishingly simple. They are subtle and original, as naturally as Monsieur Jourdain spoke prose. They tried to tell the truth, but inevitably saw it through the distorting lens of their own idiosyncrasies. With a sure instinct, they eschewed topics of temporary interest, which with the passage of time lose their import; they dealt with the subjects of enduring concern to mankind: God, love and hate, death, money, ambition, envy, pride, good and evil; in short, with the passions and instincts common to all from the beginning of time, and it is on that account that from generation to generation men have found in these books something to their purpose. It is because these writers saw life, judged and described it as their unusual personalities revealed it to them, that their works have the tang, the individuality, which continues so powerfully to attract us. In the final analysis, all the author has to give is himself, and it is because these several authors were creatures of peculiar force and great singularity that their novels, notwithstanding the passage of time, bringing with it different habits and life and new ways of thought, retain their fascination.

One odd thing about them is that, though they wrote and re-wrote, and for the most part endlessly corrected, they were not great stylists. Flaubert alone seems to have made efforts to write well. It is an irony that *Madame Bovary*, on which he spent such enormous pains, should now, just on account of its style, be less appreciated by the French intelligentsia than the carelessly written letters. Years ago, Prince Kropotkin, talking to me about Tolstoy and Dostoevsky, told me that Tolstoy wrote like a gentleman and Dostoevsky like Eugène Sue. If he meant that Tolstoy wrote in the conversational style of a well-bred and cultivated man, that, it seems to me, is a very good one for a novelist to adopt. I should say that Miss Austen wrote very much as we may suppose a gentlewoman in her day talked, and it is a style that admirably suits her novels. A novel is not a scientific treatise. Every novel demands its own particular style, as Flaubert very well knew, and so the style of *Madame Bovary* differs from that of *Salammbô* and that of *Salammbô* from that of *Bouvard et Pécuchet*. No one, so far as I know, has ever claimed that Balzac, Dickens and Emily Brontë wrote with distinction. Flaubert said it was impossible for him to read Stendhal, because his style was so bad. Even in translations it is obvious that Dostoevsky's style was slovenly. It looks as though to write well were not an essential part of the novelist's equipment; but that vigour and vitality, imagination, creative force, keenness of observation, knowledge of human nature, with an interest in it and a sympathy with it, fertility and intelligence are more important. All the same, it is better to write well than indifferently.

But strange as it may be that these distinguished authors did not write their respective languages better than they did, what is stranger still is that they wrote at all. There is nothing in their heredity to account for their talent. Their families, more or less respectable, and perfectly common-place, were neither particularly intelligent nor particularly cultivated. They themselves were not in youth thrown in contact with persons interested in arts and letters. They knew no authors. They were not inordinately studious. They joined in the amusements and occupations of the girls and boys of their age and station. There was nothing to show that they had unusual capacity. With the exception of Tolstoy, who was an aristocrat, they belonged to the middle class. With their environment and upbringing one would have expected them to become doctors or lawyers, government officials or business men. They took to writing as the new-fledged bird takes to the air. Surely it is very strange that of two members of a family, Cassandra and Jane Austen, Fyodor and Michael Dostoevsky, for example, brought up in the same way, leading very much the same sort of lives, exposed to the same circumstances and bound together by mutual affection, one, and not the other, should be endowed with a supreme gift. I think I have shown that the great novelist needs a variety of parts, not only creativeness, but quickness of perception, an attentive eye, the power to profit by experience, and above all an absorbing interest in human nature, by the happy conjunction of which to become just the sort of novelist he is. But why these faculties should be meted out to one person rather than to another; why, against all likelihood, they should be possessed by the daughter of a country parson, the son of an obscure doctor, the son of a pettifogging attorney or of a shifty government clerk, is a mystery which, so far as I know, is insoluble. How these novelists came by their rare gifts, none can tell. It seems to depend on the personality, and the personality, with few exceptions, seems compounded of estimable qualities and sinister defects.

The artist's special gift, his talent or, if you wish, his genius, is like the seed of the orchid that comes to rest, at haphazard it would seem, upon a tree in the tropical jungle, there to burgeon, deriving no nourishment from it, but from the air, and then to bring forth a strange and beautiful flower; but the tree is cut down to be made into logs or floated down the river to a sawmill, and the wood on which grew the rich, fantastic flower is no different from a thousand other trees in the primeval forest.

This book, designed by
William B. Taylor
is a production of
Edito-Service S.A., Geneva

Printed in Switzerland

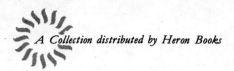